Strategies for Teaching in the Content Areas

A Handbook for K-8 Teachers

Marjorie J. Wynn
University of South Florida—Lakeland

Allyn & Bacon
is an imprint of

Boston • New York • San Francisco
Mexico City • Montreal • Toronto • London • Madrid • Munich • Paris
Hong Kong • Singapore • Tokyo • Cape Town • Sydney

Acquisition Editors: Kelly Villella Canton and Darcy Betts Prybella
Senior Managing Editor: Pamela D. Bennett
Editorial Assistant: Annalea Manalili and Nancy J. Holstein
Project Manager: Sarah N. Kenoyer
Production Coordinator: Michael Krapovicky, Pine Tree Composition, Inc.
Design Coordinator: Diane C. Lorenzo
Cover Design: Diane Y. Ernsberger
Cover Image: Artville Royalty Free CD
Operations Specialist: Susan W. Hannahs
Director of Marketing: Quinn Perkson
Marketing Manager: Darcy Betts
Marketing Coordinator: Brian Mounts

For related titles and support materials, visit our online catalog at
www.pearsonhighered.com

Library of Congress Cataloging-in-Publication Data

Wynn, Marjorie J.
Strategies for teaching in the content areas : a handbook for K-8 teachers / Marjorie
J. Wynn.—1st ed.
        p. cm.
    Includes bibliographical references and index.
    ISBN–13: 978-0-13-159970-3 (alk. paper)
    ISBN–10: 0-13-159970-4 (alk. paper)
1. Content area reading—Handbooks, manuals, etc. 2. Language arts—Correlation with
content subjects—Handbooks, manuals, etc.. I. Title.
    LB1050.455.W96 2009
    428.4071'2—dc22

                                                                    2008027433

Printed in the United States of America

10 9 8 7 6 5 4 3 2 1   BRR 12 11 10 09 08

Allyn & Bacon
is an imprint of

www.pearsonhighered.com

Preface

Strategies for Teaching in the Content Areas: A Handbook for K–8 Teachers is designed to fill the need for a single resource book that is organized for quick and ready access to specific instructional strategies to meet the lesson planning needs of both novice and experienced teachers. This handbook provides a quick and ready reference to more than 175 strategies that actively involve students in meaningful, motivational learning experiences. This handbook provides a wealth of information to help you survive and succeed in the classroom.

Strategies in this resource book are generically designed for "pick-me-up possibilities." Implemented with well-known children's classics and award-winning literature, these techniques are readily transferable to other literature selections and textbook reading. Furthermore, the strategies are easily modified for use in more than one content area as well as across grade levels and curriculum.

The initial inspiration for this handbook came from Julie, a student teacher, who visited my home one Friday evening for help with lesson planning. Julie knew the curriculum content, or *what* she wanted to teach; she just needed some guidance and reminders on *how* to teach the content using specific instructional strategies. She was looking for activities that are effective with students and practical for classroom implementation. Julie had been introduced to innumerable teaching strategies in earlier education methods courses but had only fuzzy recollection of some of these techniques.

Julie's dilemma mirrors the problem I observe in my classroom visits each week with both pre-service and in-service teachers whose fundamental concern is lesson planning. Where novice teachers struggle to remember teaching strategies, experienced teachers search for a new angle or idea to get students excited about learning. Time constraints in lesson preparation place teachers in situations where at times their lesson presentations do not meet their own personal, professional expectations. Teachers do not have time to go to through files, magazines, books, and journals in search of the perfect strategy. A survey of 350 educators, including student teachers, classroom teachers, and college instructors, confirmed the need for such a handbook.

This handbook is an ideal resource for college courses and professional development seminars. This book provides access to a vast array of specific instructional strategies. These strategies are research-based, classroom tested, and practical; they actively involve students in learning. Organized by content areas for easy accessibility, this handbook concludes with a chapter on mysteries, that demonstrates using core books with an integrated, across the content areas of reading, writing, social studies, math, and science, thematic approach to learning. Especially noteworthy, in light of the drug abuse/addiction pandemic facing our nation, are the drug-prevention possibilities found in Chapter 7. Teachers pursuing excellence will find this book invaluable in planning exciting educational experiences designed to stimulate students' academic growth.

UNIQUE FEATURES

Chapter Organizers

- Chapter-opening charts for Chapters 2–8 provide a visual overview for the strategies highlighted in each chapter. This feature allows ready access in locating a strategy for a given content area.

Accessible and Predictable Chapter Organization

(Chapters 2–7)

- Each chapter focuses on one of the following content areas: Reading, Writing, Language Arts, Social Studies, Mathematics, and Science.
- Each chapter includes a research-based introduction to the content area.
- Each chapter includes national standards information appropriate for the content area. For additional information, website references are included.
- Each content area is broken down into five representative topics that are appropriate for most elementary and middle-school curricula. For most topics there are concrete, real-world, hands-on experiences when possible and vicarious experiences when concrete experiences are not feasible.
- In Chapter 2 there are five core literature selections from a variety of genre with a focus across representative cultures.
- Each representative content area topic or literature selection in Chapters 2 through 7 includes an introduction and specific, literature-based strategies for each of the following:

 Artistic Adventures provide linguistic, spatial, and bodily-kinesthetic learning experiences. Students have opportunities to artistically invent and share literary responses using strategies such as paper folding, bookmaking, stationery, and puppets.

 Gamut of Games provide logical-mathematical, bodily-kinesthetic, and interpersonal learning experiences. Students have opportunities to create and participate in board games, television shows, learning centers, cooperative groups, and every student participation (ESP) strategies.

 Ocular Organizers provide spatial and often logical-mathematical or naturalist learning experiences. Ocular organizers are means to graphically organize and visually represent information with tables, charts, formulas, webs, and outlines.

 Dramatic Debut provides bodily-kinesthetic, interpersonal, musical, and linguistic learning experiences. Dramatic debut provides occasions to develop oral language skills through creation and participation in role playing, musicals, and puppet shows.

 Creative Composition provides intrapersonal, linguistic, and often musical and naturalist learning experiences. Creative composition is a time to express thoughts on paper through sentences, paragraphs, stories, commercials, poetry, and song lyrics.

Chapter 8: Mysteries Across Content Areas

- Mysteries are the most popular literary genre.
- The chapter opens with an introduction to mysteries, often exciting whodunit crimes, that intrigue novice detectives as they seek to ferret out the culprit by searching for clues, interrogating witnesses, and verifying evidence.
- Chapter 8 focuses on five different mystery selections.
- Each mystery provides an example of literature-based, thematic integration with specific instructional strategies for reading, writing, social studies, math, and science.

Strategies May Be Adapted and Implemented in Multiple Ways:

Across Curriculum	May be plugged into most programs.
Across Content Areas	May be used in more than one content area.
Across Grade Levels	Are applicable in most grade levels as well as across developmental levels.
Across Literature	Are readily adaptable to other children's literature, basal stories, or textbook selections.
Across Modalities	Include visual, auditory, and kinesthetic experiences.
Across Intelligences	Involve a variety of multiple intelligence approaches.

Strategies May Be Implemented with the

- Whole class
- Cooperative groups
- Individualized instruction

Differentiating Instruction

Embedded within each chapter, there are specific suggestions for differentiating instruction for younger students, older students, at-risk learners, as well as English as Second Language Learners (ESL).

Appendices

- *Appendix A: Activity Appendix*   Includes detailed directions for specific instructional strategies presented in this handbook with multiple applications for many of these strategies.
- *Appendix B: Music Appendix*   Includes guidelines for creating song innovations, a list of familiar songs, and lyrics for learning literary elements and literature genre.
- *Appendix C: Poetry Appendix*   Includes formats for more than twenty types of poetry that are implemented in this handbook.
- *Appendix D: Lesson Planning*   Includes a Pickle Picnic Reading/Listening Lesson Plan Format as well as a Purdom-Wynn Lesson Plan Format.

Acknowledgements

Acknowledgement of contributions to this handbook is shared using an original poetic format, "The Mystery of You-niqueness."

The Mystery of You-niqueness

Who are they?
*They are kids, classroom teachers, college students,
Professors, computer experts, and reviewers.
They are special!
Sometimes I ask:
Why do they care enough to implement these strategies in their classrooms?
Why do they care enough to read reflectively by the hour and give quality feedback?
Why do they care enough to design creative computer images?
Sometimes these educators exclaim:
These strategies are research-based.
These strategies meet National Standards.
And deep down they also know that:
Kids are having fun!
Kids are learning!
Who are they?
They are:
Kristi Cox, Sherry Mosier, and Janet Vorderburg (classroom teachers);

Richard Austin, Barry Morris, Kathleen Riley, and others (university professors);
Judy Monahan: computer expert extraordinaire;
Kimber Pepper: amazing administrative assistant;
Classroom Teachers; College Students;
And most important of all, CLASSROOM KIDS!
They are You-nique!

*Poetry Appendix C, pages 363–364; Text pages 242; 263; innovation/reformatted

REVIEWERS

I would like to thank the reviewers for their contributions to this handbook. They are: Richard A. Austin, University of South Florida; Linda F. Balog, SUNY College at Brockport; Barbara Biglan, Chatham College; Becky Birdsong, LeCourneau University; Laurel Burgia, Western Illinois University; Monique Davis, Arizona State University; Virginia W. deThy, Richard Stockton College of New Jersey; Lois K. Draina, Marywood University; Joyce W. Frazier, University of North Carolina at Charlotte; Randa A. Gick, Arizona State University; Roy Hurst, The University of Texas of the Permian Basin; Nonor Keirans, Chestnut Hill College; Melissa J. Marks, University of Pittsburgh at Greensburg; John McIntyre, Southern Illinois University; Barry Morris, William Carey College; Pamela Murray, Mary Baldwin College; and Fara Nizamani, City University.

Dedication

Strategies for Teaching in the Content Areas: A Handbook for K–8 Teachers is dedicated to my husband, Chuck. This dedication is shared in a poetic format, a limerick:

There once was a great guy named Chuck
Who said, "Write a book, not some yuck.
Your ideas are just great!
Write now; don't you wait!"
Then he cooked, cleaned, critiqued. He was stuck!

Limerick Poetry Appendix C, page 363; Text page 225

Contents

NOTE: Every effort has been made to provide accurate and current Internet information in this book. However, the Internet and information posted on it are constantly changing, so it is inevitable that some of the Internet addresses listed in the textbook will change.

CHAPTER 1

Introduction to Content Area Strategies: Theory and Practice

The Inspiration of Theory

The Wisdom of Experience

The Value of Differentiated Instruction

Inspiration from Unexpected Places

Selection of Strategies for This Handbook

Think of one teacher from your past.
Classify the teacher as outstanding, average, or below average.
Why do you remember this teacher?

OVERVIEW

Most of the students in my college classes remember an outstanding teacher. A few remember a below average teacher. Rarely does a student remember an average teacher. Then students respond to, "Which kind of a teacher would you like to be?" First, they dismiss the possibility of becoming an average teacher. Who wants to be average? No one will remember you. Next, after a discussion on quirks that cause a teacher to be classified as below average, they dismiss that possibility because, in the rare instance you are remembered, the memories are not positive. Finally, they discuss the characteristics of an outstanding teacher. Outstanding teachers touch lives in a personal way. Outstanding teachers make learning fun! Outstanding teachers actively involve students in classroom lessons. This discussion provides the impetus for investigating ways to become an outstanding classroom teacher.

Each of our classes begins with a Thought for the Day (TFD). In the first class, the TFD is

Tell me; I forget

Show me; I remember

Involve me; I understand

Ancient Chinese Proverb

Students discuss why they often forget what a parent or spouse tells them. Then they discuss the sense of hearing and why, even though they can physically hear, they don't always internalize the message. Then they focus on the sense of sight. Often when they see something, they remember it—at least for a while. However, there are times when they may not remember all the details. Finally, they wrestle with the sense of touch, the kinesthetic modality, and how writing notes to themselves improves memory. Often, they don't even have to go back and read the note because involvement in writing the note is sufficient to trigger memory. The class then discusses the value of involving students in multisensory learning experiences to promote long-term retention of information and academic achievement.

Barbe and Swassing's (in Guild & Garger, 1985, pp. 62-63) research on instructional methods found that modalities usually refer to the sensory channels through which we receive and communicate messages. These researchers identified auditory, visual, and kinesthetic/tactile modalities as significant sensory channels for learning. For learning style characteristics of auditory, visual, and kinesthetic learners, see Figure 1.1.

Memories from a workshop Dr. Barbe led many years ago include this imperative: *If a child doesn't understand, teachers must present the material in a new and different way, preferably employing a different modality.* Unfortunately, when a student doesn't understand, the teacher's tendency is to reteach *the same way* using his or her own preferred modality. The only difference is, he gets *louder* and goes more *s-l-o-w-l-y*. My classroom observations reveal that, even though there is overwhelming research support for multisensory teaching, a teacher's preferred mode of teaching is to talk … and talk … and talk with an occasional *visual* thrust into the lesson. Rarely is the kinesthetic modality employed, allowing students to become actively involved in learning. After all, kinesthetic learning is noisy and often messy.

Multimodal teaching is evident in the Purdom-Wynn Lesson Plan Format (see Lesson Planning Appendix D) in which strategies for student learning include auditory, visual, and kinesthetic stimuli. Remediation experiences for students who do not accomplish the lesson plan objective are presented using a different strategy and a different modality with concepts and skills broken down into smaller, simpler steps. Even though early educational research and professional intuition support multimodal teaching as a stimulus for academic success, there has to be more to the story. It's time to examine the inspiration of theory, the wisdom of experience, the value of differentiated instruction, inspiration from unexpected places, and finally, selection of strategies for this handbook.

FIGURE 1.1 Learning Style Characteristics

Auditory Learners	Visual Learners	Kinesthetic/Tactile Learners
Tell Me or I'll Tell You Learners	**Show Me or I'll Show You Learners**	**Let's Do It Learners**
• Prefer to discuss skills and concepts	• Prefer to see or visually represent skills and concepts	• Prefer to be physically active when learning
• Learn through oral repetition by themselves or others	• Find graphic organizers such as webs, graphs, and data charts helpful	• Have difficulty sitting still and are often a teacher's worst nightmare
• Subvocalize when asked to read silently	• Are motivated by opportunities to represent academic concepts artistically	• Often take copious notes or doodle and sketch
• Are distracted by environmental sounds	• Insist on an uncluttered, attractive environment	• Learn when participating in games, drama, and art experiences
• Learn by participating in discussions, musical experiences, and drama		

Based on information from Guild & Garger (1985).

THE INSPIRATION OF THEORY

The mediocre teacher tells.
The good teacher explains.
The superior teacher demonstrates.
The great teacher inspires.

William Arthur Ward

Come with me on a journey along the Yellow Brick Road where our travels take us from Barbe's multimodal workshop, not to the Wizard of Oz but to Howard Gardner's research on multiple intelligences (1983, 1991). His theory, as well as the practical implementation of his findings in the classroom (Armstrong, 1994, 2003; Campbell, 1997), will certainly assist in understanding *why what works, works.* Along the Yellow Brick Road we will also visit the research of Susan Kovalik (1994) and Susan Jones (1998). Both researchers focus on brain research and the brain-compatible classroom. Cratty's (1971) active learning games and Armstrong's (1998) challenge to awaken the genius within provide additional insight into the understanding of *why what works, works.*

Howard Gardner shows us how to reach the unique intelligences in each of our students. His research on multiple intelligences (1983, 1991) expands earlier research on multisensory learning. He stresses that *all students learn, BUT not all students learn in the same way.* In other words, the *what*, or content, remains the same, but the *how*, or instructional strategies for presenting and learning the content, must differ to meet each student's preferred learning style. His research, and the subsequent research of Armstrong (1994, 2003), Campbell and Campbell (1999), and Checkley (1997), determine that no one approach works for every student. Learning occurs when a variety of approaches with choices and opportunities for personalization are employed.

Gardner identifies eight intelligences: linguistic, logical-mathematical, spatial, musical, bodily-kinesthetic, interpersonal, intrapersonal, and naturalist. His current research focuses on even more intelligence possibilities. He suggests that each of us has all eight intelligences but in differing amounts. Thus each of us has different strengths. He suggests that we each look different, have different personalities, and have different kinds of minds. We can all learn, but each of us learns differently. *No single approach works best for every*

FIGURE 1.2   Multiple Intelligences: Questions and Instructional Strategy Suggestions for Lesson Planning

1. **Linguistic Intelligence**
   How can I stimulate the use of the spoken or written word?
   - Write a poem, fable, myth, or legend.
   - Participate in storytelling, debates, and interviews.

2. **Logical-Mathematical Intelligence**
   How can I bring numbers, calculations, logic, classification, or critical thinking into my lessons?
   - Develop a classification system for a given type of plant life.
   - Create story problems related to the thematic unit.

3. **Spatial Intelligence**
   How can I use visual aids, visualization, color, art, metaphor, or visual organizers?
   - Make a chart, map, web, or graph.
   - Create advertisements.

4. **Musical Intelligence**
   How can I bring in music or environmental sounds, or set key academic points in a rhythm or melody?
   - Sing a song that explains an academic concept.
   - Participate in a musical drama.

5. **Bodily-Kinesthetic Intelligence**
   How can I involve the whole body or provide hands-on learning experiences?
   - Invent a board or floor game.
   - Participate in an academic drama experience.

6. **Interpersonal Intelligence**
   How can I engage students in peer or cross-age sharing, cooperative learning, or large group simulation?
   - Coach a friend who needs help.
   - Participate in a small group research project.

7. **Intrapersonal Intelligence**
   How can I evoke personal feelings or memories or give students choices?
   - Make daily entries in a personal journal.
   - Write a poem about a personal experience.

8. **Naturalist Intelligence**
   How can I stimulate student discovery of patterns in nature?
   - Keep an observation log.
   - Participate in an outdoor field trip related to the class thematic focus.

Based on information from Armstrong (1994); Campbell & Campbell (1999).

student. Gardner's research, as well as that of his colleagues, suggests questions teachers might ask themselves when planning lessons and selecting instructional strategies for each of the eight intelligences (see Figure 1.2).

While studying six schools that focus on implementing multiple intelligences strategies, Campbell and Campbell (1999) found that students experience success when participating in programs focusing on *art, music, dance,* and *creative writing*. In these schools, students are interactively involved in hands-on, multimodal learning. As a result of *diversified instructional approaches,* students participate in real-world, thematically focused, personalized learning experiences. These researchers discovered that in all six schools, no matter what the diversity or economic status, the disparity among white and minority academic achievement is substantially reduced or eliminated through differentiated instruction.

In her research on brain-compatible classrooms, Susan Kovalik (1994) reminds us that each of us has a unique brain with differing amounts of the seven (now eight) intelligences identified by Gardner. She emphasizes the need for a classroom curriculum that consists of concepts, skills, and attitudes/values taught within a real-world context. She notes the differences in methods used in gifted classrooms as opposed to the methods employed in other classrooms. The focus in gifted programs is on providing enrichment while teachers in other programs seem to feel the constraints of a traditional, textbook-driven curriculum. Thus gifted classrooms are exciting, and other classrooms are b-o-r-i-n-g! Kovalik reminds us that,

> Ditto's don't make dendrites! That is to say, neither dittos nor the textbook or workbooks create an enriched environment which activates the brain at the level of powerful learning. In other words, every minute spent on what students experience as boring or as "seat work," is a minute spent NOT building intelligence. (p. 85)

Kovalik emphasizes Glasser's findings on learning retention in which students who hear the information retain only 10 percent of what they hear, while students who attempt to teach others retain 90 percent of the information (see Figure 1.3).

During a presentation on brain research findings and their implications for the classroom at a Florida Association for Supervision of Curriculum and Development (FASCD) workshop, Susan Jones (1998) shares the characteristics of a brain-compatible classroom: novelty, emotion, ritual, and challenge. She suggests that knowledge should be

- Connected to the learner's background template of experiences.
- Retrievable so that the listener may revisit the knowledge.
- Adaptable to other situations.

She stresses employing novelty as the brain loathes monotony. She cautions teachers against teaching isolated facts. Students must feel that what they are learning is relevant to their own lives. Students need firsthand, hands-on learning experiences. She emphasizes, *Sameness and uniformity kill the love of learning.*

While contemplating a creative learning environment, answer *"true"* or *"false"* to the following statement: *Learning is occurring in a quiet, orderly classroom.* "It depends," is not an acceptable answer on a true/false test. However, in this case the test item is not fair (*no wonder my college students complain about true/false tests*). Some students in a quiet, orderly classroom may well be learning, *but* there are also students who may not be learning. Why? They need to move. Bryan Cratty's classic research (1971) establishes a child's need for movement. Cratty comes to the logical conclusion: If children need to move, why not take advantage of this need and provide motivational, meaningful, movement through active academic learning games? Cratty's book includes a wide variety of these games. Most are geared toward younger children but may be readily adapted to older students. For example, in Chapter 4, *Spelling Cheers* were inspired by one or more of Cratty's suggestions. In assessing movement needs of students, Gardner, Campbell, and Kovalik would probably say, "Let's provide learning experiences in which these students can use their bodily-kinesthetic intelligence."

FIGURE 1.3   Continuum of Retention

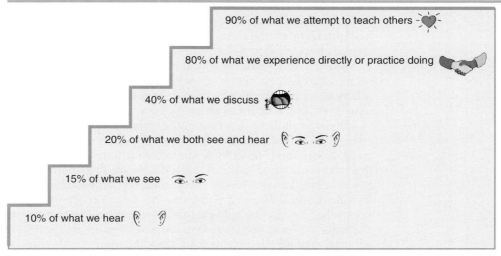

90% of what we attempt to teach others

80% of what we experience directly or practice doing

40% of what we discuss

20% of what we both see and hear

15% of what we see

10% of what we hear

Based on information from presentation by Pat Roy (1992); in Kovalik (1994).

Armstrong (1998) challenges teachers to awaken the genius within and make learning a joy for each and every student. The chorus of "Amens!" you hear are from Campbell, Checkley, Cratty, Gardner, Jones, Kovalik, and other researchers who have devoted their professional lives to stimulating students' academic, social, and emotional growth. Even Plato from the distant past challenges us: "Do not then train youths to learning by force and harshness, but direct them to it by what amuses their minds so that you may be better able to discover with accuracy the peculiar bent of the genius of each."

THE WISDOM OF EXPERIENCE

To learn you must want to be taught.

Jewish Proverb

While traveling along the Yellow Brick Road, we encounter my research with at-risk beginning readers (Wynn, 1993) and collegial research involving second language learners' literacy acquisition (Wynn & Laframboise 1996). Findings in these studies support the premise that lyrics lead to literacy. When singing well-known children's songs as well as creating innovative lyrics set to familiar tunes, students experience academic success. Sight vocabulary increases significantly. Melody and lyrics of songs become embedded in memory. Advertisers make use of this phenomenon in developing commercials that have repetition, rhythm, and rhyme in both tune and lyrics. Listeners are easily caught up in these catchy ditties and often find themselves humming and singing along. Appeal to musical intelligence when singing about academic concepts occurs when singing parts of speech (Chapter 4), spelling (Chapter 4), math facts (Chapter 6), and other academic skills and concepts found throughout this book. Academic *singspirations* dramatically promote academic growth.

One of the best things about singing with students is they don't care if you can carry a tune. They just appreciate a joyful noise! During my classroom visits, students' enthusiasm for music is evident in their repeated requests, "Please sing with us!" Taking advantage of this request, we often burst into an academically grade-level appropriate song.

As an example of expanding learning and teaching possibilities, consider how the digestive system is traditionally taught. Most of my college students agree that the traditional assignment is to ask classroom students to read a textbook chapter and answer the questions at the end of the chapter in complete sentences. After completing this assignment, are students able to remember the structure and sequence of the digestive system? Probably not. We brainstorm alternative strategies for teaching the digestive system: research on the Internet, videotapes, DVDs, transparencies depicting the human body, or a plastic model of the body to trace the digestive system, for example. Next, volunteers are asked to explain the digestive system. Oops! Some have a vague idea, but most recollections are hazy.

My understanding of the digestive system was just as hazy when, as a first-grade teacher, I was asked to serve on a committee designing a unit to teach the digestive system to cafeteria paraprofessionals. Surely the prime responsibility of those on duty in the cafeteria is to stop kids from thumping peas at each other and stomping on milk cartons. Is there a way to get this staff excited about the digestive system when their number one concern is preventing food fights?

When all else fails, try songs, puppets, and drama. These strategies work in the classroom, so they will probably work with paraprofessionals. Mysteriously, lyrics and a related drama script with puppets appear on my computer screen. Soon resounding throughout the school, visitors hear the digestive system songs (see Figure 1.4).

Many years later in a fifth-grade classroom, one of my interns is teaching a lesson on editing. She tells the students to be sure they use capital letters and punctuation marks correctly. She reminds them to be sure all words are spelled correctly. She tells them to check their papers. End of lesson. Oops! Where are the components of the Purdom-Wynn Lesson Plan (see Lesson Planning Appendix D) that have been modeled repeatedly in the college classroom? Where are the visuals? Where is the interactive learning? We meet and discuss her lesson. She tells me that there are *no* interesting ways to teach editing. What a challenge! "Would you like me to work with your students?" With her permission and the permission of her directing teacher, I ask the students, "Would you like me to tell you about

FIGURE 1.4 "My Digestion Song"

Title: "My Digestion Song"
Tune: "She'll Be Coming Round the Mountain"
When you take a bite of food, chew it well. Chew! Chew! (2X)
When you take a bite of food, you don't want to be rude.
When you take a bite of food, chew it well. Chew! Chew!
　Your saliva will dissolve food; yes, it will. Spit! Spit! (2X)
Your saliva will dissolve food. (2X)
Your saliva will dissolve food; yes, it will. Spit! Spit! Chew! Chew!
(Follow the same pattern for each succeeding verse.)
　The food slides down the esophagus, way, way down. Slide! Slide!
　It lands in the stomach where it's squeezed. Squeeze! Squeeze!
　Digestive fluids in the intestines make it smaller. Scrunch! Scrunch!
　It travels in the intestines all around. Round! Round!
　It gets smaller, smaller, smaller, all the time. Itty, bitty!
　Then into the bloodstream, it will go. Swish! Swish!
　Then it's used by your cells, to make you grow. Grow! Grow!

the book I'm writing?" They are delighted. After all, this means they get a break from the dreadfully dull task of checking their papers for capital letters, punctuation, and spelling.

As a teller-of-tales, I launch into a wild yarn about the book I have been slaving over for weeks. Chapter 1 is just about complete. The editor must be impressed if she is going to publish my book. The students discuss some of the writing techniques that will impress the editor: well-written sentences, sticking to the topic, using capital letters and punctuation correctly, and so on. With these findings as a foundation, we discuss the publishing headquarters edifice in New York City. This four-story building has an editing office on each floor. A drawing of a four-story building appears on the board. On each floor there is an office to which my chapter must be sent (see Figure 1.5).

- First, the chapter is sent to the office on the third floor, now labeled **O** for the *Organization Editor.* This editor is trying to ferret out any revision or editing organizational problems. We discuss types of organizational goofs for which this editor might be searching such as sequencing problems, missing information, and unnecessary information.
- Next, the chapter is sent to the office on the first floor, now labeled **S** for the *Spelling Editor.* This editor searches diligently for any spelling errors.
- Then the chapter is sent to the second-floor office, which is now labeled **P** for the *Punctuation Editor.* This editor slaps on her punctuation hat and scrutinizes each and every sentence trying to detect any punctuation errors. By this time I am really nervous. If my chapter can make it through the office on the fourth floor without any errors, the editor will publish my work.
- Finally, the chapter is sent to the office on the fourth floor, now labeled **C** for the *Capitalization Editor.* A student screams, "Cops!" Once I regain control of the class, we discuss this editor, who has a magnifying glass and peers closely at each sentence in hot pursuit of any punctuation errors. We all need to be editing COPS.

Why do lyrics lead to increased academic achievement in the areas of sight vocabulary, parts of speech, spelling, and math facts? Why do singing, puppets, and drama get paraprofessionals excited about the digestive system? Why do discussion, drawing on the board, and a little drama get kids excited about editing? Face it, none of these topics is of high interest to the learner. However, reflection on these and many other classroom scenarios reveals enthusiasm and academic achievement are enhanced when enticing thrice through

　　👁 👁 eyes,

　　👂 👂 ears,

　　❤ and emotions.

FIGURE 1.5   Editing Offices

Capitalization Editor (fourth floor) [C]

Organization Editor (third floor) [O]

Punctuation Editor (second floor) [P]

Spelling Editor (first floor) [S]

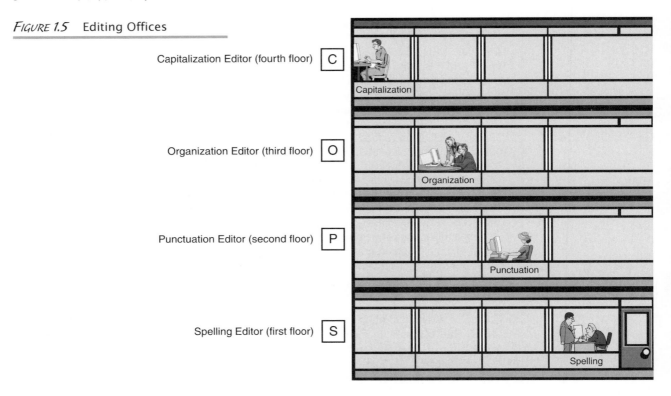

THE VALUE OF DIFFERENTIATED INSTRUCTION

*The essence of education is not to stuff you with facts but
to help you discover your uniqueness,
to teach you how to develop it, and then
to show you how to give it away.*

Leo Buscaglia

As we continue our journey along the Yellow Brick Road, we encounter research in the area of differentiated instruction. *Differentiated instruction* includes a wide variety of meaningful, motivational, memory-friendly methods designed to enhance retention of information. Differentiated instruction allows the teacher to *meet and greet* each student where he or she is and then to facilitate his or her educational journey through stretching like a rubber band from personal background knowledge, through familiar context, and toward an individual, academic goal. Franklin (2002) and Willis and Mann (2000) stress the importance of flexible grouping within a differentiated classroom as well as choices for each student in demonstrating individual knowledge. Rather than a *one-size-fits-all* mentality, the teacher realizes that within the classroom, each of the students has a unique pattern of learning.

In her book, *The Differentiated Classroom: Responding to the Needs of All Learners*, Tomlinson (1999) emphasizes the need to modify content, process, and products to meet diverse needs. Adaptations include:

- **Content:** The core content or *what* for all students is the same. The complexity of the content is adjusted based on background experiences and diverse needs. Teacher scaffolding is adjusted accordingly.
- **Process:** The activities, strategies, or methods are selected based on an individual's unique learning style, background experience, diverse needs, and personal interests. In other words, adaptations are made in relation to *how* the student learns best.
- **Product:** Academic assessment is based on a student's culminating project. Based on personal choice, the student demonstrates learning through a self-selected product. For each student, expectations are high as students tend to live *up* to or *down* to meet the teacher's expectations.

During her presentation at the 2003 International Reading Association Conference, Beth A. Olshansky (2003) provided the audience an opportunity to experience life without differentiated instruction. Each participant was asked to

- Write your name as if you were signing a check.
- Write your name in cursive using your nondominant hand.
- List your observations during the second experience.
  Observations included difficult, took more time, looked at peer's work, noise level built, had to think about, frustrating, uncomfortable.
- Consider that your frustration is the same as that experienced day in and day out by at-risk visual/kinesthetic learners stuck in a world where the majority of classroom instruction is designed for auditory and verbal learners.
- Imagine what your life would be like if you had to work all year using your nondominant hand? Many at-risk learners go through the school year in a *nondominant-hand-mode* because they are living in an auditory and verbal world in which they are expected to function in a nondominant learning mode.

Olshansky shares the positive impact of the artists/writers workshop on the academic achievement of diverse learners, including at-risk populations. Especially noteworthy in her presentation is the need to provide visual and kinesthetic learners with the tools to support their acquisition of reading and writing skills. She reminds the audience that pictures are a universal vehicle for thinking that transcend learners' facility with language. She suggests using art and dance strategies to build students' self-esteem, reminding the audience that success breeds success. Certainly, no one wants to go through life in a nondominant-hand mode.

INSPIRATION FROM UNEXPECTED PLACES

The brain loves novelty.
The brain loathes monotony.
Adapted from Susan Jones

While contemplating the inspiration of theory, the wisdom of my experience, and the value of differentiated instruction, dance with me down the Yellow Brick Road to visit a Jazzercise teacher who has large classes of satisfied customers. What secret power does this teacher possess that lures me back to class week after week? She follows *the principles of teaching* that assure we are all **REDI** to learn:

- **Risk:**   As a student, I am willing to take risks because I am in a situation in which no one is going to criticize me. Even when the rest of the class dances to the right and I dance to the left, there is no reprimand. Usually, I catch on quickly (self-assessment) and run the other direction.
- **Enthusiastic:**   This Jazzercise teacher believes that enthusiasm is caught not taught. She is Jazzercising when I get to class, and she is Jazzercising when I crawl out the door after class. She even has me enthusiastic about exercise, and I hate to exercise.
- **Different:**   Each week is a different routine. Pain through variety. Exercising at home with a videotape is a possibility, but the routines would all be the same.
- **Involved:**   The whole class is actively involved. We have *joy* (if you can call it that) in learning each of these routines. Our interpersonal intelligence is getting a work out. After all, misery loves company! We are moving to music! We are employing our bodily-kinesthetic and musical intelligences.

To retain these theoretically and educationally sound principles, sing

Title: The Principles of Teaching
Tune: "Turkey in the Straw/Do Your Ears Hang Low"

Kids should be <u>**Risk**</u> takers.
Then successful they will be.
Teachers should be role models.
Teaching <u>**Enthusiastically**</u>.
With <u>**Different**</u> strategies

Variety is the key
Kids **Involved** in projects
As they learn effectively.

SELECTION OF STRATEGIES FOR THIS HANDBOOK

*More important than the curriculum is the question
of the methods of teaching and the spirit
in which the teaching is given.*

Bertrand Russell

As we near the end of our journey along the Yellow Brick Road, contemplate Armstrong's (1998) twelve qualities of genius: curiosity, playfulness, imagination, creativity, wonder, wisdom, inventiveness, vitality, sensitivity, flexibility, humor, and joy. You will find embedded in the purpose for each strategy one or more of these qualities as well as stimulation of one or more of the multiple intelligences. As you journey with your students along the Yellow Brick Road, be sure your adventures include opportunities to entice thrice through

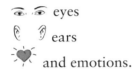 eyes

ears

and emotions.

To assure learning within all communication systems, selected strategies fall within and across one or more of the communication systems. The Communications Systems Chart (Table 1.1) that follows conveys interrelationships and includes information from the three communication systems[1]—*oral, written, and visual*—identified by The International Reading Association (IRA) and The National Council of Teachers of English (NCTE) (1996). Additional communication systems—*musical, kinesthetic,* and *emotional*—supported by Gardner (1983, 1991), Armstrong (2003), and others.

Strategies selected for this handbook cross the gamut of these communication systems. For example, *viewing* strategies include: looking at a Venn diagram to compare two characters in a story (Chapter 2), examining a data chart to compare and contrast information about Native Americans (Chapter 5), and seeing and comparing the effects of illegal drugs (Chapter 7). Examples of the *visually representing* strategies include creating a biographical character using the eightfold person technique (Chapter 5) and developing a pie quivalent chart while studying fractions (Chapter 6). Motivational *musical* experiences abound throughout the book, including those found in the Music Appendix B. Dramatic debut stimulate kinesthetic communication, while a gamut of games provides interactive *emotional* experiences with others.

TABLE 1.1   *Communication Systems Chart*

System	Multiple Intelligence	Receptive	Expressive
Oral	Linguistic	Listening	Talking
Written	Linguistic	Reading	Writing
Visual	Spatial	Viewing	Visually Representing
Musical	Musical	Listening to Music	Singing; Playing an Instrument
Kinesthetic	Bodily-Kinesthetic Naturalist	Imagery	Drama, Movement, Dancing
Emotional	Interpersonal; Intrapersonal	Listening to others; self-reflection	Sharing with and responding to others

Strategies selected for this handbook are

Multisensory
Multi-intelligence
Multipurpose providing for differentiated instruction
Across Curriculum
Across Content Areas
Across Grade Levels
Across Literature Selections to meet the
Multi-Needs of diverse students through
Multicommunication systems.

References

Armstrong, T. (1994). Multiple intelligences: Seven ways to approach curriculum. *Educational Leadership, 52* (3), 26–28.

Armstrong, T. (1998). *Awakening genius in the classroom.* Alexandria, VA: Association for Supervision and Curriculum Development.

Armstrong, T. (2003). *The multiple intelligences of reading and writing: Making the words come alive.* Alexandria, VA: Association for Supervision and Curriculum Development.

Campbell, L. (1997). Variations on a theme: How teachers interpret MI theory. *Educational Leadership, 55* (1), 14–19.

Campbell, L., & Campbell, B. (1999). *Multiple intelligences and student achievement: Success stories from six schools.* Alexandria, VA: Association for Supervision and Curriculum Development.

Checkley, K. (1997). The first seven … and the eighth: A conversation with Howard Gardner. *Educational Leadership, 55* (1), 8–13.

Cratty, B. J. (1971). *Active learning games to enhance academic abilities.* Englewood Cliffs, NJ: Prentice-Hall.

Franklin, J. (2002, March). The art of differentiation: Moving from theory to practice. *Education Update, 44* (2), 1, 3, 8.

Gardner, H. (1983). *Frames of mind: The theory of multiple intelligences.* New York: Basic Books/Harper Collins.

Gardner, H. (1991). *The unschooled mind: How children think and how schools should teach.* New York: Basic Books/HarperCollins.

Guild, P. B., & Garger, S. (1985). *Marching to different drummers.* Alexandria, VA: Association for Supervision and Curriculum Development.

International Reading Association & National Council of Teachers of English. (1996). *Standards for the English Language Arts.* Retrieved February 6, 2008 from www.ira.org

Jones, S. (1998, April 4). *Presentation on brain research.* Florida Association for Supervision of Curriculum and Development. St. Leo University, St. Leo, Florida

Kovalik, S. (1994). *Integrated thematic instruction: The model* (3rd ed.). Kent, WA: Susan Kovalik & Associates.

National Council of Teachers of English. (1996). *Standards for the English language arts.* Urbana, IL: National Council of Teachers of English and the International Reading Association.

Olshansky, B. A. (2003, May 6). *Picturing writing: Fostering literacy through art.* Presentation at the International Reading Association Conference, Orlando, FL.

Roy, P. (1992, November 17). *Presentation on Revisiting Cooperative Learning.* Outcomes-Based Education Conference, Phoenix, AZ.

Tomlinson, C. A. (1999). *The differentiated classroom: Responding to the needs of all learners.* Alexandria, VA: Association for Supervision and Curriculum Development.

Willis, S., & Mann, L. (2000, winter). Differentiating instruction: Finding manageable ways to meet individual needs. *Curriculum Update,* 1–3; 6–7.

Wynn, M. (1993). Lyrics lead to literacy. *NERA Journal, 29* (3), 18–27.

Wynn, M., & Laframboise, K. (1996). Shared experiences to scaffold second language learners' literacy acquisition. *NERA Journal, 32* (2), 3–9.

Websites

Brain Research and Education

Fad or foundation? Information on teaching, learning, and assessment.

www.mcli.dist.maricopa.edu/forum/fall03/brain.html

Differentiated Instruction

Individual differences intrigue and challenge educators. Includes suggestions for dealing with these differences.

www.ascd.org/pdi/demo/diffinstr/differentiated1.html

Multiple Intelligences

Specific suggestions for tapping into multiple intelligences in the classroom.

www.multipleintelligences.com

CHAPTER 2 GENRE/CULTURE/ LITERATURE SELECTIONS	Artistic Adventures	Gamut of Games
Traditional Lit Asian *Yeh-Shen: A Cinderella Story from China*	Character Growth Sleeve Puppets **DR** *During Reading*	Vocabulary Puzzles **VE** *Vocabulary Enrichment*
Non-Fiction Native American *If You Lived with the Hopi*	Sketch-to-Summarize Shape Book **DR**	WOW Word Wall **VE**
Historical Fiction African American *I Thought My Soul Would Rise and Fly*	Eight Fold Person Character Web Personal Prediction Story **PR**	Questioning the Author (QtA) **DR**
Contemporary Realistic Fiction European American *Bridge to Terabithia*	Book & Author Focus Trifold Brochure **AR**	Stump the Teacher/ Stump the Student Literature Circles **PR**
Modern Fantasy Jewish *The Devil's Arithmetic*	Choose-a-Word Step Book **VE**	Summary Story **DR**

Reading

Ocular Organizers	Dramatic Debut	Creative Composition
Venn Diagram Compare & Contrast Data Chart **EE** *Extension & Enrichment*	Word Picture Charades **PR** *Pre-reading*	Story Sequel ABC Story Sequel Acrostic Summary Pyramid Poem for a Story Summary **AR** *After-Reading*
KWL Strategy **PR**	Role-Playing Problem and Solution **AR**	Diamante Poetry **E&E**
Context Clue Guru Bulletin Board **VE**	Readers' Theater **EE**	Simulated Journals **AR**
Plot Structure Chart Personal Paragraphs &/or Stories **DR**	Commercials **EE**	Simile Search Four-Flap Flip-Flop Book **VE**
Headline Highlights Headline Highlights Bulletin Board **PR**	Story Theater **AR**	Theme Senses Poem Thematic Senses Poem **EE**

Nobody on earth can know everything,
But when you can read, you can learn anything.

OVERVIEW

Reading is a critical life skill that contributes to success in school, on the job, and in society. Through reading we learn to understand ourselves, others, and our world. *Reading* is meaningful interaction with print in which the reader constructs meaning based on background knowledge brought to the text and information in the text. The background knowledge of the reader is strengthened through classroom strategies that activate prior knowledge and experiences related to the topic. Good readers learn to skillfully integrate information in the text with what they already know. Through class discussion and sharing, the reader's background information is linked with information provided by classmates to develop an expanded pool of knowledge for all students. It is incumbent upon teachers to provide background-building experiences because

The more information the reader brings to the printed page,
The less information the reader must get from the page.

Traditionally reading was taught by asking students to read a story or expository text and answer questions. This was practicing reading, not teaching students *how* to read. Research has determined that text comprehension is enhanced when the reader develops *metacognition*, or comprehension monitoring. Students develop metacognitive awareness as they become cognizant of their own reading comprehension abilities and needs and learn specific strategies for monitoring and adjusting reading behaviors to fit their personal comprehension needs (Reutzel & Cooter, 1992). Pressley (2000) suggests that students self-regulate their reading by asking, Does what I'm reading make sense? From a *constructivist point of view*, a reader is a meaning-maker who builds meaning based on his experiences and knowledge (Flood, Lapp, & Fisher, 2003). When self-monitoring, the reader might ask him- or herself the following questions:

What am I learning?
What is confusing?
What should I do when what I'm reading doesn't make sense?

BEST PRACTICES IN A READING PROGRAM

The more you read,
The more you know;
The more you know,
The more you grow,
The smarter you grow,
The stronger your voice
When speaking your mind
Or making a choice.

Anonymous

Suggestions for best practices in a reading program include findings from the research of Billman (2002); Fisher, Frey, and Williams (2002); Ivy (2002); Pressley (2000); and Zemelman, Daniels, and Hyde (1998). Best practices should include the following:

1. Reading *to* students
2. Reading *with* students
3. Reading *by* students
4. A beginning reading program that includes:
   - Building a firm phonics foundation
   - Increasing sight word repertoire
   - Developing word attack skills
5. Reading about reading

Reading to Students

The Teacher's Read-Aloud Commandment:
You shall read to your students everyday.

Hearing books read aloud is the beginning of learning to read. Picture books are an essential component in a read-aloud program. They often introduce and provide background knowledge for a topic. Although there is a perception that picture books are written for younger students, this is not always true. Many picture books deal with complex issues and difficult concepts and are designed for mature audiences (Billman, 2002). For example, in the picture book *Who Belongs Here? An American Story*, (Knight, 1993), Nary, a Cambodian refugee, experiences intolerance in a U.S. school. An illustration with empty lockers and empty halls in a school is accompanied by interdependent text and asks these compelling questions, *What if everyone who now lives in the United States, but whose ancestors came from another country, was forced to return to his or her homeland? Who would be left?*
     Advantages of the teacher reading aloud include the following:

1. Inspiring students to read.
2. Building and extending background knowledge.
3. Providing access to information from texts that are too difficult for students to read; this is especially important for at-risk readers and English as second language (ESL) students.
4. Expanding vocabulary knowledge.
5. Modeling fluent reading.
6. Modeling **how** to read by thinking aloud and verbalizing
   - Predictions
   - Connections to personal background experience
   - Understanding of text
   - Confusion about text
   - Procedures to take when confusion occurs
7. Introducing new books.
8. Building interest and excitement about literature for independent reading.

Reading with Students

The Teacher's Reading-With Commandment:
You shall read with your students everyday.

Reading with students includes shared and guided reading experiences. *Shared reading* is a reading experience in which a teacher models expressive, fluent reading while students follow the text and often join in repeated choral readings. Multiple copies of the text or an enlarged text in a big book, on a chart, or projected by an overhead projector or computer allow all to see. A pointer such as a flashlight, yardstick, or laser light helps focus students' attention on the text and allows students to make an aural-visual association between the words they are hearing and the words they are seeing. Shared reading at home is an opportunity for both parent and child to sit close together while simultaneously choral reading a book. Shared reading experiences are motivational and effective with at-risk readers and students whose first language is not English (ESL).
     Literacy strategies that are successful with monolingual English-speaking students are also beneficial for ESL students. A colleague and I (Wynn and Laframboise, 1996) found that when scaffolding and support are provided by the teacher and peers, the following strategies are effective with ESL kindergarten-second grade students:

- **Shared** Concrete Experiences:
  Example: Making chocolate chip cookies and peanut butter and jelly sandwiches
- **Shared** Reading of Predictable Books:
  Example: Reading *Peanut Butter and Jelly* (Wescott, 1987)

- **Shared** Singing of Predictable Songs:
  Example: Singing "Old MacDonald Had a Farm"
- **Shared** Writing of Story Innovations:
  Example: Transforming *Good-Night Owl* (Hutchins, 1972) into *Good-Night Elephant*

The predictable patterns, repeated refrains, and rhythms in books and songs provide a supportive framework for students' emerging reading and writing. The concrete experiences and visuals are important in building concepts and vocabulary. Culturally responsive instruction for all students is necessary to meet diverse student needs and promote literacy acquisition.

Guided reading strategies promote interest and active involvement in understanding of the text during silent and oral reading. During guided reading, the teacher actively guides the reading experience using strategies incorporated in the Pickle Picnic Reading Plan (see Lesson Planning Appendix D).

The classic study, *Becoming a Nation of Readers: The Report of the Commission on Reading* (Anderson, Hiebert, Scott, & Wilkinson, 1985), found that the heart of reading instruction in U.S. classrooms is the small group reading lesson in which the teacher works with a small group of students while the rest of the class is working on independent reading assignments at their desks, in cooperative groups or at learning centers. Flexible groups may be established based on student interest or ability.

Reading By Students

The Teacher's Independent Reading Commandment:
Students shall read silently everyday.

"Simply providing interesting books for children is the most powerful incentive for reading" (Krashen, 1998, p. 21). An effective reading program exposes students to a wide and rich array of print and goes beyond the use of the basal reading program. Making decisions within this print-rich environment is imperative, because making choices is an integral part of literate behavior. Research suggests that the amount of independent silent reading children do in school is significantly related to gains in reading achievement and reading fluency.

Guidelines for independent reading include the following:

- Prioritize class time so independent reading will occur. Anderson et al. (1985) suggest 2 hours of independent reading per week by third or fourth grade.
- Establish an environment that is quiet and comfortable. A reading nook with beanbag chairs, pillows, and lamps is inviting.
- Use product positioning; display books not with the spine, but with the front of the book facing the potential consumer. According to Jim Trelease (2003), kids do judge a book by its cover. He suggests displaying books face-front in rain gutters. The gutters can be attached to a wall at varying heights and in space-appropriate lengths. View gutters in the classroom on the Jim Trelease website.
- Provide discussion time for students to share books they are reading independently.
- Plan dramatic book sales in which students create commercials (see later in chapter) to entice others to read their book. Design lit links, as an alternative to dreadfully dull book reports, to stimulate excitement (see Chapter 4).
- Encourage WOW word adventures in which students share *WOW words*, words that are unusual, interesting, and significant to text understanding, from their independent reading (see Wow Word Wall later in chapter).
- Document independent reading experiences at home and school on Reading Record Forms (see Figure 2.1).
- Increase interest in independent reading by encouraging each student to establish a personal reading goal that might be number of books, pages, or minutes to read daily. Design developmentally appropriate bar graphs where students chart their progress.
- Reward goal achievement with inexpensive stickers or free homework passes.
- Provide multilevel books for a given topic. This allows students to read about a topic from a variety of texts using a wide range of reading levels and text formats rather than from a single text. Multilevel texts are especially advantageous for at-risk and ESL learners.

FIGURE 2.1   Reading Record Form

_____ (student's name)

_____ (book title)

_____ (number of minutes) _____ (number of pages)

_____ (signature)

Jim Trelease (2003) says when we improve the print climate in the home, we increase reading achievement. He suggests a National Guilt Campaign, which he likens unto the National Smoking Campaign, in which educators point out the dangers of not reading in the home. Educators should also emphasize that in homes where reading is valued, where books are available, and where library use is encouraged, children have higher test scores. In this day and age, *when tests scores speak, parents listen.* Trelease suggests a daily reading diet of 20 minutes per day, six days per week. Krashen (1998) agrees with many of Trelease's suggestions and emphasizes building equity in books through increasing the number of books in school and public libraries and promoting greater student use.

An overarching goal in the reading program is developing *lifelong readers.*

The question *is not*, "Can they read?"
The question *is*, "Will they read?"

Beginning Reading

Beginning reading instruction should provide children with many opportunities to interact with print. "Phonics instruction is just the first step toward the ultimate goal of fast, accurate word identification and fluent reading" (Anderson et al., 1985, p. 46). Students in kindergarten through second grade should have well-structured instruction in phonics. As decoding skills become automatic, students have more capacity for comprehension.

Building a Firm Phonics Foundation

A strategy that works well in mastering phonics skills is singing. The vowel song that follows and the phonics ditty in Figure 2.2 are from my kindergarten through second-grade classes.

Certainly vowel sounds and their spellings are challenging. Our class created objects with movable parts to illustrate each short vowel sound: Ally Alligator who eats apples; Elly Elephant who eats eggs; Illy Impala who ingests iguanas; Olly Octopus who eats olives, and Ully Umpire who has underwear (always good for a giggle). When singing the vowel song, we pointed to each representative artistic creation and sang:

Title: Vociferous Vowels
Tune: "When the Saints Go Marching In"
Oh * *Ally Alligator* who eats *apples.* (2X)
When you want to know the **/<u>a</u>/ sound
Oh *Ally Alligator* who eats *apples.*
* *Note: Substitute Elephant, Octopus, Impala, and Umpire phrases in subsequent verses.*
** *Note: Sing /a/ or appropriate phonetic sound not the name of the letter.*

Increasing Sight Word Repertoire

A sight word repertoire is a collection of instantly recognized reading words. This knowledge is essential for a student to achieve fluency in reading. High-frequency words that occur repeatedly in reading are an important component in this collection. Many high-frequency

FIGURE 2.2   Alphabet Animals

Title: Alphabet Animals
Tune: "Doe a Deer\Do Re Mi"

Verse 1
A an anteater (sing letter name)
An A (sing letter name) says /a/ (sing phonetic sound)
B a bear; a B says /b/ C a cat; a C says */c/
D a dog; a D says /d/

Note: C does not have its own sound but steals the /k/ or /s/ sound

Chorus:
I know all my phonics sounds, and I know my letters too.
When you sing this silly song, then I'll sing along with you.

Verse 2 (continue sequence with verse then chorus)
E an elephant; F a fox; G a goat; H a horse
Note: G has either the /g/ and /j/ sound

Verse 3
I an iguana; J a jaguar; K a koala; L a lion

Verse 4
M a monkey; N a nyala; O an otter; P a panther

Verse 5
Q a quail; R a rhinoceros; S a seal; T a tiger

Verse 6
U a unicorn; V a vulture; W a walrus; X an x-iger
(students may invent a different "X" animal)

Verse 7
Y a Yak; Z a Zebra; U sang beautifully today
Let's just shout, "Hooray! Hooray!"

words are structure words, such as *the, what,* and *where,* which are difficult to define and have meaning only within context, yet they occur repeatedly in reading.

To increase students' sight word repertoire, a music program is easy and inexpensive to implement. Using well-known children's songs in which students are exposed to high-frequency words within dependable musical contexts allows students to participate in a motivational learning experience while increasing reading memory. A wide variety of familiar children's songs such as "Twinkle, Twinkle, Little Star," "The Wheels on the Bus," and "The Eency, Weency Spider," are available on audiotapes, videotapes, CDs, DVDs, in songbooks, and on charts. Any song text may be easily enlarged and written in big books, on charts, on transparencies, or using computer programs. Predictable language patterns in music are easily adaptable to a variety of innovations as teachers and students become lyricists. For example, "The Wheels on the Bus" may be transformed to "The Tires on the Bike." Music may be an integral part of thematic units.

In a Lyrics Lead to Literacy Program with at-risk kindergarten through second graders (Wynn, 1993a), my students demonstrated significant gains in sight word vocabulary when singing songs with predictable patterns. I found that many students progress developmentally from listening *to* singing *to* reading *to* composing.

Implement a sight/spelling word singspiration experience. Divide your class into two groups. The first group sings the words and letters in the song. The second group has strips of paper on which they write down the letters being sung. Then each student in the second group holds up the word as the song is sung a second time. During a second rendition of the song, the groups reverse responsibilities and sing a verse about a different word. For ideas see Spelling/Sight Word Songs in Figure 4.8. Optional sight word/spelling participation possibilities include students writing words on individual chalkboards, on whiteboards, or with an erasable pen on wipe-off photo pages before, during, or after singing.

Developing Word Attack Skills

During reading, what should students do when they confront a word with which they are not familiar? Teach students the **COPS** strategy for attacking these unknown words:

> Context—use surrounding information in the text to determine the word and the word's meaning.
> Others—ask friends or the teacher for help.
> Phonics—sound out the word.
> Skip—ignore the word.

Reading About Reading

To promote the value of reading and appreciate the lengths to which some people have to go to learn to read, read about reading. The following literature selections are sure to entice the reader/listener thrice as they appeal to the 👁 👁 eyes through illustrations, the 👂 👂 ears through listening, and the 💓 emotions through identifying with the protagonists:

- *More Than Anything Else* by Marie Bradby (1995): More than anything else Brooker T. Washington wanted to read. Though ignorance and adversity abound, Brooker learns to read.
- *The Wednesday Surprise* by Eve Bunting (1989): Seven-year-old Anna plans a surprise for her Dad's birthday. On Wednesday nights, she secretly teaches her Grandma to read.
- *Thank You, Mr. Falker* by Patricia Polacco (1998): Trisha looks forward to first grade and learning how to read. But, the letters and numbers get jumbled. "Dummy!" her classmates shout. Then Mr. Falker, a fifth grade teacher, comes into her life, and Trisha learns to read.
- *Aunt Chip and the Great Triple Creek Dam Affair* by Patricia Polacco (1996): What happens in a town where television reigns? What happens to books in a town where no one reads? In Triple Creek, books are used to build a dam. And then one day, a book is removed …

Differentiated Instruction

Billman (2002) and Rasmussen (2000) suggest that at-risk and ESL students often need additional support to understand and master essential literacy skills. Strategies they recommend include the following:

- Adjusting the language demands.
- Relating instruction to students' experiences.
- Providing texts on multilevels.
- Introducing different types of text organization.
- Using graphic organizers.
- Participating in cooperative groups.
- Selecting literature and projects that meet students' interests.

For ESL Krashen (1998) finds that developing literacy in their primary language assists students in developing literacy in their second language. Since they should read in their primary language, having books in this language is essential. Unfortunately, there is often a scarcity of books in limited-English-proficient homes. Books must become available. Both students and their families should be aware of books in their primary language as well as how to use libraries to obtain these books.

IRA/NCTE STANDARDS FOR THE ENGLISH LANGUAGE ARTS

The International Reading Association (IRA) and the National Council of Teachers of English (NCTE) established twelve key standards (IRA & NCTE, 1996; see Figure 2.3). They are closely interrelated, student-centered, and encourage the development of curriculum and instruction through building on the emerging literacy abilities that children bring to the classroom. The standards are also designed to be general in nature allowing ample room for innovation and creativity in teaching and learning. These standards are designed to capture the essential elements of teaching and learning language arts.

FIGURE 2.3   IRA/NCTE Standards for the English Language Arts 1996

Standards for the English Language Arts, by the International Reading Association and the National Council of Teachers of English, Copyright 1996 by the International Reading Association and the National Council of Teachers of English. Reprinted with permission.

(www.ira.org and www.ncte.org)

1. Students read a wide range of print and nonprint texts to build an understanding of texts, of themselves, and of the cultures of the United States and the world; to acquire new information; to respond to the needs and demands of society and the workplace; and for personal fulfillment. Among these texts are fiction and nonfiction, classic and contemporary works.
2. Students read a wide range of literature from many periods in many genres to build an understanding of many dimensions (e.g., philosophical, ethical, aesthetic) of human experience.
3. Students apply a wide range of strategies to comprehend, interpret, evaluate, and appreciate texts. They draw on their prior experience, their interactions with other readers and writers, their knowledge of word meaning and of other texts, their word identification strategies, and their understanding of textual features (e.g., sound-letter correspondence, sentence structure, context, graphics).
4. Students adjust their use of spoken, written, and visual language (e.g., conventions, style, vocabulary) to communicate effectively with a variety of audiences for different purposes.
5. Students employ a wide range of strategies as they write and use different writing process elements appropriately to communicate with different audiences for a variety of purposes.
6. Students apply knowledge of language structure, language conventions (e.g., spelling and punctuation), media techniques, figurative languages, and genre to create, critique, and discuss print and nonprint texts.
7. Students conduct research on issues and interests by generating ideas and questions, and by posing problems. They gather, evaluate, and synthesize data from a variety of sources (e.g., print and nonprint texts, artifacts, people) to communicate their discoveries in ways that suit their purpose and audience.
8. Students use a variety of technological and informational resources (e.g., libraries, databases, computer networks, video) to gather and synthesize information and to create and communicate knowledge.
9. Students develop an understanding of and respect for diversity in language use, patterns, and dialects across cultures, ethnic groups, geographic regions, and social roles.
10. Students whose first language is not English make use of their first language to develop competency in the English language arts and to develop understanding of content across the curriculum.
11. Students participate as knowledgeable, reflective, creative, and critical members of a variety of literacy communities.
12. Students use spoken, written, and visual language to accomplish their own purposes (e.g., for learning, enjoyment, persuasion, and the exchange of information).

How Should You Teach Reading?

Get Ready!
Get Set! To
Read, Respond, Retell, and Remember

PICKLE PICNIC READING/LISTENING LESSON PLAN

A **Pickle Picnic Reading/Listening Lesson Plan** is a musical reading and listening lesson plan organizer that incorporates components of the classic reading programs: directed reading activity (DRA) and directed reading-thinking activity (DR-TA). The DRA focuses on setting a purpose for reading, building background knowledge, introducing vocabulary, reading, and answering questions at the literal, inferential, and critical levels (Betts, 1946). The DR-TA focuses on prediction cycles: reading a selection and proving, disproving, or modifying the predictions (Stauffer, 1969). Successful strategies that increase reading comprehension are also effective in developing listening comprehension, as listening and reading are both receptive language modes. To help cement these components in forever memory, sing the Pickle Picnic Song in Figure 2.4.

Note: The Pickle Picnic Reading/Listening Lesson Plan (see Appendix D) was developed to ensure that all essential components were included in my student teachers' reading plans. Prior to incorporating this acrostic format, one or more components were often missing from lesson planning and presentations.

INSTRUCTIONAL ACTIVITIES THAT PROMOTE COMPREHENSION

Flood and colleagues (2003) suggest several types of instructional activities that promote comprehension. All of these are or may be included in a Pickle Picnic Reading Plan.

1. Preparing for reading activities
2. Developing vocabulary activities
3. Understanding and using text structure knowledge activities

FIGURE 2.4   Pickle Picnic Song

Title: Pickle Picnic Song
Tune: "Doe a Deer/Do Re Mi"
Note: This song is written from the student's point of view.

Purpose:	What do I want to know?
Interest:	What captivates me?
Concepts:	Ideas I need to know.
Knowledge:	Info inside of me.
Location:	The setting in a story.
Expression Expansion:	Vo-cab-u-lar-y.
Gee I'm learning how to read	
And, it's so eas-y!	
Prediction cycles:	Making guesses
Inquire:	Answers I need to know
	Some right there.
	Some seek and find.
	Some decisions as I go.
Confirm:	My guess, hey I was right!
Negate:	A wrong turn somewhere.
Inflate:	Extension of the text.
Capsulize:	A summary there.

4. Questioning activities
5. Information processing activities
6. Summarizing activities
7. Note-taking activities
8. Vocabulary or recreational reading

PROGRESSIVE READING INSTRUCTION

Progressive reading instruction includes *pre-reading strategies* that get students ready to read, *during-reading strategies* that include shared and guided reading experiences, *after-reading strategies* that provide follow-up to the story and include informal assessment, and *extension and enrichment strategies* that go beyond the lesson objective. *Vocabulary enrichment* may occur before, during, or after reading a selection.

Pre-Reading

Pre-reading strategies are experiences that activate students' prior knowledge, provide for construction of a shared knowledge base, and build bridges to new knowledge and concepts pertinent to comprehension of the text. Pre-reading strategies are used before reading a story as well as before reading individual chapters in a story. The students' purpose for reading significantly influences the degree of intensity with which they concentrate and thus their reading comprehension (see Pickle Picnic Song sections *P-I-C-K-L*).

During Reading

During-reading strategies promote interest and active involvement in understanding of the text during silent and oral reading by focusing student attention on specific information (see Pickle Picnic Song *prediction cycles*).

After Reading

After-reading strategies allow students and teachers to *assess* comprehension and enhance long-term memory of text concepts (see Pickle Picnic Song *capsulize* section).

Vocabulary Enrichment

The acquisition of proprietary vocabulary is enhanced through a variety of meaningful activities. *Proprietary vocabulary* is a collection of words over which the owner has mastery of understanding in listening and reading and mastery of use in speaking and writing (Wynn, 1993b). The traditional approach to vocabulary acquisition is

1. Look the word up in a dictionary.
2. Write a definition for the word.
3. Use the word in a sentence.

This approach provides exposure to words; however, there is minimal transfer to students' oral communication and written composition. Because vocabulary knowledge is a significant predictor of reading comprehension (Irvin, 2001), there should be a classroom focus on expanding a student's vocabulary repertoire. Enhanced vocabulary increases not only reading and listening comprehension but also verbal and written communication (see Pickle Picnic Song *expression expansion* section).

Strategies for proprietary vocabulary acquisition should meet one or more criteria in the eclectic **MODE** of instruction:

<u>M</u>eaningful Context
<u>O</u>pportunities to Use
<u>D</u>ifferent Activities
<u>E</u>xposure and Experience

Extension and Enrichment

Extension and enrichment strategies provide opportunities for students to respond to concepts in the story and go beyond the text in applying new knowledge to a variety of situations (see Pickle Picnic Song *inflate* section).

Literature Selections for the Chapter

Each literature selection provides a core book around which to build reading experiences. Literature selections come from a variety of genres with a focus across representative cultures. The books are developmentally sequenced from a picture book appropriate for younger readers to selections in nonfiction, historical fiction, and contemporary realistic fiction that are appropriate for a more mature reader, to a modern fantasy selection for older readers. Each Gamut of Games strategy is designed for cooperative group learning experiences.

TRADITIONAL LITERATURE

Cinderella comes to us from the oral tradition. According to Louie (1982) and Yen Mah (1999), the oldest versions of Cinderella come from Asia, not Europe. There are more than 700 variants of this fairy tale. They are representative of our diverse world and cross many cultures. Students will revel in studying different cultures through their folktales. They might look at a selected culture and examine a number of folktales from that culture or, as in the case of Cinderella, study a given tale as told across cultures.

There are a wide variety of sub genres included in traditional literature. Although not all literature experts agree, the following are suggested as sub genres: fairy tales, fables, myths, legends, tall tales, and traditional poetry such as epics, ballads, and Mother Goose. To find out more about picture books, multicultural literature, and traditional literature, sing the first nine verses of the "Literary Genre Dynamic Ditty" found in the Music Appendix B.

Yeh-Shen: A Cinderella Story from China

Yeh-Shen: A Cinderella Story from China is a traditional Cinderella tale retold in picture book format by Ai-Ling Louie (1982) and illustrated by Ed Young. In this variant, significant in Yen-Shen's life are a pet fish, the bones of the fish, a wise sage, golden slippers, and a king. Especially interesting is the inclusion of an early edition of the story written in Chinese.

An alternative Cinderella tale that will appeal to mature readers is *Chinese Cinderella: The True Story of an Unwanted Daughter* (Adeline Yen Mah, 1999). This autobiographical chapter book will bring tears to the readers' eyes as they experience the tragedies that occur in a *real* Cinderella's life.

Artistic Adventures

Character Growth/Sleeve Puppets

Students should be aware of *character growth* in stories. They need to observe that characters mature as they set goals, confront roadblocks, overcome obstacles, and progress toward goals. As students identify with characters in stories, they develop strategies for dealing with personal roadblocks while advancing toward their own personal goals. Singing the "Character Chant" will assist in careful observation of character growth (see "Literary Elements" in the Music Appendix B). Students learn to make the connections between literature and life by comparing characters in stories with people they know.

Puppetry provides a medium through which students convey some of their most intimate thoughts as they tackle difficulties in their own lives. Speaking through puppets, students are able to reflect on and share growth in their own lives as they encounter problems, mature, and make plans to attain a goal. Discuss how facial expressions show our own feelings and how puppets' facial features express their feelings. Talk about changes in facial expressions as situations get better or worse.

Students make *sleeve puppets* with a face on the front portraying their own feelings before growth in a particular situation and a different face on the back portraying feelings they have after growth in that situation. Directions for making sleeve puppets are in the puppet section of Activity Appendix A.

Literature-Based Example

While reading Yeh-Shen, *students make sleeve puppets to portray the feelings of the character when an obstacle is faced and later overcome. The face on front of the puppet shows initial feelings when facing the obstacle. Later, students draw a face on back of the puppet to reveal the feelings the character has after overcoming the obstacle.*

Character growth for Yeh-Shen might be:

I used to be *scared of making my stepsister mad.* (front)

But now I am *confident and know I have a mind of my own.* (back)

Gamut of Games

Vocabulary Puzzles

Have students construct vocabulary puzzles. Draw a picture from the story on the front of a piece of poster board. On the back of the poster board randomly write vocabulary terms. Next to each term write a definition or draw an illustration to display the meaning of the term. Draw puzzle lines between each term and the definition or illustration. Cut apart along puzzle lines to make a vocabulary puzzle. (See Activity Appendix A for puzzle pleasers directions.) Group members share each others' puzzles.

Literature-Based Example

Choose vocabulary terms from Yeh-Shen. *Use these terms along with definitions for a vocabulary puzzle.*

Vocabulary Term	Definition
Sage	wise person
Entranced	fascinated; spellbound
Transformed	changed into something different

As an alternative, create a story puzzle. Write questions and answers about the story or chapter. Draw lines between each question and answer to form puzzle pieces. Students exchange puzzles and discuss vocabulary terms or answer their friends' questions.

Ocular Organizer

Venn Diagram/Compare and Contrast/Data Chart

A *Venn diagram* is a graphic organizer that allows comparison of similarities and contrasts between different characters, different stories, and different versions of the same story. To

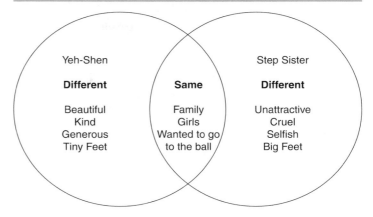

FIGURE 2.5   Venn Diagram for Comparing and Contrasting Traits of Yeh-Shen and Her Stepsister

create a Venn diagram, draw two circles so that they overlap. Put one character or story name on the left side of the left circle. List traits that are unique to this character or story under the name. Put the name of the other character or story to be contrasted on the right side of the right circle. List traits that are unique to this character or story under the name. Use the overlapping section of the two circles for traits that are the same or similar for both characters or stories.

Literature-Based Example

As an introduction to creating Venn diagrams, compare and contrast traits of Yeh-Shen and her stepsister (see Figure 2.5).

For extension and enrichment experiences compare and contrast two or more variants of Cinderella using a Venn diagram or a data chart (see Figure 2.6).

Dramatic Debut
Word Picture Charades

From the story, students or the teacher select interesting *word pictures*, phrases that draw mental pictures in the mind. Write these phrases on slips of paper. Teams of students play charades. Team members take turns drawing a slip of paper and acting out the word picture. The member acting out the word picture is not allowed to talk. Team members have to guess which word picture is being acted out.

Literature-Based Example

Before reading Yeh-Shen, *look for word pictures in a traditional version of Cinderella such as the Caldecott Award–winning variant translated and illustrated by Marcia Brown (1954). Using a traditional variant will build and expand background knowledge and set the stage before reading Yeh-Shen or variants from other cultures.*

Have students act out the following word pictures:

- Cinderella's father was tied hand and foot to his wife's apron strings.
- The step-sister's jewelry was not to be sneezed at.
- The prince fell head over heels in love with the owner of the slipper.

FIGURE 2.6   Data Chart to Compare and Contrast Variants of *Cinderella*

Title Author Illustrator	*Cinderella* **Marcia* *Brown* 1955 Caldecott Award	*Yeh-Shen: A* *Cinderella* *Story from* *China* Ai-Ling Louie *Ed Young	***Cendrillon: A*** ***Caribbean*** ***Cinderella*** Robert D. San Souci *Brian Pinkney	***Cindy Ellen:*** ***A Wild*** ***Western*** ***Cinderella*** Susan Lowell Jane Manning
Country	France	China	West Indies	America
Protagonist	Cinderella	Yeh-Shen	Cendrillon	Cindy Ellen
Setting	Once upon a time	Cave in southern China	Martinique, an island in the Caribbean	Wild, wild west
Source of Conflict	Stepmother Stepsisters	Stepmother Stepsister	Stepmother Stepsister	Stepmother Stepsisters
Goal	Go to the ball	Attend the Spring Festival	Go to birthday ball for Paul	Attend a rodeo, a Western fandango
Stumbling Blocks	No coach No horses No coachmen No clothes	No clothes No shoes	No carriage No horses No footmen No coachman No gown	No clothes No fine horse No stagecoach No stagecoach driver No stagecoach guard
Magic Source	Fairy godmother Wand	Bones of her pet fish	Godmother Wand	Godmother Pistol
Resolution	Cinderella marries the prince	Yeh-Shen marries the king	Cendrillon marries Paul	Cindy Ellen and Joe Prince got hitched

*Caldecott/Caldecott Honor Illustrator

Creative Composition

Story Sequel/ABC Story Sequel/Acrostic Summary/Pyramid Poem for a Story Summary

A *story sequel* is another book, chapter, or event that sequentially follows the plot of the story. Students choose one event and work cooperatively to develop the sequel or decide on several events and have different group members write about these events. Another possibility is to write another book and continue the narrative of the preceding story, thus beginning a series of books with the same characters. Students develop an outline for the book and assign sections of the book to be written by different group members.

FIGURE 2.7   ABC Story Sequel and Acrostic Summary for *Yeh-Shen: A Cinderella Story from China*

As the years went
By
Cinderella (Yeh-Shen) was
Determined to
End the
Family feud. She
Gave gifts to
Her family
Insisting that
Joy not jealousy was to be. The
King
Loved Yeh-Shen to distraction
Making the
Nobles
Obey her every command. Her loving
Personality
Quelled any
Rebellion
She might have faced
Twins of the royal couple were soon
Under foot with
Vivaciousness bringing
Wonderment and
EXcitement for
Years to come. The royal family
Zestfully reigned happily ever after.

Cinderella (Yeh-Shen) had
Internal beauty.
Negating her desire for revenge, a wise sage told her to
Dwell not on things of the past. She
Entered the
Royal family when the king
Enticed her to marry him. She
Lived in a
Loving relationship
Always seeking good for the kingdom.

Literature-Based Examples

1. The following questions could provide the stimulus for a story sequel for *Yeh-Shen*:
   - What happens in Yeh-Shen's life after she marries the king?
   - What changes will the stepmother and stepsister make in their own lives if they escape from the shower of flying stones?
2. Compose an *ABC Story Sequel*. (see Figure 2.7).
3. Create an *Acrostic Story Summary* (see Figure 2.7).
4. Design a *pyramid poem for a story summary*, a pyramid-shaped outline that includes information for literary elements such as character, setting, and plot, thus creating a story summary. The pyramid poem format is found in the Poetry Appendix C. Challenge students to make careful vocabulary choices for each line of the pyramid (Macon, Bewell, & Vogt, 1991). Display one or more summaries on a square pyramid (see Three-D-Geometry in Activity Appendix A).

A pyramid poem for a Story Summary for Yeh-Shen:
Yeh-Shen (1)
Hardworking, beautiful (2)
Cave to castle (3)
Spring Festival attendance forbidden (4)
Stepmother, stepsister cruel, crafty, jealous (5)
Fish bones, sage, wish come true (6)
Prince adores, she flees, slipper lost, search (7)
Slipper fits, rags transformed, lives happily ever after (8)

———————————————

 # NONFICTION

The purpose of nonfiction or expository text is to pass on or impart knowledge. Nonfiction literature includes a practical presentation of facts. Often nonfiction text is formatted as descriptive, sequence, compare and contrast, cause and effect, or problem and solution. For additional information, sing the nonfiction verse in the "Literary Genre Dynamic Ditty" found in the Music Appendix B and see the Informational Writing section in Chapter 3.

If You Lived with the Hopi

If You Lived with the Hopi (Kamma, 1999) is a nonfiction informational book that enlightens the reader about Native Americans. Facts include information about food, clothing, housing, religion, customs, and Hopi history. Chapter titles are written in a question format. Additional books in this Scholastic Native American Series include *If You Lived with the Sioux Indians*, *If You Lived in the Alaska Territory*, *If You Lived with the Cherokee*, and *If You Lived with the Iroquois*. Scholastic also has a similar information book series about other cultures.

Artistic Adventure
Sketch-to-Summarize/Shape Book

Summarizing is an important skill in assessing whether a reader has understood text information. After reading a passage, one way to condense the information is to draw a sketch. Students design a sketch for each chapter or section of a story to represent a synopsis of the information. Bind a collection of these sketches in a shape book.

To design a shape book, choose a shape that is representative of the story and make a front and back cover in that shape from poster board. For each chapter or section of the story make a shape page. On each page create a sketch to summarize the information for one chapter or section of the story (see Shape Books in Activity Appendix A).

———————————————

Literature-Based Example

For If You Lived with the Hopi, *make a shape book in the form of a Hopi house, similar to an apartment building with a flat roof. Cut a shape page for each chapter of the text. On each page create a sketch to represent the information for that chapter.*

———————————————

 ### *Gamut of Games*
WOW Word Wall

Working in cooperative groups, select *WOW words*, words that are unusual, interesting, and significant to text understanding. Jot WOW words on sticky notes and place next to the appropriate sentence in a literature selection. The sentence does not have to be copied. Then share the context in which the word occurs with your group. After sharing, place sticky notes on the class *WOW word wall*, a vocabulary bulletin board. Next, develop a classification system for the WOW words on your WOW word wall.

Literature-Based Example

The following vocabulary terms might be selected from If You Lived with the Hopi: *cistern, clan, Hopi, kachinas, kiva, mesa, metates, pueblo, reservation, spring, and washes. Additional words may be added as Hopi research expands. An initial classification possibility for a WOW word wall might look like this:*

Food and Water	Shelter	Family	Tradition	Jobs
Spring	Pueblo	Clan	Kachinas	Pottery
Cistern	Mesa			Jewelry
Washes	Kiva			Baskets
Metates	Reservation			

Ocular Organizers
KWL Strategy

The *KWL strategy* (What we *K*now; What we *W*ant to know; What we *L*earned) is an effective technique to use before reading (Ogle, 1986). A KWL chart is organized in three vertical columns:

Column 1: Enter information students already *K*now about the topic, thus establishing a common background of prior knowledge.
Column 2: List questions students *W*ant answered. Questions may be added to this column as the reading progresses.
Column 3: Record information students *L*earn as reading progresses.

The KWL is a practical, easy-to-implement, effective teaching strategy at all grade levels. For additional KWL application ideas, see Informational Writing in Chapter 3.

Literature-Based Example

An example of a pre-reading chart for If You Lived with the Hopi *might look like this;*

KWL Chart

What we **K**now about the Hopi tribe	What we **W**ant to know about the Hopi tribe	What we **L**earned about the Hopi tribe.
The Hopi are Indians who lived a long time ago.	Are there still Hopi today?	
	Where did the Hopi live?	
	Did the Hopi scalp people?	

Dramatic Debut

Role-Playing/Problem and Solution

Role-playing is a dramatic activity that allows the participants to assume a character's persona and participate in life's experiences from that character's point of view. To incorporate role-playing as an after-reading activity, cooperative groups receive or develop *vignettes*, short literary sketches, that relate to situations confronted in the text.

Stimulate critical thinking by acting out potential solutions to problems characters in the text encounter. Several small groups may receive the same problem to discuss and role play. As different groups discuss and act out their vignettes, a variety of solutions for any given conflict become apparent.

The following vignette may be used as an introduction to problem-and-solution role-playing. Students often experience rejection in new social situations. To identify with this student, role play the following:

> *You are the new student in a school. You are not accepted by the other students. What could you do? How do you feel?*

Literature-Based Example

Now experience problems and solutions with the Hopi. You are a member of the Hopi tribe. There is no newspaper, no television, no telephone. How do you get the latest news? Each village has a town crier whose job is to shout out the latest news as well as problems needing the attention of villagers. The problems that follow are some you hear. In your group figure out potential solutions to these problems, and plan a vignette presentation.

- *We're in the middle of the drought. What should we do?*
- *Our village has no school. How will our children learn?*
- *We want to preserve our history, but writing is not yet part of our culture. How can we preserve our history?*

Creative Composition

Diamante Poetry

A *diamante* is a diamond-shaped poem that emphasizes contrast and provides an interesting way to develop vocabulary choices and review parts of speech. A diamante poem is sometimes written to contrast a protagonist and an antagonist. The antagonist may be another character, the setting, society, or conflicts within the character. The diamante format is found in the Poetry Appendix C.

Literature-Based Example

For an extension and enrichment experience, compare and contrast other Native American tribes to the Hopi tribe. Create diamante poetry to reveal your findings. In the following modified diamante poem, lines 2 and 6 contrast housing. Lines 3 and 5 contrast characteristics. Line 4 contains social values for each tribe.

Hopi
Living in an apartment
Farming, Eating Corn, Settling
Peace and cooperation are imperative; War is a game and time of honor.
Hunting, Eating Buffalo, Traveling
Living in a tipi
Sioux

HISTORICAL FICTION

Hansen (1997) delineates the value of historical fiction when she notes, "the details are based on the diaries, journals, oral histories, and narratives of people who lived through those tumultuous times (p. 196)," thus the historical information is accurate. As is often true in historical fiction, the protagonist is fictional. Patsy, a lame, timid, friendless girl, is a figment of the author's imagination. Historical fiction adds interest and motivation to social studies classes. For a musical experience, sing the historical fiction verse in the "Literary Genre Dynamic Ditty" found in the Music Appendix B.

I Thought My Soul Would Rise and Fly

I Thought My Soul Would Rise and Fly: The Diary of Patsy, a Freed Girl (Hansen, 1997) is the winner of the Coretta King Award. Written in a diary format, the reader experiences life from a freed—or is she free?—African American slave's point of view.

Artistic Adventures

Eight Fold Person/Character Web/Personal Prediction Story

Before reading, create an *eightfold person* (see Activity Appendix A) for a character in the text. Develop the character's appearance based on information that is gleaned as the story is read. Inside the jacket of the eightfold person, develop a *character web*, a graphic organizer on which the name of a character is centered in the nucleus of the web and categories related to the character radiate out from the nucleus forming a web. The *four As* provide one possibility for categories:

1. **Appearance:** what the character looks like
2. **Action:** what the character does
3. **Articulation:** what the character says
4. **Attitudes:** how the character feels about him- or herself and how other characters in the story feel about him or her

As the story is read, add appropriate information to the web. To reinforce character information, sing the "Character Chant" located in the Music Appendix B. After completing the story, students might use information from the web to write a paragraph or two summarizing the webbed information and place this information on a card mounted inside the character's jacket.

Personal prediction stories take advantage of the power of premonition to lure predictors into the story. Before reading or hearing a book read, the class, cooperative groups, or individual students write a personal prediction story using assigned clue words. The story tells what the writer thinks is going to happen. The story is initially shared and later compared and contrasted to the original story.

Literature-Based Example

An initial character web for Pasty, the protagonist in I Thought My Soul Would Rise and Fly *is based on information in her first diary entry (see Figure 2.8). Make additional web entries as the story is read.*

Suggested terms for an initial personal prediction story for the story are: diary, free, games, joke, legal, Pasty, read, slave. A personal prediction story might be:

Patsy is a *slave*. She can't *joke*, or play *games*.
She wants to be *free* but that isn't *legal*.
One day she finds a *diary*, but she can't *read* it.

Compare and contrast this personal prediction story after reading several diary entries in the book.

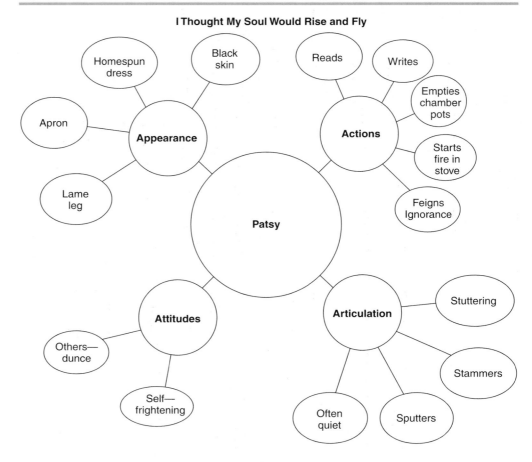

FIGURE 2.8 Initial Character Web for Patsy in *I Thought My Soul Would Rise and Fly*

Gamut of Games

Questioning the Author

Questioning the author (QtA) is a method designed to facilitate understanding of text ideas while simultaneously challenging the authority of the author (McKeown & Beck, 1999). QtA is a method compatible with the *constructivist approach* to learning, which focuses on having students actively involved in constructing their own personal knowledge. The teacher is collaboratively involved in the role of facilitator. To implement QtA, the teacher reads the text, determines the message or information students should take from the text, anticipates problems students may encounter in understanding the text, and develops queries for class discussion.

Beck, McKeown, Hamilton, and Kucan (1997) differentiate questions from queries. Traditionally, *questions* are used after reading an assignment, an after-the-fact retrieval system. Students' answers are used to check understanding and *assess* comprehension. On the other hand, *queries* are used at predetermined intervals during a reading assignment allowing students to participate in shared inquiry. Queries are designed as challenges that provoke students' thinking as they grapple with the author's ideas. Students also build understanding that includes explaining information, connecting information to previous knowledge, and subsequently using the information to assist in developing a greater depth of understanding.

The following are samples of queries designed by Beck et al. Queries are initially modeled by the teacher and later developed by small group discussion leaders.

Initiating Queries
- What is the author trying to say here?
- What is the author's message?

Follow-up Queries
- What does the author mean here?
- Does the author explain this clearly?
- Does this make sense with what the author has told us before?

Narrative Queries
- Character
- How do things look for this character now?

Plot
- How has the author let you know something has changed?

The teacher selects, adapts, and designs queries to fit the text and students' developmental level. Queries are written on sticky notes and placed at appropriate stopping places in the text. As students become adept at QtA, they gradually assume responsibility for developing queries in their cooperative groups.

Literature-Based Example

Based on the first diary entry in I Thought My Soul Would Rise and Fly, *Friday, April 21, 1865, use QtA to develop background knowledge about the historical time frame and what is happening in Patsy's life.*

Query 1: (Paragraphs 1-4): What is the author telling us about Patsy?
Possible Answer: Patsy is a slave who secretly knows how to read.
Query 2: (p. 4): What additional information does the author provide the reader?
Possible Answer: Even though Annie and Charles think Pasty is a dunce, she is really smart and can write as well as read.
Query 3: (p. 5): What secrets are the plantation owners keeping? How does this impact Patsy's life?
Possible Answer: The slaves are now free, but Patsy's life of servitude continues as it always has.

 Ocular Organizers

Context Clue Guru Bulletin Board

A *context clue guru* attempts to stump the class by seeking and finding sentences with examples of interesting vocabulary terms. The guru must be sure the sentence context lends itself to determining the word and the word's meaning. The context clue sentence is displayed on the context clue guru bulletin board, leaving a blank for the vocabulary term.

Loyal followers attempt to ascertain the missing term. They write prediction possibilities on sticky notes and place them on the sentence display. The context clue guru then shares the author's word choice. Discussion ensues about possible reasons for the author's word choice and whether other synonym options change or enhance the meaning of the sentence and story.

Literature-Based Example

Context clue sentences from I Thought My Soul Would Rise and Fly:

- I thought Mistress would slap her, but she turned as red as a beet and _____ away with Nancy flouncing behind her. *(Possibilities: ran; rushed; hurried. Author's choice: stomped)*
- Thomas is two years old and like a little _____ . Nancy has to run behind him. *(Possibilities: brat; imp; monkey. Author's choice: hurricane)*

For additional adventures, make an accordion book (see Activity Appendix A). Place each context clue sentence with a blank on a separate page of the accordion book. List possibilities for the missing word under the sentence. Hide the author's word choice on another page in the accordion book. For at-risk, ESL, or younger students, the teacher may choose to put the sentences on an overhead transparency and implement this strategy as an oral class experience.

Dramatic Debut
Readers' Theater

Readers' theater is a dramatic experience in which the students practice and read their assigned parts (Shepard, 1994). There is no attempt to memorize the script, rather, the emphasis is on expressive oral reading. Participants sit or stand during a performance, but they do not act out their parts. At times background scenery and minimal props are used. Students take turns reading different parts.

Where do you get readers' theater scripts? Purchase commercial scripts; look for free scripts on the websites in the reference section; or create class scripts using a story text. When developing class scripts, model writing these scripts. Instructions could sound like this:

> Use dialogue from the story to help you construct the script. You may add some words for characters if the book simply describes what the character is thinking or feeling. You will want the character to actually say words that portray these feelings and thoughts.

> Anonymous

Later, cooperative groups or individual students will enjoy creating their own scripts.

Literature-Based Example

Begin a readers' theater script as extension and enrichment for I Thought My Soul Would Rise and Fly *as follows:*

Phillis:	I know I am young, but I can read, write, cook, wash, and teach. I should be able to find work and care for myself.
Ruth:	Remember what I taught you a long time ago. You must ask for what you want to have.
Phillis:	Yes, and the first thing I want is to get an education. Then I want to teach school.
Brother Solomon:	You will be the first teacher in our new village school. We'll call our village Libertyville, because we're so glad to be free.

Creative Composition
Simulated Journals

A *simulated journal* is a written account of daily experiences from another person or character's point of view. In a simulated journal the writer gains insight into a character's emotions and develops an understanding of the character's actions while assuming that character's persona. Students may choose different characters for their simulated journal writing. When reading chapter books, students could write a simulated journal entry after reading each chapter.

Pairs of students may write simulated journals. When writing simulated journals in peer pairs, each student assumes the persona of a different character in the book. Then the characters dialogue with each other.

Literature-Based Example

The following simulated journal entries from Nancy's mother and Nancy are based on diary entries from Wednesday, May 10, 1865.

Nancy's Mother: I'm so excited. I just found out where you are. We were separated when you were only four years old. You must be about fifteen by now. I can hardly wait to take you home.

Nancy: I've been the maid for the lady of the house for a lot of years. She treats me well most of the time. Certainly my life is better than the other freed slaves. I get to live in the big house and eat pretty well.

Nancy's Mother: I can't believe it! You hid behind the lady of the house and refused to speak to me. What's a mother to do?

Nancy: I don't know if you're my mother or not. But I do know, I have it pretty easy. I don't want to give this all up to go live in a hut and eat practically nothing.

CONTEMPORARY REALISTIC FICTION

Contemporary realistic fiction could happen in our everyday world. The author draws us into a believable world with a believable plot. The only problem is that this story is real only in our imaginations. The author has made up the story for our enjoyment and edification. Sing about contemporary realistic fiction using the lyrics in the "Literary Genre Dynamic Ditty" in Music Appendix B.

Bridge to Terabithia

Written by Katherine Patterson (1977), this book is a Newbery Award–winning classic. Many schools have multiple copies to use in small groups or with a whole class. There is a powerful friendship theme throughout the story. As the reader is drawn into the story, tears will flow as events take a logical but unexpected twist. As in life, both the protagonist and reader learn that what we get in life is not always what we want.

Artistic Adventures

Book and Author Focus/Trifold Brochure

During a *book and author focus*, cooperative groups of students choose another book written by the selected author, or they choose a book with a similar theme. After reading the book, students design a *trifold brochure* (see Activity Appendix A). The purpose of the brochure is to build interest and entice other students to read the book. The teacher should stress that the ending of the story must not be given away.

For a book and author focus, create an inviting reading center for the classroom with an attractive display of books. A beanbag chair, bathtub, sofa, rocking chair, and child's swimming pool all contribute to inviting reading corners.

Literature-Based Example

During a book and author focus on Katherine Patterson, choose, read, and develop a trifold sales brochure for one her books. Possibilities include Come Sing Jimmy Jo, Consider the Lilies, The Crane Wife, The Great Gilly Hopkins, Jacob Have I Loved, The Master Puppeteer, Of Nightingales That Weep, Park's Quest, The Sign of the Chrysanthemum, *or* Tale of the Mandarin Ducks.

For trifold brochure suggestions for Katherine Patterson's Newbery Honor book, *The Great Gilly Hopkins* (1978), see Figure 2.9.

FIGURE 2.9 Trifold Brochure for *The Great Gilly Hopkins*

A Tri-Fold Brochure for *The Great Gilly Hopkins* (1978) might contain the following information as well as illustrations:

Author, Illustrator, Brochure Creators *The Great Gilly Hopkins* By: Katherine Paterson This book has been determined by our million dollar sales force, Charles, Connie, and Brent, to be one of the best books they have ever read.	Main Character, Problem, and Goal *Main Character:* **G**ruesome **G**um Smacking **R**ebellious **I**ntelligent **E**xasperating **L**oud **A**bandoned **L**onely **T**alented **Y**elling *Problem:* Gilly causes chaos in foster homes and at school. *Goal:* Gilly's goal is to live with her "real" mother.	*Event* - Gilly meets her new family. Gilly meets her new foster mother, Trotter, "a huge hippopotamus of a woman". She is introduced to William Ernest, a nearsighted, stubby-nosed, shy, slow reader. Gilly encounters Mr. Randolph, the blind neighbor with the brown face who eats dinner every night at Trotter's house.
Title Page: page 1	page 2	page 3
Event - Gilly enrolls in a new school Gilly has encounters at her new school with the principal, her new teacher, and the students.	*Event* - Gilly runs away. Gilly steals money and runs away to find her "real" mother.	"Tidbits to Tempt Your Taste Buds" Comments by Suzie: "*The Great Gilly Hopkins* is the best book I have ever read in my whole entire life! I challenge you to read the book."
page 4	page 5	Back of Brochure: page 6

Gamut of Games

Stump the Teacher/Stump the Student/Literature Circles

Stump the teacher (StT), an adaptation of the request procedure (Manzo, 1969), is a highly motivational strategy in which the teacher and students read the same text and attempt to stump each other as they alternate asking each other questions. When participating in StT, the first rule is that no one may have read the selection previously. You and your students must read new-to-you material, perhaps several pages. Then close your books. An announcer might shout, "Let the questioning begin!" Alternate asking and answering questions. Initially, most student questions may be at a literal or factual level. As you model higher-order questions, your students will begin asking higher-order questions. Undoubtedly, you will be embarrassed at times when you can't answer the students' questions. Your self-esteem may suffer. You are now on the same "hot seat" you often provide for your students. Your students will appreciate your willingness to take risks.

StT is fun for students, but the level of involvement for each student is low when each has to wait for a turn to ask a question. To increase student involvement, adapt StT to *stump the student (StS)*. Within *literature circles* of four, form two pairs. Then follow the sequence of silently reading several pages, closing the books, and alternately asking and answering questions. There may be several literature circles in a classroom each reading the same or different books.

Literature-Based Example

The teacher and student read the first four pages of The Bridge to Terabithia. *Then they close their books and alternate asking questions such as:*

Teacher:	Why did Jess run everyday?
Student:	He wanted to be the fastest runner in fifth grade.
Student:	Why did the kids make fun of Jess?
Teacher:	He liked to draw.
Teacher:	What did the author mean when she said no one had more grit than Jess had? (moving questioning to higher order)
Student:	Hm … I'm not sure. I think that grit is like dirt.

Ocular Organizer

Plot Structure Chart/Personal Paragraphs and/or Stories

A *plot structure chart* is a graphic organizer that allows students to analyze or plan the action of an incident, chapter, or story. A plot structure chart is a stair-step organizer that includes a problem, goal, events, a climax, and a conclusion. Plot structure charts are read from the bottom to the top.

Students choose an incident in the story. They use a plot structure chart to organize their thoughts. Based on this incident, they write *personal paragraphs and/or stories*. The paragraph or story may start, "Once upon a time. …"

Literature-Based Example

Story Incident

In The Bridge to Terabithia, *the Burke family is very intelligent in many ways that are unique to Jess. They have goals that focus on personal growth. Their family structure is very different from that of the other families in the town. Leslie Burke struggles with her unique family background and her desire for peer acceptance.*

Plot Structure Chart

Conclusion: 1 1/2 friends
Climax: Befriends school bully
Event 3: Teacher's pet
Event 2: No TV
Event 1: Hobby—scuba diving
Problem: Everyone thinks she's weird
Goal: To be accepted by peers
Character: Leslie

Personal Paragraph

Leslie is new at school. She desperately wants to be accepted by her peers. Unfortunately, everyone thinks she's weird. Her hobby is scuba diving. Whoever heard of a girl doing that? She has no television set at home. Everyone else does. She's the teacher's pet. That's no way for her to impress anyone. Then she befriends the school bully. She is overjoyed. She tells Jess, "Thanks to you, I think I now have one and one-half friends at Lark Creek School" (p. 76).

Dramatic Debut
Commercials

Commercials are advertisements designed to sell a prospective consumer a product. Commercials make use of a variety of propaganda techniques. Three popular techniques are testimonial, bandwagon, and reward. The *testimonial technique* employs a popular person, like an athlete or film star, to convince people to purchase a product. The *bandwagon technique* claims that everyone is using the product, and you should use it too. The *reward technique* offers something to a person for buying a particular product. Have students investigate these propaganda techniques and then design commercials to sell Katherine Paterson's books. For additional propaganda ideas, see Persuasive Writing in Chapter 3.

Students make television sets from cardboard boxes or poster board and request "air time" to broadcast advertisements for their favorite books. An additional challenge in developing commercials is to use *alliteration*, words beginning with the same initial sound.

Literature-Based Example

Testimonial: I, F. Bertram Johnston, tell you that *The Great Gilly Hopkins* by Katherine Paterson is the *greatest* book I have ever read. Why, I was just a poor, struggling cashier at a sub shop when, one day, a customer gave me a copy of this book. After reading about Gilly and her "grit and granite" outlook on life I told myself, "If Gilly can do it, I can do it too!" You see where I am today—living the "lifestyle of the rich and famous"—all due to my encounter with Gilly.

Bandwagon: All the members of the world famous National League baseball team, "The Great Gilly Gutsers," are grateful to Gilly for the guidance she gave them in *The Great Gilly Hopkins.* Their grandstand plays are a tribute to Gilly, who taught them that great feats are possible with grip and grit.

Reward: Hurry! Hurry! Read all about her! *The Great Gilly Hopkins* has grandiose plans for those who read about her gregarious guise and gradual growth as she comes to grip with life's challenges. Gilly will give you not one, but two, free Katherine Paterson books when you purchase the anniversary edition of *The Great Gilly Hopkins.*

Creative Composition
Simile Search/Four-Flap Flip-Flop Book

A *simile* is a comparison in which two unlike things are compared using the words *like* or *as*. Often the two things being compared appear to be unrelated *(e.g., she was as cool as a cucumber)*. Similes allow the reader to form vivid mental images and gain fresh insight into the objects being compared. Go on a *simile search* and locate similes in the story. Use the first half of the story simile and compose a new second half for the simile thus creating an *original student simile*.

Make a *four-flap flip-flop book* (see Activity Appendix A). Write the first half of each story simile on the top of a flap. Write the original student ending and illustrate the original student simile under the flap. Write the story simile on the back of the flap. Compare the original student simile with the story simile.

Literature-Based Example

Go on a simile search in The Bridge to Terabithia *(Paterson, 1977). Devise original student similes and compare to those composed by Katherine Paterson.*

- **Story Simile:** *The boys quivered on the edges of their seats like moths fighting to be freed of cocoons (p. 24).*
- **Original Simile:** *The boys quivered on the edges of their seats like rabbits waiting to flee from a hound.*
- **Story Simile:** *She was sitting straight up in her seat, looking as pleased with herself as a motorcycle rider who's just made it over fourteen trucks (p. 74).*
- **Original Simile:** *She was sitting straight up in her seat, looking as pleased with herself as if she had won a hundred dollars.*

MODERN FANTASY

Fantasy allows the reader to suspend disbelief. Thus, the reader accepts impossible characters, setting, or both as true. Tiny characters as in *The Borrowers*, animated toys as in *Pinocchio*, talking animals as in *Peter Rabbit*, an out-of-this world setting as in *A Wrinkle in Time*, and preposterous characters and setting as in *Alice in Wonderland* are all believable to the reader. The time warp in *The Devil's Arithmetic* allows the characters and reader to move back and forth across periods of time.

The Devil's Arithmetic

In a time warp, Hannah is swept back to the time of the Holocaust, to the place of *The Devil's Arithmetic* (Yolen, 1988), a death camp, a place of unspeakable horrors. Why deal with this heart-wrenching issue? Because as Hannah says, "You must remember, too, so that whoever of us survives this place will carry the message into that future. What message? That we will survive. The Jews. That what happens here must never happen again (p. 157)." This saga is Yolen's powerful protest against man's inhumanity to man. If *The Devil's Arithmetic* is too graphic for your students, as an alternative and a more gentle dealing with the Holocaust, consider *Number the Stars*, Lois Lowry's Newbery Award winner (1989).

Artistic Adventures
Choose-a-Word/Step Book

Students and teachers choose interesting words or phrases from the story to add to proprietary vocabulary. Students make *step books* and write a vocabulary word or phrase on each step of the book (see Activity Appendix A). The word meaning is illustrated above the word and beneath the preceding step. As an alternative, a riddle is written on each step of the book. The answer to the riddle, the focus vocabulary term, is illustrated above the riddle and beneath the preceding step.

Literature-Based Example

A step book for The Devil's Arithmetic *might include the following words or phrases with their story-appropriate meanings or story context along with appropriate illustrations.*

1. **Chosen:** "A person is not killed here, but *chosen*" (p. 128).
2. **Processed:**   "They are not cremated in the ovens, they are *processed*" (p. 128).
3. **Foreknowledge:**   "What use was her special *foreknowledge* if no one would listen? Maybe they thought her strange or sick or even crazy, but she was none of that. She was from the future, somehow" (p. 91).

Gamut of Games
Summary Story

A *summary story* is an adaptation of story impressions and GIST (generating interactions between schemata and text) strategies found in *Reading Strategies and Practices: A Compendium* (Tierney, & Readence, 2000). This sequential, condensing, integrating, and summarizing approach provides motivational challenge. The summary story method includes the following steps:

1. Discuss the title, author, and illustrator.
2. Read the first part or chapter of the story.
3. Summarize part 1 of the story or Chapter 1 in 15 words or less.
4. Read the second part of the story or Chapter 2.
5. Summarize parts 1 and 2 of the story or Chapters 1 and 2 in 15 words (or summarize Chapter 2 or section 2 by itself).
6. Read the third part of the story or Chapter 3.
7. Summarize these three parts in 15 words (or summarize Chapter 3 or section 3 by itself).
8. Continue the sequence.
9. Share summaries.

Variations:
- For long chapters increase the number of words.
- Each summary section may consist of three lines without a word count.
- At-risk, ESL, or younger students may summarize with pictures or with the teacher acting as scribe.

Literature-Based Example

A summary story for Chapters 11 and 12 of The Devil's Arithmetic *might look like this:*

Chapter 11

Boxcars.	*Death.*	*Thirst.*	*March!*	*Schnell!*
I	*will*	*last.*	*Strip.*	*Hope.*
Showers.	*Shiver.*	Never	*cry*	*again.*

Chapters 11 and 12

Thinking	*dangerous.*	*Choose*	*clothes.*	*Tattoo*
numbers.	*Laughter.*	*Hope.*	*Life.*	*Jew*
smoke.	*Remember*	*name*	*not*	*number.*

Ocular Organizer

Headline Highlights/Headline Highlights Bulletin Board

Introduce *Headline Highlights* by asking, "Why do viewers watch Headline Highlights, for example, CNN, rather than a longer television news show?" Numerous reasons are possible, including newscasters come straight to the point, they get right to the heart of the matter, viewers are not bogged down with trivial details, and the all-time, number one viewing reason, Headline Highlights is less time consuming to watch. Study the format of headline news shows. Listen to information presented by news commentators. Read succinctly framed phrases. Watch text that rolls across the bottom of the screen often with weather or safety disaster information. Cooperative groups may devise Headline Highlights news programs using a subject area focus in social studies, science, or other content areas.

Develop a *Headline Highlights bulletin board* to promote interest in news programs. Display attention-capturing titles, subtitles, quick quotes, and illuminating illustrations. Broadcast Headline Highlights news throughout the school via closed circuit television.

Literature-Based Example

In the pre-reading phase, building background knowledge is essential for enhancing comprehension. The Holocaust is a time in history about which most students have little knowledge. Working in cooperative groups to research and report on this time in history will give students an introduction to and an informational foundation for the Holocaust.

Introduce the Holocaust through picture books. These books will provide a gentle introduction to the complex issues and difficult concepts for this horrific time in history. Choose age-appropriate books with historical accuracy. Many students will have questions for which there will be no answers. For example, how could the Nazis hang people and then burn them in gas ovens?

Develop a Headline Highlights news program such as:

There is tragic news regarding the Holocaust. Ladies and gentlemen, we regret to inform you that friends and family members are disappearing left and right. As we search for a common thread in why some people are chosen and others are left, one thing stands out, all those who have disappeared are Jews. Apparently, the Nazis arrive in town, the Jews are told they're being resettled, the Jews are loaded into trucks, and they are heard from no more. Stay tuned. We will update you as these tragic events unfold.

Create a Headline Highlights bulletin board on which to display Holocaust information. Include questions such as, "How is the Holocaust like the story of Hansel and Gitl? Search the internet for actual pictures from this time period to display. Creating rolling text using adding machine tape with dowels to roll the tape on.

Dramatic Debut
Story Theater

Story theater is a dramatic experience in which a narrator reads the text while participants assume characters' roles and act out what is being read. The participants' focus is on action, and they do not have speaking parts. Story theater occurs at designated places within a story, at the end of a chapter, or at the end of the book. While the narrator reads the text, students reenact the scene and gain insight into the unfolding drama and emotions of the characters.

Literature-Example

Each participant assumes the role of one of the characters in The Devil's Arithmetic. *Create passports for each death camp inmate. Design a death camp midden, garbage dump, using crumpled newspapers, empty food cartons, and other trash. Wear double layers of clothes such as torn shirts, skirts, and jackets. Wear flip flops. When diving into the midden throw off the outer layer of clothes and flip flops beside the midden. Use dolls or stuffed animals to represent small children being carried into the midden.*

As a narrator reads selections from pages 122–123, participants make clucking sounds to warn the children that the commandant is coming and others grab small children and jump in the midden.

> Rivka....a penetrating clucking noise...From all over the camp...crazed crickets...children...scrambling...raced toward the midden...skinned out of their clothes and dove...(pp. 122-123)

Note: Additional midden information is available on pages 116–117, 123–124, 138–140 and other places in the story.
Near the midden, set up a kitchen with a table and big pots. Each participant should have a bowl, a used plastic food container, that is essential for daily existence. Reenact the uses of the bowl:

> You must take good care of your bowl ...I call them Every Bowls because they are everything to us. Without the bowl, you cannot have food, you cannot wash, you cannot drink. Memorize your bowl—its dents, its shape. Always know where you have put it. There are no replacements (pp. 107–108).

Creative Composition
Theme/Senses Poem/Thematic Senses Poem

A *theme* is the unifying meaning of the story and often answers the question, "What is the story's message?" Because readers bring different background experiences to a story, they may not all agree on the central meaning. Themes are determined by observing the main character's growth and development in overcoming conflict and reaching goals. Students may be introduced to the theme before reading the story. This allows them to focus on the central theme while reading. On the other hand, students may be asked to decide what they think the theme of the story is as they read and after reading the story. This challenge will provide insight into each student's depth of observation. Differences of opinion will stimulate fascinating discussion.

A *senses poem* is a poem that focuses on the sight, sound, smell, taste, and touch (feel or feelings) of a person, place, or thing (see Poetry Appendix C). Younger students enjoy composing senses poems about concrete objects such as an apple, cookie, or marshmallow. From this experience, students progress to creating a senses poem about the setting or one of the characters in a story. A *thematic senses poem* is a poem that focuses on the sight, sound, smell, taste, and touch (feel or feelings) of the theme of a story.

Literature-Based Example:

"Remember" is a central theme in The Devil's Arithmetic. *The following is a senses poem for this theme:*

Remember

Remember *looks* like cattle going to the slaughter, a corpse hanging on the gate.
Remember *sounds* like wailing and weeping.
Remember *smells* like the garbage dump, burning flesh.
Remember *tastes* like watery soup and sometimes stale bread.
Remember *feels* like skin and bones.
We must **remember**, lest we forget.

> *Those who cannot remember the past*
> *Are condemned to repeat it.*
>
> Santayana

Literature References

Bradby, M. (1995). *More than anything else*. New York: Orchard Books.

Brown, M. (1954). *Cinderella*. New York: Charles Scribner's Sons. Caldecott Award.

Bunting, E. (1989). *The Wednesday surprise*. New York: Clarion Books.

Hansen, J. (1997). *I thought my soul would rise and fly: The diary of Patsy, a freed girl*. New York: Scholastic. Coretta Scott King Award.

Hutchins, P. (1972). *Good-Night owl*. New York: Aladdin Books.

Kamma, A. (1999). *If you lived with the Hopi*. New York: Scholastic.

Knight, M. B. (1993). *Who belongs here? An American story*. Gardiner, ME: Tilbury House.

Louie, A. (1982). *Yeh-Shen: A Cinderella story from China*. New York: Penguin.

Lowell, S. (2000). *Cindy Ellen: A wild western Cinderella*. New York: Harper/Collins.

Lowry, L. (1989). *Number the stars*. New York: Dell. Newbery Award.

Paterson, K. (1977). *Bridge to Terabithia*. New York: Harper & Row. Newbery Award.

Paterson, K. (1978). *The Great Gilly Hopkins*. New York: Avon Books. Newbery Honor.

Polacco, P. (1996). *Aunt Chip and the great Triple Creek Dam affair*. New York: Philomel.

Polacco, P. (1998). *Thank you, Mr. Falker*. New York: Philomel.

San Souci, R. D. (1998). *Cendrillon: A Caribbean Cinderella*. New York: Simon & Schuster.

Stevens, J. (1995). *Tops and bottoms*. Orlando, FL: Harcourt, Brace & Company. Caldecott Honor.

Westcott, N. B. (1987). *Peanut butter and jelly*. New York: Dutton.

Yen Mah, A. (1999). *Chinese Cinderella: The true story of an unwanted daughter*. New York: Delacorte Press.

Yolen, J. (1988). *The devil's arithmetic*. New York: Puffin Books.

References

Anderson, R. C., Hiebert, E. H., Scott, J. A., & Wilkinson, I. A.G. (1985). *Becoming a nation of readers: The report of the Commission on Reading.* Champaign, IL. The National Academy of Education. The National Institute of Education. The Center for the Study of Reading.

Beck, I. L., McKeown, M., Hamilton, R. L., & Kucan, L. (1997). *Questioning the author.* Newark, DE: International Reading Association.

Betts, E. A. (1946). *Foundations of reading instruction.* New York: American Book.

Billman, L. W. (2002). Aren't these books for little kids? *Educational Leadership, 60* (3), 48–51.

Fisher, D., Frey, N., & Williams, D. (2002). Seven literacy strategies that work. *Educational Leadership, 60* (3), 70–73.

Flood, J., Lapp, D., & Fisher, D. (2003). Reading comprehension instruction. Sponsored by International Reading Association & National Council of Teachers of English. In J. Flood, D. Lapp, J. R. Squire, & J. M. Jensen (Eds.), *Handbook of research on teaching the English language arts (2nd ed.,* pp. 931–941). Mahwah, NJ: Lawrence Erlbaum Associates.

International Reading Association (IRA) & National Council of Teachers of English (NCTE). (1996). *Standards for the English Language Arts.* Urbana, Illinois: Author.

Irvin, J. L. (2001, May). Assisting struggling readers in building vocabulary and background knowledge. *Voices from the Middle. 8* (37–43)

Ivy, G. (2002). Getting started. Manageable literacy practices. *Educational Leadership, 60* (3), 21–23.

Krashen, S. (1998). Bridging inequity with books. *Educational Leadership, 55* (4), 18–22.

Macon, J. M., Bewell, D., & Vogt, ME. (1991). *Responses to literature grades K-8.* Newark, DE: International Reading Association.

Mazano, A. V. (1969). The request procedure. *Journal of Reading,* 12, 123–126.

McKeown, M. G., & Beck, I. L. (1999). Getting the discussion started. *Educational Leadership,* 25–28.

Ogle, D. M. (1986). K-W-L: A teaching model that develops active reading of expository text. *The Reading Teacher, 39,* 564–570.

Pressley, M. (2000). What should comprehension instruction be instruction of? In M. L. Kamil, P. B. Mosenthal, P. D. Pearson, & R. Barr (Eds.), *Handbook of reading research, Volume III* (pp. 545–561). Mahwah, NJ: Lawrence Erlbaum Associates.

Rasmussen, K. (2000, Summer). Give me shelter: Reading and English proficiency learners. *Curriculum Update,* 4–5.

Reutzel, R. D., & Cooter, R. B. (1992). *Teaching children to read: From basals to books.* New York: Macmillan.

Shepard, A. (1994). From script to stage: Tips for Readers Theatre. *The Reading Teacher, 48* (2), 184–185.

Stauffer, R. G. 1969. *Directing reading maturity as a cognitive process.* New York: Harper & Row.

Tierney, R., & Readence, J. E. (2000). *Reading strategies and practices: A compendium.* Boston Fifth Edition: Allyn and Bacon.

Trelease, J. (2003). *Some things reading educators might learn from Oprah, Barnes & Noble, and the grocery store.* Presentation at the 2003 International Reading Conference, Orlando FL.

Wynn, M. J. (1993a). Lyrics lead to literacy. *NERA Journal, 29* (3) 48–57.

Wynn, M. J. (1993b). Proprietary vocabulary acquisition: A creative thematic adventure. *Reading Horizons, 33* (5), 389–400.

Wynn, M., & Laframboise, K. (1996). Shared experiences to scaffold second language learners' literacy acquisition. *NERA Journal, 32* (2), 3–9.

Zemelman, S., Daniels, H., & Hyde, A. (1998). *Best practices: New standards for teaching and learning in America's schools, (2nd ed.)* Portsmouth, NH: Heinemann.

Websites

American Library Association: Great Websites for Kids

The American Library Service to Children (ALSC), a division of the American Library Association, maintains this website, which includes suggestions on information about animals, literature and languages, sciences, the arts, history and biography, mathematics and computers, and social sciences.

www.ala.org/greatsites

International Reading Association (IRA)

Look for association news, research bulletins, publications, and conference announcements

www.ira.org

Jim Trelease

Includes a wide variety of information on reading aloud to kids. To view rain gutters in the classroom, click on to this site.

www.trelease-on-reading.com

National Council of Teachers of English (NCTE)

Look for information on reading, literature, and writing.

www.ncte.org

The Partnership for Reading

Questions about reading instruction. Teachers, administrators, parents, researchers, and others interested in scientifically based reading instruction are invited to submit questions. Information about reading comprehension, independent reading, vocabulary, assessment, differentiated instruction, and reading fluency.

www.nifl.gov/partnershipforreading/
questions/questions_about.html

Read Write Think

IRA/NCTE site that has extensive information in the following areas: lessons, standards, web resources, and materials. Included are ideas in literacy engagements in learning language, learning about language, and learning through language.

www.readwritethink.org

Readers' Theater

Full-text scripts found at this site are adapted by the author, Aaron Shepard. They are aimed primarily at grades 3-9 and include basic production suggestions such as reading/grade level. A guide to storytelling is also available.

www.aaronshep.com

Free readers' theater scripts for classroom use are available at:

www.aaronshep.com;

www.readinglady.com;

www.loiswalker.com;

www.storycart.com; and

www.lisablau.com

CHAPTER 3 TOPICS	Artistic Adventures	Gamut of Games
Personal Writing	Autobiography Accordion Books	Postcards Secret Pen Pal Postcards
Narrative Writing	Step Book Story Organizer	Campfire Tales Story Box with Story Starters
Informational Writing	Descriptive Writing Biography Bugography Blottos	Sequential Writing Board Games Bug-a-Mania
Persuasive Writing	Advertisements Junk Art	Interviews Interview Summary
Poetry	Picture Poems	Formula Sentence Poems Poetry Pass

Ocular Organizers	*Dramatic Debut*	*Creative Composition*
Friendly Letters Letter Larry Enveloptionery	Pass-It-On Autobiographical Stories Auto Organizers	Journal Writing Journal Jackets
Plot Poems Plot Plan	Picto Map Theater Book	Tall Tales Tall Tale Tunes Tall Tale Book
Compare and Contrast Writing Create-a-Chart Alphabetical Research Writing Sequence	Problem and Solution Writing Picnic Possibilities	Cause and Effect Writing Learning Log Bug Log
Business Letter 3.5 Persuasive Paragraph Organizer 3.5 & 3.8 Paragraphs	Persuasive Puppets Persuasive Script	Before and After Writing Attitude Adjustment Arranger Class Cloud Books
Poetry Place Limerick	Poetry Party Poetry Pocket Plate Mobile Invitation Poem	Patterned Poetry

*I find that if students have one good teacher of writing
in their entire career, irrespective of grade level,
they can be successful writers.
Be that one teacher!*

(Graves, 1993, p. 14)

OVERVIEW

Throughout life we write lists reminding us of things to do, items to buy, and appointments to keep. We write notes and letters to friends and family to inform them of significant events in our lives. We write to influential political and business figures to persuade them to accept our point of view. Sometimes we write stories about our world or the world as we would like it to be. We write poetry and journal entries to express our innermost thoughts. Certainly learning to communicate effectively through writing is an invaluable life skill.

When students enter school, they *believe* they can write. Young children often make a series of carefully formed scribbles and read them confidently to anyone who will listen. These scribbles, which might be called *pretend writing*, are evidence that children are in an early developmental stage in writing. Some teachers have students read their scribbles and write the child's interpretation under the scribbles. Teachers need to take advantage of students' confidence in their ability to write and encourage them to write daily. Students rapidly learn,

*"If I can say it, I can write it.
If I can write it, I can read it."*

Elbow (2004) suggests that writing before reading is an effective approach to literacy. Whereas first graders can read only words they have previously learned to read or sound out—a small lexicon—they are in a better to position to write in that they can write all the words they can say. Elbow points out, when summarizing the findings of Calkins (1994), Graves (1994) and others, that very young children

- Can write before they can read
- Can write more than they can read
- Can write more easily than they can read because they
- Can write anything they can say

Allen (2003) says that writing is act of discovery. He points out,

From the first scribbles a child makes while imitating grownups to that final signature on a last will and testament—not to mention all the reports, essays, and letters that are a part of school, work, and home life in between—the ability to express one's thoughts in writing is an essential part of being educated (p. 1).

Traditional writing instruction focused on producing a *product*. Writing was taught by having students write about an assigned topic and then turning in their compositions. The teacher took red pen in hand, assessed the compositions, circled any errors, and then assigned grades. This *assign/assess/assign* system did not teach students *how* to write. In fact, many students react negatively to having their papers covered with red marks.

Moving from a *product* orientation to a *process* orientation, progressive writing instruction focuses on the *process* of learning *how* to write rather than on producing a finished product. Progressive writing instruction immerses students in writing for meaningful purposes. Real-life situations such as making a shopping list of ingredients needed in baking cookies, leaving a note for a friend, and documenting observations in a science experiment provide meaningful writing situations. Students should have a variety of opportunities to write about personal experiences that are significant in their own lives such as a new pet, a family trip, or a secret wish.

Graves (1983) notes,

Surprises come when children begin to control writing as a craft. ... A craft is a process of shaping material toward an end. There is a long, painstaking, patient process demanded to learn how to shape material to a level where it is satisfying to the person doing the crafting. Both craft processes, writing and teaching, demand constant revision, constant reseeing of what is being revealed by the information in hand; in one instance the subject of the writing, in another the person learning to write. The craftsperson is a master follower, observer, listener, waiting to catch the shape of the information. (pp. 1, 6)

STAGES OF WRITING

For developing the craft of writing, research suggests a process writing model with five stages (Allen, 2003; Calkins, 1994; Graves, 1983; 1994; Henk, Marinak, Moore, & Mallette, 2004/2005; National Writing Project, 2004). This writing process is recursive in that students may move back and forth between the stages as the need arises.

Process Writing Stage 1: Prewriting

In the prewriting stage the writer brainstorms ideas about which to write. Brainstorming includes both oral discussion and jotting down lists of ideas. The ideas are later refined and organized into categories. Webbing is an effective way to develop these categories. Authors should spend a great deal of their writing time in the prewriting stage investigating topics to write about and determining the answers to the questions What, Why, Who, and How?

Who?	Who is my audience?
What?	What is my topic?
Why?	Why am I writing about this topic, or
	What is my purpose in writing?
How?	How am I going to present my information, or
	What format am I going to use?

The format the author chooses to convey thoughts depends on the audience and purpose of the composition. If the reason for writing is to record personal thoughts and feelings, the author may choose journals or poetry. If the reason for writing is to share with others, depending on the writing objective, the author may choose from a variety of formats including a letter, research report, or story.

Process Writing Stage 2: Drafting

In the drafting stage, the author begins to put thoughts, phrases, and sentences on paper. This draft is often called a "sloppy copy." The focus of the drafting stage is getting thoughts down on paper. The author should leave spacing on the paper to allow insertion of additional ideas as they occur.

Students keep their drafts in individual writing folders. These writing folders contain lists of personal writing topics and all of their written work. Work in these folders serves as a resource of writing ideas as well as documentation of progress in writing skill. Every piece of writing in the folder will not result in a published product. Often the student will write several sloppy copies and then choose a favorite to take to stages 3, 4, and 5.

Process Writing Stage 3: Revising

In the revising stage, the author focuses on effective word choices and organization and sequence of information. The author uses editing marks, such as arrows, to indicate a rearrangement of text. An alternative method of reordering the text is to cut the composition into pieces, rearrange the pieces, and paste the pieces down. If the author is using a word processing program on a computer, she could utilize the "cut-and-paste" feature to rearrange text. Conferencing with peers and teachers provides feedback for refining compositions. Reading the composition aloud or hearing a peer read the composition aloud enables the author to make changes if the writing does not sound right.

Process Writing Stage 4: Editing

In the editing stage, the author moves from the content focus in stages 1, 2, and 3 to a polishing focus. To check for spelling, punctuation, and grammar problems, three stages of editing take place: *self-editing* in which the author checks for errors, then *peer-editing* in which peers check each other's papers for errors, and finally *top-editing* in which the teacher checks for errors.

Process Writing Stage 5: Publishing

In the publishing stage, the author shares the product with an audience. The author may sit in an *author's chair,* a prestigious chair designated for use on special occasions, while reading to peers. After listening to the composition, peers and teachers make positive comments and suggestions. This is an effective form of publishing. Publication takes a variety of other forms: personal books, class books, journals, bulletin boards, a class newspaper (see Activity Appendix A for publishing ideas). In personal and class books, students enjoy including a *Dedication Page,* an *Authors' Page* with autobiographical information, and a *Read by . . . Page,* which friends and relatives sign after reading the book.

A song that reinforces the process writing stages and which students delight in singing is:

> *Title: Best Seller*
> *Tune: "This Old Man"*
> Process Writing, Process Writing
> This method is really exciting.
> We'll **web, draft, revise, edit**
> Conference with a friend.
> **Publish** a best seller in the end.

IRA/NCTE STANDARDS FOR THE ENGLISH LANGUAGE ARTS

Four of the IRA/NCTE Standards for the English Language Arts have a specific writing focus (see Figure 2.3; IRA & NCTE, 1996). Standards 4 and 5 stress communicating effectively with a variety of audiences for a variety of purposes. The prewriting stage in process writing provides opportunities for the writer to identify her audience based on the purpose of the composition and then to select an appropriate format.

Standard 7 focuses on students researching issues of interest to them. Students generate ideas, questions, pose problems, then gather, evaluate, and synthesize data from a variety of sources. They communicate their discoveries in a variety of ways that suit their purpose and audience. The informational section in this chapter focuses on student research and reports. Science, social studies, health, and other content areas provide opportunities for research. Writing across the curriculum helps students focus and learn. Franklin (2003) cites a study in which students participating in writing across the curriculum programs had higher test scores, no failures, and a more positive attitude toward learning.

Standard 12 emphasizes students' use of spoken, written, and visual language to accomplish their own purposes. In this chapter personal writing experiences such as autobiographies, postcards, friendly letters, journal writing, persuasive writing, and poetry all provide opportunities for enjoyable communication experiences.

How Should You Teach Writing?

BEST PRACTICES IN WRITING

*Teachers who write are
Better teachers of writing*

Integrating the qualities of best practices in teaching writing identified by Zemelman, Daniels, and Hyde (1998), with findings from other researchers (Graves, 1994; Henk et al., 2004/2005; National Writing Project, 2005; Ray, 2004; Villaume & Brabham, 2001), results in the following guidelines for writing instruction:

- All students can and should write in a classroom climate conducive to writing. Writing tools such as a dictionary, thesaurus, and rhyming dictionary should be available. Graphic organizers assist those with language challenges.
- Teachers must help students find real purposes to write. All students have stories to tell, ideas to share, and opinions to voice. They need opportunities to make choices about writing topics. Students from varied cultural backgrounds can build on their personal literacy experiences.
- Students need to take ownership and responsibility. Students are often stalled in a stale sameness. They need a *nudge*, a slight push in the right direction to try new things and experiment with new skills. They need to take a risk and step out of their comfort zones.
- Effective writing programs involve the complete writing process. Students learn that as authors, they approach a writing project as one that occurs in a series of stages, stages they can revisit as the need arises.
- Teachers can help students get started. When students are stalled, ideas are stimulated by personal lists of topics in their writing folders, wall chart topics, reading about topics, questions, discussion, and group brainstorming.
- Teachers help students draft and revise. Charts delineating stages of the writing process as well as other ideas and suggestions are on display.
- Grammar and mechanics are best learned in the context of actual writing. Editing checklists assist in the polishing of mechanics. Implement teacher-guided mini-lessons as the need occurs.
- Students need real audiences and a classroom context of shared learning. Conferences may occur with a peer, small group, the class, or a teacher. During author sharing, peer conversation might take the *TAG* format (Villaume & Brabham, 2001):
  - **T**ell what you like
  - **A**sk questions
  - **G**ive ideas
- Writing should extend throughout the curriculum. Students value and use writing more when it is used *across content areas*. Writing is one of the best tools for stimulating academic growth because writing activates thinking.
- Effective teachers use evaluation constructively and efficiently. They maintain a writing folder or portfolio for each student. The teacher and/or student uses a scoring rubric to evaluate writing samples.
- Students should write daily, thus living in a constant state of composition. Students need a scheduled, predictable time to write, and teachers need time to teach writing.
- Student writing should be on display. When encouraged to think of themselves as authors, student achievement soars. When invited to publish their writing in books or display their writing on bulletin boards, student motivation for writing excels. Calkins (1994) suggests "Publication Celebrations."
- Teachers should demonstrate the writing process. Graves (1994) points out the value of modeling,

   Students can go a lifetime and never see another person write, much less show them how to write. Yet it would be unheard of *for an artist not to show her students how to use oils by painting on her own canvas, or for a ceramist not to demonstrate how to throw clay on a wheel and shape the material himself. Writing is a craft. It needs to be demonstrated to your students in your classroom, which is a studio, from choosing a topic to finishing a final draft. They need to see you struggle to match your intentions with the words that reach the page (pp. 109–110).*

- Teachers should participate in training for process writing instruction. There is evidence that students in classrooms with trained teachers score higher on writing tests, especially if they write more than one draft of a composition and maintain a personal writing portfolio.
- Teachers should invite others to observe and give feedback. Henk and colleagues (2003) have a detailed observation instrument that includes the process writing stages as well as other components. This instrument provides a common language and shared goals for writing instruction and provides a repertoire of instructional strategies.
- Teachers should write because teachers who write are better teachers of writing.

THEMATIC, LITERATURE-BASED WRITING

Students enjoy thematic, literature-based writing experiences. Teachers and students should make personal choices of literature and/or theme based on students' interests, developmental appropriateness, and grade level curriculum. In this chapter, real-world, meaningful, thematic, literature-based writing experiences are implemented for the following:

Type of Writing	Theme
- Personal Writing	- Me, Myself, and My Family
- Narrative Writing	- Storytelling
- Informational Writing	- Science/Bugs
- Persuasive Writing	- Ecology
- Poetry	- People

PERSONAL WRITING

Personal writing provides an opportunity for students to convey their thoughts, feelings, attitudes, and emotions using words. Personal writing may be as informal as a journal entry in which authors write as they would speak. This type of writing allows authors to build fluency and encourages the development of written communication skills. Because journal entries are not graded, students are free to express themselves without fear of receiving negative feedback. They are not overly concerned about spelling, grammar, and sentence construction. Some personal writing is more formal as in writing autobiographies and friendly letters. The theme chosen for personal writing is *Me, Myself, and My Family*.

Artistic Adventures

Autobiography/Accordion Books

An *autobiography* is a written account of an author's personal life. Writing autobiographies can be motivational for students, because they are writing about a topic that they know well—themselves. Personal experiences and significant events shaping their own lives become the focus of the writing.

Autobiographies include information about the author's family, early childhood, pets, and school experiences. Students might also share favorite family activities, books, games, foods, and television shows. Some questions that stimulate ideas for autobiographies include: What do you want to be when you grow up? What do you like to do in your free time? What sports activities do you enjoy? What bothers you? What makes you happy? What people have influenced your life?

Autobiographies are often written in chronological order, but students may choose to focus on a *piece of life* and develop that particular facet of their lives. Tomie de Paola did this when writing *The Art Lesson* (1989). He concentrated on his own school art experiences in kindergarten and first grade. Another possibility is writing about what happens when one has had a horrendous day as Alexander did in the fictional account written by Judith Viorst, *Alexander and the Terrible, Horrible, No Good, Very Bad Day* (1972).

To organize ideas for an autobiography, students develop an auto web. They compose their autobiographies using the webbed information. Each event of the completed story is entered on a page in an *accordion book* (see Activity Appendix A) or on a page in a journal. Each entry is enhanced with appropriate illustrations.

Literature-Based Example

After reading the book When I Was Young in the Mountains *by Cynthia Rylant (1982) and examining Rylant's use of the repetitive phrase, "When I was young in the mountains ...," students create an auto web for their own particular environment and write a personal autobiography. Potential topics for the web are family, hobbies, school, and unusual events (see Figure 3.1).*

An example of a student autobiography for life in Lakeland, Florida is the following:
Title: When I Was Young in Lakeland
Page 1: When I was young in Lakeland, my Dad worked at the phosphate mines. He would come home dirty every night. My Mom would have a glass of freshly squeezed orange juice waiting for him.
Page 2: When I was young in Lakeland, we would go fishing in different lakes. We would catch fish, clean them, and have a big fish fry out in our back yard. We would invite all the neighbors over for fish and grits.
Page 3: When I was young in Lakeland, my first grade teacher would read to us everyday. She helped us write stories about what we wanted to be when we grew up.
Page 4: When I was young in Lakeland, we would go to the Strawberry Festival in Plant City every year. We would eat a big bowl of strawberry shortcake, ride all the midway rides, and sometimes I would get sick.

Gamut of Games

Postcards/Secret Pen Pal Postcards

One form of friendly letter writing is postcard writing. Students write short, friendly messages to their family and friends. As they write *postcards*, they develop skills in writing brief messages, using correct letter format, writing addresses correctly, and creating illustrations

FIGURE 3.1   Auto Web for "When I Was Young in Lakeland."

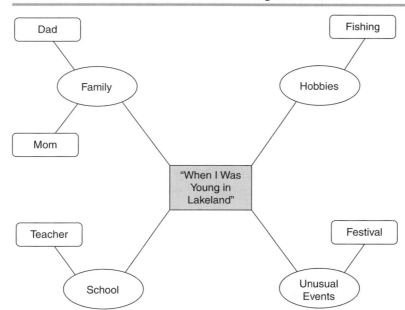

to convey a message. Rectangular index cards may be used for postcards. Divide one side of the card in half widthwise. The left side is for the message, and the right side is for the address. Draw an illustration on the reverse side of the card.

One postcard possibility is writing *secret pen pal postcards*. A random drawing of names determines the secret pen pal pairs. The class formulates secret pen pal guidelines that might include keep the name of your secret pen pal confidential, send your secret pen pal two postcards each week, and find a way to deliver your cards so that your secret pen pal will not be able to determine who you are. (You may engage the help of the postmaster/teacher in this endeavor.)

Literature-Based-Example

Read Alexander and the Terrible, Horrible, No Good, Very Bad Day *by Judith Viorst (1972) for secret pen pal postcard ideas. Make a two-column chart of ideas. In the left column list reasons for a terrible, horrible, no good, very bad day (use THNGVBD because space on a postcard is limited). In the right column list reasons for a wonderful, fantastic, super, very good day (use WFSVGD). Design postcard pictures to cheer the recipient.*

Postcard entry possibilities:

- "I noticed you are having a THNGVBD. I just wanted to cheer you up. I think you are wonderful because ..."
- "Thank goodness! Today you are having a WFSVGD. Aren't you glad the teacher decided not to give us homework? We'll have a lot of free time this afternoon to ..."

Another postcard possibility is writing postcards as part of a social studies unit. Post-cards may be sent to or from various geographical locations. Stringbean's Trip to the Shining Sea *by Vera Williams (1988) is a book made of postcards that tells a story of the trip made by a family as they travel from Jeloway, Kansas, to the Pacific Ocean.*

Ocular Organizers
Friendly Letters/Letter Larry/Enveloptionery

A *friendly letter* to the class or personal letters to each student (with the help of a computer) delivered by a mail person will capture the attention of students and stimulate interest in letter writing. My sixth-grade students enjoyed getting letters from Oscar, a large, rubber head that sat on top of the storage cabinets in our classroom. One morning when they arrived in class, there was a message on the chalkboard. It read:

> Somewhere Elementary School
> 3001 Anywhere Street
> Plant City, Florida 33565
> October 10, 1982
>
> Dear Class,
>
> I am <u>convinced</u> that many of you will soon look like me. Your behavior <u>indicates</u> a lack of willingness to do your homework. Many of you even <u>resent</u> having to do it. You forget that people who don't study will end up <u>ignorant</u>.
>
> As smart as you are, it is <u>deflating</u> my opinion of you to see you goofing off. Let's <u>conspire</u> together to get busy, and soon Mrs. Wynn will note <u>remarkable</u> improvement in your work.
>
> I don't mean to <u>complicate</u> your life by grumping, but if you had to live in here after school with Mrs. Wynn ... Oh, is she a pain when you're not doing your best!
>
> Your friend,
>
> The Late Oscar

The students loved the letter and immediately began corresponding with Oscar. Each time Oscar responded he would add another "Late" to his closing (The Late, Late Oscar; The Late, Late, Late Oscar) until finally his closing was the Late, Late, Late... Oscar. The underlined words in Oscar's letters are from class basal stories. Lively discussions about their meaning within the context of the letter provided a stimulus for students' proprietary vocabulary acquisition. *Proprietary vocabulary* is a collection of words over which the owner has mastery of understanding in listening and reading and mastery of use in speaking and writing (Wynn, 1993). The students progressed from writing to Oscar to independent letter writing.

Our class discussed how much fun it is to receive letters and communicate with friends who are far away. Our discussion included answering the following questions:

1. Do you like to get letters? Why?
2. Who sends you letters?
3. What messages are in the letters?
4. Does the person sending you a letter anticipate a reply? Why?

Answering these questions establishes one of the purposes for learning to write letters: If you expect to receive letters, you have to write and respond to letters. On the basis of class discussion, the definition of a friendly letter might be a *letter* is a message that is personal, often handwritten, and usually comes in the mail, in an envelope with a stamp. Sharing examples and non-examples of friendly letters reinforces this definition. Non-examples include advertisements that come in the mail, flyers that come with the newspaper, and telephone messages.

Learning to write letters is essential if students wish to respond to letters they receive. *Letter Larry* makes letter writing fun. Draw Letter Larry on a transparency (see Figure 3.2). Label each of his five letter parts with a transparency marker and discuss the components of each part of a friendly letter. A beginning comment could be, "A letter is very much like our profile." Use the following questions to stimulate class discussion:

1. What does Letter Larry have on the very top of his profile? (Head for "heading")
   What goes in the heading of a letter?
2. What does Letter Larry use when he sees close friends?
   (Hands and mouth for the "greeting")
   What goes in the greeting of a letter?
3. What is the largest part of Letter Larry's profile? ("Body") What goes in the body of a letter?
4. What keeps Letter Larry's tennis shoes closed?

FIGURE 3.2   Letter Larry

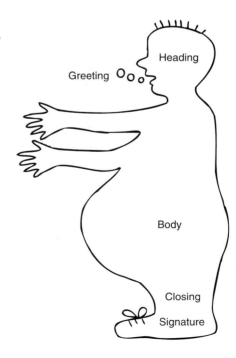

(Laces or hook-and-loop fasteners for "the closing")
What goes in the closing of a letter?
5. What do we expect to find on our tennis shoes near the bottom?
(Brand name for "signature")
Why does a letter need a signature?
A possibility for exciting letter writing is using enveloptionery (see Activity Appendix A). An *enveloptionery* is a piece of stationery that folds to make its own envelope. Write a note on the stationery and fold the paper into an enveloptionery. Unfold the envelope, and the letter magically appears.

Literature-Based Example

Based on the story Dear Mr. Henshaw *(1983), write to Leigh Botts, the main character in the story, about his invention. Seek his advice in developing an invention to deal with a school problem. Write the letter on enveloptionery.*

> 10 Anywhere Drive
> Charlotte, North Carolina 11111
> June 10, 2008
>
> Dear Leigh,
>
> Your invention to protect your lunch from the lunch box thief is wonderful. Could you help me with a problem I'm having at school? The other kids are picking on me, because I am so short. Could you help me think of an invention that would make me taller?
>
> Desperately yours,
>
> Shorty Sam

The Jolly Postman or Other People's Letters *(1986) and* The Jolly Christmas Postman *(1991) by Janet and Allan Ahlberg contain a variety of letter formats that students will enjoy. Each book has a number of envelopes that contain unique letters.*

Dramatic Debut

Pass-It-On/Autobiographical Stories/Auto Organizers

Pass-It-On is a game in which the students spin a yarn, tell personal *autobiographical stories*, and develop their storytelling ability. Students are able to concentrate on making their stories interesting and exciting to the audience, because they are telling familiar stories about themselves. As a result, their oral language fluency and verbal expressiveness improve.

Play Pass-It-On in *small groups* (3 to 5 players). Before playing the game, each group member prepares an **auto organizer** (see Figure 3.3). To help the players organize their thoughts, the auto organizer may have auto starters such as:

Turn 1: *When I was little. ...*
Turn 2: *Then as I grew I learned to ...*
Turn 3: *Next, I. ....*
Turn 4: *Finally I . ...*

To prepare for the game, get a long piece of string and a can with a plastic lid (a coffee can with a plastic lid works well). Tie knots in the string at three-foot intervals. There should be four knots for each group participant (if there are four participants,

FIGURE 3.3   Auto Organizer

When I was little...

1. _____
2. _____
3. _____
4. _____

Then as I grew I learned to...

1. _____
2. _____
3. _____
4. _____

Next, I...

1. _____
2. _____
3. _____
4. _____

Finally, I...

1. _____
2. _____
3. _____
4. _____

there will be 16 knots). Place the string in the can, and start the end through a small hole in the lid.

During the game each group member takes turns spinning his or her personal yarn. While pulling the string through the hole in the lid of the can, the first player begins spinning a yarn. When the first knot comes through the can lid, the storyteller quickly builds to an exciting part of the story and then stops—leaving the idea open ended and the audience in suspense. Group members shout, "Pass it on!" and the can is passed to the second player. This player begins spinning a new, personal yarn while pulling the string, reaches the knot, builds quickly to an exciting part of the story, stops, and then the group shouts, "Pass it on!"

After the first cycle of sharing is complete and each group member has had a turn, the players stop and add information to their auto organizers. Many times ideas peers have shared stimulate thoughts that allow players to expand their *auto thoughts*, ideas about themselves. Then a second cycle of turns begins. The game continues through as many cycles of play as time permits, as interest remains high, and as is age appropriate. At the end of Pass-It-On, auto organizers are completed. On the basis of auto organizer information, students may further expand their ideas and write an autobiography to publish in a variety of forms such as journal jackets, pop-up techniques, accordion books, eightfold persons, etc. (see Activity Appendix A).

Literature-Based Example

After reading Sam, Bangs, & Moonshine *by Evaline Ness (1966) to the class, use the following as an example of Sam's spinning a yarn:*

Turn 1: When I was little, my mother died. Many times I would pretend my mother was still alive. I would tell moonshine (lies) about my mother...

Turn 2: Then as I grew older, I told my friend Thomas that I had a baby kangaroo. I would send Thomas different places looking for my pet kangaroo.

Turn 3: Next, I told Thomas my mother and pet kangaroo were at Blue Rock. Thomas and my cat, Bangs, went to search for them ... when ... My father came running out of the storm into the house dripping wet. "Oh no!" I screamed, "Thomas and Bangs have gone to Blue Rock! They'll drown!" My dad ran out of the house...

Turn 4: Finally, I realized that telling moonshine wasn't a very good idea.

Creative Composition
Journal Writing/Journal Jackets

A *journal* is a record of personal experiences and observations of daily life. The author expresses thoughts and feelings in words and records his or her thinking on paper. A list of personal topics is kept in the front of the journal to stimulate thinking when the author experiences "blank page syndrome." Students may draw pictures in their journals and then write about their drawings. Time is designated in the daily classroom schedule for journal writing, since the values of journal writing include (1) building *writing fluency*, ease and flow in writing, and (2) building self-confidence, "I can do it! I do have something important to say!"

An author may choose to share a journal entry by reading the entry aloud to peers, or the entry may remain private. Journal entries are written only once and are not intended to progress through the five process writing stages. However, an author may choose an entry that is of particular interest to expand into a published product.

Students appreciate the importance of journal writing when they read about famous people whose journals became source material for information about their lives and historical times. Books that include examples of young people's journal writing are *A Gathering of Days: A New England Girl's Journal, 1830–1832* by Joan Blos (1979), *Harriet the Spy* by Louise Fitzhugh (1964), *My Side of the Mountain* by Jean Craighead George (1959), and *Three Days on a River in a Red Canoe* by Vera B. Williams (1981).

Dialogue journals are written conversations that a student has with a teacher, peer, or parent. Students enjoy writing notes to each other, and dialogue journals provide this opportunity. When the classroom teacher corresponds with students in journals, motivation for journal writing is high, and student and teacher communication is enhanced. At times teachers may want to write journal entries to the entire class.

There are a variety of ways to make journals. Spiral-bound notebooks work well and are readily available. A journal is easily made by folding a piece of construction paper in half to make a cover and stapling paper inside. Students delight in making their own *journal jackets* using contact paper, wall paper, and wrapping paper (see Activity Appendix A).

A song about journal writing that students enjoy singing is:

Title: Journal Jive
Tune: "Supercalifragilisticexpialidocious"

You're having a terrible, horrible, no good, very bad day.
Seems like things you try to do,
Aren't working out your way.
Oh ... when you have a day like this,

You know what you should do?
Just write an entry in your journal
Expressing a thought or two.
Oh, W-R-I-T - - -I-N- G
Writing in your journal
Will help your troubles flee.
So, when you have a day like this,
Here's what you should do…
Just get those thoughts on paper
Writing will help you!!!

Literature-Based Example

While reading Dear Mr. Henshaw *(Cleary, 1983), students may write journal entries about personal family problems. They will discover the therapeutic value of expressing their fears and concerns on paper. Writing these entries has merit similar to that discovered by readers who write to advice columnists.*

Leigh Botts, the protagonist in Dear Mr. Henshaw, *begins his experiences with personal writing when, as part of a school assignment, he writes a letter to an author. Mr. Henshaw answers many of Leigh's questions. Then he asks Leigh to answer some questions. Leigh is furious and refuses to answer the questions until his mother finds out. She says Leigh must answer.*

From letter writing, Leigh progresses to journal writing. Initially, he experiences "blank page syndrome" until he addresses his journal entries, "Dear Mr. Pretend Henshaw." Through Leigh's letter and journal writing, the reader observes Leigh's social and emotional growth in dealing with his parents' divorce and problems encountered at school.

The following questions that Mr. Henshaw asked Leigh would provide good "journal starters":

1. Who are you?
2. What do you look like?
3. What is your family like?
4. Where do you live?
5. Do you have any pets?
6. Do you like school?
7. Who are your friends?
8. Your favorite teacher?
9. What bothers you?
10. What do you wish?

The following is an example of a student's journal entry:

It bugs me that when I get home from school, I have to do my homework right away. I am not allowed to go outside. My Mom has to work, and she won't let me go out until she gets home. All my friends get to go outside and have a good time while I am stuck in the house.

◎ *NARRATIVE WRITING*

Narrative writing is written storytelling in which an author creates a sequential story based on personal experiences and imagination. "Once upon a time …" is a favorite story opener that children recognize. Whether students hear or read this familiar phrase, they know a story will follow. Children develop a sense of story from listening to stories being read and later from reading themselves. They quickly learn that stories have a beginning, middle, and end. Young listeners begin to identify story elements that are essential for the development of a story: *character*, *setting*, and *plot*. As students' understanding of story structure matures, they develop a more sophisticated knowledge of these elements as well as an understanding of three additional story elements: *theme*, *style*, and *point of view*.

Students examine how authors use each of these six story elements as they listen to and read stories. On the basis of their findings, they begin to organize their own stories like those of the authors they hear and read. Singing the song "Literary Elements" (see Music Appendix B) will reinforce story elements that answer the 5 Ws + H questions: Who? What? When? Where? Why? and How? (Wynn, 1994)

Oral storytelling was the earliest means of passing on family history and culture. Stories passed down orally from generation to generation had fast moving, captivating plots designed to capture the attention of an audience and help the listeners hold the story in memory. There were brief descriptions of the characters, and the setting was not well defined. Stories from the oral tradition provide a foundation for writing the folktales found in children's literature today.

Folktales provide a structure for students to follow in developing their own stories. At the beginning of the story the main character (protagonist), setting, problem, and goal are introduced. In the middle of the story, the protagonist goes through a series of events and setbacks in attempts to solve a problem. The setbacks may be conflicts the protagonist has within, with other people, with nature, or with society. At the end of the story, there is a solution to the problem and attainment of the goal.

Artistic Adventures

Step Book Story Organizer

After reading a folktale, examine the story elements by creating a *step book story organizer* using *four* sheets of paper (see Step Book in Activity Appendix A). Write the title for the story on top flap. Label the first step *Character*, and above the label and under the preceding flap hide information about the main character. Label the second step *Setting*, and above the label and under the preceding flap hide information about the setting. Label the third step *Problem/Goal* with appropriate information. The fourth, fifth, and sixth steps have *Event 1*, *Event 2*, and *Event 3* with information about each event. The seventh step has *Resolution* with information about solving the problem.

Literature-Based Example

Read Tikki Tikki Tembo *by Arlene Mosel (1968), a Chinese folktale about a little boy whose long name almost causes disaster. Afterward, discuss the importance of people's names. Make a class step book story organizer for* Tikki Tikki Tembo. *Then have each student devise a personal name that is long and difficult to say. Using a step book story organizer, plan a personal name story that includes a series of events that almost result in disaster and cause a shortening of the name. An example of a personal "name story" is:*

> *Margie Pargie Um Pa Largie was once my name. I hated this name and wished I could have a new name. Would you want to be called Margie Pargie Um Pa Largie? Whenever my Mom was mad at me, she always yelled, "Margie Pargie Um Pa Largie, you come here right this minute!"*
>
> *Unfortunately, trouble always seemed to find me. One day I dropped a dozen eggs on the floor. What a mess! I took off! Soon you could hear my Mom yelling, "Margie Pargie Um Pa Largie, you come here right this minute!" I was really getting tired of this name.*
>
> *Then one day while my Mom had the door open and was yelling for me, my little sister crawled out the door and toward the road. Fortunately, I came running through the yard just in time to grab my little sister. My Mom said, "Thank you,*

Margie Pargie Um Pa Largie! You know what? I think we better shorten your name. How would you like to be called Margie?

Gamut of Games
Campfire Tales/Story Box with Story Starters

Campfire tales are stories that were told by storytellers at the end of a hard day's work. Families would gather around a campfire after supper, and children would listen in awe as parents and grandparents spun yarns about the *good old days*. Family history and cultural values were essential elements in these tales, and children developed an understanding of their heritage and culture as they listened in rapt attention to the storyteller.

The African American people have a strong tradition of storytelling that enriches their culture. Wandering storytellers traversed the country sharing stories as they traveled. Storytellers sometimes wore hats with items dangling from the brim. Each item would represent a story. Other storytellers carried story nets that had objects tied to them. Each object represented a story. The audience would choose an object, and the storyteller would begin the story. The audience often participated in these stories by repeating a familiar story's beginning or ending and repetitive words, phrases, or sentences (Norton, 1995).

For a classroom campfire tales experience, instead of a hat or net, students make *story boxes* (see Activity Appendix A). These boxes contain *story starters*, small objects or pictures that represent a collection of stories they are willing to tell during campfire tales. Campfire tales could be a classroom experience with blankets spread on the floor and students sitting on the blankets in a circle around an imitation fire. Campfire tales can also be a school/family outing at night, when parents come and sit around a real campfire to hear their children participate in storytelling. Students bring their story boxes with story starters to campfire tales, so the audience can choose an object for a story. (Students may have only one object for their first experience at campfire tales.)

Literature-Based Example

The People Could Fly: American Black Folktales by Virginia Hamilton (1985) contains a collection of folktales divided into animal tales, exaggerated tales, supernatural tales, and slave tales of freedom. One of these tales, "Doc Rabbit, Bruh Fox, and Tar Baby," features Bruh Rabbit as the trickster. When sharing this story, the storyteller could begin the tale by showing a related object from a story box. Students will enjoy reading other Bruh Rabbit stories and creating their own versions of Bruh Rabbit's adventures to share during campfire tales.

Ocular Organizers
Plot Poems/Plot Plan

A *plot poem* is a poem composed of seven couplets arranged on six ascending stairsteps and one descending stairstep. (see Poetry Appendix C) Each step couplet focuses on a different literary element—step 1: Problem; step 2: Goal; step 3: Event 1; step 4: Event 2; step 5 Event 3; step 6: Climax, and step 7: Resolution. To create a *plot plan*, draw seven stairsteps on which to organize the plot poem. The poem is read from step 1 up to step 6 (from the bottom to the top) and then down to step 7 for the last couplet.

A *couplet* is a pair of lines in which the words at the end of each line rhyme with each other. Before composing plot poems brainstorm pairs of rhyming words for couplets. Younger students may compose a plot paragraph by writing a sentence on each step on the plot plan rather than using couplets.

Literature-Based Example

The following plot poem (Wynn, 1994) was developed after reading A Story A Story *by Gail E. Haley (1970).*

6. The captives were wrapped tightly
and delivered high.
To the throne of the god who was in the
sky. *(Climax)*

5. He tricked a fairy who was dancing by.
Stuck to the gum baby she gave a cry.
(Event 3)

4. He crept through the woods—though not too far.
Caught some hornets in a calabash jar. *(Event 2)*

3. He tied a leopard to a branch on a tree.
To the sky god's home you will go with me. *(Event 1)*

2. The spider man traveled to his home in the sky.
Do three things for me, and these stories you can buy. *(Goal)*

1. Once upon a time there were no stories on land.
The sky god had them in a box with a band. *(Problem)*

7. The stories were released
and tumbled down to earth.
With each retelling they are
given new birth. *(Resolution)*

Students may develop plot plans for changes in the story they have read. For A Story A Story *they might begin by changing the three tasks given by the sky god, thus changing the couplets for steps 3, 4, and 5. After becoming proficient in making changes in a story, they might progress to creating personal plot plans and plot poems.*

Dramatic Debut
Picto Map/Theater Book

A *picto map* is a graphic organizer that allows a reader or listener to create pictures to analyze story elements within a story. The picto map has four rows of pictures: row 1 has three pictures one for character, another for goal, and the third for setting; row 2 has one picture for the problem; row 3 has three pictures for three events; and row 4 has one picture for the resolution to the problem. Creating a picto map allows reader or listener to visualize each event as it occurs and provides an opportunity for the teacher to assess listening or reading comprehension. Authors also use picto maps to organize stories they want to write. Students will enjoy drawing pictures and symbols to organize their thoughts.

Using information from a picto map, students write a story innovation for a *theater book*, a book created from a file folder (see Activity Appendix A). The back of the file folder forms a backdrop for movable scenery pages. The story innovation is made into a class book and mounted on the floor of the file folder. As the book is read, scenery pages are changed at appropriate places.

Literature-Based Example

After listening to or reading Hawk, I'm Your Brother *by Byrd Baylor (1976), students draw a picto map for the story (see Figure 3.4). Next they write a story innovation based on the picto map.*

Page 1: Hawk, I'm Your Brother *Story Innovation*
Written and Illustrated by Miss Kitty's Class
(title, author, illustrator)

Page 2: Rudy Soto lives in the Santos Mountains. Rudy has a dream of learning to fly.
(character, goal, setting)

Figure 3.4 Picto Map for *Hawk, I'm Your Brother*

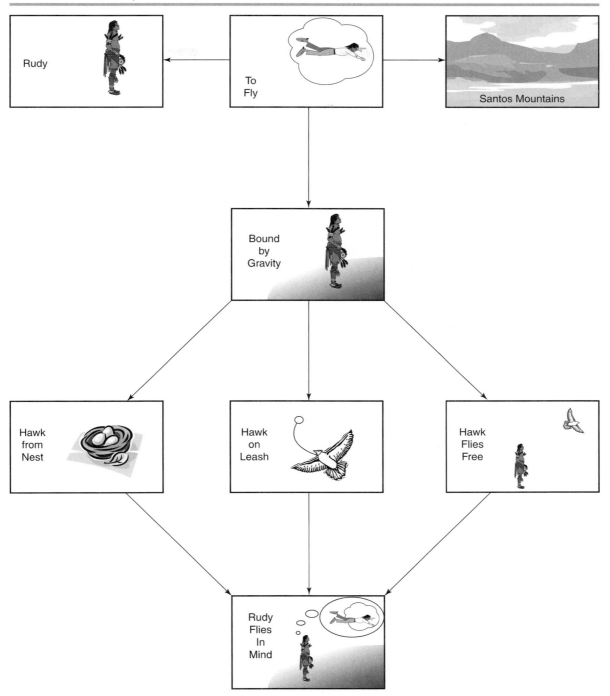

Page 3: Family and friends discourage Rudy. They tell him people can't fly. (problem)

Page 4: One day Rudy takes a young hawk from his nest.
 (event 1)

Page 5: He keeps the hawk in a cage or tied to a leash. The hawk is never free to fly wherever he wants to fly.
 (event 2)

Page 6: Rudy is never able to make the hawk completely happy, until one day, he lets the hawk go free.
(event 3)

Page 7: The hawk soars happily, and Rudy Soto achieves his dream to fly. He learns to fly in his mind! (resolution to the problem)

Students then draw scenery pages to go with the story. As the story is read, the scenery pages are changed at appropriate places.

Creative Composition
Tall Tales/Tall Tale Tunes/Tall Tale Book

Tall tales are humorous stories that stretch the truth about characters, plot, and setting. Some tall tales are based on real people and events, and some are pure fiction. In tall tales the characteristics and abilities of the hero or heroine are exaggerated until they are bigger than life. A great deal of the history and growth of the United States during pioneer times is incorporated in tall tales.

Many tall tales began as stories that were shared around a campfire. The storyteller would begin a story about a real person, and before you could bat an eye, the truth had been stretched—just a little. The next time the tale was told, the truth was stretched—just a little more. After numerous retellings, the facts became totally unbelievable. Some well-known tall tales from our U.S. heritage feature Pecos Bill, Paul Bunyan, John Henry, Johnny Appleseed, Davy Crockett, and Calamity Jane.

In learning to share tall tales, students must make the audience believe everything in the story really happened. Logical explanations for the exaggerations are incorporated within the tale. Students will enjoy the opportunity to stretch the truth and attempt to convince the listeners that this story really did happen. When creating a tall tale, students may start with a real character and event and then stretch the truth for both the character and event.

Composing *tall tale tunes* will motivate even the most reluctant writer. Composers begin by selecting a favorite song and using the melody for their composition (see Familiar Songs in Music Appendix B). They examine the rhyme scheme as well as the number of syllables in each line of the original song. Using the pattern of the original song as a model, they compose lyrics for a tall tale tune (see Guidelines for Creating Song Innovations in Music Appendix B). At times liberal *lyric license* must be taken to match lyrics to the melody. Lyrics for a simple tall tale tune using music from "The Mulberry Bush" could be:

> *Look at Davy Crockett stare.*
> *Look at him stare. Look at him stare.*
> *Look at Davy Crockett stare.*
> *He stared down a bear.*

Literature-Based Example

After reading Pecos Bill *by Steven Kellogg (1986), students compose a tall tale or tall tale tune that they write and illustrate on a* tall tale book *(see wrap-over book variation in the Activity Appendix A). Authors reveal the tall tale character's adventures while unwrapping the book and singing:*

> **Title: Pecos Bill**
> **Tune: "When the Saints Go Marching In"**
>
> *Oh, Pecos Bill was a cowboy*
> *And he was strong as he could be*
> *He fell out of a wagon*
> *When just a little ba-by.*

Oh, he was found by a coyote
Who raised him as a little cub.
He learned to howl at the mo-on
And to hu-nt with a club.

A wandering cowboy came along
He told Bill, "You're a man like me
Pecos Bill didn't believe him
Until his reflection he did see.

He rode a huge, bucking mustang
A rattlesnake was his las-so.
He rounded up wild bron-cos
Everywhere that he did go.

He met a gal upon the range
And her name was Sluefoot Sue.
They fell in love and got married
Now they live in Texas too.

INFORMATIONAL WRITING

Informational writing is factual, nonfiction writing that is built upon the accumulation of research gathered on a specific topic. Science, social studies, health, and other content area textbooks contain informational writing. The purpose of informational writing is to pass on or impart knowledge. Students gain knowledge for informational writing through reading, studying, and personal experience. Sharing of information may take place in learning logs, research reports, biographies, and newspapers

The *KWL Strategy* (What We **K**now; What We **W**ant to Know; What We **L**earned) is an effective technique to use when investigating a specific topic for informational writing (Ogle, 1986). A KWL chart is organized in three vertical columns. The first column lists information students already know about the topic being investigated. Information in this column is entered at the beginning of the research report. The second column lists questions the students want answered about the topic. Questions may be added to this column as the research progresses. The third column contains information the students learn as they read and study about the topic. Information is entered in this column as the investigation progresses (see example in Reading chapter, p. 29)

Know	**W**hat?	**L**earned
What we Know about (the topic)	**What we Want to know about (the topic)**	**What we Learned about (the topic)**

During the study, investigators collect facts and organize these facts into meaningful categories of information. Although informational writing is considered a practical presentation of facts, novice researchers learn to present their findings in an interesting and informative manner. This process provides the building blocks necessary for research projects in middle school and beyond.

Tompkins (2005) suggests five text patterns to use in informational writing: (1) description, (2) sequence, (3) comparison, (4) problem and solution, and (5) cause and effect. Included in this chapter is an explanation and examples for using each of these patterns. Students examine these text patterns in trade and textbooks as they research a topic.

Through informational writing, students learn about a subject and expand their background knowledge. They become "experts" on meaningful topics within content areas. *Bugs* by Nancy Winslow Parker and Joan Richards Wright (1987) was the resource book used for the science topic, bugs.

Artistic Adventures

Descriptive Writing/Biography; Bugography/Blottos

Descriptive writing is a portrayal of a subject in words that allows the reader to form a visual image of the subject. The writer uses characteristics of the subject to enhance the mental picture formed by the reader. Sensory words are useful in descriptive writing in helping the reader see, hear, smell, taste, and feel the subject.

A *biography* is an author's factual account of someone else's life. Biographies about famous people, past and present, are often written descriptively to enable the reader to form a visual image and impression of the person. A biographical web, *bio web*, may be used to collect information about the person. Some of the categories radiating out from the nucleus of the web could be family, characteristics, beliefs, and contributions (see example in the Social Studies chapter, pp. 150–151). An informational biography may also be written about animals, fish, insects, for example. An *animal web* would include information about appearance, traits, habitat, and food.

A *blotto* is made with drop or splatters of paint pressed between the folded sides of a piece of paper. When the paper is opened, an interesting shape is revealed. Features are added to the shape using a marker or pen. The resulting blotto is cut out and used in a variety of artistic adventures.

Literature-Based Example

Create a blotto and add features to fashion a blotto bug. *Transform an animal web into a bug-a-web (see Figure 3.5) for the blotto bug using information from* Bugs, Demi's Secret Garden *(1993), and other research sources.*
Write a bugography for the blotto bug.

Andy's Bugography

My pet, Andy the Ant, is red all over with two antennae on his head. He lives in an ant farm that my aunt gave me for my birthday. The ant farm, or colony, is home to many of Andy's relatives and his queen. She depends on him to find food. I give him and his relatives my leftover peanut butter sandwich and sometimes a sugar cube. They store their food in special chambers for the winter. Andy is the queen's hardest worker, but watch out! He BITES!

Gamut of Games

Sequential Writing/Board Games/Bug-a-Mania

Sequential writing is a series of instructions or events written in a consecutive arrangement and presented in either a numerical or chronological order. Using sequential writing improves linear thinking and deductive reasoning skills. Recipes, directions, and folktales are examples of sequential writing.

Board games, which are popular with people of all ages, always need directions. A basic *board game* contains a game board with spaces on which to move, playing pieces, sets of cards with rewards and penalties, dice or a spinner to indicate the number of spaces to move, and a set of directions (see Game Board in Activity Appendix A). Board games with academic questions and answers need an answer key. When students read and write directions for board games, they learn to write sequentially.

FIGURE 3.5   Bug-a-web

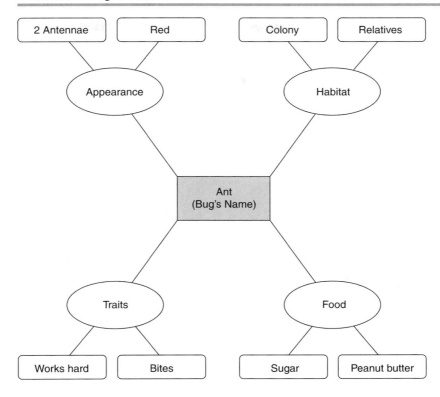

Literature-Based Example

Students create the game "Bug-a-Mania" by making a bug board (see Figure 3.6). They write sequential directions for the game. Using information from bug books, students and teacher develop questions and an answer key for the "Exterminator" and "Bug Bite" cards. Each card contains one question. The difficulty level of questions is determined by students' interest, background, and ability. An example of directions for Bug-a-Mania follows.

Directions for Bug-a-Mania

1. Choose a bug as a playing piece.
2. Place piles of Bug Bite and Exterminator cards face down on the spaces indicated.
3. Throw the dice. The player with the highest number goes first.
4. Player 1 rolls the dice and moves forward the number of spaces indicated on the dice.
   A. If the bug lands on a space labeled Exterminator, the player turns over the top card in the Exterminator pile, answers the question correctly, and moves forward two spaces. If the question is answered incorrectly, the player's bug remains on the space. An example of an exterminator question is What are the body parts of an insect?
   B. If the bug lands on a space labeled Bug Bite, the player turns over the top card in the Bug Bite pile, answers the question correctly, and remains on the space. If the question is answered incorrectly, the player's bug moves back two spaces. An example of a Bug Bite question is: You discover an anthill. There are a dozen ants on the hill. One-third of them run into the hill. How many are left on the hill?
5. The first bug to reach the safety of "Bug Spray Free Island" wins the game.

Figure 3.6   Bug-a-Mania game.

The game board contains the following spaces:

Space	Card
16	Bug Bite
17	
18	Exterminator
19	Bug Bite
20	
21	
22	Exterminator
23	Bug Bite
24	
25	

Space	Card
15	
14	Exterminator
13	Bug Bite
12	
11	Exterminator
10	
9	Bug Bite
8	
7	Exterminator
6	
5	Exterminator
4	
3	Bug Bite
2	
1	

Bug Bite Cards

Exterminator Cards

Bug Spray Free Island

Space	Card
50	
49	Bug Bite
48	
47	Bug Bite
46	
45	Exterminator
44	
43	Bug Bite
42	
41	Exterminator
40	Bug Bite

Space	Card
26	
27	Exterminator
28	Bug Bite
29	Exterminator
30	Exterminator
31	
32	Bug Bite
33	
34	Exterminator
35	Exterminator
36	Bug Bite
37	
38	Exterminator
39	

Start

Ocular Organizers

Compare and Contrast Writing/Create-a-Chart/Alphabetical Research Writing Sequence

Compare and contrast writing is the examination of similarities and differences of two or more objects or people. Charting information provides a visual representation of these similarities and differences. Information for the chart is gathered from a variety of sources and written on separate index cards or sticky notes (fact cards). After all the fact cards are completed, they are spread out on a piece of poster board and arranged and rearranged until a logical organization emerges. Then the cards are attached to a *create-a-chart*.

Cooperative groups of students may work on a research project following the *alphabetical research writing sequence*:

A. —**Assess class interest:**   Discuss a broad topic within a content area. (e.g., science/animals)

B. —**Build background knowledge:**   Encourage students to contribute information they have about the topic to a class pool of knowledge.

C. —**Choose a topic:**   Narrow the broad topic to a manageable size that students will research. (e.g., animals to endangered animals)

D. —**Divide the topic into research sections:**   Subdivide and select a focus for each group to investigate. (e.g., Each group chooses one endangered animal.)

E. —**Establish guidelines for collecting information:**   Establish a series of specific questions to be answered. (e.g., Why is this animal endangered?)

F. —**Find facts:**   Find sources of information such as reference books, magazines, computer resource services, videotapes, and experts in the field. Write information on fact cards.

G. —**Group information:**   Group the fact cards on the create-a-chart.

H. —**Huddle and write:**   Write, revise, and edit. (e.g., Each group works together to produce one section of a class research book.)

I. —**Inform others:**   Share with others by publishing a class research book.

Literature-Based Example

As a class project, students investigate bugs. Allow each cooperative group to select a specific bug. Some questions students might ask and research in bug books include:

- Where does my bug like to live?
- What does my bug eat?
- What is unusual about my bug?

Write bug facts on individual fact cards. Have group meetings to organize these facts into a logical order. Hold a class meeting to create a bug-a-chart (see Figure 3.7).

From the information on the chart, write compare and contrast research reports. For example:

Fireflies and dragonflies have many similarities and differences. Both insects are harmless to man, and both insects fly. The firefly sometimes eats other fireflies, while the dragonfly prefers to dine on mosquitoes and bees. An unusual characteristic of the male firefly is that he blinks off and on at night to attract a mate. An unusual characteristic of the dragonfly is that it captures its food with its long legs while flying.

Dramatic Debut

Problem and Solution Writing/Picnic Possibilities

Problem and solution writing involves investigating a dilemma and searching for potential resolutions. Students may view this type of writing as asking a question and discovering

FIGURE 3.7   Bug-a-chart.

Bug	Habitat	Food	Unusual
Firefly	Fields, woods, backyards All over United States	Other fireflies Larvae eat worms, snails, & soft insects	Male blinks at night to attract mate Called lightning bugs
Dragonfly	Marshes and ponds All over North America	Mosquitoes Bees	Long legs capture insects while in flight

potential answers to the question. Organize problem and solution writing on a *problem and solution planner*:

Problem	Possible Solutions	Justification for Solutions
Low homework grades	Study with friends Complete right after school	Support from peers Complete before other activities take place

Literature-Related Example

Picnic possibilities *is dramatic exploration of problems and solutions one might encounter on a picnic. Many students have picnic experiences to share; others will enjoy learning about picnics and going on a picnic. As no picnic is complete without bugs, bugs will be expected as uninvited guests.*

Students enjoy planning a class picnic and having the foresight to anticipate catastrophic events before they occur. On the basis of their predictions, investigate potential problem solutions. A picnic planner aids in organizing several picnic committees (cooperative groups) to be in charge of a destination site, food, supplies, serving, and other activities. Picnic props include a picnic basket (check garage sales), paper goods and utensils, blanket, insect repellent, and food. Add information to the following picnic planner.

Committees	Responsibilities	Potential Problems
Destination site	Locate place that has tables, benches, & make reservations	Bugs at site

Based on information on the picnic planner, each committee creates or receives a potential problem related to its responsibility. Each group is responsible for acting out a scenario about its problem and possible solutions. Some committee members will take the part of picnic guests; others take the part of bugs. Students will enjoy reacting to bug bites with swats, repellent (water), running, screaming, stomping, and first aid. (Teachers will probably want to have the picnic outside.) No talking is allowed. The rest of the class must guess what the problem and solutions are (see example in Reading Chapter p. 30). The culmination of picnic possibilities is a REAL picnic.

Creative Composition
Cause and Effect Writing/Learning Log/Bug Log

Cause and effect writing involves answering the questions *What?* and *Why?* in a particular situation. Topics for cause and effect writing are found in science, social studies, and other content areas. Examples of cause and effect questions and answers follow:

What happened? (effect)	Why did this happen? (cause)
Good report card	Studied consistently
Pretty flowers	Watered and fertilized

As students examine different situations, they enter cause and effect statements in a learning log. A *learning log* is a journal in which students record facts, findings, and feelings. A good practice to follow in writing an entry is the *5 Ws + H*:

1. **Who** or what is being investigated?
2. **What** happened? (effect)
3. **Why** did this happen? (cause)
4. **When** did this happen?
5. **Where** did this happen?
6. **How** did this happen?

Write a cause and effect summary paragraph on the basis of the learning log data. For example, students observe and record plant growth (effect) as they expose the plants to various amounts of sunlight, water, and nutrients (causes). One possibility for making learning logs is the journal jacket technique (see Activity Appendix A).

Literature-Based Example

An ant farm provides the impetus for bug log *entries. As students observe the trails made by ants, they record their findings in bug logs.*

Bug Log Entry   **Date: March 26**

1. **What** is being investigated? Ants
2. **What** happened? (effect)
   The ants made trails on the side of the jar.
3. **Why** did this happen? (cause)
   Maybe the ants were trying to get to the light.
4. **When** did this happen?
   The ants made the trails during the last week.
5. **Where** did this happen?
   The ant trails are in a jar in our classroom.
6. **How** did this happen?
   The ants pushed the sand out of the way.

Bug Log Summary Paragraph

Our class has an ant farm in a jar. We have been observing our ants for a week. The ants made trails (effect) up the side of the jar. Maybe the ants were trying to get to the light. We have to investigate this *cause* in our ant resource books to see if we are right. We think they pushed the sand out of the way to make the trails.

PERSUASIVE WRITING

Persuasive writing is a form of composition used to influence another's thoughts or course of action. In persuasive writing, the author attempts to convince the reader to respond in a desired manner. Usually persuasive writing deals with the author's position on an issue and support for this opinion in an attempt to "sell" the reader on this point of view. The author may use one or more of the following persuasive tactics:

1. *Intellectual tactics* use arguments that are factual, logical, and reasonable. There is emphasis on cause and effect statements. For example, "If you smoke, research has shown that your chances of getting throat cancer increase dramatically."
2. *Emotional tactics* employ arguments that deal with personal feelings. The writer may emphasize feelings of happiness, sadness, aggravation, and so on. There is an emphasis on personal benefits. For example, a child might say, "If you let me have a candy bar, I will do my homework."
3. *Social tactics* stress what others think, say, and do. Celebrities lend credence to the author's opinion. For example, a leading sports figure promoting a brand of tennis shoes might say, "As a result of wearing Brand X, I can jump higher, run faster, and outmaneuver members of any opposing team."

Parents are convinced that children are born learning to speak persuasively. When children want to see a television program their parents disapprove of, they very quickly learn to say, "But **all my friends** watch this program." A substitute teacher hears, "**My regular teacher** doesn't do it that way." Persuasive writing is a natural outgrowth of students' well-developed ability to speak persuasively.

Essays, business letters, friendly letters, and advertisements make use of persuasive writing techniques. Authors develop a strong sense of audience and judge the effectiveness of their persuasive writing as they note whether they are able to sway readers' opinions and/or receive favorable reactions to their position on a given issue (Tompkins, 2005). Burkhalter (1995) notes, "Because persuasive writing demands higher-level thinking skills, has a more difficult organization, and calls for increased attention to audience, most persuasive essays are extremely short, almost always shorter than any narrative produced under similar conditions" (p. 193).

Ecology is the theme selected for the persuasive writing section. As a nation, we are concerned about the conservation of our natural resources. We must protect our environment and not waste the resources with which we are blessed. A critical shortage of landfill space is a major environmental problem. Kids can make a difference when they study environmental problems and put into action three well-known conservation strategies:

1. **Reduce:** Buy fewer, well-made items that will last. For example, buy fewer but well-constructed toys that will last.
2. **Reuse:** Use items again or share them with someone who will use them again, so they don't become part of the trash in our landfill. For example, use plastic margarine tubs as containers for paper clips and rubber bands.
3. **Recycle:** Save used items and take them to businesses who turn them into new products. For example, set up recycling bins and separate trash into glass, paper, aluminum cans, and other trash. Take glass, paper, and aluminum to recycling stations.

Artistic Adventures
Advertisements/Junk Art

Advertisements are a form of persuasive writing in which the advertiser attempts to convince consumers to purchase a particular product. In an attempt to exert influence over the buyer, the advertising executive designs advertisements with intellectual, emotional, and social appeal.

One advertising strategy, sometimes recognized as having negative connotation, is propaganda. *Propaganda* is a persuasive writing technique in which the advertiser may stretch or deliberately distort the truth to sell potential buyers a product. Commercials often use propaganda techniques such as testimonial, bandwagon, and reward to convince consumers to buy their products (see example in Reading Chapter p. 38). Students develop critical thinking skills and become critical consumers as they analyze advertisements and commercials looking for persuasive writing tactics and propaganda techniques.

Using persuasive writing tactics and propaganda techniques, students produce advertisements to sell their own personal junk art. Create each piece of *junk art* from items found in and around the house. Rather than throwing these items away, reuse them for junk art creations. Use plastic containers such as two-liter drink bottles, milk jugs, soap scoops, and yogurt cups. Styrofoam containers such as fruit trays, take-home boxes, and egg cartons become part of the junk art creations. Bottle caps, milk lids, and old buttons have decorative possibilities. Students should be sure these items are clean before creating their art.

Literature-Related Example

Students become members of an advertising agency in which they, as advertising executives, plan advertising campaigns to sell their junk art to art connoisseurs. They design an art gallery with spotlights (flashlights) to highlight each exquisite item. Spotlight each piece of "art" while reading an advertisement such as the following:

Welcome to The *(Teacher's Name)* Class Art Gallery. Today *you will have the privilege of viewing many of the art world's greatest Junk Art creations. These treasures are from the furthermost corners of the earth. Don't let the term Junk Art mislead you. The design of these exquisite masterpieces is surpassed by none.*

The widely acclaimed artist Kimber Pepper created our first masterpiece. As you can see, Kimber's work is unique and imaginative! Using just an ordinary two-liter drink bottle, a few straws, milk lids, and paint, Kimber has created a luxury car with all the appeal of the latest technology. You will want to be the one who owns this unusual collector's item. All your friends will be envious. They will flock to your home to see this work of art prominently displayed on the coffee table in your living room.

Gamut of Games
Interviews/Interview Summary

An *interview* is a conversation in which the inquirer is seeking information on an issue from the person being questioned. The person being interviewed may be an expert on the issue or have opinions "inquiring minds want to know." The information obtained may be fact or opinion, based on the person's expertise and feelings about the issue. The inquirer (interviewer) should be aware of these differences. Use interviews from television shows as examples.

The inquirer should plan questions for the interview carefully. Before the interview, create an interview planner with questions, leaving spaces between the questions for notes. Some general questions, which can be made more specific based on the issue being investigated, are:

1. **Who** are you? (background, areas of expertise, education, etc.)
2. **What** is your position on _____? (issue)
3. **Why** do you feel this way? (reasons)
4. **How** do you think we should deal with this issue?

The interviewer should take notes during the interview. If possible, audiotape or videotape the interview.

An *interview summary* is a synopsis of information on an issue obtained during the interview as well as opinions on the issue that have been influenced by the person being interviewed. To build interest in an issue, experts with opposing viewpoints may be invited to share these opinions in a panel discussion or debate.

Literature-Based Example

After reading The Great Kapok Tree *by Lynne Cherry (1990), students assume the parts of different characters in the story: boa constrictor, bee, monkeys, birds, frogs, jaguar, porcupines, anteaters, sloth, child, and man. They may also create parts for the tree and the owners of the construction company. Plan interviews with each of these characters.*

An interview with the bees might go something like this:

Question: **Who** are you?
Response: I'm a bee who lives in the forest.
Question: **What** is your opinion about chopping down the great kapok tree?
Response: I don't want the tree chopped down. I need the tree more than the loggers do.
Question: **Why** do you feel this way?
Response: I've lived in the forest for a long time. My home is in a hive in the tree. From this hive, I fly to other trees and flowers pollinating them and providing for plant growth.
Question: **How** do you think the loggers should get trees to make lumber with which to build houses?
Response: Perhaps planting groves of trees just for lumber and cutting the trees on a rotating schedule would provide lumber for everyone.

 Ocular Organizers

Business Letter/3.5 Persuasive Paragraph Organizer/3.5 and 3.8 Paragraphs

A *business letter* follows the format of a friendly letter (see Figure 3.2, Letter Larry p. 55) with the addition of an inside address. The message in the letter is more formal than the message in a friendly letter. Writing a business letter persuasively often convinces a person in authority to make changes or take action on a given issue. For example, if a customer is displeased with an item purchased in a store, the customer may write a letter to the store manager listing problems with the item and requesting a refund.

A *3.5 persuasive organizer* contains a visual listing or sentences about three feelings or three actions an author wants taken on a given issue. This information is then used to develop a 3.5 paragraph. To increase interest use color-coding. For example,

Sentence 1 What I believe. Write a position statement with three feelings about the issue or actions to be taken: A (green), B (red), and C (blue).

Sentence 2 Sentence about feeling or action A (green)
Sentence 3 Sentence about feeling or action B (red)
Sentence 4 Sentence about feeling or action C (blue)
Sentence 5 Summary statement—the three feelings or actions are listed again (color code)

Once the 3.5 persuasive paragraph organizer is complete, the student writes a persuasive paragraph based on the information in the organizer. Older students may develop a 3.8 persuasive organizer that also has three feelings or actions but is developed into eight sentences. Two supporting sentences are written for each feeling or action. This information may also serve as an outline for a five-paragraph essay in which there is an introductory paragraph, a separate paragraph for each of the feelings or actions, and a summary paragraph. An eight-paragraph essay would include two supporting paragraphs for each feeling or action.

Literature-Based Example

After reading 50 Simple Things Kids Can Do to Save the Earth *(1990) and* 50 Simple Things Kids Can Do to Recycle *(1994) by the Earthworks Group, students develop a 3.5 persuasive organizer and write a business letter to the school principal. For example,*

Sentence 1: School should conserve natural resources
    (A) Reduce, (B) Reuse, (C) Recycle
Sentence 2: (A) Reduce—use paper front and back
Sentence 3: (B) Reuse—use old file folders for projects
Sentence 4: (C) Recycle—set up containers
Sentence 5: Work together to preserve our earth

3001 Anywhere Street
Dallas, Texas 11111
June 20, 2008

Mr. Donnovan Jones, Principal
Highland City Elementary School
3001 Anywhere Street
Dallas, Texas 11111

Dear Mr. Jones,

We, the students in Mrs. Hall's class, believe that our school should **reduce, reuse,** and **recycle** to conserve our natural resources. We could **reduce** our paper consumption by writing on both the front and back sides of our paper. We could **reuse** old file folders and make them into Journal Jackets and Theater Books. We could set up **recycling** containers to divide our garbage into trash that can be recycled and waste that cannot be recycled. Through a concerted effort on the part of the staff and students at Highland City Elementary to reduce, reuse, and recycle, we will have a part in preserving our earth for those who follow us.

Sincerely,

Mrs. Hall's Class

Dramatic Debut
Persuasive Puppets/Persuasive Script

Persuasive puppets are puppets that are created by reusing items that would otherwise become part of the trash and end up in a landfill. Make puppets from clean socks, panty hose and coat hangers, etc. (See Puppets in the Activity Appendix A). A persuasive puppet's responsibility is to *sell* the audience on a given point of view through a persuasive script and actions.

Literature-Based Example

Based on the story of The Lorax *by Dr. Seuss (1991), create persuasive puppets for the Lorax, the Once-ler, Brown Bar-ba-loots, Swomee Swans, Humming Fish, and YOU. It is the responsibility of each of these puppets to persuade the Once-ler to close down his Thneed Factory and stop chopping down Truffula Trees. The persuasive script might read:*

Lorax:	Mr. Once-ler, please listen to each of my friends. Your Thneed Factory is gonna be each of their ends.
Brown Bar-ba-loots:	Mr. Once-ler, you've gotta stop chopping down Truffula Trees. We're hungry and sick and need shade if you please.
Swomee Swans:	Mr. Once-ler with all of the fogs and the smogs, We can't sing a note; our throats' full of clogs.
Humming Fish:	We have to leave, you've polluted our water Stop chopping trees; you just know that you oughter.
Once-ler:	I'm sorry you're sick, and I'm sorry you're mad, But Thneeds make the most money I've ever had.
You:	Mr. Once-ler, what good will your money do If all your friends leave, and there is just you? **UNLESS** you let me replant Truffula Trees now Environmental contamination will take over and how!

Creative Composition

Before and After Writing/Attitude Adjustment Arranger/Class Cloud Books

Before and after writing is a form of persuasive writing that examines attitudes before and after an attitude adjustment. An *attitude adjustment* is a change in an opinion that occurs when one is persuaded to alter thoughts or a course of action based on intellectual, emotional, and social persuasive tactics. The author's goal in before and after writing is to convince the reader to make an attitude adjustment and support his or her position on an issue.

Organize before and after writing on an *attitude adjustment arranger* (AAA) in three vertical columns. The first column lists initial attitudes about an issue. The second column lists attitude adjustments. The third column lists attitudes after attitude adjustments. An example of an AAA is the following:

Attitude Adjustment Arranger

Before	Attitude Adjustment	After
Homework (HW) is a pain	Homework (HW) is important for reinforcement	Do HW to learn

Before and after writing may follow an "I used to think … but, after an attitude adjustment, I now think … format." The first entry above might read, "I used to think that homework was a pain. After a class discussion on the importance of completing homework to reinforce information learned in class, I had an attitude adjustment. I now think that doing homework is important for learning."

A *class book* is a book to which each student or group of students in the classroom makes contributions. Class books provide an opportunity for students to share their attitude adjustments with others. A collection of class books increases a classroom library. Make class books using large sheets of poster board, punching holes on one side, and placing metal rings through the holes to hold the book together. Another type of class book is a photo album with self-adhering pages under which students place their writings. Include a *dedication page*, an *authors' page* with authors' autobiographical information and signatures, and a *read by . . page* which friends and relatives sign after reading the book. The readers may include comments about the book.

Literature-Based Example

After reading Just a Dream *by Chris Van Allsburg (1990), students make entries about ecology issues on an AAA. The AAA might look like the following:*

Attitude Adjustment Arranger

Before	Attitude Adjustment	After
Littering is all right	Littering clutters our environment	Be careful and deposit litter in trash containers
Throw away fruit trays	Must conserve our natural resources	Reuse fruit trays for picture frames
Put all trash in same container	Turn items into new products	Recycling bins

A class cloud book is a shape book in which the pages are silhouettes of clouds (see Shape Books in Activity Appendix A). Using the well-known saying, "Behind every cloud is a silver lining," each student or group of students composes two pages for the book. The first page is cloudy representing feelings before an attitude adjustment. Using black chalk and a cotton ball, smudge the edge of this page to give a dark, cloudy effect. The second page represents positive feelings after an attitude adjustment. Use a gray crayon or glitter on the edges of this page to give a silvery effect.

Based on the above AAA, a Class Cloud Book contains the following pages:
Title page: Behind Every Cloud is a Silver Lining
         By: Mrs. Vorderburg's Class
Dedication page: *Dedicated to Natural Conservationists Everywhere*
Page 3: *Before we had an attitude adjustment, we used to throw litter everywhere. When we finished eating candy bars, we would throw the wrappers on the ground. We would also . . .*
Page 4: *After an attitude adjustment, we know that litter clutters our environment, and we are careful to deposit litter in trash containers.*
(Continue alternating page sets for each class member or group of students)
Authors' page: *Tammi is in the sixth grade at New York City Elementary School. Tammi likes to read and ride her bike. Tammi is currently writing a story that she plans to publish soon. (Each author contributes a paragraph to this page.)*
Read by ... page: *Signature of each person who reads the book as well as comments by each reader.*

POETRY

> Poetry is words that
> Paint pictures in your mind
> Poetry is rhythm
> Poetry is rhyme. ... sometimes
> Poetry is feelings
> Poetry is experiences
> Poetry is concise
> Poetry s-t-r-e-t-c-h-e-s your imagination.

Most students enjoy hearing poems read aloud to them by enthusiastic teachers. Their early experiences with nursery rhymes provide a foundation for the enjoyment of poetry. "Reading a poem is the way, to start each and every day," is a reminder that teachers should read poetry daily with their students.

The Random House Book of Poetry (1983), edited by Jack Prelutsky and illustrated by Arnold Lobel, is a collection of more than 550 poems for children. Poems by many well-known children's poets, including Aileen Fisher, Mary Ann Hoberman, Myra Cohn Livingston, David McCord, Jack Prelutsky, Shel Silverstein, and others, are found in this collection. This book is an excellent resource for a teacher's professional library. The varieties of poetic formats provide examples for both reading and writing.

Actively involve students not only in the listening and reading of poetry but also in writing. Many poems written for children rhyme, leading to an assumption that poems must rhyme. When students write their own poetry, they often have difficulty finding rhyming words that "make sense" in their compositions. One solution to this dilemma is the use of a rhyming dictionary. Another alternative is introducing students to a variety of poetic formats that do not require rhyming words. Students are often very successful poets using these alternative formats. Poetry Appendix C includes formats, for more than 20 types of poetry.

Poetry writing appeals to the novice as well as the experienced writer. Because most poetry compositions are short, even reluctant writers will experiment with writing poems. Looking for just the right word to make poetry revisions is generally not time consuming, thus writers are willing to make changes in their poems. Publishing poetry is easy and fun.

Artistic Adventures

Picture Poems

A *picture poem* is a poem written in the shape or on the shape of an object. These poems are sometimes called shape poems or concrete poems, because the words are written to create a picture characterizing the object. The poet may use free verse, alliterative words (words beginning with the same sound), or alphabetical words (an "A" word, then a "B" word, etc.) to describe the object and create the picture poem (see Figure 3.8).

Sketching a picture lightly on paper and using the pencil lines as a guide when writing will aid the poet in creating an object that is recognizable. Using a pattern of an object and writing around the edges or across the object is an even easier way to assure a poet's pleasure in the appearance of the product. Die cut machines that cut out multiple shapes are a great timesaver for the teacher. The outer edges of the paper from which the shape is cut may be mounted on a contrasting color of paper and the poem written within the silhouette.

Literature-Based Example

The book People *(1980) by Peter Spire is a valuable multicultural resource that provides ideas for people picture poems. These poems are written on the shape or in the shape of a person. Students may want to use the multiple men technique (see Activity Appendix A)*

FIGURE 3.8   People Picture Poems

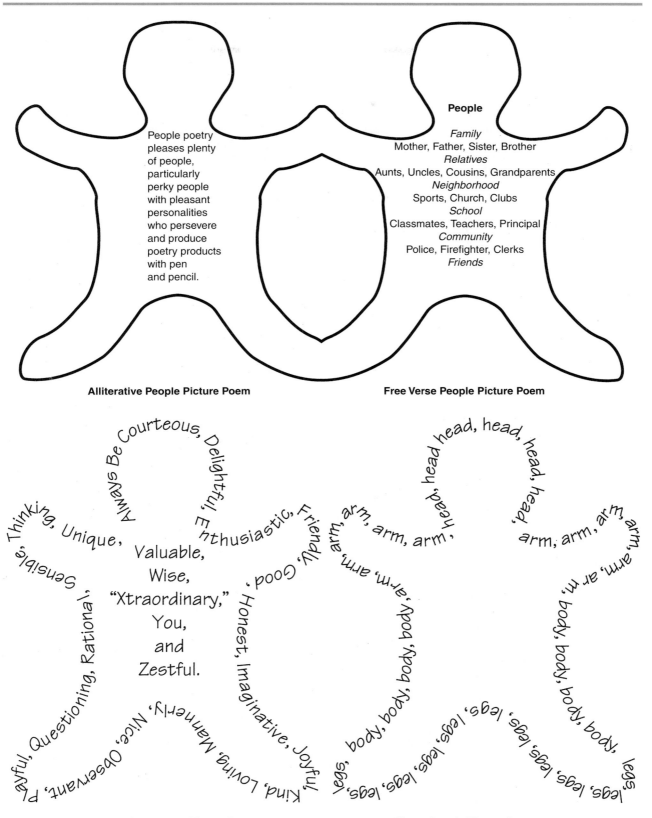

People poetry pleases plenty of people, particularly perky people with pleasant personalities who persevere and produce poetry products with pen and pencil.

People

Family
Mother, Father, Sister, Brother
Relatives
Aunts, Uncles, Cousins, Grandparents
Neighborhood
Sports, Church, Clubs
School
Classmates, Teachers, Principal
Community
Police, Firefighter, Clerks
Friends

Alliterative People Picture Poem   **Free Verse People Picture Poem**

Always Be Courteous, Delightful, Enthusiastic, Friendly, Good, Honest, Imaginative, Joyful, Kind, Loving, Mannerly, Nice, Observant, Playful, Questioning, Rational, Sensible, Thinking, Unique, Valuable, Wise, "Xtraordinary," You, and Zestful.

head, head, head, head, head, arm, arm, arm, arm, ar.m, body, body, body, body, legs, legs, legs, legs, legs, arm, arm, arm, arm, arm, body, body, body, body, legs, legs, legs, legs, legs,

Alphabetical People Picture Poem   **Shape People Picture Poem**

to make several people on which to write their poems (see Figure 3.8). Students may write a different poem on each person, or they may continue one poem across several people.

Gamut of Games
Formula Sentence Poems/Poetry Pass

Formula sentence poems have a structure or pattern within which students create their poems. Each line or thought begins with the same words, providing repetition for the poem. Because the structure provides an outline for the poem, the author focuses attention on making effective thought and word choices. Examples of formula sentence poetry formats are the following:

1. ***Is/Are Poems* … (definition poems)**
   People are …
   People are the same and different
   People are good and bad
2. ***I Wish* …**
   I wish I had a million dollars …
   I wish all the people in the world would …
3. ***If I were* …**
   If I were the principal, I would. …
   If I were a person in Alaska, I would . .
4. ***I used to be … but now I am* …**
   I used to be short but now I am tall.
   I used to think all people should be alike, but now I know differences are important.

Poetry Pass is a game in which a group of players composes a collaborative formula poem. First, the players choose a topic for the poem and write the topic at the top of a sheet of paper. Then they write the beginning words for each line of the poem several times in a column down the left side of the paper. The first player completes the first line and says, "Poetry Pass," and passes the paper. The second player completes the second line, says, "Poetry Pass," and passes the paper. As the paper is passed from player to player, each makes a written contribution to the poem, says, "Poetry Pass," and gives the paper to the next player. The last player writes a summary line for the poem. Use an egg timer to determine the length of time for each player's turn.

Literature-Based Example

After sharing the book People, *a group of students plays Poetry Pass and composes a people poem using the formula:*
People are alike because …
People are different because …

People

Player 1: **People are alike because** they all have eyes.
Player 2: **People are different because** their eyes are different colors.
Player 3: **People are alike because** they all like to eat.
Player 4: **People are different because** they like to eat different food.
Player 5: It is important for people to be both alike and different.

Ocular Organizers

Poetry Place/Limerick

A *poetry place* has a poetry outline made in masking tape lines on the floor. The poetry format determines the number and length of the lines. For example, the lines for a diamante poem (see Poetry Appendix C) look like this:

```
                    ____

            ____         ____

        ____       ____        ____

    ____      ____       ____       ____

        ____       ____        ____

            ____         ____

                    ____
```

Write a rough draft of the poem before using the masking tape lines. When the draft is satisfactory, write words for the poem on word cards or sentence strips and place them on the masking tape lines on the floor or carpet. Another possibility for using an outline on which to create a poem (especially if the custodians object to masking tape on the floor or carpet) is to draw the lines on a transparency. Show the lines on the board using an overhead projector. If available, use a computer program to project lines on the board. Students fill in the lines and write their poem on the board. An alternative is to draw the outline on large sheets of tag board and then laminate the tag board. Write poems with water-soluble markers on the tag board.

A *limerick* is a humorous poem with five lines. The words at the ends of lines 1, 2, and 5 rhyme with each other. The words at the ends of lines 3 and 4 rhyme with each other. Often lines 3 and 4 are shorter. Usually line 5 has a surprise ending. For an outline for a limerick see the Poetry Appendix C. Help students in their initial limerick writing by providing sets of rhyming words such as:

eye, cry, dinner, thinner, sigh
hair, scare, fright, sight, bear

Literature-Based Example:

A limerick about people that students might compose to put on an outline in the Poetry Place is:

> *People*
> Each of us has a different nose.
> Each of us wears different clothes.
> We each have a different name.
> None of us looks the same.
> But when sleepy, we all doze.

Dramatic Debut

Poetry Party/Poetry Pocket Plate Mobile/Invitation Poem

Poetry parties provide an opportunity to share poems and music (a form of poetry) with family and friends. A poetry party may take place either in the classroom or as a special event at

FIGURE 3.9   Invitation Poem

Party Time!

WHO: YOU are invited to a

WHAT: POETRY PARTY

WHEN: On MONDAY, JUNE 01 at 10:00 A.M.

WHERE: In ROOM 3 at WILSON ELEMENTARY SCHOOL

WHY: To have FUN and SHARE poetry

HOW: Through EXPRESSIVE READING, SINGING, and
           DRAMATIC POETRY PRESENTATIONS

Please bring a favorite poem to share.

a parent-teacher program. Use poems written by class poets to decorate party hats, table-cloths, and placemats. Display additional poems in *poetry pocket plate mobiles*, a paper plate container designed to hold students' poems (see Pocket Plate Mobile in Activity Appendix A). Display students' poems in the pocket as well as on the back of the whole paper plate.

Deliver *invitation poems* by hand to prospective guests (see Figure 3.9). Write these poems on enveloptionery (see Activity Appendix A). A poetry party is the culminating activity for a poetry unit.

Creative Composition
Patterned Poetry

Patterned poetry writing uses an existing poem as a model and substitutes alternative words in the model to write a poetry innovation. Young poets often make changes in familiar poems and songs that they have memorized. Using the predictable language patterns, students try different words in the poem or song. They write the new words on sticky notes and place over the original text. After reading *Brown Bear, Brown Bear What Do You See?* by Bill Martin Jr. (1983), students substitute the names of animals in the story. The next innovation makes changes in the color words.

Literature-Based Example

In writing patterned poetry about people, the song, "Where Is Thumbkin?" could become:
    Line 1: Where is my friend? Where is my friend?
    Line 2: I'm right here. I'm right here.
    Line 3: I'm an African American. I'm an African American.
    Line 4: We are friends. We are friends.

For line 3, substitute Hispanic American, Native American, European American. Add cultural groups appropriate for your classroom, neighborhood, city. The summarizing verse might be:

Where are all my friends? Where are all my friends?
We're right here. We're right here.
We are all together. We are all together.
We are friends. We are friends.

After reading Jack Prelutsky's (1984) poem "Homework! Oh, Homework!" in The New Kid on the Block *(1984), students might create a poetry innovation that focuses on people.*

People! Oh, People!

People! Oh, People!
I love you! You're great!
I pray that destruction
Will not be our fate.
If only a bomb
Won't explode us to bits.
Tension on earth
Is giving us fits.
I'd rather be free
To take walks in the park,
Than worry whenever
Outside it is dark.
Violence around us
All of the time.
Yet freedom from fear
Should always be mine.
People! Oh, People!
If we're to exist
And live in freedom
Violence must desist
When peace on earth reigns
It will tickle me pink
People, Oh, People!
Love's the missing link.

Literature References

Ahlberg, J., & Ahlberg, A. (1991). *The jolly Christmas postman*. Boston: Little, Brown and Company.

Ahlberg, J., & Ahlberg, A. (1986). *The jolly postman or other people's letters*. Boston: Little, Brown and Company.

Baylor, B. (1976). *Hawk, I'm Your Brother*. New York: Macmillan. Caldecott Honor.

Blos, J. W. (1979). *A gathering of days: A New England girl's journal, 1830–1832*. New York: Macmillan. Newbery Award.

Cherry, L. (1990). *The great kapok tree*. New York: Harcourt Brace Jovanovich.

Cleary, B. (1983). *Dear Mr. Henshaw*. New York: Dell. Newbery Award.

Demi. (1993). *Demi's secret garden*. New York: Henry Holt.

de Paola, T. (1989). *The art lesson*. New York: Putnam.

EarthWorks Group. (1994). *50 simple things kids can do to recycle*. Berkeley, CA: EarthWorks Press.

EarthWorks Group. (1990). *50 simple things kids can do to save the earth*. New York: Andrews and McMeel.

Fitzhugh, L. (1964). *Harriet the spy*. New York: Dell.

George, J. C. (1959). *My side of the mountain*. New York: Penguin Books. Newbery Award.

Haley, G. E. (1970). *A story a story*. New York: Macmillan. Caldecott Award.

Hamilton, V. (1985). *The people could fly: American black folktales*. New York: Alfred A. Knopf.

Kellogg, S. (1986). *Pecos Bill*. New York: Mulberry Books.

Martin Jr., B. (1967). *Brown bear, brown bear, what do you see?* New York: Holt, Rinehart, and Winston.

Mosel, A. (1968). *Tikki Tikki Tembo*. New York: Henry Holt.

Ness, E. (1966). *Sam, Bangs & Moonshine*. New York: Henry Holt. Caldecott Award.

Parker, N. W., & Wright, J. R. (1987). *Bugs*. New York: Mulberry Books.

Prelutsky, J. (Ed.). (1983). *The Random House book of poetry for children: A treasury of 572 poems for today's child*. New York: Random House.

Prelutsky, J. (1984). "Homework! Oh, homework!" In *The new kid on the block*. New York: Greenwillow Books.

Rylant, C. (1982). *When I was young in the mountains*. New York: E. P. Dutton. Caldecott Honor.

Seuss, Dr. (1991). The Lorax. In *Six by Seuss: A treasury of Dr. Seuss classics*. New York: Random House.

Spire, P. (1980). *People*. New York: Doubleday.

Van Allsburg, C. (1990). *Just a dream*. Boston: Houghton Mifflin.

Viorst, J. (1972). *Alexander and the terrible, horrible, no good, very bad day*. New York: Macmillan.

Williams, V. (1988). *Stringbean's trip to the shining sea*. New York: Greenwillow.

Williams, V. (1981). *Three days on a river in a red canoe*. New York: Greenwillow.

Professional References

Allen, R. (2003, Summer). Expanding writing's role in learning: Teacher training holds key to change. *ASCD Curriculum Update*. Alexandria, VA

Burkhalter, N. (1995). A Vygotsky-based curriculum for teaching persuasive writing in the elementary grades. *Language Arts, 72*, 192–199.

Calkins, L. M. (1994). *The art of teaching writing*. Portsmouth, NH: Heinemann.

Elbow, P. (2004). Writing first. *Educational Leadership, 62* (2), 8–13.

Franklin, J. (2003, Summer). Breaking the barriers: How writing across the curriculum program helps students and teachers. *ASCD Curriculum Update*. Alexandria, VA.

Graves, D. (1983). *Writing: Teachers & children at work*. Exeter, NH: Heinemann.

Graves, D. H. (1994). *A fresh look at writing*. Portsmouth, NH: Heinemann.

Henk, W. A., Marinak, B. A., Moore, J. C., & Mallette, M. H. (Dec 2004/Jan 2005). The writing observation framework: A guide for refining and validating writing instruction. *The Reading Teacher, 58* (4), 322–333.

International Reading Association & National Council of Teachers of English. (1996). *Standards for the English Language Arts*. Urbana, IL. National Writing Project, (2004) Retrieved June 30, 2005. www.writingproject.org.

Norton, D. E. (1995). *Through the eyes of a child*. New York: Merrill.

Ogle, D. M. (1986). K-W-L: A teaching model that develops active reading of expository text. *The Reading Teacher, 39*, 564–570.

Ray, K. W. (2004). When kids make books. *Educational Leadership, 62* (2), 14–18.

Tompkins, G. E., (2005). *Language arts patterns of practice* (6th ed.). Englewood Cliffs, NJ: Merrill.

Villaume, S. K., & Brabham, E. G. (2001). Conversations among writers in authors circles. *The Reading Teacher, 54* (5), 494–476.

Wynn, M. J. (1993). Proprietary vocabulary acquisition: A creative thematic adventure [Themed Issue: Exemplary Teaching and Exemplary Teachers]. *Reading Horizons, 33* (5), 389–400.

Wynn, M. J. (1994). Experiencing literary elements in stories through music and poetry. *The Florida Reading Quarterly, 31* (2), 5–11.

Zemelman, S., Daniels, H., & Hyde, A. (1998). *Best practices: New standards for teaching and learning in America's schools* (2nd ed.). Portsmouth, NH: Heinemann.

Websites

International Reading Association (IRA)

Look for association news, research bulletins, publications, and conference announcements.

www.reading.org

National Commission on Writing

Includes resources on helping children learn to write, supporting the teaching of writing, and expert tips for parents and students. Reports to Congress include *The Neglected "R"* and *Writing: A Ticket to Work...Or a Ticket Out, A Survey of Business Leaders*.

www.writingcommission.org

National Council of Teachers of English (NCTE)

Look for information on reading, literature, and writing.

www.ncte.org

National Writing Project (NWP)

The mission of the National Writing Project (NWP) is to improve the teaching of writing and improve learning in the nation's schools. NWP builds the leadership, programs, and research needed for teachers to help their students become successful writers and learners.

www.writingproject.org

Read Write Think

IRA/NCTE site that has extensive information in the following areas: lessons, standards, web resources, and materials. Included are ideas in literacy engagements in learning language, learning about language, and learning through language.

www.readwritethink.org

CHAPTER 4 TOPICS	Artistic Adventures	Gamut of Games Centers
Listening	Listen and Draw	Listen and Learn Centers
Lit Links	Quilts	Lit Link Centers
Grammar	Grammacrostics Banner Book	Great Grammar Centers
Spelling	Media Mix	Spelling Success Centers
Handwriting	Squiggles	Practically Perfect Penmanship Places

Language Arts: Scaffolds, Skills, and Centers

Ocular Organizers	Dramatic Debut	Creative Composition
Prediction Chart	Obstacle Course Experience Life from Phillip's Point of View	Listen, List, and eLaborate
Lit Link Legends	Felt Board	Freedom Trail Freedom Facts Chart Freedom Folio
Grammar Grid Tongue Twisters	Grammar Cop, Laws, Tickets, and Skits	Sentence Expansion Sentence Schematic Wrap-Over Book
Dictionary Display	Spelling Cheers Spelling Sports	Spelling Songs
Belly Button Buddy	Notes in a Nutshell "The Case of the Messy Message"	The Important Job The Important Thing About Me

OVERVIEW

Just as scaffolds are structures for supporting a worker during the construction of a building, listening, lit links, grammar, spelling, and handwriting are the scaffolds that support a student during the construction of effective reading and writing skills. Teachers facilitate the building of these scaffolds by encouraging students to use the listening and oral language skills they bring with them to the classroom. *Listening* develops through hearing the voices of friends, relatives, and even broadcast media. A sense of story emerges while listening to stories. Often young children respond spontaneously to stories by putting on a play, coloring a picture, or telling the story to a friend. *Lit links* are a variety of strategies for reflecting and sharing creatively exciting encounters with books. Thus, lit links are natural extensions of literary experiences.

Children develop a sense of syntax, sentence structure, and *grammar* usage through observation and imitation of language patterns. Eventually, verbal patterns become models for writing. As students write, they become aware of the need for *spelling* and *handwriting skills* to ensure effective communication with an audience. Thus, grammar, spelling, and handwriting become essential scaffolds to support young authors' compositions. These scaffolds continue to provide support as writing proficiency develops.

The *IRA/NCTE Standard for the English Language Arts* that specifically mentions knowledge of language structure and language conventions (e.g., spelling and punctuation) is standard 6 (see Figure 2.3). Many researchers suggest teaching these scaffolding skills within the context of process writing. They also note the importance of implementing mini-lessons for direct instruction as the need arises (Calkins, 1994; Graves 1994). For example, Allen (2003) notes that lack of quality penmanship has a negative effect on a student's ability to write, self-confidence, and desire to write. Thus, direct instruction is needed. Experiencing difficulties with grammar usage and spelling can also impede effective communication and may necessitate mini-lesson instruction.

Scaffolds and skills for effective language arts communication are often reinforced in centers. *Centers* are activity areas set aside in a classroom where students go to practice, review, or extend skills. In this chapter each Gamut of Games section has three suggested center activities. One advantage in using centers is the efficient use of class time. While students work independently, in peer pairs, or in small groups at centers, teachers conduct conferences with individual students and small groups of students. Another advantage of using centers is that center activities do not require grading. Many activities are self-corrective, using answer keys or matching symbols, thus providing immediate feedback to the student. Other activities do not require feedback (e.g., making a puppet).

Centers may be organized in a variety of ways. The centers in the room may all relate to one scaffold (e.g., all listening centers), or the centers may be a combination of scaffolds and skills (e.g., one center for grammar, another for spelling, another for listening). There are several options to determine the center in which students will participate. Three options are (1) free choice, (2) assigning students to centers based on academic need, and (3) assigning students to groups that rotate through the centers. This may be a weekly rotation with five centers, so that group 1 begins in center 1 on Monday, on Tuesday goes to center 2, and so on, while group 2 begins in center 2 on Monday and completes the rotation in center 1 on Friday. On Monday, group 3 begins in center 3, group 4 begins in center 4, and group 5 begins in center 5, and each group continues the rotation.

This chapter is devoted to the supportive components of language arts that are essential in effective communication across content areas. The theme of this chapter is *self-esteem*, developing confidence in one's ability to do well in any given situation. The literature choices focus on character growth in attitude about self. Thus, students are examining a character's growth in self-esteem while developing academic skills. As students develop self-confidence in listening, grammar, spelling, handwriting, and creating exciting lit links, academic skills as well as self-confidence in communication are enhanced.

 # LISTENING

When you talk, you repeat what you already know;
When you listen, you often learn something.

Jaren Sparks

A large percentage of classroom time is spent in *listening to learn;* therefore, it is imperative that students *learn to listen.* *Listening* is the ability to comprehend a spoken message. This ability to convert language to meaning in the mind is based on the listener's background knowledge and the speaker's information. Listening includes both *hearing,* the physical capability to perceive sounds, and *comprehension,* the ability to make meaning from the sounds. Listening comprehension is an essential component in learning.

Listening is the first learned and most frequently used language mode. Young children respond to parents' voices. They listen as parents read and tell stories. When students enter school, they can listen, and teachers assume that they know how to listen. Therefore, little, if any, instructional time is spent in helping students develop effective listening skills, and teachers' manuals typically include minimal information on listening strategies.

Teachers quickly discover that the degree of intensity with which a student listens is determined by the student's interest in the subject and purpose for listening. Students are very adept at determining *when* and *if* they will listen. At times they may choose to suffer from *selective hearing loss,* tuning out a spoken message. One cause of this malady is disinterest in the topic of discussion. The teacher should promote meaningful purposes for listening on topics of interest to students, provide opportunities to build background information, and model good listening skills. Both teachers and students must strive to improve the listening atmosphere in the classroom.

Classroom conditions as well as the speaker's skills and listener's skills affect listening. A *classroom environment* that is conducive to attentive listening includes:

1. Comfortable temperature
2. Minimal noise and interruptions
3. Varied activities
4. Intermittent changes in seating arrangements
   (opportunities to move around the classroom)
5. Clear desks and hands

A *speaker's skills* that promote listeners' auditory retention include:

1. Capturing the attention of the audience
2. Speaking clearly and at a comfortable volume
   (neither too loudly nor too softly)
3. Speaking with intonation and not in a monotone
4. Choosing vocabulary and information that is appropriate for the audience
5. Using visuals such as webs, charts, and pictures
6. Organizing information
   a. *Introduction*: Tell audience what you are going to say
   b. *Content Presentation*: Tell audience the information in a sequential manner
   c. *Summary*: Tell audience what you said
7. Involving audience in the presentation and discussion of open-ended questions
8. Reviewing frequently

A *listener's responsibilities* include:

1. Focusing on the speaker
2. Forming visual pictures in the mind of what the speaker is saying
3. Taking notes

4. Summarizing the information mentally, verbally, and in writing
5. Asking questions

Students must develop listening skills at literal, inferential, and critical levels. They should also develop appreciative listening skills. A song that differentiates and explains these levels is:

Title: Levels of Listening Comprehension
Tune: "Supercalifragilisticexpialidocious"

Oh, Level One in listening is **Literal** you see.
Knowledge level listening; facts for you and me.
Listen to directions; sequence carefully.
Main ideas, details are easy for you and me.
  Oh, Level Two in listening is **Inferential** you see.
Bringing facts and prior knowledge together carefully.
Cause, effect, prediction, problem, solutions, too.
We can make an educated guess in everything we do.
  Oh, Level Three in listening is **Critical** you see.
Analyzing, evaluating, judgments made carefully.
Watch out for emotions, propaganda too.
Check out the speaker's background before making a decision or two.
  Oh, another level in listening is **Appreciative** you see.
Lit Links to stories you hear are made personally.
You may do innovations with music, drama, or art.
All you need is quality lit to give you a good start.

Students should be actively involved in listening. Class discussion to increase awareness of the importance of listening and a variety of strategies enable students to improve their listening skills. If students are going to *listen to learn,* they must *learn to listen.*

The literature focus for listening is a classic, *The Cay* (1969), and *Timothy of the Cay: A Prequel-Sequel* (1993) by Theodore Taylor. *The Cay* is the story of an old black man, Timothy, and a blind boy, Phillip, marooned on a small Caribbean island. Timothy devotes his life to preparing Phillip to survive on the island. Phillip's attitudes about others change, and his self-esteem is enhanced as he lives with Timothy and learns survival skills. *Timothy of the Cay* is a prequel that deals with Timothy's life before being stranded on the cay and a sequel that deals with Phillip's life after he is rescued. The chapters alternate between prequel and sequel.

 ## *Artistic Adventures*

Listen and Draw

Listen and Draw is a game in which one player gives directions for drawing a picture to another player who is blindfolded or wearing dark glasses. Aluminum foil over dark glasses cuts out any light and enhances the feeling of blindness. The player who is drawing experiences the frustration of being blind. This game requires attentive listening to directions to draw what is being described. An additional challenge is to draw with different colors of crayons or markers. Place the crayons or markers in a line, and the player giving the directions must tell the position of a given color (e.g., "The blue crayon is the fourth crayon from the left").

Literature-Based Example

After reading about Phillip and Timothy's cay, the blindfolded player draws a picture of the cay based on a partner's description. The partner could suggest drawing the cay so that it almost fills the sheet of paper and then give descriptions of a hut, small fire, signal fire, bushes, fishing hole, palm trees, Stew Cat, and other features. After the blindfolded player sees the picture, he or she may choose to redraw the picture without the blindfold.

Gamut of Games

Listen and Learn Centers

Listen and learn centers are centers that have activities designed to enhance a student's listening skills.

Listen and Learn Center 1

Timothy's Trip to the Cay is a game in which students take turns telling what they would take on a trip to a cay. The items are given in alphabetical order. Each player adds an item to the list and must also name all of the previous items in the correct order. This game helps students develop short-term auditory memory.

Directions

1. The first player says, "My name is Timothy, and I'm going on a trip to a cay. I'm going to take *arrows*." (Item beginning with an A)
2. The second player says, "My name is Timothy, and I'm going on a trip to a cay. I'm going to take *arrows* and a *bow* to shoot the arrows." (Item beginning with a B)
3. Continue taking turns, repeating previous items, and adding items in alphabetical order.

Listen and Learn Center 2

Show and Tell is an activity in which a speaker shares information about one or more topics or items. Listeners benefit from show and tell as they develop listening skills while focusing on what the speaker is saying, learning information about a topic or item, and asking questions to increase their understanding. Show and tell helps the speaker develop skill in planning and presenting information orally to an audience. Information shared relates to the literature and content area focus in the classroom.

Directions for the Speaker

1. Choose an item you would need to survive on an island.
2. Share two ways this item is beneficial to you on an island.
3. Ask your audience to share other ways this item might be beneficial.

Directions for Listeners

1. Form pictures in your mind of what the speaker is saying.
2. Take notes on ways the item is beneficial.
3. Place your notes in a folder for a later class discussion when class members will compare and contrast item choices and their uses.

Listen and Learn Center 3

Investigative Listening is a game in which players listen through earphones to a story on an audiotape and answer teacher-generated questions about the story. Questions at the literal level often answer the question What. Questions at the inferential level often answer the question How. Questions at the critical level often answer the question Why.

Literature-Based Example

Timothy (T) did several things to prepare Phillip (P) to live independently on the cay. As students listen to the story on the audiotape, they might fill in the chart as follows:

What survival skill did T help P develop?	*How* did the survival skill help P?	*Why* was this skill important?
Follow vine rope	Find signal fire	Attract rescuers
Use cane	Move around island	Find food, fire, and shelter
Fishing with pole and hooks	Catch fish for food for Stew Cat and himself	Food is essential for survival

Ocular Organizers

Prediction Chart

A *prediction chart* is a graphic organizer with three columns:

> *Column 1: What? Questions about the story and predictions.*
> *Column 2: Why? Evidence for predictions.*
> *Column 3: Verify or Modify? Evidence to support, modify, or reject predictions after listening to the story or a chapter or section of the story.*

Predictions require the listener to make use of inferential skills by using personal background knowledge and information given in the story. Making predictions promotes listener involvement, as the listener has an investment in listening carefully to confirm, modify, or reject predictions. Predictions help the listener focus on the plot of the story.

Use the following steps when making predictions about picture books and chapter books (Note: Teacher reads text; students listen).

Picture Books
1. Ask initial questions based on the title and illustrations.
2. Record predictions with the teacher acting as scribe.
3. Read to a predetermined stopping point.
4. Verify, modify, or reject predictions based on evidence in the text and illustrations.
5. Ask new questions based on the next section of the story.
6. Continue steps 2 through 5 for each section of the story.

Chapter Books
1. Ask initial questions based on the title and illustration on the cover of the book.
2. Record predictions.
3. Read the first chapter of the book.
4. Confirm, modify, or reject predictions based on evidence in the chapter.
5. Ask new questions based on this information for the next chapter of the book.
6. Continue steps 2 through 5 for each chapter.

Literature-Based Example

Before reading The Cay, *make initial entries on the prediction chart. After completing Chapter 1, verify, modify, or reject initial predictions. Continue making chart entries for each chapter. On the sample chart there are initial entries before listening to the first chapter and entries before listening to Chapter 13.*

Prediction Chart for <u>The Cay</u>

What?	Why?	Verify or Modify?
Before Listening to the Chapter 1		
*What is the book about?		
**An adventure at the beach	Picture of ocean in background	
*Characters?		
** A black man, a white child, and a cat	Pictures on cover of book	Phillip (P), white boy, is with his parents on an island during war So far there is no black man and no cat
* Problems?		
**The black man's cat runs away and the boy helps him find the cat	The man is lovingly holding the cat	Problem is war
Before Listening to Chapter 13		
(Note: in Chapter 12 Timothy (T) is struck with malaria. (P) rescues him)		
*What is the chapter going to be about?		
(T) is going to die	(T) never regains his strength	
(P) will be all alone	Because he is blind, (P) will not be able to take care of himself	(T) conducts a survival course for (P); teaches (P) to get fish; encourages him to climb coconut tree
		(P)'s last question in the chapter, "(T), are you still black?"

 ## Dramatic Debut

Obstacle Course/Experience Life from Phillip's Point of View

An *obstacle course* is a route containing a series of hurdles that hamper progress and which must be overcome to reach a goal. The hurdles in an obstacle course may be physical barriers, directions to follow, or questions to answer. As participants meet the challenges in an obstacle course, an appropriate sound track tape helps establish mood.

Literature-Based Example

Students experience life from Phillip's point of view as a blind person when they wear dark glasses or a blindfold and participate in an obstacle course designed as the cay. Because they are blind, students are dependent on feeling, listening, and the assistance of others as they make their way through the hurdles. A sound track of water, wind, and waves provides dramatic effect. Students use a cane and hold onto a vine (twine) as Phillip did on the cay as they continue through the obstructions on the course. Initially, partners help by giving verbal directions, which include north, south, east, and west, as well as walking them around the cay for orientation. The goal is to complete five tasks on the obstacle course designed for survival and rescue. These tasks include:

1. Walk to the palm tree and untie the fishing pole. Tie a hook (magnet) to the end of the string on your pole. Walk to the fishing hole and catch a fish (paper fish with paper clip that will attach to magnet).
2. Take the fish you caught and go to the fire near your hut (made of cardboard boxes). Put the fish on the end of a stick and cook it.
3. Find out what the hurricane deposited on your cay. Identify it and plan how to use it (can, piece of wood, string, canvas, etc.).
4. Listen !! An airplane is coming. Take a small piece of firewood from the fire in front of your hut, proceed to the signal fire on the beach, and light the fire. Add wood to the fire.
5. Check the stones on the beach where you wrote HELP to make sure they are in place.

Creative Composition

*Listen, List, and eLaborate

Listen, List, and eLaborate (LLL) is a note-taking strategy in which students *listen* to a question, *list* information to answer the question, and *eLaborate* on their answers. This strategy, which strengthens note-taking skills, focuses student attention on important aspects of narrative and informational material. After making a list of answers, students *eLaborate* and apply this information to other situations. LLL is an especially effective strategy for noting character growth and attitude adjustments. On the basis of information from LLL notes, students write compositions.

Literature-Based Example

Phillip's attitude toward black people undergoes a dramatic change during his experience on the cay. Listen to an audiotape of The Cay *and use LLL to examine this change. The following chart shows examples of changes in Phillip's attitude.*

Listen	List	eLaborate
What initial attitudes does Phillip have about black people?	Prejudiced Didn't like Unsure of	Mother didn't like, and he adopted her attitude; didn't associate with
What changes occur in Phillip's attitude?	Appreciation Understanding	Timothy took care of Phillip, endangering his own life
What attitude does Phillip adopt at the end of the story?	Skin color does not make any difference; we are all the same	Phillip asked Timothy if his skin was still black; grieved his death

---

LIT LINKS

In a very real sense, people who have read good literature
Have lived more than people who cannot or will not read.
It is not true that we have only one life to live;
If we can read, we can live as many more lives and
As many kinds of lives as we wish.

S. I. Hayakawa

Lit links are a variety of strategies for reflecting and creatively sharing exciting encounters with books. Lit links include artistic, dramatic, and written experiences to extend and enrich listening to or reading a book. Lit links are motivational alternatives to the traditional book report handout that requires students to answer questions such as: Who is your favorite character? What happened in the story? Would you recommend this book to a friend? In the past book reports have often been a terribly tedious task.

Lit links provide opportunities to stimulate independent reading and participation in creative reading experiences. Independent reading increases proprietary vocabulary, reading comprehension, and knowledge about our world. Students become familiar with sentence and text patterns through independent reading. The classic study, *Becoming a Nation of Readers: The Report of the Commission on Reading* (1985) by Anderson, Hiebert, Scott, and Wilkerson, stresses the importance of independent reading and the fact that classroom teachers are instrumental in prioritizing class time, so that independent reading will occur. Many schools have implemented a daily scheduled time for independent reading. The teacher's goal is to get students "hooked on books."

Lit links are motivational, making reading an exciting challenge. Literature choices include books about Harriet Tubman, an African American who struggled to lead her people from slavery to freedom on the Underground Railroad. She developed and maintained self-esteem during very trying times and is an exemplary role model for all students. The following are focus choices: *Aunt Harriet's Underground Railroad in the Sky* by Faith Ringgold (1992), *Follow the Drinking Gourd* by Jeanette Winter (1988), *Harriet and the Promised Land* by Jacob Lawrence (1993), *Harriet Tubman* by Bree Burns (1992), *If You Traveled on the Underground Railroad* by Ellen Levine (1988), and *Sweet Clara and the Freedom Quilt* by Deborah Hopkinson (1993).

Lit link strategies are readily adaptable to other literature selections (e.g., younger students might study railroads in a transportation unit and use several of the lit link strategies).

(Note: Not every book read or listened to should have a lit link. Sometimes reading books is just for fun.)

Artistic Adventures

Quilts

Quilts are handmade bed coverings made from squares of cloth sewn together in a predetermined pattern. Each square in a quilt has special meaning and is reminiscent of a significant person or event. Quilts are a tradition in many cultures. They are often given as wedding or baby presents and then passed down from generation to generation. Often family and friends have quilting parties where they gather to socialize, reminisce, and sew scraps of fabric together to form squares and then sew the squares together to make a quilt. Sometimes the pictures in the squares on the quilt tell family stories, and they are frequently arranged in chronological sequence.

Students can make their own quilts from squares of fabric or paper. Decorate quilts made from fabric with stitching, fabric crayons, or fabric paint. Join squares by sewing them together. Decorate quilts made from paper with miscellaneous decorative materials. Glue squares to a large piece of paper or poster board. Plan squares so that the outer edges fold under on all four sides of each square. Then staple the squares together underneath before gluing them to another surface. This technique gives a finished appearance.

Literature-Based Example

Based on stories about Harriet Tubman, students working in peer pairs design squares for significant events in Harriet's life, important events during the historical time, and thought-provoking vocabulary words for these events. Join these squares to make a quilt. Use the quilt as a visual when sharing stories about Harriet Tubman.

Gamut of Games

Lit Link Centers

Puppets, plays, pictures, and parades are lit link centers where students work individually, in peer pairs, or in small groups to reflect on as well as extend and enrich their experiences with books. Puppets, plays, pictures, and parades provide motivational opportunities for students to create, and then share with peers and others, exciting encounters with books. As peers observe and listen to the sharing of a book, they are enthusiastic and want to read the same book; thus, independent reading is encouraged. Often, students enjoy simultaneously reading the same book with a friend and then working together to create a lit link.

Lit Link Center 1

Puppet productions provide opportunities to extend experiences in reading books, writing scripts, listening to others while planning productions, and speaking expressively while participating in the puppet plays. Create bathroom tissue tube puppets from bathroom tissue tubes that are wrapped with construction paper. Decorate with crayons, markers, and miscellaneous decorative materials. Concoct facial features, hats, and clothing that are appropriate for the character. Attach popsicle sticks or tongue depressors to assist in moving the puppets. For other possibilities see puppets in Activity Appendix A.

Directions for this center might include the following:

1. Plan a puppet play.
2. Produce a script.
3. Prepare puppets.
4. Practice your production.
5. Present your puppet play.

Lit Link Center 2

Create a *Four-Fold Flip-Flop with Handle* to share five or more bits of information from a literature experience (see Activity Appendix A). Label the handle with the title, author, and illustrator of the book. Label each flap with a bit of information, and on the back of the flap and under the flap are places for two pictures about this bit of information. The following chart shows three possibilities for labeling the flaps.

	Possibility 1	**Possibility 2**	**Possibility 3**
Flap 1	First	Characters	Main Character
Flap 2	Next	Setting	Event 1
Flap 3	Then	Problem	Event 2
Flap 4	Finally	Solution	Event 3

Lit Link Center 3

Parades are processions to honor a significant event, anniversary, or person. *Floats*, vehicles bearing displays, are essential in a parade. Plan a class parade with floats representing books students read. During the parade, while each float stops in front of the grandstand and television cameras (video camera), a famous commentator reads a description of the float and the book it represents.

Directions for this center might include the following:

1. Place a cardboard shoebox so the open side is down.
2. Decorate the sides and top (formerly bottom) of your shoebox float.
3. Punch a hole in one narrow end of your float and attach a piece of string for a float pull.
4. Write a brief description of your float and why it represents the book you read.
5. Line your float up for the class parade.
6. Pull your float down the parade route (tables), and stop your float in front of grandstand while a description of your float is read.

Ocular Organizers

Lit Link Legends

Lit Link Legends is a classroom bulletin board that displays individual, independent reading records for each student in the class. The objective for each class member is to read an established number of books to reach a personal goal and become a lit link legend. Thus, to become a legend (hero) in our times, the student must read a number of stories (legends). The number of books and difficulty of the books are jointly determined by the teacher and each student. Student motivation is high when individual achievement is visible, and there may be a tangible reward when the student reaches a personal goal.

Independent reading occurs in the classroom, at home, or anywhere a student chooses. Reading record forms are available for independent reading (see Figure 2.1). When a book is read at home, the parent signs and sends the form to school. Forms are also signed when students read in peer pairs, or older students are invited to the classroom to listen to younger students read.

Literature-Based Example

The theme of the lit link legend bulletin board is determined by the thematic focus in the classroom. When reading about Harriet Tubman and the Underground Railroad, place individual railroad cars for each student along a train track on the bulletin board. The student fills out a ticket (reading record form) for each book read. Indicate the number of tickets for each student by tally marks on the side of his or her railroad car. When the student reaches a personal goal, move his or her railroad car to freedom in Canada at the top of the bulletin board. He or she then becomes a conductor to help guide others (listen to others read). He or she also receives a second railroad car to move toward freedom in Canada through independent reading.

Dramatic Debut

Felt Board

Students delight in telling stories while manipulating figures on a felt board. A *felt board* is a storytelling backdrop made using felt as a surface covering. Mount the felt on a large piece of cardboard or a piece of steel (metallic hot pads for countertops or large cookie sheets) for large group stories. Students can also make smaller felt boards on a file folder (see Journal Jacket in the Activity Appendix A) or a steel lap tray to use for small group stories. Lap trays have legs, so that the felt board will stand up (see Figure 4.1). The advantage of a lap tray or other steel surface is that the felt board may be used with either magnetic or felt objects.

Make characters and scenery for the story from felt or Pellon® (a thin fabric that will adhere to the felt and may be used when tracing pictures). Use fabric or paper for figures when the board is magnetic. To give body to these items, glue them to paper or file folder scraps and attach a magnet or piece of magnetic stripping.

FIGURE 4.1 Felt Board

Literature-Based Example

After reading about Harriet Tubman, students plan and present a felt board story and make necessary scenery, props, and people such as the following:

Scenery, Props, and People	Purpose
Passengers/Slaves	Wanted freedom
Railroad Agents	Helped slaves escape
Stations	Houses and barns/slaves hid
Wagon with hay	Transport hidden slaves
Harriet Tubman	Conductor or guide to freedom

Creative Composition

Freedom Trail/Freedom Facts Chart/Freedom Folio

A *freedom trail* is a symbolic road to equality and independence. For anyone who travels a freedom trail, there are many people, places, and events that contribute to equality and independence. Historically, there have been many freedom trails. One such path to freedom was the *Underground Railroad,* a secret escape route which slaves traveled when seeking emancipation.

As students research a particular time in history, they examine freedom facts: persons, places, and events that contribute to equality and independence. Organize these freedom facts on a *freedom fact chart*:

Contributions to Freedom		
People	**Places**	**Events**

Organize information from the freedom fact chart in chronological order on a freedom trail, a long roadway drawn on a piece of paper. Along the roadway are buildings, people, and symbols representing events. From the visual information on a freedom trail, students write about independence and place their compositions in a *freedom folio,* a class collection of essays. Decorate an accordion file folder with patriotic symbols to make an appropriate folio.

Students may create personal and historical freedom trails. On personal freedom fact charts and freedom trails, students list, sketch, and then write about people, places, and events that are contributing to their own contemporary and future freedom.

Literature-Based Example

After reading several books about Harriet Tubman, students develop a freedom facts chart and a freedom trail with railroad tracks representing the escape route to freedom known as the Underground Railroad (see Figure 4.2). Using this information, students write freedom essays that they enter in the class freedom folio.

FIGURE 4.2   Freedom Trail

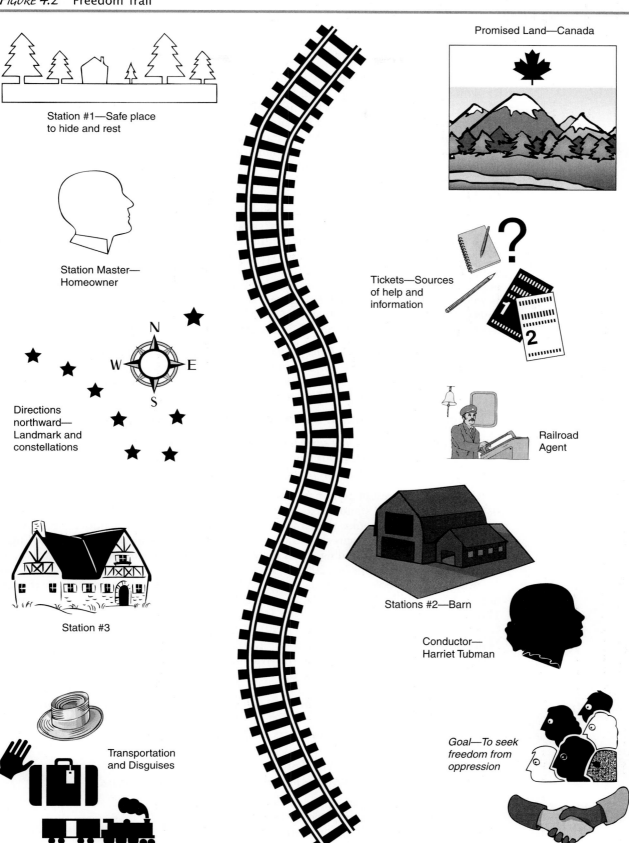

Station #1—Safe place to hide and rest

Station Master—Homeowner

Directions northward—Landmark and constellations

Station #3

Transportation and Disguises

Promised Land—Canada

Tickets—Sources of help and information

Railroad Agent

Stations #2—Barn

Conductor—Harriet Tubman

Goal—To seek freedom from oppression

GRAMMAR

We often judge a book by its cover
And a person by the way he speaks and writes.

Grammar is an established system of rules for a language and is concerned with *syntax*, rules for sentence construction and sentence patterns, as well as *usage*, socially acceptable ways of speaking. Grammar includes the mechanics of writing and speaking. The study of grammar provides an opportunity for enhancing effective communication skills.

Tompkins (2005) suggests that, "Grammar is probably the most controversial area of language arts" (p. 568). *Traditional* grammar instruction focused on teaching skills in isolation, often using a dreadfully dull *skills and drills* approach. Kane (1997) has concerns about using isolated sentences that are not set within context such as daily oral language *fix-the-errors* assignments. In these exercises, students copy and correct stilted sentences with innumerable grammar errors. Implementing a traditional approach often results in a lack of transfer of grammar skills to students' speaking and written compositions.

An alternative approach to grammar instruction is using a variety of strategies within the meaningful context of reading and writing. By examining sentence structure and word usage as they read literature, students are then able to employ the effective grammar skills observed in their own written compositions. Kane (1997) collects sentences from literature as well as her students' writing. Using these sentences as models, students develop an innate ability to express themselves effectively as well as correctly. She often uses first and last sentences from literature. For example, in the classic, *Charlotte's Web* (White, 1952):

First sentence: *"Where's Papa going with that ax?" said Fern to her mother as they were setting the table for breakfast.*
Last two sentences: *It is not often that someone comes along who is a true friend and a good writer. Charlotte was both.*

From the Newbery Award winner, *Maniac Magee* by Jerry Spinelli (1990)

First two sentences: *They say Maniac Magee was born in a dump. They say his stomach was a cereal box and his heart a sofa spring.*
Last sentence: *He knew that finally, truly, at long last, someone was calling him home.*

A renewed interest in grammar instruction has been stimulated by an increased emphasis on writing on state standardized tests (Schworm, 2005). As teachers seek and dust off ancient grammar textbooks, there may be a return to the grammar school concept of days long ago. However, the focus should be on making intuitive knowledge about the English language explicit and providing labels for words within sentences, parts of sentences, and types of sentences (Tompkins, 2005).

Ruth Heller's books provide a colorful and creative approach when examining the function of words within the English language. Each book focuses on a different part of speech. These books include: *About a Cache of Jewels and Other Collective Nouns* (1987), *Merry-Go-Round: A Book About Nouns* (1990), *Kites Sail High: A Book About Verbs* (1988), *Many Luscious Lollipops: A Book About Adjectives* (1989), and *Up, Up and Away: A Book About Adverb* (1991). Students enjoy the vivid illustrations that stimulate interest and learning.

Grammar strategies focus on the following literature choices: *Amazing Grace* by Mary Hoffman (1991), *The Star Fisher* by Laurence Yep (1991), and *The Sign of the Beaver* by Elizabeth George Speare (1983). In each of these stories, one or more characters develop self-esteem.

The following song reinforces parts of speech:

Title: Parts of Speech Medley
Tune: "If You're Happy and You Know It Clap Your Hands"
Oh, a noun is a person, place, or thing. (clap, clap)
Oh, a noun is a person, place, or thing. (clap, clap)
Oh, a noun is a person. Oh, a noun is a place.
Oh, a noun is a person, place, or thing. (clap, clap)

Oh, a verb shows action or is linking. (clap, clap)
Oh, a verb shows action or is helping. (clap, clap)
Oh, a verb shows action. Oh, a verb shows action,
Oh, a verb is action, helping, or linking. (clap, clap)

Oh, an adjective modifies a noun. (clap, clap)
Oh, an adjective modifies a noun. (clap, clap)
It gives you a picture. It gives you a picture.
Oh, an adjective modifies a noun. (clap, clap)

Oh, an adverb tells how, when, where, to what extent.
(clap, clap)
Oh, an adverb tells how, when, where, to what extent.
(clap, clap)
Oh, an adverb tells how. Oh, an adverb tells where.
Oh, an adverb tells how, when, where, to what extent.
(clap, clap)

Artistic Adventures

Grammacrostics/Banner Book

An *acrostic* is a series of words or lines of words in which the first, last, or an intermediate vertical line of letters forms a word. A *grammacrostic* is an acrostic in which the words are a particular part of speech or the words form a sentence. Personal grammacrostics use a person's name for the vertical line of letters and the chosen words describe or relate to the person. For example, the name "Greg" in an adjective grammacrostic reads:

G-*regarious*
R-*easonable*
E-*nergetic*
G-*reat*

Composing grammacrostics challenges students and motivates them to use the dictionary and thesaurus as they seek appropriate words that fit the grammacrostic format. Publish grammacrostics in a *banner book*, an accordion-folded book with three banner sections for entries and illustrations (see Activity Appendix A).

Literature-Based Example:

Read Amazing Grace *by Mary Hoffman (1991). Students collaborate to compose grammacrostics about Grace. Afterwards, students write personal grammacrostics using their own first names. An additional challenge is using middle and last names. Younger students may do only one or two grammacrostics using the format that is easiest for them.*
The following are grammacrostic entries for a banner book using the name Grace:

Adjective Grammacrostic
G-regarious
R-esolute
A-damant
C-reative
E-nthusiastic

Noun Grammacrostic
G-enius
R-arity
A-ctress
C-hild
E-nchantress

Verb Grammacrostic
G-ives
R-esolves
A-ttempts
C-aptivates
E-xplores

Challenging Grammacrostics

Mid Grammacrostic
Ima -   **G** - inative
Dete - **R** - mined
Am -   **A** - zing
Pra -   **C** - ticing
Indep - **E** - ndent

Ending Grammacrostic
Challengin - **G**
Supe -   **R**
Hiawath -   **A**
Fantasti -   **C**
Invincibl - **E**

Sentence Grammacrostic
G - race
R - esolved to
A - lways meet
C - hallenges with
E - nthusiasm

_____

Gamut of Games
Great Grammar Centers

Great Grammar Center 1

Great grammar grabbers are center activities that are organized in grab bags. *Grab bags* are paper sacks that are not labeled, so the person selecting from among the sacks has a random chance of selecting any of the grab bag activities. Change objects in the bags and other game pieces periodically to maintain interest and relate them to different literature and content area focus. The following are two examples of grab bag possibilities.

Grab Bag 1

Grammatives (adjectives)

Directions

1. Do not peek.
2. Reach into the grab bag.
3. Feel the item in the bag.
4. Describe the item based on what you feel with your hand.
5. Have your partner make a list of the words you use. How many descriptive words did you use?
6. Can your partner guess what is in the bag?

Example: Baseball Cap

Adjectives: rough, stiff, silky, plastic

Grab Bag 2

Grammaction (verbs)

Directions

1. Do not let your partner see what is in the bag.
2. Look in the bag at the object or a picture of the object.
3. Use action words to tell what the object does. Have your partner make a list of these action words. How many action words did you use?
4. Can your partner guess what is in the bag?

Example: Toy figurines or a picture of a person

Verbs: talks, sits, stands, bends, eats

Great Grammar Center 2

Grammacards is a card game in which sentences are formed using the words written on the cards. Make grammacards using a deck of standard playing cards with color-coded pieces of construction paper or labels adhered to the face of each card or use color-coded index cards. Each color represents a different part of speech. Laminate the cards before writing words on them, so that old words may be erased and new words written using water-soluble markers. Choose words for the grammacards on the basis of current thematic and literature focus.

Directions

1. Shuffle the cards and place the stack face down on the table.
2. Draw ten cards.
3. Within three to five minutes, make as many different sentences as possible using the words on the ten cards. You may use a grammacard in more than one sentence but not twice within the same sentence.
4. Make a list of the sentences.
5. Point system:
   a. Each grammacard word used in a sentence is worth one point (a name is worth one point).
   b. Jokers are wild cards and used for any words needed but are not worth any points.
   c. Noun determiners (e.g., the, a, an, this, these) may be inserted into a sentence, but they are not worth any points since they are not included in the deck.

Literature-Based Example

Below are suggestions for words related to Chapter 3 in The Star Fisher *(Yep, 1991), a story of a Chinese American family adjusting to life in a community that does not welcome them. This family struggles to establish a business and maintain self-esteem.*

Adjective	Noun Pronoun	Verb	Adverb	Preposition (Purple) Conjunction
(Green)	(Blue)	(Red)	(Orange)	(Yellow)
merry	Joan	gave/give	accidentally	at (P)
brief	Mama	run/ran	slowly	to (P)
heavy	Papa	stumble/d	very	with (P)
	Emily	stagger/ed	suspiciously	against (P)
	Bobby	ask/ed	quickly	for (P)
	Miss Lucy	look/ed	repeatedly	
	water	had		
	door	sloshed		
	laugh			
	explanation			and (C)
	bucket			

A student might draw the following ten grammacards: (1) Miss Lucy, (2) accidentally, (3) sloshed, (4) Joan, (5) water, (6) slowly, (7) very, (8) shouted, (9) laughed, (10) ran. The student could make the following sentences and earn 23 points in the allotted time limit:

Miss Lucy sloshed (the) water accidentally.
(4 points)
Miss Lucy shouted. (2 points)
Joan sloshed water very slowly. (5 points)
Joan ran very slowly. (4 points)
Miss Lucy ran very slowly. (4 points)
Joan laughed very slowly. (4 points)

Great Grammar Center 3

A *grammasong* is a song with missing words for which students individually, in peer pairs, or as a class collaboration provide words, pictures, and possibly actions.

Directions

1. Choose words to fill in the blanks for the grammasong. Be sure to choose words that are the proper part of speech and relate to the story you are reading in class.
2. Write and illustrate your word choices on word cards.
3. As you share your song with the class, hold up the word cards.
4. If you compose a song with partners, alternate taking turns and holding up word cards while singing the song.

The following grammasong is for the five members of the Lee family in *The Star Fisher* sung to the tune of, "If You're Happy and You Know It, Clap Your Hands."

Nouns

Oh, a Chinese American is a <u>man</u>, a <u>woman</u>, a <u>colleague</u>.
(clap, clap)
Oh, a Chinese American is a <u>boy</u>, a <u>girl</u>, a <u>baby</u>.
(clap, clap)
Oh, a Chinese American is a <u>classmate</u>.
Oh, a Chinese American is a <u>worker</u>.
Oh, a Chinese American is a <u>friend</u>, a <u>citizen</u>, a <u>neighbor</u>. (clap, clap)

Verbs

Oh, Joan can <u>translate</u>, <u>study</u>, and <u>clean</u>. (clap, clap)
Oh, Mama can <u>iron</u>, <u>cipher</u>, and <u>fuss</u>. (clap, clap)
Oh, Bobby can <u>dart</u>. Oh, Emily can <u>scowl</u>.
Oh, Papa can <u>wash</u>, <u>write</u>, and <u>read</u>. (clap, clap)

Adjectives

Oh, Joan is <u>smart</u>, <u>brave</u>, and <u>ambitious</u>. (clap, clap)
Oh, Mama is <u>scared</u>, <u>tough</u>, and <u>independent</u>. (clap, clap)
Oh, Bobby is <u>friendly</u>. Oh, Emily is <u>stubborn</u>.
Oh, Papa is <u>ambitious</u>, <u>wise</u>, and <u>optimistic</u>. (clap, clap)

Adverbs

Oh, Joan translates <u>quickly</u>, <u>quietly</u>, and <u>well</u>. (clap, clap)
Oh, Mama fusses <u>loudly</u>, <u>excitedly</u>, and <u>now</u>. (clap, clap)
Oh, Bobby plays <u>loudly</u>. Oh, Emily sleeps <u>soundly</u>.
Oh, Papa washes <u>daily</u>, <u>carefully</u>, and <u>today</u>. (clap, clap)

Prepositional Phrases

Oh, Joan tells stories <u>about the star fisher</u>. (clap, clap)
Oh, Mama burns rice <u>in the pot</u>. (clap, clap)
Oh, Bobby is clever <u>with wood</u>.
Oh, Emily has tea <u>at Miss Lucy's</u>.
Oh, Papa wipes words <u>from the fence</u>. (clap, clap)

Ocular Organizers
Grammar Grid/Tongue Twisters

A *grammar grid* is a chart on which the number of vertical columns is determined by parts of speech being studied, and the number of horizontal rows is determined by the number of letters in a name or object. Label each vertical column with a part of speech. Label each horizontal row with a letter from the name or object; the words in the row begin with that letter. Reading the first letter in each row vertically forms a name or object acrostic.

Tongue twisters are sentences in which every word or almost every word begins with the same phonetic sound. Write tongue twisters using words from the grammar grid. Students enjoy developing grammar grids and creating tongue twisters with their own names.

Literature-Based Example

The following grammar grid and tongue twisters are based on the name Matt. *Matt is the protagonist in* The Sign of the Beaver. *He lives independently for many months in the wilderness and is able to endure because of his bravery and survival skills. Attean is his Native American friend.*

Matt's Grammar Grid

	Adjective	Noun	Adverb	Verb	Noun
M	Motivated	Matt	Magnificently	Managed	Maine
A	Ambitious	Attean	Almost	Admitted	Attack
T	Thinking	Time	Tolerantly	Teaches	Tasks
T	Terrible	Trials	Thoroughly	Tested	Tempers

Matt's Tongue Twisters
Motivated Matt magnificently managed Maine.
Ambitious Attean almost admitted attack.
Thinking time tolerantly teaches tasks.
Terrible trials thoroughly tested tempers.

Dramatic Debut
Grammar Cop, Laws, Tickets, and Skits

A *grammar cop* is a classroom officer of the law who is authorized to uphold the grammar laws of our land and issue grammar tickets to those who break grammar laws. *Grammar laws* are rules that are established for formal language usage. Develop grammar laws based on the students' background knowledge and the school curriculum. *Grammar tickets* are citations issued to those who break grammar laws (see Figure 4.3).

A grammar cop is often the classroom teacher. The grammar cop's uniform may be real or a shirt and slacks the color of the uniform worn by local law enforcement officers. A set of real or toy equipment such as a badge, handcuffs, whistle, radio, and dark glasses provide dramatic effect.

A *grammar skit* is a short play designed to combat grammar law abuse. The teacher or the teacher and students write the skit. Assign individual script parts to class members (who, of course, are highly incensed when issued grammar tickets for breaking grammar laws). Deliberately create examples of incorrectly written text material on transparencies and display them at the appropriate time.

FIGURE 4.3   Grammar Ticket

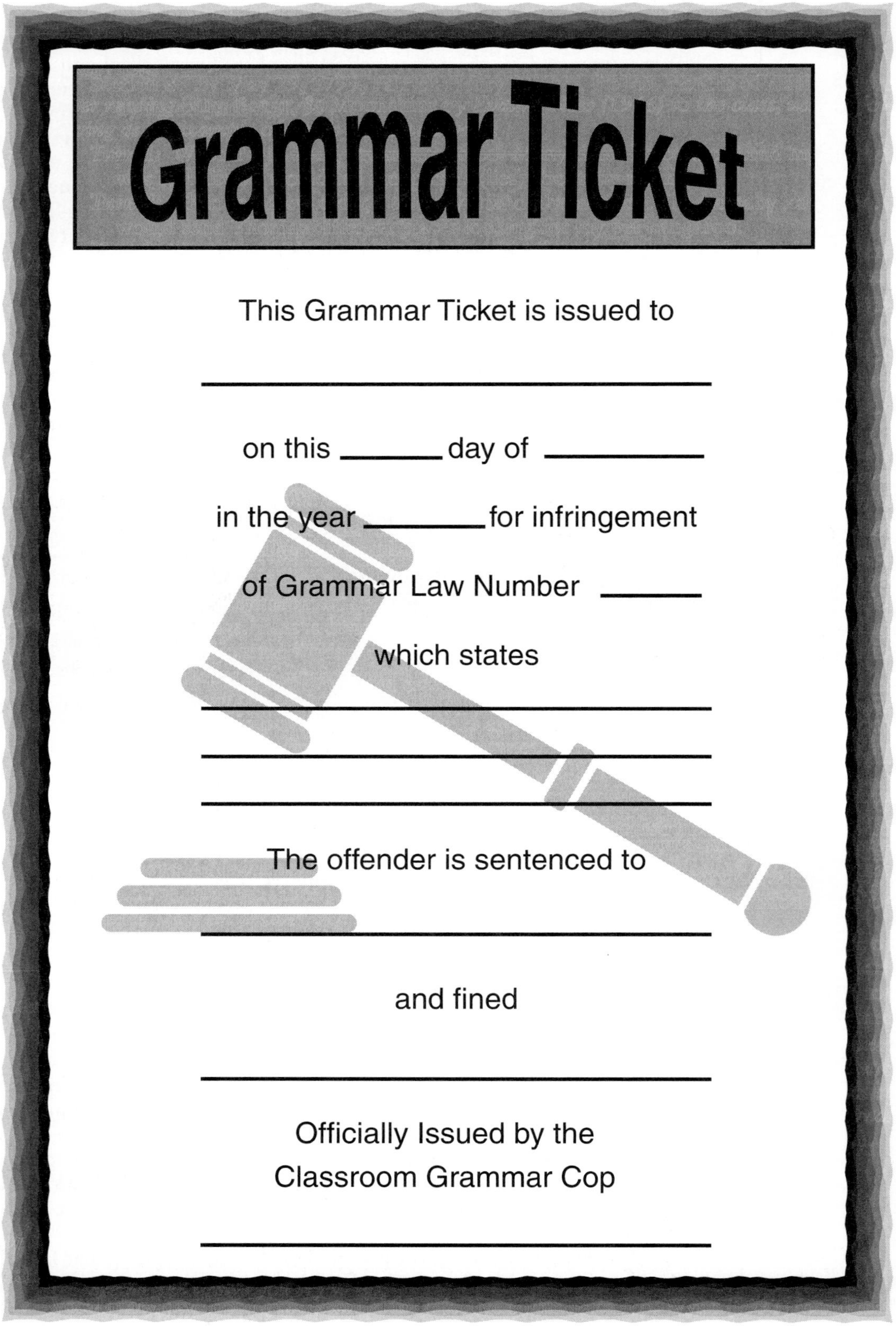

Grammar Ticket

This Grammar Ticket is issued to

_____

on this _____ day of _____

in the year _____ for infringement

of Grammar Law Number _____

which states

_____

_____

_____

The offender is sentenced to

_____

and fined

_____

Officially Issued by the
Classroom Grammar Cop

_____

The following is a sample skit

Narrator:	Are you a grouchy, grammar grump?
	Do you gripe about grammar laws?
	Does grammar cause you grief?
	For great grammar grades, you need
	GRAMMAR COP!!!
Grammar Cop:	Thank goodness! I've been called here to the scene of great grammar grief. I understand there are some grammar grumps here today. It's time to investigate and issue grammar tickets to those of you who are not following the great grammar laws of our land. Lisa, have you done your grammar homework?
Lisa:	I <u>ain't</u> done my homework yet.
Grammar Cop:	Grammar Grief! Grammar Grief!!
	Lisa, I hereby issue you a grammar ticket for breaking Grammar Law Number 6.325, the use of an inappropriate word.
Lisa:	I can't believe it! I don't deserve this ticket.
Grammar Cop:	Now remember, you have the right to remain silent. Anything you say can and will be used against you in a court of classroom law. Pam, have you completed your homework?
Pam:	Well, Mari-Elean and <u>me</u> <u>done</u> it last night.
Grammar Cop:	Grammar Grief! Grammar Grief!!
	I can't believe it! Not only have you broken Grammar Law Number 5.132 regarding the correct use of pronouns, you have also broken Grammar Law Number 3.186 regarding the proper use of verbs.
Pam:	Good grief!!! Another grammar ticket!
Grammar Cop:	Laura, let me see your homework.
	(Display on overhead)
	<u>w</u>e went to the movie yesterday
	Grammar Grief! Grammar Grief!!
	Look at that! Laura, you get two grammar tickets. You have broken Grammar Law Number 1.986 regarding beginning all sentences with a capital letter, and you have broken Grammar Law Number 9.768 regarding ending all sentences with a punctuation mark.
Laura:	But I didn't know...
Grammar Cop:	Ignorance of the grammar law is no excuse.
	Candy, let me see your work. (Display on overhead)
	Carolyn <u>give</u> Richard and Cindy many good ideas. Candy, you have broken Grammar Law Number 3.184 regarding the correct use of verbs. Here's your grammar ticket.
Candy:	I <u>ain't gonna</u> pay this ticket.
Grammar Cop:	Then it's off to the Grammar Slammer!
	A Grammar Cop's life is never easy!

Creative Composition

Sentence Expansion/Sentence Schematic/Wrap-Over Book

Sentence expansion is adding details to a kernel sentence to make the sentence more interesting. A *kernel sentence* is a sentence that contains only a noun and a verb. An *expanded sentence* contains a kernel sentence plus adjectives and adverbs. Expanded sentences help the writer to express thoughts precisely and to make the intended meaning clear and interesting to the reader. An equation for an expanded sentence is the following:

Kernel Sentence + Adjectives + Adverbs = Expanded Sentence

Expanded sentences may be organized on a *sentence schematic*, an ocular organizer designed to aid in composing interesting sentences. When using a sentence schematic, ask:

1. *Who* or *what* is the sentence about?
   (Fill in noun)
2. *Describe* the who or what. (Fill in adjective)
3. What did the who or what *do*? (Fill in verb)
4. *How, when, where,* or *to what extent* did this action occur? (Fill in adverb)

Literature-Based Example

Using The Sign of the Beaver *(Speare, 1983) ask the following questions, fill in the sentence schematic, and write expanded sentences.*

1. Who is the story about? (Matt)
2. Describe Matt. (brave, adventurous)
3. What did Matt do? (survived)
4. When? Where? How? did Matt survive?
   (for several months, in the wilderness, using skill and wit)

Adjective (2)	Noun (1)	Verb (3)	Adverb (4)
brave adventurous	Matt	survived	for several months in the wilderness using skill and wit

Kernel Sentence   Expanded Sentence

Kernel Sentence	Expanded Sentence
Matt survived.	Brave, adventurous Matt survived for several months in the wilderness using skill and wit.

Publish kernel sentences and expanded sentences in a wrap-over book (see Activity Appendix A). As the wrap-over book unfolds, each sentence is longer and has more detail. Each succeeding illustration has more detail.

Text 1: Matt survived. (kernel sentence with appropriate illustration on adjacent page)

Text 2: Brave, adventurous Matt survived. (kernel sentence + adjectives with appropriate illustration on adjacent page

Text 3: Brave, adventurous Matt survived for several months in the wilderness using skill and wit. (expanded sentence with appropriate illustration on adjacent page)

 SPELLING

> How do you spell relief?
> R-O-L-A-I-D-S
> Don't believe it? Check it out on television.
>
> Cleary (1979), p. 104

Spelling is the correct order of letters to represent a word. In the *traditional* textbook approach to spelling approximately 30 minutes per day was spent on spelling assignments. The weekly program included:

Monday: Assign a list of phonetically related words from the spelling textbook. Write the words five to ten times each, or write a different sentence for each word.

Tuesday: Assign textbook exercises that include language arts skills incorporating the spelling words. Students usually grade the exercises in class.

Wednesday: Textbook assignment and grading of assignment.
Thursday: Textbook assignment and grading of assignment.
Friday: Test.

The objective of the traditional approach to spelling was for students to score 100 percent on the Friday spelling test. Teachers noted, however, that even when students did well on spelling tests, often they did not incorporate the correct spelling of these same words into their written work (Gentry, 2001; Klein, 2006).

A *progressive* approach to spelling requires approximately 10 to 15 minutes per day for spelling assignments, implementing a test-study-test sequence (Cunningham, 1978; Zutell, 2007 …). The weekly program includes:

Monday: Pretest that students self-correct.
Tuesday: Spelling activities. The focus of these activities is to practice the spelling of each word especially those missed on Monday's pretest.
Wednesday: Spelling activities.
Thursday: Spelling activities.
Friday: Posttest.

The objective of the progressive approach to spelling is for students to incorporate the correct spelling of these words into their written work. Spelling words for a progressive program come from a variety of sources, such as:

1. Lists of the most frequently used words. The Dolch Word List (see Dolch Word website www.dolch-words.com/) is an example of such a list.
2. Words misspelled in journal writing.
3. Everyday words such as months of the year and days of the week.
4. Content area words that are used routinely in writing.
5. Literature words that are used routinely in writing.
6. Spelling textbook words that are phonetically related.

Students go through several developmental stages as they move toward the correct spelling of words (Bear & Templeton, 1998; Templeton & Pikulski, February 9, 2007). Generally, students progress from lines of scribbles, to spaces between scribbles, to adding some letters, to invented spelling using phonics sounds, and eventually to correct spelling. As students progress through these stages, it is important for them to practice spelling words that they need to use in daily writing experiences. Participation in the following sequence is often helpful:

1. **Look** at the word correctly written. Have a print-rich environment in the classroom with displays of words on charts, webs, and lists.
2. **Write** the word while looking at a model of the correctly written word on the board or on a spelling list.
3. **Cover and Write** the word without looking at the model.
4. **Check** the word against the model and self-correct any errors.

An overemphasis on correct spelling forces students to choose words they can spell. Often the easiest word to spell is not the most effective word choice. For example: Tina is a *marva, marve, marvlous* (oops) friend. Tina is a *remarkeabl, remaka, remakeeble* (oops) friend. Tina is a *good* friend. After struggling with the spelling of *marvelous* and *remarkable,* the author chooses *good,* because the spelling is familiar.

A spelling activity my students at all grade levels enjoyed began as a survival technique (discipline gimmick). I spelled one of the words in a sentence aloud. For example, "I hope I don't have to Y - E - L - L today." Students listened carefully to decipher auditorily what was being spelled. This worked so well that soon students were spelling to me. For example, "It's time to S - I - T." The students replied, "At our D - E - S - K - S." Concentrating on a word that is being spelled verbally builds visual imagery as a student creates a picture of the word in his or her mind's eye. Of course, the words being spelled, as well as the rate of spelling, are determined by the age and experience of the students.

Games are beneficial for increasing interest in spelling. Variations of board games where the student must spell a word to advance on the board are fun. Concentration games using pairs of word cards builds visual images of correct spelling. Spelling activities in this chapter may be used with any spelling words.

Artistic Adventures

Media Mix

Media mix is a spelling activity in which individual letters are cut out from newspapers, magazines, and advertisements to make spelling words. Letters are available in a variety of sizes and shapes. Assemble and arrange the letters in the correct order and attach to a piece of paper or an index card (see Figure 4.4). In an alternative activity, students sketch a picture that represents the spelling word and attach letters to the picture thus forming a concrete picture of the word (see Figure 4.4).

Figure 4.4   Media Mix

Gamut of Games
Spelling Success Centers

Spelling Success Centers are centers where students practice their spelling words independently or with peers. Activities at the centers should be changed periodically to maintain interest.

Spelling Success Center 1

A *spuzzle* is a puzzle in which each puzzle piece contains a letter or letters of a spelling word. When the spuzzle is put together, a spelling word is made (see Figure 4.5). Use rectangular strips of construction paper of various colors for spuzzles. Store spuzzles in envelopes or spuzzle boxes (see Story Box in Activity Appendix A). For younger students, indicate the spuzzle piece with the first letter of the spelling word with a star or a number one. Students exchange spuzzles and put each other's spuzzles together.

Spelling Success Center 2

Thumbprint things is a motivational activity in which students make their spelling words using thumbprints (see Figure 4.6). Use inkpads with washable ink and a variety of colors. Students may also create pictures to illustrate their spelling words. *Ed Emberly's Great Thumbprint Drawing Book* (1977) provides a wide variety of thumbprint possibilities.

Spelling Success Center 3

Stock a spelling success center with a variety of *media materials* such as watercolor paint, colored pencils, a variety of pens, shaving cream, crayons, fabric crayons or paint, chalk, paper clips, fabric scraps, and colored paper. Make spelling necklaces and bracelets using

FIGURE 4.5 Spuzzles

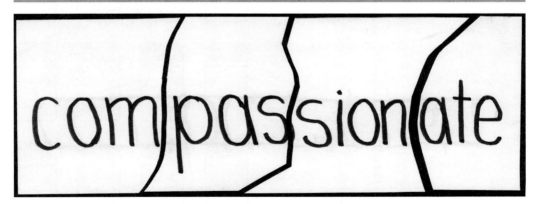

FIGURE 4.6 Thumbprint Things

paper clips chained together. Tape a small piece of construction paper around each paper clip, and write a letter or letters for a spelling word on each piece of paper. Have students practice their spelling words using media material they choose. They might even paint one word, use crayon for a second word, or try a gel pen for the third word.

Ocular Organizers

Dictionary Display

A *Dictionary Display* is a visual display of words students use as a reference when writing. Arrange words alphabetically for quick and easy access. Determine word choices based on the needs and interests of the students.

A system for displaying the words should provide for ease in rearranging words quickly to maintain alphabetical order. One possibility is using index cards with words written on them. Make a hole in the end of each card with a hole punch. Hang on push-pins in alphabetical order on a bulletin or around the walls in the classroom (adaptation of Scratch in Cunningham, 1978; see Figure 4.7).

Dramatic Debut

Spelling Cheers/Spelling Sports

A *cheer* is an established choral chant that spectators shout at an athletic event to demonstrate enthusiastic support for the participants and event. A *spelling cheer* is a choral chant

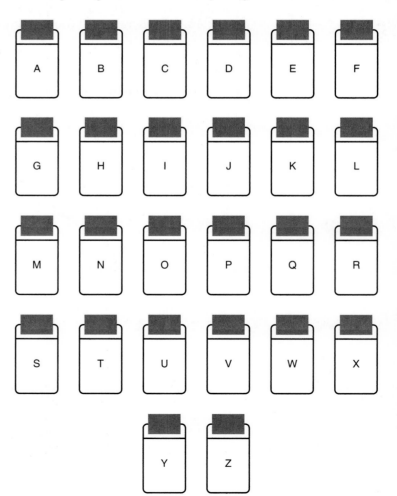

FIGURE 4.7   Dictionary Display

students shout during *spelling sports*, an event at which students demonstrate enthusiasm for spelling participants and the correct spelling of words.

In preparation for spelling sports, assign cooperative groups of students (3 to 6 students) or have students select spelling words. Group members prepare letter cards with one large letter per card for each of the individual letters in their words. Each group appoints a head cheerleader and determines in which order group members must stand to hold letter cards for each word. Depending on the length of the word, group members may need to hold two letter cards, or with very long words, recruit volunteers from the audience to hold some of the letter cards.

Group members line up in the correct order with their letter cards and turn their backs to the audience. As the head cheerleader calls out a letter, the participant with that letter turns around and holds the letter card in the air. Then the class shouts out the name of the letter. (Suggestion: To maintain peace and harmony in the school, hold spelling sports outside.) After all letters are visible, the entire class shouts out the word.

Literature-Related Example

The following is a suggested spelling sport script for the word friend.

Cheerleader:	Give me an F !
First Group Member:	(Turns and holds up F)
Class:	F
Cheerleader:	Give me an R !
Second Group Member:	(Turns and holds up R)
Class:	R
(Continue until all the letters are named.)	
Cheerleader:	What have you got?
Class:	**FRIEND!**

Creative Composition
Spelling Songs

Spelling songs are lyric innovations for familiar tunes that incorporate the letter-by-letter spelling of words within the song. Students enjoy singing their spelling words and composing lyrics for the class to sing. These songs also increase sight word vocabulary (see Figure 4.8). Holiday melodies, as well as other familiar tunes (see Music Appendix B), are well known, and many are readily adaptable to spelling lyrics. The following holiday tunes work for three-letter words in the "at" and "ug" word families:

Title: "Jingle Spell"
Tune: "Jingle Bells"

B-A-T; B-A-T; B-A-T spells bat.
R-A-T; R-A-T; R-A-T spells rat.
C-A-T; C-A-T; C-A-T spells cat.
H-A-T; H-A-T; H-A-T spells hat.

Title: "Spelling Words Are Coming to Town"
Tune: "Santa Claus Is Coming to Town"

Oh, we better watch out; we better not cry.
We better not pout; the teacher's telling us why.
Spelling words are coming to town. (Verse 1)

We're making a list; checking it at night.
Making sure our words are spelled right.
Spelling words are coming to town.

We know that H-U-G spells hug,
And B-U-G spells bug.

FIGURE 4.8   Sight/Spelling Word Songs

Four-Letter Sight/Spelling Words:
Tune: "Frere Jacques or Are You Sleeping?"
B – l – u – e. B – l – u – e.
That spells blue. That spells blue.
B – l – u – e. B – l – u – e
That spells blue. That spells blue.

Five-Letter Sight/Spelling Words:
Tune: "B I N G O"
There was a class that had some *spelling words.
And this was one of them.
S-u-p-e-r; s-u-p-e-r; s-u-p-e-r
Super was one of them.

Six-Letter Sight/Spelling Words:
Tune: "Happy Birthday to You"
Y-e-l-l-o-w. Y-e-l-l-o-w. Y-e-l-l-o-w
Yellow's our spelling word.

Seven-Letter Sight/Spelling Words
Tune: "Camptown Races"
S-p-e-c-i-a-l; Special! Special!
S-p-e-c-i-a-l; spells *special* today.
T-w-i-n-k-l-e; Twinkle! Twinkle!
T-w-i-n-k-l-e; spells *twinkle* today.
Goin' read all night! Goin' spell all day.
Yes, I know my spelling words.
All the Doo-dah Day!

Eight-Letter Sight/Spelling Words
Tune: "Oh, Dear! What Can the Matter Be?"
D-i-n-o-s-a-u-r
D-i-n-o-s-a-u-r
D-i-n-o-s-a-u-r
Dinosaur's my spelling word.

Note: reading may be substituted for *spelling* in most of these songs.

We know that D-U-G spells dug,
And R-U-G spells rug. (repeat verse 1)

Note: Substitute different spelling words.

HANDWRITING

Cursive is dumb. It's all wrinkled and stuck together,
and I can't see why I am supposed to do it...
I will not enjoy it...all those loops and squiggles.
I don't think I'll do it.

Cleary (1990), pp. 8–9

Handwriting, a support skill for effective written composition, is the formation of alphabetic symbols on paper (Tompkins, 2005). When students have interesting opportunities to practice their handwriting, there is improvement in *legibility,* ease in reading, as well as *fluency,* ease in writing. Legible handwriting increases the effectiveness with which a reader comprehends a message. Without fluency, too much of the writer's cognitive energy is focused on letter formation rather than content.

Handwriting is a neglected skill in the classroom as well as in college courses for teachers. Handwriting trauma leads to ineffective writing skills that inhibit the ability to compose, lower self-esteem, and result in shorter, less developed compositions (Allen, 2003). On the other hand, once the mechanics of writing are under control, students can devote their attention to information, to sentence structure, and to the content of their letters, poems, and stories (Graves, 1994).

Good handwriting embellishes the appearance of written work. The appearance of assignments often affects their evaluation and assessment. In many instances, students who struggle academically have improved their performance as their handwriting skills improve. When teachers write positive notes about penmanship progress, students' self-esteem grows, and they take pride in their compositions.

Instruction in letter formation should follow these steps:

1. **Demonstration:** The teacher demonstrates the formation of a letter on the board or an overhead projector transparency. Overhead projectors have the following advantages: (a) writing on a flat surface, (b) writing in the same proportion and size as writing on paper, (c) facing the class to observe class understanding and potential management problems, (d) using colored pens for interest and emphasis, and (e) providing letter strokes that are easily seen by students.
2. **Visualization:** Students carefully observe the formation of a letter.
3. **Verbalization:** Students give the teacher directions for writing a letter, and the teacher follows the student directions. The students correct any deliberate or unintentional mistakes the teacher makes while forming the letter.
4. **Application:** During short practice sessions, students practice forming the letter while the teacher moves around the classroom observing letter formation as well as paper and pencil position.
5. **Self-Evaluation:** Students write several letters and indicate (e.g., with a star, happy face, etc.) their best letters.

Paper and pencil positions are very important. It is incumbent upon teachers of younger students to make necessary changes early, because once a student practices a particular pencil grip and positions paper in a certain way, changes are difficult to make. A right-handed student angles the lower left corner of the paper toward the belly button (belt buckle), while a left-handed student angles the lower right corner of paper toward the belly button (belt buckle). Adjust the angle of the paper to meet individual needs. Students grip a pencil on top of the middle finger, hold it between the thumb and index finger, and rest it in the curve between the thumb and index finger.

A song that reinforces the steps in handwriting instruction, directionality guidelines for manuscript writing, and the importance of legibility and fluency is the following:

Title: Practically Perfect Penmanship
Tune: "This Old Man"
H-and-writing, circles, sticks.
Practice, fuss, and errors fix.
Counterclockwise circles.* Sticks from the top down.
Left-to-right, but never frown.

De-mon-stra-tion; I'll show you how.
Please *look* at this letter now.
Tell me how this letter is made.

---

*Note: Some manuscript programs make all circles counterclockwise. Other programs make lowercase b and p with clockwise circles.

Do not ever be afraid.

Practice now; *ap-pli-cation*!
Star your best; *self-e-val-u-ation*!
Practice! Practice! Do your best.
No-w, give your hand a rest.

Legibility; fluency, too.
What do these words mean to you?
Easy to read. Easy to write.
My handwriting's quite a sight!

Good handwriting skills are essential to ensure effective communication with an audience and to enhance self-esteem. Literature focus includes *The Terrible Thing That Happened at Our House* by Marge Blaine (1975) and *The Important Book* by Margaret Wise Brown (1949).

Artistic Adventures

Squiggles

Squiggles provide interesting opportunities for students to practice their penmanship with their own names and other words that are important to them. Make squiggles on a sheet of construction paper that is folded lengthwise. Have students write their names in cursive with a broad-tipped marker using the folded edge of paper as a base line. The letters should be attached to each other. If the name contains any letters that drop below the base line, set the name above the fold or handle the letter dropping below the line creatively. Cut the name out on the outside of the marker lines. Mount the resulting squiggle on a contrasting color of construction paper and decorate as a realistic or imaginative creation. Mount the silhouette from which the name is cut on a contrasting color of construction paper and make into another imaginative squiggle (see Figure 4.9).

For younger students, a variation of squiggles is to write a name or an important word in the center of a sheet of paper. Using different-colored crayons or markers, color around

FIGURE 4.9   Squiggle

the name several times—each time with a different color. The colors radiate out from the name in the center of the paper, creating an interesting design.

Gamut of Games

Practically Perfect Penmanship Places

Practically Perfect Penmanship Places are centers where students go to practice perfecting their handwriting skills. There are plenty of possibilities for perfecting penmanship and moving toward letter-perfect handwriting.

Practically Perfect Penmanship Place 1:

Shaving cream is a motivational media in which to practice perfect penmanship. An added advantage of shaving cream is that it cleans the desk or writing surface. Use unscented shaving cream for students who have allergies. When practicing, squirt a dab of shaving cream on the desk top or a cookie sheet. Practice perfecting penmanship using a finger. Wipe the desktop clean with a damp sponge.

Practically Perfect Penmanship Place 2

Small *photo albums* with plastic, self-adhering pages are inexpensive. Place samples of handwriting under the clear pages. Include interesting tidbits of information such as riddles, short poems, or tongue twisters. Students trace the letters writing on the plastic page with a washable marker. An alternative to the photo album is to laminate handwriting samples to trace.

Practically Perfect Penmanship Place 3

Practice by *painting with water* for practically perfect penmanship. Dip a small paintbrush into water contained in a pop-top soda can. The small opening in the can lid provides a way to remove excess water from the brush as it is pulled through the opening in the can. Paint letters and words on the classroom chalkboard or individual chalkboards. Make individual chalkboards using chalkboard contact paper and the Journal Jacket technique (see Activity Appendix A). Watch your letters and words magically disappear. An alternative to painting with water is using watercolor paints.

Ocular Organizers

Belly Button Buddy

A *belly button buddy* is a character placed on lined writing paper that teachers and students refer to when discussing the positioning of lines, circles, and curves in letter formation (See Figure 4.10). The belly button buddy has a hairline (headline), footline (baseline), and belly button line (midline). The belt buckle line is an alternative label for the midline. The belly button buddy is an especially meaningful reference for younger students because they can easily relate to hair on the top of their heads, feet on the floor, and belly buttons in the middle of their bodies. Placing a belly button buddy at the left end of each set of handwriting lines is helpful for beginning writers.

FIGURE 4.10 Belly Button Buddy

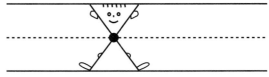

Using the overhead projector, the teacher models letter formation while students verbalize letter formation with the help of their belly button buddy. For example, when making a lowercase manuscript *h*, the teacher and students would say, "Start at the hairline and draw a straight stick down through the belly button line, stopping at the footline. Trace the stick back up to the belly button line and make a hump going back down to the footline." When making a lowercase manuscript *d*, the teacher and students could say, "Make a circle starting at the belly button line, going toward the belly button buddy, down to the footline, and back up to the belly button line. Go up to the hairline (away from the Belly Button Buddy) and draw a straight stick from the hairline, through the belly button line (just touching the circle), and stopping at the footline." Students may use the belly button buddy as a reference in both manuscript and cursive handwriting.

Dramatic Debut

Notes in a Nutshell/"The Case of the Messy Message"

Notes in a nutshell are short personal messages written to family and friends that give concise information in a few words. These notes provide a vehicle for meaningful communication as well as emphasis on the importance of legible handwriting. A classroom focus on communication with parents and closer family relationships through notes in a nutshell will encourage and increase parent/child communication.

To begin a notes in a nutshell focus, have a class discussion about the importance of parent/child communication. Include questions such as the following:

1. What are some topics you and your parents like to talk about?
2. Are there times when you would like to tell your parents something, but there just doesn't seem to be time?
3. What is another way you could tell your parents something rather than talking about it? (Teacher comment: Notes in a nutshell are a way to communicate with your parents in writing. It's fun to leave surprise notes in unexpected places.)
4. Where are some places you could leave a note in a nutshell? (refrigerator, lunchbox, briefcase, purse, pillow, taped to bathroom mirror, car, family bulletin board, etc.)
5. When writing a note, how are you going to be sure your parent can read the note? (Teacher comment: Of course, you'll have to practice your practically perfect penmanship.)

To introduce a notes in a nutshell focus and emphasize the importance of practically perfect penmanship in notes, create a skit entitled, "The Case of the Messy Message." Include examples of misunderstandings that occur when the reader is unable to decipher the message or the message is misinterpreted due to illegible handwriting. Have students initiate notes in a nutshell communication with a family member as a surprise and report reactions to receiving the messages. Notes in a nutshell may be written on enveloptionery (see Activity Appendix A).

Literature-Based Example:

"The Case of the Messy Message" is based on The Terrible Thing That Happened at Our House *by Marge Blaine (1975), a story about the frustrations experienced by a girl when her mother goes to work and is no longer at home full time. The family has been very dependent on her. Many students will relate to having a working mom and wishing she would stay home full time. Using this story as a stimulus, students examine ways to establish closer relationships and communication in their family using notes in a nutshell.*

Mom: Wow, I got a note in a nutshell from Jan. I love getting notes from my kids. I wonder what it says? Oh no, she says she wants me to . . . , and I can't read the rest. I've got to leave for work right away, and I just don't know what she wants me to do.

Dad: I got a note in a nutshell too. Isn't it great that our kids write notes to us? My note is from Nancy. She says Jan wants . . . , but I can't decipher the rest. I don't know what Nancy and Jan want.

Jan: I wonder why my Mom didn't pick us up after play practice. I left her a note. She could come right by here on her way home from work. Maybe Dad will come. I asked Nancy to leave him a note.

Creative Composition

The Important Job/The Important Thing About Me

Detailed observation of letter formation is important in developing good handwriting skills. Self-esteem is the theme of this chapter. Combining these two factors with ideas gleaned from *The Important Book* by Margaret Wise Brown (1949), students discover the importance of filling out job applications accurately using their very best handwriting.

To introduce this job search experience, collect job applications from a variety of businesses such as fast food restaurants, car dealerships, big box stores, grocery stores, and pet stores. Fill out one or more of these applications using messy, illegible handwriting, and provide incomplete information or leave some spaces blank. Discuss why a business owner would probably not hire someone who does not have neat, legible handwriting and who is careless in filling out an application.

Next, discuss why neat, legible handwriting will help a job applicant make a positive first impression. Have students practice filling out job applications using their very best handwriting. Have students write a short paragraph about why they want the job and why the business should employ them.

For younger students, develop job applications for classroom responsibilities. For example, have students apply for the following positions: handout distributor, board cleaner, book arranger, etc.

Literature-Based Example

When writing personal paragraphs for a prospective employer using ideas from The Important Thing About Me, *students might follow the sequence,*

The important thing about me is that I _____

I can _____

I look like _____

But the important thing about me is that I _____

Literature References

Blaine, M. (1975). *The terrible thing that happened at our house.* New York: Scholastic.

Brown, M. W. (1949). *The important book.* New York: Harper & Row.

Burns, B. (1992). *Harriet Tubman.* New York: Chelsea House.

Cleary, B. (1990). *Muggie Maggie.* New York: Scholastic.

Cleary, B. (1979). *Ramona and her mother.* New York: Dell.

Emberley, E. (1977). *Ed Emberley's great thumbprint drawing book.* Boston: Little, Brown.

Heller, R. (1987). *About a Cache of Jewels and Other Collective Nouns.* New York: Grosset & Dunlap.

Heller, R. (1988). *Kites Sail High: A Book About Verbs.* New York: Grosset & Dunlap.

Heller, R. (1989). *Many Lucious Lollipops: A Book About Adjectives.* New York: Grosset & Dunlap.

Heller, R. (1990). *Merry-Go-Round: A Book About Nouns.* New York: Grosset & Dunlap.

Heller, R. (1991). *Up, Up, and Away: A Book About Adverbs.* New York: Grosset & Dunlap.

Hoffman, M. (1991). *Amazing Grace.* New York: Dial.

Hopkinson, D. (1993). *Sweet Clara and the freedom quilt.* New York: Alfred A. Knopf.

Lawrence, J. (1993). *Harriet and the promised land*. New York: Simon & Schuster.

Levine, E. (1988). *If you traveled on the underground railroad*. New York: Scholastic.

Ringgold, F. (1992). *Aunt Harriet's underground railroad in the sky*. New York: Crown.

Speare, E.G. (1983). *The sign of the beaver*. New York: Houghton Mifflin. Newbery Honor.

Spinelli, J. (1990). *Maniac Magee*. New York: Little, Brown. Newbery Award.

Taylor, T. (1969). *The cay*. New York: Doubleday.

Taylor, T. (1993). *Timothy of the cay: A prequel-sequel*. New York: Harcourt Brace.

White, E.B. (1952). *Charlotte's web*. New York: Harper & Row.

Winter, J. (1988). *Follow the drinking gourd*. New York: Alfred A. Knopf.

Yep, L. (1991). *The star fisher*. New York: Morrow Junior Books.

Professional References

Allen, R. (2003, Summer). Expanding writing's role in learning: Teacher training holds key to change; Handwriting mastery: Fluent form is crucial for expression. *ASCD Curriculum Update*. Alexandria, VA.

Anderson, R.C., Hiebert, E.H., Scott, J.A., & Wilkinson, I. A. G. (1985). *Becoming a nation of readers: The report of the Commission on Reading*. Champaign, IL: Center for the Study of Reading.

Bear, D.R., & Templeton, S. (1998). Explorations in developmental spelling: Foundations for learning and teaching phonics, spelling, and vocabulary. *The Reading Teacher, 52*(3), 222–242.

Calkins, L. M. (1994). *The art of teaching writing*. Portsmouth, NH: Heinemann.

Cunningham, P.M. (1978). Scratch, scribe and scribble. *Teacher*, 68–79.

Gentry, J.R. (2001). Ten false assumptions about teaching spelling. In February 12, 2008.
http://jrichardgentry.com/text/ten-false-assumptions.pdf.

Graves, D.H. (1994). *A fresh look at writing*. Portsmouth. NH: Heinemann.

Kane, S. (1997). Favorite sentences: Grammar in action. *The Reading Teacher, (51)*, 1, 70–72.

Klein, G. (2006, May 30). *What's the big deal about spelling?* 2/2/07.
www.newsadvance.com/servlet/

Schworm, P. (April 3, 2005). *War of words: In class, grammar rears its ugly head*. February 2, 2007.
www.boston.com/news/local/articles/2005/04/03/war_of_the_words_in_class-grammar_rears_its_ugly_head/

Templeton, S., & Pikulski, J. J. *Building the foundations of literacy: The importance of vocabulary and spelling development*. February 9, 2007.
www.eduplace.com

Tompkins, G.E. (2005). *Language arts: Patterns of practice* (6th ed.). Columbus, OH: Pearson/Merrill Prentice Hall.

Zutell, Jerry. February 9, 2007. *A student-active learning approach to spelling instruction*.
www.zaner-bloser.com

Websites

America on Line

Includes online educational resources for teachers: lesson plans, classroom tools, and textbook activities; online resources for students: research topics, news and current events, subject resources, and science fairs. Organized K–2; 3–5; 6–8; and 9–12.

www.aolatschool.com

A to Z Teacher Stuff

Thousands of resources, lesson plans, and thematic units. Wide selection of language arts lesson plans. Arranged by subject and grade level; K–12.

www.Atozteacherstuff.com

Dolch Word List

The Dolch word list contains the 220 most common words and 95 nouns in children's literature. Dolch words, or "sight" words, provide an excellent base for reading at an early age. They are often called sight words because a lot of them can't be read phonetically and need to be learned by sight.

www.dolch-words.com/

Dr. Grammar

The Dr. Grammar Frequently Asked Questions page contains answers to questions previously asked of Dr. Grammar that may provide help with your grammar questions.

www.drgrammar.org/faqs/

Lesson Plans Page

Language arts, math, science, and more. Original lesson plans, all subjects and all grade levels. Wide variety of themes, topics, and skills. Included are lesson plans on parts of speech, spelling, and sentences and paragraphs

www.lessonplanspage.com

Read Write Think

IRA/NCTE site that has extensive information in the following areas: lessons, standards, web resources, and materials.

www.readwritethink.com

Teach Net

Includes lesson plans organized by subject area. Language arts lesson plans are categorized as reading, writing, spelling, speaking, terminology, ESL, and poetry. Includes a variety of book report and grammar suggestions

www.Teachnet.com

Web English Teacher

Includes teaching research, lesson plans, activities, biographies, jokes, and other materials. Has a wide variety of creative alternatives to traditional book reports along with writing ideas, including grammar and mechanics.

www.webenglishteacher.com

CHAPTER 5 TOPICS	Artistic Adventures	Gamut of Games (Cooperative Groups)
Civics and Government	Double Banner Flip Book	Think/Pair/Share Controversial Issues
Communities: Families, Cities, States, and Countries	Miniature Communities Fold-a-Building	Concentration Game
Travel and Map Skills: Optional	Optional: Vacation Destination Wrap-Over Book	Optional: Vacation Destination-O Bingo
Multicultural Diversity	Pop-Up Books Pop-Up Plans	Storytelling Tribal Tales and Traditions
Famous People: Past and Present	Biographical Web Biopoem Eightfold Person	Hero Hunt Wanted Posters
Long, Long Ago: Medieval Times	Coat of Arms	Vocabtionary Print, Praise, 'n' Pass

Social Studies

Ocular Organizers	Dramatic Debut	Creative Composition
Complete-a-Chart Governmental Organizer Pass-a-Law Organizer	Election Experiences	The Power of Political Persuasion Trifold Brochures
Community Data Chart Research Acrostic Mobiles Optional: Trip-plans	Take-a-Tour Tour Brochures Tour Guides Optional: Cyclorama Sites	Step Book Research Report Optional: Journey Journal Teeny Tiny Book
Research Chart	Plays, Puppets, and Paper Plate Stages	Circle of Cinquains Roll Over and Over Book
Time Line Mural	Heroes' Hall of Fame	Birthday Biography Birthday Biography Roll Over and Over Book
Then and Now Lifestyle Organizer	Mesmerizing Musical	Poems to Paragraphs File Folder Display

Without history, there can be no wisdom
Without geography, there can be no understanding of people and places
And without citizenship education, there can be no democracy

Paraphrased from quote by Walter Parker

OVERVIEW

What is social studies? According to the National Council for Social Studies (NCSS website), *social studies* is the integrated study of social sciences and humanities to promote civic competence. Within the school program, social studies provides coordinated, systematic study drawing upon such disciplines as anthropology, archeology, economics, geography, history, law, philosophy, political science, psychology, religion, and sociology, as well as appropriate content from the humanities, mathematics, and natural sciences. The *primary purpose of social studies* is to help young people develop the ability to make informed and reasoned decisions for the public good as citizens of a culturally diverse, democratic society in an interdependent world.

CURRICULUM STANDARDS FOR SOCIAL STUDIES

The NCSS has identified ten thematic strands that provide a program framework for social studies. The NCSS recommends that social studies programs include experiences that provide for the study of

   I. Culture
  II. Time, Continuity, and Change
 III. People, Places, and Environments
 IV. Individual Development and Identity
  V. Individuals, Groups, and Institutions
 VI. Power, Authority, and Governance
 VII. Production, Distribution, and Consumption
VIII. Science, Technology, and Society
 IX. Global Connections
  X. Civic Ideals and Practices

These strands are interrelated; for example, to understand strand VI, Power, Authority, and Governance, one must also be familiar with strand X, Civic Ideals and Practices. The standards are also interdisciplinary in that they draw from a variety of social science disciplines; for example, strand X draws from the disciplines of history, political science, cultural anthropology, and the humanities.

For each of these ten thematic strands the NCSS has established performance expectations or benchmarks for

- Early Grades
- Middle Grades
- High School

To assist in putting standards into practice, specific vignettes with examples of integrated classroom implementation are included (Parker & Jarolimek, 2001).

To ascertain how well her social studies program was meeting the NCSS standards, Tarry Linquist (1996), a fifth-grade teacher, developed a self-assessment quiz. She selected samples of performance expectations for each of the ten thematic strands and transformed the performance statements into questions. For example,

Culture: Do your students have opportunities to show how language, folktales, music, and art express culture and influence behavior?
Global Connections: Can your students describe how language, music, and belief systems facilitate global understanding or cause misunderstanding?
Time, Continuity, and Change: Can your students create, interpret, use, and distinguish various representations of the earth, such as maps, globes, and photographs?

Individual disciplines within social studies have established specific standards to further assist in curriculum planning by providing focused and enhanced content detail. To locate information on these standards, see Websites at the end of the chapter.

IS SOCIAL STUDIES DESTINED TO BE BORING?

A *traditional* approach to social studies instruction is textbook centered with a focus on facts, figures, faces, and places. Students read, memorize, and later recall this information. No wonder students develop a negative attitude about social studies! This is an ideal approach when preparing students to be contestants on *Jeopardy*, but not when preparing them to become caring, contributing citizens in our world. As Seif (2003/2004) emphasizes, "Current social studies programs based on state standards, traditional textbooks, and the lecture model do not adequately prepare U.S. students for productive citizenship in the 21st century" (p. 54).

When surveyed and asked, "How do you feel about social studies?" many students reply, "BORING!" When asked, "What do you do in your social studies class?" many students answer, "We read a chapter in the textbook and answer questions at the end of the chapter in complete sentences." As Onosko (1992) points out, "Poor student performance in social studies is due primarily to lack of engagement and motivation, not deficiencies in students' mental capacities, abilities or prior knowledge" (p. 194).

During my sojourn as a sixth grade teacher, a colleague and I paired to teach science and social studies. She taught social studies to her class for a week while I taught my class science. The next week we swapped. She taught my class social studies while I taught her class science. Theoretically swapping classes is beneficial for both students and teachers. Teachers can devote more time to planning for one subject rather than two. Students benefit from each teacher's expertise. However, *the students loved the hands-on science with an experimental emphasis. They were less than enthusiastic about social studies with a textbook focus. How did my students deal with this dilemma? Each Monday they insisted that is was their week for science.*

Is social studies destined to be boring? Rather than boring, social studies should be one of the most intriguing subjects students encounter. A motivational approach to social studies focuses on *themes*, topics or units of interest around which student learning is centered. With thematic investigation, a teacher is no longer a dispenser of knowledge, rather, a facilitator who encourages student exploration.

BEST PRACTICES IN SOCIAL STUDIES

Suggestions for best practices in social studies are based on the research of Zemelman, Daniels, and Hyde (1998); Johnson and Ebert (1992); Onosko (1992); Rasmussen (1999a, b); and Seif (2003/2004). They suggest best practices should include:

- Investigation: Thematic Integration
- Exploration of Great Guiding Questions
- Construction on Prior Knowledge Foundation
- Collaboration in Cooperative Groups
- Communication Suggestions
- Appreciation for the Past; Participation in the Present; Preparation for the Future

Investigation: Thematic Integration

Select a meaningful, worthwhile, authentic, age-appropriate controversial problem, issue, or concept. You may want to incorporate the selected problem, issue, or concept into a broader curriculum-appropriate thematic unit. Themes should be broad enough to allow integration of content area standards, grade-level skills, and age-appropriate information. They should provide opportunities for

Horizontal learning: Broadening background knowledge.
Vertical learning: Increasing in-depth knowledge.

An in-depth thematic focus results in higher-order thinking and longer-lasting learning. A thematic approach to curriculum planning encourages the logical integration of language arts, math, science, the arts, and other content area skills.

Thematic planning should occur across grade levels to assure a wide range of thematic strand exposure. However, within a given grade level, the number of units should be streamlined to assure an in-depth investigation. A thematic unit should focus on:

- Big Ideas
- Essential Questions
- Enduring Understandings
- Lifelong Learning Skills

Post information related to essential questions and enduring understandings in the classroom as a visual stimulus for recall and retention.

Ogle and McMahon (2003) focus on authentic content for learning through thematic integration:

The rationale for integrating the language arts with other content areas is that language is central to the meaning making process both within schools and within other communities. Therefore integration fosters a more authentic context for learning. Putting students into settings where they use language to explore and learn about topics or problems of interest stimulates their interest in and development of language abilities. Both exploratory and performance oriented talk are essential in units where students begin framing questions, observing, collecting data and constructing meaning together. (pp. 1048–1049)

Exploration of Great Guiding Questions

In the skillful use of the question,
more than anything else,
lies the fine art of teaching.

Charles DeGarmo

All our knowledge results from questions,
which is another way of saying that
question-asking is our most important intellectual tool.

Neil Postman

Inquiring minds want to know. Inquiring minds foster exploration into important issues and controversies. To focus inquiry, ask one or two succinct, significant guiding questions. Organize thematic units and lessons around these questions. A great guiding question should meet the *PONG* criteria:

Purpose—establishes a focus for the lesson or thematic unit from the student's point of view
Open-ended—allows numerous answers
Nonjudgmental—remains neutral; does not take sides
Grabs—captures attention both emotionally and intellectually

"What" and "how" questions often meet the PONG criteria. For example, a great guiding question for a thematic unit on citizenship might be, "*What is government?*" This question meets the PONG criteria because:

Purpose—Inquiring student minds want to know about government.
Open-ended—There are numerous response possibilities.

Nonjudgmental—Nothing in the question indicates that government is good or bad.

Grabs—Most students have personal opinions about what government is, as well as whether government is good or bad, often based on their parents' perceptions. Students' intellectual knowledge may be limited, but motivation for investigation is high when discovery focuses on the good, the bad, and the ugly of government.

Construction on Prior Knowledge Foundation

Build an expanded structure of information on top of students' prior knowledge foundation. How do you know what students already know? Ask them. Better yet, plan a collaborative class KWL (What We Know; What We Want to Know; What We Learned) experience to guide students in finding out what they already know about a topic. See both the Reading and Writing chapters for more information about the KWL strategy.

What do you <u>K</u>now about government?	What do you <u>W</u>ant to know about government	What have you <u>L</u>earned about government?
Government makes laws	How come the government can tell me how fast I can drive?	
	How can I change laws I don't like?	

You may want to modify the KWL chart, and have a PKWL experience.

People we <u>K</u>now in government	People we <u>W</u>ant to meet in government	What we <u>L</u>earned about new government people we meet
Our president	Our state's governor	
	Our city's mayor	
	Our police chief and fire chief	

Time lines, wall charts, maps, and daily journals provide additional possibilities for recording prior knowledge and adding additional information during the study.

Collaboration in Cooperative Groups

> *Cooperation, like other things,*
> *Can be learned only by practice:*
> *and to be capable of it in great things,*
> *a people must be gradually trained to it in small.*
> *Now, the whole course of advancing civilization*
> *is a series of such training.*
>
> John Stuart Mill

What is the best way to learn (see Chapter 1 for additional information)? We learn and retain

10% of what we **hear**
15% of what we **see**
20% of what we both **see** and **hear**
40% of what we **discuss**
80% of what we **experience** directly or **practice** doing
90% of what we attempt to **teach others**.

> *Susan Kovalik (1994)*

By teaching others in **cooperative** groups, students learn to

<u>C</u>onnect through a caring community, resulting in
<u>O</u>utcomes that benefit both the small groups and large group in using
<u>O</u>rganizational structures that
<u>P</u>romote problem solving,
<u>E</u>ncourage critical thinking,
<u>R</u>aise the bar on
<u>A</u>cademic achievement, and promote
<u>T</u>rust through teamwork. Students learn to
<u>I</u>nvest in positive interdependence while
<u>V</u>aluing the diversity of their peers, thus providing
<u>E</u>nhanced self-confidence as well as a sense of security within the learning community.

Cooperative learning allows students to build skills and habits needed for lifelong responsible learning within a collaborative, problem-solving community. For example, within the classroom community, each group may investigate one aspect of a problem. Incorporating the findings from each group, the class makes a collaborative decision on how to best to solve the problem. Another possibility: In the middle of a class discussion stop and have each group summarize the information presented and/or discuss potential solutions to the problem. For additional information on cooperative learning see Wynn (in press).

As you ponder taking time for students to develop long-lasting relationships with peers, the curriculum, and the community, visit with Mrs. Olinski and the Souls, her sixth academic team, in *The View from Saturday* (Koningsburg, 1996). This team learns to prioritize time as evidenced by, "Maybe—just maybe—Western Civilization was in a decline because people did not take time to take tea at four o'clock" (p. 125).

Communication Suggestions

Reading

Textbook Challenges   Social studies textbooks are often difficult to read and understand. The result of this quandary? Student frustration. One successful strategy to lessen frustration and enhance comprehension is Questioning the Author, QtA (Beck & McKeown, 2002). QtA is designed to build understanding of text ideas by making queries during the reading experience. Queries may include: What is the author telling you? Why is the author using this example? For more information on QtA, see the Reading Chapter (pp. 32–33).

Trade Book Inspiration   Use trade books to enhance the social studies experience. Select a picture book to introduce a thematic unit. The value of picture books is to promote interest, provide background knowledge, or ease students into a hard-to-understand topic. Trade books are available at a variety of reading levels, thus meeting the comprehension needs of each and every student.

There is a plethora of interesting literature from which to choose for an in-depth exploration of any given theme. Through active involvement in motivational, literature-based activities, students participate vicariously in the lifestyle of a specific time period. Each student should experience the feeling of "I am there!" One example of literature where teachers might find support for a selected social studies theme is Amy Cohn's *From Sea to Shining Sea: A Treasury of American Folklore and Folk Songs* (1993). Students need opportunities to learn from the past and study the impact of the past on planning for the present and preparing for the future.

Writing

Have students write for a minute or two at the beginning of class to summarize information from homework or from the last class discussion. Younger students may summarize these experiences through drawing. At the end of the class period, have students summarize and reflect on what they have learned or have them respond to a question or two. Use these notes for review before assessing student learning.

Appreciation for the Past; Participation in the Present; Preparation for the Future

Appreciation for the Past

Historically, students study their own lives in relation to the past and realize their indebtedness to those who preceded them. As they view their place in history, they come to realize that change is natural and essential. They discover that people throughout the ages have had the same basic needs, wants, and desires. People want to be respected, to be loved, and to feel secure. Through historical investigation, students come to understand our common heritage, the interdependence of mankind, and the necessity of learning from past mistakes.

Norby (2003/2004) suggests the study of different people with different points of view living and working in the same place in history. Each cooperative group might work with a variety of primary source material. The Smithsonian Institution has websites, a magazine, and teacher workshops available to assist in lesson planning (see Websites). When handling this source material, having students wear white gloves, as museum curators do, emphasizes the significance of the material.

Participation in the Present

When students wrestle with real-world problems that have personal relevance, these encounters make them wiser. As students examine controversial personal, family, school, and community issues, they discover inevitable quandaries:

Which should take precedence?

- My personal freedom or the good of community
- The good of my cultural group or the best for all cultural groups
- Governance by the local community, the state, or the nation

Dealing with controversial issues may involve:

- Debating an issue
- Drafting letters and proposals
- Seeking actual changes
- Setting up committees to accomplish goals

An essential life skill is making wise choices within established parameters. Setting priorities challenges each and every one of us. To assist in this endeavor, guide students in establishing a list of hot topics within appropriate grade-level parameters. Discuss and debate the value of an in-depth study of each topic. Come to a class consensus on which issue to study. Provide a list of research project possibilities, including wall data charts, journal entries, research reports, wanted posters, news broadcasts, interviews, plays, skits, diary entries, newspaper publication, debates, speeches, speakers, and fieldtrips. Keep in mind, making choices within parameters is both motivational and educational.

Preparation for the Future

In preparation for students' becoming lifelong responsible citizens, rather than rewarding the memorization of a laundry list of decontextualized facts, focus on students developing higher-order, critical-thinking skills. With the overarching goal of social studies education, preparation for responsible democratic citizenship, assist students in following the **IDEA** for informed decisions:

Inquiry
Decision making
Evaluation
Action

How Should You Teach Social Studies?

So much to cover
So little time

A thematic unit is a vehicle for learning about social studies themes while integrating related language arts components. Content area concepts and skills from math, science, health, safety, music, and art may be integrated into the selected theme to provide meaningful learning experiences. Guidelines for thematic planning are found in Figure 5.1. A thematic unit planner is found in Figure 5.2.

Social studies issues are often pondered and discussed during cooperative group experiences. In this chapter, each Gamut of Games section includes opportunities for collaborative learning. As students work together, they are developing lifelong team skills.

This chapter focuses on active student investigation of social studies themes through a variety of enjoyable and meaningful experiences. These representative themes for thematic strands are found across the school curriculum:

Theme	NCSS Thematic Strand
Civics and Government	VI & X
Communities: Families, Cities, States, and Countries; Travel and Map Skills	I & IV
Multicultural Diversity	I & IV
Famous People Past and Present	II & III
Long, Long Ago: Medieval Times	II & III

FIGURE 5.1   Guidelines for Thematic Planning

1. Identify thematically appropriate content area standards.
2. Select a meaningful, worthwhile, authentic, age-appropriate controversial problem, issue, or concept. Incorporate the selected problem, issue, or concept into a broader theme when age/curriculum appropriate.
3. Organize your thematic unit around a great guiding question, a burning question that begs to be answered. When developing the question, establish the **Purpose** of the lesson from the student's point of view and follow the *pong* criteria (see pages 126–127).
4. Establish an appropriate **Environment**.
5. Plan an appropriate **Attention** grabber.
6. Locate thematically related resources. Resources may include textbooks, trade books, media materials, and information from colleagues, parents, students, and the Internet.
7. **Review** to assess students' background knowledge. Build a common core of background experience.
8. Plan thematically related, curriculum appropriate mini-lessons for selected concepts and skills. Direct instruction with shared and guided practice will promote academic achievement (see Reading Chapter pages 15–16).
9. Determine the best use of individual learning, class collaboration, and cooperative group experiences. Follow the sequence of:

    Do For   Teacher modeling

    Do With   Shared and guided experiences with the class and teacher

    Do By Myself   Do independently
10. Provide opportunities for differences and decisions through motivational, interactive, thematically appropriate projects.
11. Develop differentiated instructional strategies to meet the unique learning needs of your students.
12. Integrate appropriate content area information and skills into your thematic unit. Do not include content area focus for subjects that don't make logical connections within the thematic unit.

FIGURE 5.2   Thematic Unit Planner

Content Area Standards

_____

_____

Thematic Focus   _____

__Purpose__/Guiding Question   _____

_____

__Environment__   _____

_____

__Attention__ Grabber   _____

_____

__Resources__

Textbook Information   _____

_____

Trade Books   _____

_____

Media Materials   _____

_____

Colleagues, Students, and Parents   _____

_____

Internet   _____

_____

__Review__/Background Knowledge

Assess   _____

_____

Concepts to Build   _____

_____

Mini-Lessons for Selected Concept and Skill Focus

    1._____

    2._____

Project Possibilities

    1._____

    2._____

Differentiated Instruction

    1._____

    2._____

Content Area Integration

    1._____

    2._____

__PEAR__ experiences

Each theme is supported with specific children's literature. Base your selection of theme and literature on student interest and grade level curriculum.

CIVICS AND GOVERNMENT

*Ideals and principles continue
from generation to generation
only when they are built into the
hearts of the children as they grow up.*

George S. Benson *(Goodman, 1997, p. 684)*

The focus of education in civics and government is to prepare students to become informed, responsible participants in political life as well as competent citizens committed to the fundamental values and principles of American constitutional democracy (NCSS website). Students develop political savvy and higher-order critical thinking skills as they evaluate our government, their rights and responsibilities, and opponents' positions on controversial issues. An integral component of this study is the power of political persuasion through the influence of media on American political life. See Figure 5.3 for an example of a Thematic Unit Planner for Government. Use the same format when planning thematic units for other topics.

Artistic Adventures
Double Banner Flip Book

*To vote or not to vote?
That is the question!*

Make a double banner book using patriotic colors (see Activity Appendix A). Fold in half parallel with the banners. Draw a horizontal line on the fold marks to differentiate the top flip and the bottom flip (see Figure 5.4). With the book right side up, write on the top three banners:

1. *I vote!*
2. *I Make a*
3. *Difference*

Flip the book upside down. Write on the banners:

1. *I Don't Vote!*
2. *I Don't Make a*
3. *Difference*

Flip the book right side up. Inside the book, above the horizontal fold-line, write reasons to vote based on information in the book *Vote* (Christelow, 2003) and other literature selections. Create lists of reasons to vote. Entries might include:

- I vote because voting is one of my American rights and responsibilities.
- I vote because I want my voice to be heard in making governmental decisions.
- I vote because I want input into how my tax money is spent.

Flip the book upside down. Inside the book, above the horizontal line, write reasons many people choose **not** to vote. Entries might include:

- Some people don't vote because they don't think their votes will make any difference.
- Some people don't vote because they are too lazy to go to the polls.
- Some people don't vote because they would rather gripe and grouch than take an active part in running our government.

FIGURE 5.3 Thematic Unit Planner for Government

Representative NCSS and Civics and Government Standards:

- What is the government and what should it do?
- Identify basic features of the political system in the United States, and identify representative leaders from various levels and branches of government
- How can Americans participate in their government?
- Examine an issue of public concern from multiple points of view.

Thematic Focus: The Government of the United States
(Subtopics: Voting; Political Savvy)

- **Purpose/Guiding Question:** What is government?
- **Environment:** Political rally setting with red, white, and blue streamers. Election headquarters for each of the opposing parties. Voters' registration booth with class-created ballots. Voting booth.
- **Attention Grabber:** Campaign regalia: badges, brochures and flyers, bulletin boards with campaign information, bumper stickers, hats, posters, and signs.

Textbook Information: Social studies/information on government

Trade Books: Vote (Christelow, 2003); *The Voice of the People: American Democracy in Action* (Maestro & Maestro, 1996);
If You Were There When They Signed the Constitution (Levy, 1987)
Media Materials: Current events newspaper article display; television and radio spot information
Colleagues, Students, and Parents: Send note or have students inquire
Internet: www.civiced.org/std_toc_intro.html
www.kidsvotingusa.org
(see chapter website references for additional information)

- **Review**/Background Knowledge

Assess: KWL (assess at appropriate times in thematic unit)
What do you know about our government?
What do you know about voting?
What do you know about political savvy?

Concepts to Build:

Constitutional organization of our national government
Voting rights and responsibilities
Persuasive political tactics

Mini-Lessons for Selected Concept and Skill Focus

- Organization of the United States government
- Controversial issues of current concern
- How to pass a law
- Voting rights and responsibilities
- The power of political persuasion

Project Possibilities

- Art: Double Banner Flip Book
- Gamut of Games: Think/Pair/Share—Controversial Issues
- Ocular Organizer: Complete-a-Chart Governmental Organizer; Pass-a-Law Organizer
- Dramatic Debut: Selection by Election
- Creative Composition: The Power of Political Persuasion in Trifold Brochures

Differentiated Instruction

- Use picture books to enhance understanding
- Add illustrations to discussion and explanations
- Include culturally appropriate issues and concerns

Content Area Integration

- Math: Campaign costs; voting numbers and percentages
- Language Arts: Speeches, debates, persuasive writing

*PEAR experiences

FIGURE 5.4   Double Banner Flip Book

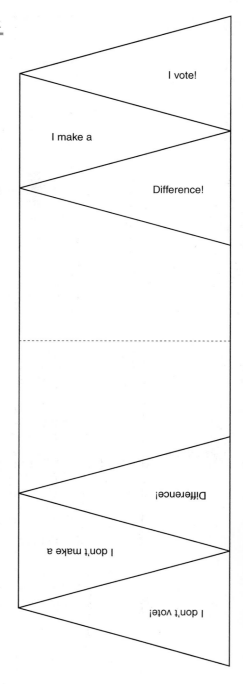

Decorate the double banner flip book appropriately. Include relevant quotes and slogans such as (from Goodman, 1997, p. 880),

Our American heritage is threatened
as much by our own indifference
as it is by the most unscrupulous office
or by the most powerful foreign threat.
The future of this republic is in the
*hands of the **American voter**.*

Dwight D. Eisenhower

> *Bad officials*
> *are elected by good citizens*
> *who do not vote.*
>
> George Jean Nathan

Gamut of Games

Think/Pair/Share (T/P/Sh)/Controversial Issues

T/P/Sh is one of the easiest cooperative learning structures to use. The strategy sequence is the following:

Think: *Contemplate an issue or question; perhaps jot a note or two.*
Pair: *Consult with a peer or partner.*
Share: *Discuss your ideas with the group.*

T/P/Sh is effective not only in cooperative groups but also as a whole class experience.

Literature-Related Examples

Controversial Classroom Issues

T/P/Sh allows inquiring minds to investigate controversial issues. Implement T/P/Sh when examining classroom rights and responsibilities.

Think about one right you should have in our classroom. Jot a note. Include ideas on responsibilities that accompany this right.
Pair with a partner to discuss your rights and responsibilities.
Share your findings with your group.

Some ideas that may emerge are the following:

I have the right to learn.
I do not have the right to interfere with the learning of others.
I have the right to my personal space.
I do not have the right to invade the space of another person.
I have the right to express my feelings.
I do not have the right to hurt other peoples' feelings.

School Dilemma

We should have pizza for lunch everyday. Implement T/P/Sh.

Community Controversy

There is only enough tax money to build either a new school or new jail. Which should we build? Implement T/P/Sh.

National Controversy

Should the entry fees to National Parks be doubled? Implement T/P/Sh.

Ocular Organizers

Complete-a-Chart/Governmental Organizer/Pass-a-Law Organizer

Complete-a-Charts include graphic organizers with space for students to enter appropriate information. As students develop expertise in completing these charts, they will progress to creating their own organizers.

Literature-Based Examples

Governmental Organizer

To understand the structure of our national government, read books such as The Voice of the People: American Democracy in Action *(Maestro & Maestro, 1996). While reading, insert information in a Complete-a-Chart/The Government of the United States on which initial entries might look like Figure 5.5.*

Pass-a-Law Organizer

Read If You Were There When They Signed the Constitution *(Levy, 1987). Study the Pass-a-Law Organizer in Figure 5.6. Decide on a bill that would make a good law for our country. Create an organizer with illustrations to demonstrate the steps a bill must go through to become a law. Additional investigation may include committees through which the bill must pass.*

Dramatic Debut
Election Experiences

Political Forum

Create a forum for political rallies. Have an election headquarters for each of the opposing parties. In one corner of the classroom, set up a voters' registration booth with class-created ballots. In another corner of the classroom, have a voting booth. Decorate with red, white, and blue streamers and campaign regalia:

- Badges: *Please take note! I vote!*
  I make a difference! I vote!
- Brochures/Flyers (see Trifold Brochure in the Activity Appendix A)
- Bulletin Boards: newspaper articles, editorials, letters to the editor, advertisements related to the election
- Bumper Stickers with slogans (e.g., *Vote for Pete; He's neat!*)
- Hats—variations of Fold and Tear Adventures (see Activity Appendix A)
- Posters and Signs

Campaign Teams

Democrat	Republican
President	President
Vice President	Vice President
Campaign Manager	Campaign Manager
Press Agent	Press Agent
Media Coordinator	Media Coordinator
Symbol—Donkey	Symbol—Elephant

Is there a balanced ticket for each party to assure broad voter appeal? Are the president and vice president from different socioeconomic backgrounds, sections of the country, and occupations? Are there candidates who are running as independents or from other political parties such as those from the past—Green Party, Libertarians, American First Party, and Progressives?

Figure 5.5   Complete-a-Chart Chart/The Government of the United States

The Constitution provides for three branches of government:

Branches	Executive Branch	Legislative Branch	Judicial Branch
Components	**The President** Serves four years; may serve one additional term **The Vice President** **The Cabinet**—Heads of government departments such as agriculture, labor, transportation, energy, education	**The Congress** *Senate—100 members 2 from each state 6 year term *House of Representatives—number per state based on population 2-year term	The Supreme Court Chief Justice and eight Associate Justices; lifetime job Lower federal courts
Jobs and Responsibilities	Executes laws and makes sure they are carried out. Directs and manages running of government. Deals with world problems and domestic issues. Nominates Supreme Court Justices.	Legislates or makes new laws; raises money to run government; can declare war. Senate must approve nominations for Supreme Court Justices and ratify treaties with other countries.	Interpreting our nation's laws; Settles questions and disagreements about the Constitution and the law
Checks and Balances Each branch has control over the other two branches	When bill arrives from both houses, the president has three options: *Sign *Veto—Congress can override with 2/3 vote *Table—Do nothing; becomes law in 10 days without signature	Bill to Committee Committee to Senate or House of Representatives Both houses must approve If approved, goes to president	The Supreme Court explains and interprets the Constitution when questions concerning particular laws arise in lower courts

Initial entry information from:
The Voice of the People: American Democracy in Action (Maestro & Maestro, 1996)
If You Were There When They Signed the Constitution (Levy, 1987)

Campaign Strategies

Plan and implement campaign strategies such as

- Meet 'n' Greet—shake hands, hold babies, hug constituents
- Walk 'n' Talk—stroll while exulting personal, political positions
- Debate 'n' Agitate—hold forums for debates and agitate opponents
- Interviews—have newspaper reporters interview candidates (see Writing Chapter for interview suggestions)
- Travel—plan trips, mileage, and expenses

FIGURE 5.6   Pass-a-Law Organizer

Pass-a-Law Organizer

A law begins as a bill in either the House of Representatives or the Senate.
Bills for taxes and military expenditures must begin in the House of Representatives.

Congress	Initiates Bill	Passes Bill	Bill Goes to	Passes Bill	Bill Goes to the President
House of Representatives	X	X	Senate	X	X
Senate	X	X	House of Representatives	X	X

President—3 choices
         *President signs and bill becomes law.
         *President does nothing; in 10 days bill becomes law.
         *President vetoes; bill goes back to Congress.

In order to override a presidential veto, the bill goes back to Congress.
Both houses must have two-thirds vote to override the veto.
Getting a two-thirds vote is very difficult.

Information from: *If You Were There When They Signed the Constitution* (Levy, 1987)
The Voice of the People: American Democracy in Action (Maestro & Maestro, 1996)

- Speeches—write and deliver campaign speeches
- Plan fundraising activities, take polls, and determine costs of advertising—all math learning experiences.

Optional

Organize a democratic classroom. Hold a mini-constitutional convention. Compose a constitution for class organization. Outline the rights and responsibilities of citizens in the class. Delineate class committees with appropriate responsibilities. According to fifth-grade teacher Nadine Rousch (Allen, 2003), the benefits in this type of classroom experience include increased awareness of the value of collaboration, a greater understanding of the necessity of teamwork in the community to achieve a common goal, and more proficiency in the art of compromise. Rousch finds democracy noisy and productive (additional information in Allen, 2003).

Creative Composition
The Power of Political Persuasion/Trifold Brochures

Look for different types of political persuasion. Guide students in evaluating the influence of the media on U.S. political life. Examine political advertisements. Listen to and view radio and television spots.

Political Ploys

Identify political ploys designed to delude the unsuspecting. Three types follow. There are certainly others.

1. **Half-truths:** Sharing only part of the story.
2. **Exaggeration:** Stretching the truth.
3. **Guilt by Association:** Intimating that the candidate has similar skeletons in the closet to those of family and friends

Political Proverbs

Collect proverbs and idiomatic expressions that have or could have political implications. For example,

* Actions speak louder than words.
* Believe only half of what you see and nothing you hear.
* Do as I say, not as I do.
* Fool me once, shame on you; fool me twice, shame on me.
* He has something up his sleeve.
* Let his record speak for itself.
* Nothing could be further from the truth.
* Truth is stranger than fiction.
* You're known by the company you keep.

Campaign Jargon

Make a Campaign Jargon Word Wall (for word wall information, see the Reading chapter). Sample entries are:

Aiding and abetting	Misrepresent
Bag of tricks	Mitigating circumstances
Complicity	Scheme
Depict in glowing terms	Slanted
Distort	Subterfuge
Embellish	Tactics
Implication	Throw up a smokescreen
Lay it on thick	Trash 'n' bash
Maneuver	Tricks of the trade
Manipulate	Twisted

Collect Campaign Advertisements

Locate campaign advertisements for a selected candidate. For each ad, identify, discuss, and write an annotation about the political ploys employed.

Trifold Brochures

Design a **trifold brochure** (see Activity Appendix A) to sell your candidate to others. Grab the voters' attention with great graphics and a catchy slogan or two on the cover. Use the *power of political persuasion* to convince the voter to support your candidate. Lay it on thick. Employ political tactics and campaign jargon. Depict your candidate in glowing terms. End on a positive, upbeat note. For example:

Cover
For joy and jubilation in Washington
Vote for Jerry Jones
Page 1: Check it out! In the last Congressional debate, I, Jerry Jones, alone, stood for the cause of education. I, alone, proclaimed the undeniable rights of our children to have an education like unto none in any other nation in the world. While my opponent was aiding and abetting the opposition, I alone was willing to go out on a

limb, rise to the occasion, take a risk and vote for education above all. Let my record speak for itself. *(half-truth)*

Page 2: Read my lips! No new taxes! In fact, I, Jerry Jones, will cut your taxes while increasing benefits to the elderly, the downtrodden, and our schools. Your vote for Jerry Jones assures joy and jubilation. *(exaggeration)*

Page 3: You know my friends and colleagues. Why, my campaign manager, Ken Kinder, is as honest as the day is long. He leaves no stone unturned, as he searches the highways and by ways seeking those who have been treated unfairly. In fact, Ken received the highest honesty award imaginable, *"The Honest Politician's Award." (honesty-by-association)*

Page 4: *(Create a collage of pictures with captions designed to impress.)*

Back of brochure
Jerry Jones is your man
Keep this man in WashingTAN.

COMMUNITIES: FAMILIES, CITIES, STATES, AND COUNTRIES

Students need to develop an understanding of *communities*, a group of people with common goals living within a given geographical location. Communities may include families, cities, states, and countries. The *traditional* approach to studying a community was choosing a topic related to the community and writing a research report about that topic, often with little guidance from the teacher. This approach often turns kids off to social studies. Exciting alternatives that may be used across grade levels for any community study include developing miniature communities, concentration games, community data charts, research acrostic mobiles, take-a-tour with tour brochures and tour guides, and step-book compositions. For research purposes, use a variety of information books.

The state of Florida is the specific community chosen for an example. *The Kids' World Almanac of the United States* by Thomas G. Aylesworth (1990) and *Flags of the United States* by Mark Lloyd (1990) were consulted for research information. Additional information came from the state tourist bureau.

To include geographical experiences, optional *Travel and Map Skills* are provided. Some students will have the opportunity to travel to faraway places. Others will not. Plan vacations so that students have vicarious vacation visits to unusual and exciting historic locations. Provide "I am here!" experiences. Map skills are essential in planning these vicarious vacations. Anticipation and exploration of a vacation destination add excitement and motivation to any social studies unit.

What better place to travel and experience history in the making than our nation's capital, Washington, DC. Every citizen will better understand our heritage and the price paid and being paid for our freedom after a vacation trip to Washington, DC. Here students explore a plethora of museums, monuments, memorials, and federal buildings. Information books, maps, travel brochures, and videotapes provide assistance in planning the trip. Specific reference information is found in the *AAA Tour Book of the Mid-Atlantic States* (1993) and the *Inside-Outside Book of Washington, D. C.* (Munro, 1987).

Artistic Adventures

Miniature Communities/Fold-a-Building

Students of all ages learn about the influence of a community on their lives and the lives of others as they explore the inner workings of the community. One way to explore a community's people and geographic features is to develop a *miniature community*. Construct houses and other important buildings in a variety of sizes using the Fold-a-Building technique (see Activity Appendix A). Use a large table or piece of poster board as the land (base) for the community. Construct roads with masking tape. Make landscaping and other important details from construction paper. Create people from pipe cleaners.

Literature-Based Example

When studying the state of Florida, make an outline of the state on a table or piece of poster board using masking tape. Construct important buildings to represent key cities. Represent the capital of Florida, Tallahassee, with a capitol building; Tampa with a University of South Florida building; Orlando with a Walt Disney World structure; Miami with a condominium on the ocean. Devise citrus, cattle, and tourist sites using construction paper and place in areas of the state where they are of economic importance.

Optional: Vacation Destination Wrap-Over Book

As students plan their vacations, discuss sites they want to visit in route to, upon arrival, and when departing from their vacation destination. Individually or in groups choose attractions to study in depth. One way to share this information with peers is a vacation destination wrap-over book (see Wrap-Over Book in Activity Appendix A). This book format allows students to write about and illustrate information for three sites. A suggested format is, "I plan to visit _____ because _____."

Literature-Based Example

Cover: Vacation Destinations
Site 1: I plan to visit the White House because this is where all of our presidents, except George Washington, have lived.
Site 2: I plan to visit the National Museum of American History because this is where the inaugural gowns of the presidents' wives are on display.
Site 3: I plan to visit the Washington Monument because this memorial is dedicated to our first president, and from the top there is a panoramic view of Washington, DC.

Gamut of Games

Concentration Game

Some facts about communities are important to remember. Students will enjoy identifying information they decide is important to remember and including this information in a concentration game.

Make a large concentration grid on a bulletin board using yarn. Mount a push-pin in the top center of each square. Write questions and answers on separate pieces of paper that have holes punched on the top. Hang these questions and answers randomly, blank side up, on the push-pins in the grid. Class teams of students play concentration. Appoint two students to turn the set of choices over as each team takes a turn attempting to match a question and the appropriate answer.

Make small game boards with a concentration grid for pairs of students to use when playing concentration. Use small pieces of construction paper for questions and answers.

Literature-Based Example

When playing Concentration, the following are examples of questions and answers for the state of Florida:

Question: What is the capital of Florida?
(**Answer:** Tallahassee)

Question: What are three of Florida's main economic resources?
(Answer: Citrus, tourism, and cattle)
Question: Where is Florida located?
(Answer: In the southeast corner of the United States)
Question: Florida is a peninsula. What is a peninsula?
(Answer: Land surrounded on three sides by water)

Optional: Vacation Destination-O Bingo

Bingo is a popular game for all ages. Vacation Destination-O Bingo *provides a means of reviewing pertinent information about map skills and geographic locations. Students contribute questions and answers for this game.*

Make copies of the Bingo Board in the Activity Appendix A. On their own individual bingo boards, students each number the small boxes in the top left corner of each square randomly from 1 to 25. For example, the top five smaller boxes across might be numbered 7, 12, 22, 18, 6. As the teacher calls out a number and a question, the student writes the answer to the question in the large corresponding box. When the student has answered five questions in a row or column correctly, he or she calls out, "Bingo."

Literature-Based Example

Here are some sample questions about Washington, DC.

Question 7: Which edifice reminds us of the atrocities of life during Hitler's reign in Germany?
(Answer: Holocaust Memorial Museum)
Question 12: Where is our currency printed?
(Answer: Bureau of Engraving and Printing)
Question 22: Where are men and women trained in law enforcement tactics?
(Answer: FBI Building)
Question 18: When traveling from Williamsburg, Virginia, to Washington, DC, in what direction do you travel?
(Answer: North)
Question 6: Where do the Senate and the House of Representatives meet?
(Answer: The Capitol Building)

 Ocular Organizers
Community Data Chart/Research Acrostic Mobiles

As individual students or groups of students read about their community, they post information on a *community data chart*. Determine appropriate headings for the chart based on the community being studied. Students add information to the chart as they explore a variety of resources. Having a limited space in which to record information reduces the temptation to "copy" information from resource books.

To create a *research acrostic mobile*, students make large tag board letters for each letter in the name of the community they are studying. These letters form a vertical chain when holes are punched in the top and bottom of each letter, and the letters are tied together with yarn. On each letter write some information about the community and illustrate the answer. Use magazine and travel brochure pictures in the illustrations.

Literature-Based Example

Fill in a Florida Community Data Chart such as the following:

Florida Community Data Chart	
Economy	Tourism, Citrus, Cattle
Educational Attractions	Kennedy Space Center; Everglades National Park; Castillo de San Marcos (fort)
Famous People	Ponce de Leon; Thomas Edison
Geography	Southeastern Corner of the U.S.; Peninsula
History	Settled in 1565 by Spain; Statehood in 1845
Sports	Fishing; Swimming; Water Skiing
Tourist Attractions	Beaches; Walt Disney World; Sea World

Create a Florida Research Acrostic Mobile (see Figure 5.7).

FIGURE 5.7   Florida Research
Acrostic Mobile

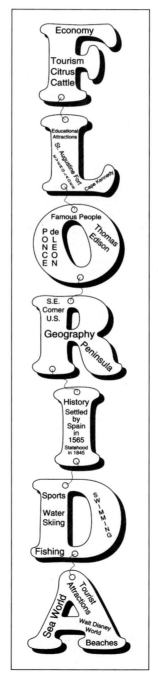

Optional: Trip-plans

Trip-plans contain individually planned travel routes with detailed information about points of interest along the route. Students develop trip-plans that detail their itinerary from the point of departure to their destination and then a different return route via historic landmarks. Essential map skills such as directions (north, south, east, and west), distance, map symbols and legends, and natural features should be part of the trip-plan development. Highlight travel routes on maps, calculate distance, and estimate travel time taking into account the type of road (interstate, two-lane, etc.), traffic congestion in densely populated areas, and natural features that enhance or inhibit travel (plains, mountains, etc.).

Literature-Based Example

A trip-plan to Washington, DC, might include an en route stopover in Williamsburg, Virginia, to visit the reconstructed historic colonial buildings. In Washington, DC, a detailed city map, with attractions labeled and highlighted, is essential. On the return route, schedule a trip to Gettysburg, Pennsylvania, to view the battlefields and cemetery.

Dramatic Debut

Take-a-Tour/Tour Brochures/Tour Guides

Students plan a tour of the community they are studying. To *sell* potential travelers on the tour, students decide on the information to include in a *tour brochure* (see Trifold Brochure in the Activity Appendix A).

An exciting experience for oral language development is the opportunity to be a *tour guide*. Certainly, a special hat indicating this position is essential! Students brainstorm and list the important qualities of a tour guide, for example, enthusiastic, able to give clear directions, knowledgeable about community. Students take turns as tour guides. Tour guides pass out tour brochures to passengers who are taking the tour and discuss sites of interest as the tour progresses.

Set up the classroom as a tour bus. Arrange chairs as bus seats in long rows. Beside the bus, to give the illusion of the bus traveling down the highway and through the community, have large pictures that can be changed or murals that are slowly pulled or rolled out.

Literature-Based Example

Ladies and gentlemen, we are now on our way through fabulous Florida. As you can see from the map in your brochure, we are leaving Tampa and heading east. If you will look out the windows of the bus, you will see Plant City (picture of strawberry fields). The fields you see from the windows on both sides of the bus are strawberry fields. Plant City is the winter strawberry capital of the United States. Next, we will be passing through Lakeland (picture of lakes, trees, flowers, and an alligator peeking out of the lake). Lakeland is well known for its many beautiful lakes. You may even see an alligator in one of the lakes. Soon we will arrive in Orlando. I know you are all looking forward to our trip to delightful Walt Disney World …

Optional: Cyclorama Sites

A cyclorama is a series of picture panels mounted on the wall around the perimeter of a circular room that give a panoramic view of a place or event. Spectators stand in the center of the room (thus in the center of the cyclorama) and turn slowly as each panel is spotlighted and discussed. Background music is used for dramatic effect.

Literature-Based Example

Construct a cyclorama of Washington, DC. Allow student volunteers to create different panels representing museums, monuments, memorials, and federal buildings. Arrange the panels in geographic positions, as much as possible, around the perimeter of the classroom. Use a flashlight or laser pointer to focus spectators' attention on each panel. The artists for each panel discuss the significance of their panel's illustrations on our country's freedom. Play patriotic music in the background. Audiotape or videotape the cyclorama presentation for future enjoyment.

Creative Composition

Step Book Research Report

Researching, writing, and illustrating information about a community is lots of fun when the information is compiled in a *step book* (see Activity Appendix A). Determine the number of pages in the step book by the number of different types of information the students are researching. On each step of the book write a community topic. Write the information about this topic over the topic and under the preceding step. Include appropriate illustrations.

Literature-Based Example

Cover: Florida
Step 1: Animal
　The state animal of Florida is the Florida panther.
Step 2: Bird
　Florida's state bird is the mockingbird.
Step 3: Capital
　The capital of Florida, Tallahassee, is located in north Florida.
Step 4: Flag
　Florida's flag has a white background with the red cross of St. Andrew and the Florida state seal in the center.
Step 5: Flower
　The state flower of Florida is the orange blossom.
Step 6: Song
　"Suwannee River" by Stephen Foster is Florida's state song.
Step 7: Tree
　The state tree of Florida is the sabal palm.
(Note: Determine the depth of information based on the curriculum and students'
　developmental levels.)

Optional: Journey Journal/Teeny Tiny Book

A journey journal contains a personal, written record of daily experiences and observations that occur before, during, and after a trip. The initial entries detail preparation and planning for the trip, including plans for food and snacks, lodging, clothing, transportation, safety, and money. A journey journal might be a spiral-bound notebook, or one could be made by folding a 12" × 18" piece of construction paper in half for a cover and stapling some paper inside (see Journal Jacket in Activity Appendix A). Make a more elaborate journey journal using the **teeny tiny book** *technique (see Activity Appendix A).*

Literature-Based Example

Before Trip Entry

This is exciting! We are really going to Washington, DC! I am going to have to save my allowance and get some extra jobs, so that I will have spending money. (This idea could be extended for math skills by determining how much money is needed for souvenirs, snacks, per day, etc.). *I need to plan my wardrobe carefully. I'm allowed one suitcase and one piece of hand luggage. We're going to be staying at motels, and I need to investigate the costs taking into consideration coupons, breakfast included in the price, charge for children, and other motel incentives* (more math possibilities). *We'll certainly be taking a first aid kit and planning to have the car safety checked.*

During Trip Entry

WOW!!! What a vacation! The trip to Williamsburg is a highlight of the trip. I got to serve on a jury during a mock trial at the Governor's Palace. The restored colonial buildings really made history come alive. I felt like I was right there with George Washington, Patrick Henry, and other patriotic heroes. Tomorrow we leave for Washington.

After Trip Entry

A lot of people have died, so that I might be free. Our trip to Arlington National Cemetery and Gettysburg taught me just how many men and women were willing to make sacrifices for my freedom. I'll never take my freedom for granted again.

MULTICULTURAL DIVERSITY

We live in a land of cultural diversity. Our forefathers came from different lands seeking freedom from many types of oppression. When they landed on these shores, they found the land inhabited by different tribes of Native Americans. Both those who migrated here and those who were native to America had basic needs for food, clothing, and shelter. They all had personal as well as community beliefs, values, customs, and goals. They chose to meet their needs and achieve their goals in a variety of ways. A study of the cultural heritage of people who came to these shores as well as those who already inhabited the land is important in understanding the history and contributions of a variety of cultures to the development of our American way of life.

Pique student interest in cultural diversity through a study of Native Americans, often called Indians. Some students may view Native Americans as either heroes or savages. An investigation of early disputes between the white men and the Indians reveals miscommunication, greed, and mistakes on both sides in squabbles over individual rights and ownership of land. Today we are seeking to reconcile these differences and develop a respect and understanding for each other's similarities and differences.

One possibility for understanding the cultural contributions of Native Americans is to examine folktales from their oral tradition. Tomie dePaola has researched many Native American legends and tales, and strategies in this section are based on his book *The Legend of the Bluebonnet* (1983), a legend of the Comanche people to explain the origin of the bluebonnet, the Texas state flower. *North American Indians* by Marie and Douglas Gorsline (1977) was used as resource for information on the research chart. *Through the Eyes of a Child* by Donna Norton (1995) was the resource book used for information on Native American storytelling.

Artistic Adventures

Pop-Up Books/Pop-Up Plans

Pop-up books, books with pictures or parts of pictures that appear to be jumping out from the page, appeal to young and old alike (see Pop-up Techniques, Activity Appendix A). Techniques abound for developing books with interesting moving pictures and picture parts. Students love the challenge of planning a pop-up product and watching the magic of motion appear on the pages.

A *pop-up plan* is essential in deciding which picture or part of a picture should be moving on the page. As students create an outline for the text, they decide which part of the illustration should be active. They also decide on background illustrations. The pop-up plan determines the number of pages in the book.

Literature-Based Example

A pop-up plan for The Legend of the Bluebonnet *includes:*

Page 1:
- *Problem:*   Drought and famine
- *Pop-Up:*   She-Who-Is-Alone holding doll
- *Background:*   Brown, parched fields and hot sun

Page 2:
- *Event 1:*   Shaman says the way to solve problem is sacrifice
- *Pop-Up:*   Shaman
- *Background:*   Dark sky, dry fields, people listening

Page 3:
- *Event 2:*   Selfishness of people
- *Pop-Up:*   People with balloons for quotations, "I'm sure I don't need to share my …"

Page 4:
- *Event 3:*   Sacrifice of doll
- *Pop-Up:*   Doll on fire
- *Background:*   Dark sky, stars, torch

Page 5:
- *Solution:*   Rain comes, people and land saved
- *Pop-Up:*   One-Who-Dearly-Loved-Her-People
- *Background:*   Fields of bluebonnets

Gamut of Games
Storytelling/Tribal Tales and Traditions

> *A man is always a teller of tales,*
> *He lives surrounded by his stories and the stories of others,*
> *He sees everything that happens to him through them; and*
> *He tries to live his own life as if he were telling a story.*
>
> Jean-Paul Sartre

You learn to be a *storyteller* by telling stories. *Storytelling* builds communication skills through reflection on as well as determining how we can best verbally convey our experiences to others. Stories may be used to (PIE):

Persuade: Stories may be used to influence the thoughts and actions of the audience as the storyteller attempts to convince his or her listeners to support his or her ideas and opinions.
Inform: Stories may be used to convey information such as how to perform a task.
Entertain: Stories may be used to amuse, excite, cheer, and stretch imaginations.

Working in cooperative groups to develop stories and storytelling ability is less intimidating to novice raconteurs than telling tales on their own. An initial telling of tales might encompass retellings of familiar tales. Tale-telling tips (Wynn, in press) include the following:

- *Picture the Place:*   Assist the audience in visualizing the setting.
- *Plan the Plot:*   Have a beginning with a goal or problem, a middle with complications, and an ending with a resolution. Plan personal stories as well as stories about family and friends. Fact and fiction stories about content area information stimulate learning.
- *Provide the People:*   Assist the audience in identifying with the characters; limit the number of characters.

- *Predetermine the Phrases:*   Use repetition, rhythm, and rhyme to aid in audience enjoyment, understanding, and participation. For example: Storyteller, "Little pig, little pig, let me come in." Audience, "Not by the hair of my chinny, chin, chin." Storyteller, "Then I'll huff, and I'll puff, and I'll blow your house in." Use sequence cues such as first, next, then, and finally.
- *Preplan a Pack-a-Punch:*   Develop the theme; at times an unusual twist or surprise adds interest and intrigue; make a moral memorable.
- *Personalize the Presentation:*   Add props, pictures, voices for characters, songs, or a storytelling vest with appropriate illustrations (see vest in Activity Appendix A).
- *Prescribe the Pace:*   Tell the story slowly and pause intermittently to allow the audience to absorb information.
- *Practice! Practice! Practice!*   Each group member may tell a portion of the story, and story-telling vests might have illustrations appropriate to sections of the story.

The preservation of *tribal traditions*, culture, and history is essential in understanding the values and beliefs of Native Americans. For many years, a tribe's traditions and history were passed from one generation to the next through oral storytelling. Folklore sharing typically occurred in the evening after a day's work was complete. Indians sat around a fire, and parents and grandparents shared tribal stories. Boys in the tribe assumed the responsibility for preserving and transmitting their heritage. They listened intently to a story, as they were expected to repeat the same tale the next evening. They were well aware that the audience might applaud or criticize their ability to tell the story.

Tribal storytellers knew they had to capture the attention of the audience, which they often did with a common story opening, humor, audience participation, and a common story ending. Listeners were not allowed to interrupt, but they could repeat the last word in a sentence or say, "Yes," to show they were attentive and appreciative. In some tribes the storyteller gave kernels of corn to members of the audience who then ate the corn during the story to aid in remembering the content and importance of the story. In some tribes the storyteller gave gifts to the audience at the end of the story to reimburse the audience for a night taken from their lives.

Literature-Based Example

Cooperative groups will enjoy researching a particular region or Native American tribe to discover the use of specific storytelling techniques. They might choose something in nature and develop a legend explaining the existence of this phenomenon. The Legend of the Bluebonnet (1983) by Tomie dePaola will serve as an example. Plan a tribal meeting around the campfire to implement the storytelling techniques and share the folktales and legends that have been created. Students may design special vests for this auspicious occasion and decorate their vests with Native American symbols (see vest in Activity Appendix A). They might choose to arrange the symbols to tell a story.

 Ocular Organizers
Research Chart

A *research chart* is an information grid that provides a graphic representation of the data collected for the topic being studied. List one set of topics at the beginning of each row down the left side of the chart. List a set of subtopics, which may be in the form of questions, horizontally for each column across the top of the chart. As students locate data, they write information in each box on the grid. A research chart provides a visual representation of data collection, information, and summarization. After collecting data, students may focus on one of the topics and make a second research chart to refine the information for that topic.

Literature-Based Example

The following research chart demonstrates the beginning of Native American region data collection. After collecting information on a region, students may decide to develop a second research chart to collect data on tribes within the region. Encourage students to study the geographical impact of weather, natural resources, and land formation on each tribe's housing, food, transportation, and way of life.

Native American Region Data

Region	Housing	Food	Transportation
Northeast	Wigwams Long Houses	Corn Squash	Canoes
Southeast	Chickees	Fish & Game Corn & Beans	Canoes
Great Plains	Teepees Earth Lodges	Corn & Beans Buffalo	Boats & Sleds Horses & Ponies
Northwest	Plank Houses Brush Huts	Fish Nuts & Seeds	Canoes
Southwest	Pueblo Hogan	Corn Buffalo	Ponies

Dramatic Debut

Plays, Puppets, and Paper Plate Stages

Write plays for production on paper plate stages. Developing a script and participating in puppet productions allow students to develop their expressive ability and creativity both orally and in writing. Construct a *paper plate stage* from paper plates (see Activity Appendix A). Mount puppets, small paper figures, on craft sticks or tongue depressors. Mount a different figure on each side of the stick, so when the stick is turned over, a different facial expression for the puppet or a different puppet person is portrayed. Use fabric, yarn, feathers, and other media to add features and interest to puppets. Create background scenery based on the story script. Design background scenery to change as the play progresses.

Literature-Based Example

Students write a play and create a paper plate stage and puppets for The Legend of the Bluebonnet. *The first background scenery might be mountains, a dark sky, and brown crops. The second set of scenery could be a bright, sunny sky with bluebonnets on the hillsides. To demonstrate her name change, make puppets for She-Who-Is-Alone (She 1) on the front of a stick and One-Who-Dearly-Loved-Her-People (She 2) on the back of the same stick. Another puppet might feature the Shaman on the front of the stick and one of the Comanche people on the back of the same stick.*

She 1: I am so afraid. My people are starving. What can we do?
Shaman: The Great Spirits have spoken. One of us must sacrifice a favored possession.
Comanche: I am sure the Great Spirits do not mean for me to give up my favorite bow.
She 1: Great Spirits, please take my doll. It is the only thing I have from my family.
She 2: Rain!!! Look at the bluebonnets!

Creative Composition
Circle of Cinquains Roll Over and Over Book

A *cinquain* is a formula poem containing five unrhymed lines that describes a subject or tells a story (see format in Poetry Appendix C). Writing a cinquain provides students with experiences in developing new and unusual comparisons as they create a unique simile for their topic. Encourage students to search for unusual and effective vocabulary words for their poems.

Individually or in groups students may design a *circle of cinquains roll over and over book* (see Activity Appendix A). Relate the cinquains to one literature selection, or base them on several stories related to the social studies topic. Mount eight cinquain poems around the circumference of the book.

Literature-Based Example

The following is a cinquain for the protagonist in The Legend of the Bluebonnet. *Create other cinquains for this story or for other Native American legends. Make a circle of cinquains book from two large grocery sacks. The roughness of the paper and the shape of the book will make the book resemble a circle of teepees.*

She-Who-Is-Alone

She-Who-Is-Alone
Lonely, Unselfish
Loving, Praying, Sacrificing
Lovely as a Bluebonnet
One-Who-Dearly-Loved-Her-People

FAMOUS PEOPLE: PAST AND PRESENT

Provide opportunities for students to get caught up in the excitement of similarities and differences in their lives and the lives of historical people. From the time period being studied, individual students or groups of students may choose from a list of historical contributors, or they may investigate important people who have made or are making significant contributions to their lives. As students study a plethora of trade books, they will discover well-known and little known facts about historical heroes. Provide a variety of motivational strategies that allow students to experience, "I am there." The focus literature selection for this section is *Where Was Patrick Henry on the 29th of May?* by Jean Fritz (1975).

Artistic Adventures
Biographical Web/Biopoem/Eightfold Person

A *biographical web* provides a visual representation and graphic organizer for the data being collected. The famous person's name forms the nucleus of the web. Radiating out from the nucleus are categories of interest relevant to the person. Some categories to include are beliefs, characteristics, childhood, contributions to society, family, profession, and quotes.

Write a *biopoem* about the person using information from the biographical web (see format in Poetry Appendix C). Several students may write individual biopoems about one famous person. Have students compare and contrast their poems.

Create an *eightfold person* for each famous character in the class study (see Activity Appendix A). Clothing, hat, and hairstyle should be representative of the time period and occupation of each historical person. The characters may hold objects related to their professions and beliefs. Write biopoems on the insides of the jackets. Display these characters with their biopoems on a bulletin board or as mobiles.

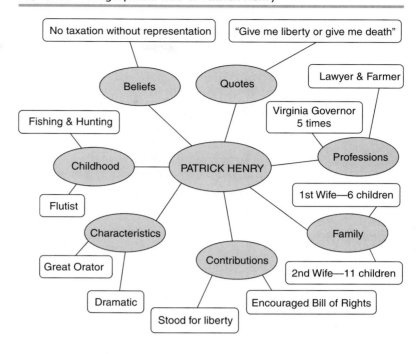

FIGURE 5.8   Biographical Web of Patrick Henry

Literature Based Example

Use information from a biographical web of Patrick Henry (see Figure 5.8) to write a biopoem.

Biopoem

Patrick
Orator, Lawyer, Governor, Planter
Lover of nature, Virginia, freedom
Who believed in individual and states' rights
Who wanted no taxation without representation, liberty, time to relax
Who used his voice and dramatic ability for his country
Who gave time, love, devotion, and loyalty to his country
Who said, "Give me liberty or give me death."
Henry

Gamut of Games
Hero Hunt/Wanted Posters

The following class discussion sets the tone for a *hero hunt*:

> *Law and order are important in our society. Unfortunately, we have notorious villains loose in our midst. They have hidden many of our famous heroes. It is our duty as dedicated citizens to rescue our heroes and apprehend the villains. To identify the heroes and villains we need* wanted posters *with pictures. These posters should include descriptions of the heroes and culprits, a list of their contributions or crimes, a reward for their return or capture, and other pertinent information. Each law-abiding citizen must do his or her civic duty in creating these posters and participating in the hero hunt (see wanted poster in Activity Appendix A).*

On "Hero Hunt Day" students dress as heroes or villains. Villains stash heroes in given locations within the school and then hide themselves. Provide written clues in riddle form for searchers to follow indicating the whereabouts of the heroes and villains, so that each villain may be apprehended and our heroes rescued.

Literature-Based Example

Patrick Henry has escaped. For information on this hero his wanted poster (see Activity Appendix A) contains the following information:

Wanted Dead or Alive
Name: Patrick Henry
Description: White male, six foot, lanky build with blue eyes and dark hair
Known for: Having a loud voice. Speaks openly against taxation without representation.
Reward: Freedom from oppression

Hero hunt clues include the following:

Clue 1: Go where you hear sweet, lilting melodies
    And seek behind the bushes and the trees.
(outside the music room; behind the shrubbery)
Clue 2: Go where your friends are at play
    And look below the ball hoop today.
(physical education court)
Clue 3: Go where the sentence is handed down
    And must be accepted without a frown.
(principal's office)
Clue 4: Oh my goodness, who do I see?
    There in the principal's closet is Patrick Henry!

 ## Ocular Organizer
Time Line Mural

Create a *time line mural* with a chronological sequence of events based on the time period being studied. Make the mural on large bulletin board paper and mount it on a wall in the classroom. Write dates across the bottom of the mural. As research proceeds, add information and illustrations to the time line mural.

Literature-Based Example

The information on this time line is based on information found in Where Was Patrick Henry on May 29th? *Additional events are added to the time line as students read other trade books.*

1736	1761	1765
Born	Began law practice	Spoke against Stamp Tax

1775	1788	1796
"Liberty Speech"	Spoke against Constitution	Retired

 ## Dramatic Debut
Heroes' Hall of Fame

Nominate significant people from the time period for the class *Heroes' Hall of Fame*. Some of these nominees will have controversial backgrounds and political positions. Nominating speeches should include information on why a person should be accepted into the Heroes' Hall of Fame. Plan rebuttal speeches to refute this information. Heroes accepted for the Hall of Fame should plan and present acceptance speeches. Create time period clothes and hats from old clothes, bed sheets, paper, and various media. In lieu of dressing the part, consider using eightfold people puppets (See Eightfold Person in the Activity Appendix A). Play patriotic music for background effect.

Literature-Based Example

Narrator: *Today we are gathered together to establish and bring forth our Heroes' Hall of Fame. Mr. Smith, I believe you are to make the first nominating speech.*

Mr. Smith: *Sir, it is my privilege to greet you and this auspicious body. It is my personal privilege and pleasure to place in nomination the name of a gentleman so forthright and worthy in character that no one, and I repeat no one, will dare question his place as an outstanding American hero. I speak, of course, of Mr. Patrick Henry, first in Virginia, first in peace, and first in the hearts of our countrymen. Mr. Henry, as you well know, is best known for his continual endeavor to make each and every one of us free. He spoke eloquently and sincerely when he said, "Give me liberty or give me death." I nominate Mr. Patrick Henry as a candidate for our Heroes' Hall of Fame.*

Narrator: *Yes, Mr. Jones?*

Mr. Jones: *How can we even consider Mr. Patrick Henry for our Heroes' Hall of Fame? Why, Mr. Henry has caused nothing but controversy. He has spoken continually against our mother country, England. He has not supported the parsons in our churches. He has had the audacity to speak out against our proposed Constitution. I, for one, and I'm sure you will all agree with me, am appalled that Mr. Henry's name should be brought before this distinguished body.*

Creative Composition

Birthday Biography/Birthday Biography Roll Over and Over Book

A *biography* is a written account of another person's life. A *birthday biography* is a biography that uses the date of the person's birthday as the hallmark in each chosen year. Discuss focus events in relation to the birthday date in that year.

Publish a birthday biography in a *birthday biography roll over and over book* (see Roll over and over Book in Activity Appendix A). Identify eight significant events in different years of a person's life. Organize these events chronologically. Write about and illustrate each event in one section of the birthday biography roll over and over book.

Literature-Based Example

Birthday Biography Book: Patrick Henry

Section 1: On May 29, 1736, Patrick Henry was born.

Section 2: By May 29, 1761, Patrick Henry had educated himself in the legal profession and was a practicing lawyer.

Section 3: By May 29, 1765, Patrick Henry was a member of the House of Burgesses, and he spoke against English taxes.

Section 4: By May 29, 1775, Patrick Henry urged his constituents to prepare for war.

Section 5: On May 29, 1777, Patrick Henry was elected governor of Virginia for the second time. He served five terms as governor.

Section 6: By May 29, 1788, Patrick Henry spoke out against the Constitution. This did not make him popular with many people. As a result of his speeches, the Bill of Rights was added to the Constitution.

Section 7: By May 29, 1796, Patrick Henry retired from public life to enjoy his farming, family, and friends.

Section 8: By May 29, 1799, Patrick Henry enjoyed the last months of his life before dying on June 6, 1799.

LONG, LONG AGO: MEDIEVAL TIMES

In social studies students are frequently introduced to people who lived long, long ago. Because students do not have a background frame of reference experience to deal with a different time period, it is often difficult for them to relate to people who lived and died long before they were born. History may be made more meaningful and students may develop a frame of reference if they are allowed to participate in the time period through a variety of cultural experiences.

The specific time period focus is the Middle Ages. Student involvement in chapter strategies will help students understand medieval society. The literature focus is *A Medieval Feast* by Aliki (1983), *I Wish I Could Be a Knight* by Duncan Crosbie (2005), *Living in Castle Times* by Robyn Gee (1991), *St. George and the Dragon* by Margaret Hodges (1984), and *Castle* by David Macaulay (1977).

Artistic Adventures

Coat of Arms

As most knights looked alike when dressed in suits of armor, there was a problem in battle when it came to identifying a knight as an ally or an opponent. A *coat of arms*, which was placed on the shield and on the front of the coat of armor, was designed to identify the knight as friend or foe. These coats of arms were personalized and identified the family of the knight as well as his individual achievements. Minor changes were made as the coat of arms was passed down in the same family through succeeding generations. Heralds responsible for royal proclamations and issuing challenges at a tournament were also medieval historians who kept records of family histories and their coats of arms. Rosemary A. Chorzempa (1987) has compiled a detailed book on the subject entitled, *Design Your Own Coat of Arms: An Introduction to Heraldry*. Books containing surnames with origins, meanings, and information on heraldic emblems for family coats of arms provide valuable information.

Literature-Based Example

Students will revel in choosing shape, color, and symbols for designing their own personal coats of arms. Designate each section of the shield with symbols representing a student's family, interests, aspirations, and accomplishments. A class herald should keep records of each coat of arms.

Gamut of Games

Vocabtionary/Print, Praise, 'n' Pass

Vocabulary development is essential for effective communication. Wynn (1993) found that acquisition of proprietary vocabulary is enhanced through active involvement in a variety of creative, thematic-based activities.

Vocabtionary is a game in which students sketch clues for selected vocabulary terms. As a team member draws clues, other team members guess what the sketch is. The illustrator does not talk. Make sketches on a chalkboard, white board, or paper. Use a timer to allow each team member an equal amount of time. Teammates rotate turns as the illustrator. Teammates attempt to guess what the sketch is until they make a correct guess and win a point or the timer goes off. If they cannot guess correctly, give another team the opportunity to guess.

Vocabtionary may be played on two levels of difficulty:

Level 1: Word Only	1 point
Level 2: Two Rhyming Words	2 points

Determine the choice of terms by their importance to the thematic unit and student interest. Write the terms on slips of paper and place them in either a Level 1 container or a Level 2 container. In Level 1, a team member draws a picture representing the term that is pulled from container 1. Younger students will probably play only at Level 1. In Level 2, team members must guess the two rhyming words for the sketch.

In the group game, *Print, Praise, 'n' Pass,* each team member selects a pen/ink color and places the pen in the holder in the center of the table. Team member 1 begins:

Print *one entry while reading the entry aloud.*
Wait for **Praise** *from team members.*
Pass *the paper.*

Team member 2 picks up her pen and repeats the sequence. Continue to rotate the paper making a single entry for each turn.

Print, praise, 'n' pass may be used with a variety of learning experiences. For example, each team member may compute a step in solving a math problem. When creating a web about a famous person, each team member may take a turn adding characteristics and details.

Literature-Based Examples

Castletionary is a vocabtionary game in which all of the terms relate to medieval times. Students and teachers choose thematic terms, write them on strips of paper, and place them in either the Level 1 or Level 2 container. Rhyming pairs may not be possible for all terms, but students will enjoy attempting to make pairs. A rhyming dictionary is an asset in developing pairs. The following terms may be used in Castletionary:

Level 1: Moat *(student draws castle with water)*
Level 2: Moat Boat *(student draws castle and boat in water)*
Level 1: Serf *(student draws person)*
Level 2: Serf Turf *(student draws person on farm with crops)*
Level 1: Page *(student draws a servant)*
Level 2: Page Rage *(student draws a mad servant)*

In praise, print, 'n' pass, create and illustrate a team ABC "Medieval Times for Me Summary." Initial team member entries might begin:

Team Member 1: *A*rmor
Team Member 2: *B*attle
Team Member 3: *C*astle
Team Member 4: *D*anger
Team Member 1: *E*nemy
Team Member 2: *F*east
Team Member 3: *G*uild
Team Member 4: *H*onor bound

Ocular Organizers

Then and Now Lifestyle Organizer

One way to develop an understanding of the lifestyles of long, long ago is to compare what life was like then with what life is like now. Comparison allows students to note differences and similarities in lifestyles.

Students decide on characteristics of an early lifestyle they wish to investigate. These characteristics might include food, shelter, clothing, education, transportation, communication, entertainment, shopping, and professions. Develop a four-column lifestyle organizer with boxes. In the first column, list lifestyle characteristics. In the second column make entries about what life was like then. The fourth column contains information about life now. The third column includes information about the similarities of life then and now.

Literature-Based Example

Then and Now Lifestyle Organizer for Medieval Times			
Characteristics	**Medieval (Then)**	**Mutual (Similarities)**	**Modern (Now)**
Communication	Messengers, Town criers	People sharing with each other	Telephone, TV, newspaper, Email
Housing	Castles, Manors, Huts	Single-Family dwellings	Apartments, Condominiums
Transportation	Horses, Carts, Carriages	Boats	Cars, Buses, Planes

Dramatic Debut

Mesmerizing Musical

A *mesmerizing musical* provides an opportunity for students to read, research, plan, and participate in a lyrical production. Students write lyrics, design scenery and props, and develop dramatic ability. They are able to enhance all their language arts skills. They *read* to gather information about the time period; they *write* the script for the production; they *listen* to others as they plan and participate in the production; they use *oral language* as they say and sing their parts. In addition they are using their visual communication skills as they create props and scenery. Musical experiences provide a variety of communications systems experiences as they entice thrice through 👁 👁 eyes, 👂 👂 ears, and 💓 emotions (see Chapter 1).

Literature-Based Example

Involvement in planning and producing a medieval musical allows students to experience "you are there." As they become one of the medieval knights, ladies of the court, serfs, or peasants in the cast, they participate vicariously in the medieval culture. Make castles, costumes, and other props using cardboard boxes, poster board, fabric, and various media materials. Sing the following song during the medieval musical. Encourage students to compose additional verses.

Title:	***The King Is Coming***
Tune:	***"She'll Be Coming Round the Mountain"***
Verse 1:	Oh, the king is coming—yes, he is! Hurrah! (2X)
	Oh, the king is coming. (3X)
	Yes, he is! **Hurrah!**

Verse 2: The manor must be cleaned—the rooms made up.
         Dust! Dust!!

Continue format. The end of the last line is Dust! Dust!! Hurrah*

Verse 3: A tremendous feast—we must prepare. **Plan! Plan!!**
Verse 4: The butter and the cheese—must be made. **Churn! Churn!!**
Verse 5: We will bake a blackbird pie—with fourteen birds.
         Chirp! Chirp!!
Verse 6: The king has just arrived—we must bow down.
         Your majesty!
Verse 7: The feast is delicious—yes it is. **Yum! Yum!!**
Verse 8: Jesters, jugglers, minstrels—entertain us.
         Ha! Ha!!
Verse 9: A good time was had by all—yes, it was. **Clap! Clap!!**

*Acting out, and singing the last two words in each verse in reverse order, provides a hilarious musical experience.

Creative Composition
Poems to Paragraphs/File Folder Display

Writing formula poetry allows students to choose precise vocabulary to express their thoughts. As students make careful word choices for their poems, their ability to express themselves creatively grows. *Formula poetry* is poetry that has a specific format, sequence, and organizational pattern. The number of lines and the number of words or syllables for each line of poetry is often delineated. Biopoems, cinquain, diamante, senses poems, and story poems are examples of formula poetry (see Poetry Appendix C). Writing formula poems and expanding these *poems to paragraphs* is a motivational technique to use in developing narrative and expository writing skills. Publish poems and paragraphs on *file folder displays* or on a Castle Shape book (see Activity Appendix A).

Literature-Based Examples

Story Poem

A story poem based on St. George and the Dragon *(1984), retold by Margaret Hodges, including background knowledge of knights and dragons, that students write might look like this.*

My Hero

Dragon
Fire-breathing; Capture maiden
Saint George
Slay dragon; Save maiden
Sharpen sword
Travel far
Good-bye dragon
Maiden saved; Live happily ever after

Poem to Paragraph

Once upon a time there was a fire-breathing dragon who captured a fair maiden and devoured many knights who tried to rescue her. Saint George decided to slay the dragon and save the maiden. He sharpened his sword. Then he traveled far. He confronted and slew the dragon. He saved the maiden, married her, and they lived happily ever after.

File Folder Display

Make a file folder display for this poem and paragraph. Notch the top of the file folder to represent the top of a castle wall. Mount a dragon, Saint George, and a maiden on pop-up notches in the display.

Literature References

AAA Tour Book of the Mid-Atlantic States. (1993). Heathrow, FL: American Automobile Association.

Aliki. (1983). *A medieval feast.* New York: Harper & Row.

Aylesworth, T.G. (1990). *The kids' world almanac of the United States.* New York: World Almanac.

Chorzempa, R.A. (1987). *Design your own coat of arms: An introduction to heraldry.* Mineola, N.Y: Dover.

Christelow, E. (2003). *Vote.* New York: Clarion Books.

Cohn, A.L. (1993). *From sea to shining sea: A treasury of American folklore and folk songs.* New York: Scholastic.

Crosbie, Duncan. (2005). *I wish I could be a knight.* New York Backpack Books.

dePaola, T. (1983). *The legend of the blue bonnet.* New York: Putnam.

Fritz, J. (1975). *Where was Patrick Henry on the 29th of May?* New York: Coward-McCann.

Gee, R. (1991). *Living in castle times.* London: Usborne.

Gorsline, M., & Gorsline, D. (1977). *North American Indians.* New York: Random House.

Hodges, M. (1984). *Saint George and the dragon.* Boston: Little, Brown and Company. Caldecott Award.

Koningsburg, E.L. (1996). *The view from Saturday.* New York: Atheneum Book for Young Readers. Newbery Award.

Levy, E. (1987). *If you were there when they signed the Constitution.* New York: Scholastic.

Lloyd, M. (1990). *Flags of the United States.* New York: Gallery Books.

Macaulay, D. (1977). *Castle.* Boston: Houghton Mifflin. Caldecott Honor.

Maestro, B., & Maestro, G. (1996). *The voice of the people: American democracy in action.* New York: Lothrop, Lee & Shepard Books.

Munro, R. (1987). *The inside-outside book of Washington, D. C.* New York: Penguin Books.

Professional References

Allen, R. (2003, Winter). Civic virtue in the schools: Engaging a new generation of citizens. *ASCD Curriculum Update.* Alexandria, VA: Association for Supervision and Curriculum Development.

Beck, I.L., & McKeown, M.G. (2002, November). Questioning the author: Making sense of social studies. *Educational Leadership, 60* (3), 44–47.

Goodman, T. (Ed.). (1997). *The Forbes book of business quotations.* New York: Black Dog & Leventhal Publishers.

Johnson, N.M., & Ebert, M.J. (1992, March). Time travel is possible: Historical fiction and biography—passport to the past. *The Reading Teacher, 45* (7), 488–495.

Kovalik, S. (1994). *Integrated thematic instruction: The model* (3rd ed.). Kent, WA: Susan Kovalik & Associates.

Linquist, T. (1996, May/June). How does your teaching rate? Social studies now. *Instructor,* 36–67.

National Council for Social Studies (NCSS). (2004). *Curriculum Standards for Social Studies.* Retrieved February 20, 2004. www.ncss.org.

Norby, S.L. (December 2003/January 2004). Hardwired into history. *Educational Leadership, 61* (4), 48–53.

Norton, D. (1995). *Through the eyes of a child.* New York: Merrill.

Ogle, D.M., & McMahon, S. (2003). Curriculum integration to promote literate thinking: Dilemmas and possibilities. In Flood, D. Lapp, J. Squire, & J. Jensen (Eds.), *Handbook of research on teaching the English language arts* (2nd ed., pp. 1035–1051). Mahwah, NJ: Lawrence Erlbaum Associates. Sponsored by the International Reading Association and the National Council of Teachers of English.

Onosko, J.J. (1992, September/October). An approach to designing thoughtful units. *The Social Studies, 83* (5), 193–196.

Parker, W.C., & Jarolimek, J. (2001). *A sampler of curriculum standards for social studies: Expectations of excellence.* Upper Saddle River, NJ: Merrill Prentice Hall. www.socialstudies.org/standards/exec.html).

Rasmussen, Karen. (1999a, Winter). Social studies: A laboratory for democracy. *ASCD Curriculum Update,* 1–3 & 8.

Rasmussen, Karen. (1999b, Winter). Teaching social studies for meaningful learning. *ASCD Curriculum Update,* 3 & 6.

Seif, E. (December 2003/January 2004). Social studies revived. *Educational Leadership, 61* (4), 54–59.

Wynn, M.J. (1993). Proprietary vocabulary acquisition: A creative thematic adventure. *Reading Horizons, 33* (5), 389–400.

Wynn, M.J. (in press). *Power-packed methods.*

Zemelman, S., Daniels, H., & Hyde, A. (1998). *Best practices: New standards for teaching and learning in American schools* (2nd ed.). Portsmouth, NH: Heinemann.

Websites

edHelper

This is an excellent collection of thousands of searchable K-12 lesson plans organized by category, WebQuests, and other educational resources.

www.edhelper.com

Education World

Statement comes from the National Council for the Social Studies. … in statements that begin "Social studies programs should include experiences that provide for the study of"

www.education-world.com/standards/
national/soc_sci/index.shtml

Kids Voting

Kids Voting USA (KVUSA) is a national nonprofit, nonpartisan organization that teaches students about the concepts of citizenship, civic responsibilities, democracy and the importance of political participation.

www.kidsvotingusa.org

Mid-Continent Research for Education and Learning

To find national standards for all subjects, including civics, economics, geography, and history (but not social studies), using a single website, see the following website from McREL

www.mcrel.org/compendium/browse.asp

National Council for Social Studies (NCSS)

Expectations of Excellence: Curriculum Standards for Social Studies

www.ncss.org/

Smithsonian Education — Students

Explore, Discover, Learn: Everything Art; Science & Nature; History & Culture; People & Places. Explore all the Smithsonian has to offer at Smithsonian Students . From interactive idea labs to homework help to strange but true facts, you'll find it here!

www.smithsonianeducation.org/students

Social Studies for Kids

This site provides activities and information for teachers and students about many social studies topics including history, geography, economics, cultures, current events, holidays and religions.

www.socialstudiesforkids.com

CHAPTER 6 TOPICS	Artistic Adventures	Gamut of Games Every Student Participation (E.S.P.)
Calculations and Computations	Paper People Practice Step Book	Paper Clip Creations Sticky Note Participation
Fraction Action	Parts Pictures	Parts of Whole Objects Parts of a Set of Objects
Dollars and Cents: Economics	Pop-Up Pleaser Holiday and Twelve-Month Pop-Up Pleasers	Bingo
Picture Perfect: Geometry, Graphing, and Data Analysis	Three-D-Geometry	Tangram
Measure Mania: Measurement, Time, and Data Analysis	Clock: What Time Is It?	Treasure Measure Hunt Pocket Books

Mathematics

Ocular Organizers	*Dramatic Debut*	*Creative Composition*
Town House Math	Card Capers Card Caper Corner	Math Log Thumbprint Thoughts
Pie Quivalent Wall Chart Money Quivalent Wall Chart	Culinary Creations	Cookbooks A Secret Ingredient Cake Shape Cookbook
Cost Comparison Charts	Dine 'n' Dash Diner	Money Memoirs Money Memoirs Circle Story
Graphs	Family Broadcasting Network Polls, Surveys, and Graphs	Tantalizing Template Tangles Tantalizing Template Tales
Class Chart of Records Class Book of Records	Gifts and Greetings Gallery	Personal Guinness Book of Records in a Teeny Tiny Book

OVERVIEW

What is mathematics? The *American Heritage Dictionary* (2000) defines mathematics as, "the study of the measurement, properties, and relationships of quantities and sets, using numbers and symbols" (p. 1080). Troutman and Lichtenberg (1995) suggest that the study of mathematics should include:

- **Computation,** which includes adding, subtracting, multiplying, and dividing
- **Application,** which includes sets of relationships that enable people to solve everyday problems
- **Topics,** which include sets of logically organized deductive systems

According to Willoughby (1990), mathematics encompasses number sense, estimation skills, ability to analyze data intelligently, knowledge of two- and three-dimensional geometry, and knowledge of probability. On the basis of this information, *mathematics* is a systematic approach to solving everyday problems using numbers, patterns, and logic.

Traditionally, the mathematics curriculum was textbook centered with a focus on computation skills. The goal of mathematics was for students to solve numerical problems and get the *right answers.* Students often moved sequentially through the mathematics textbook page by page completing a myriad of worksheets, solving computation problems, and hopefully getting the right answers. Students in kindergarten were most likely to use manipulatives to solve these problems, but as these students progressed up through the grades, fewer and fewer manipulatives were used. With this procedural emphasis on computational skills, students often progressed too quickly from concrete examples that provide meaningful experiences and understanding of mathematical problems to memorizing a pattern for symbol manipulation. As Hyde and Bizar (1989) point out, they were pushed into *premature and excessive symbolism.*

To provide application and problem-solving strategies, story problems were often added at the end of each textbook chapter or included in the enrichment section of the chapter and often intended for more advanced students. To solve these story problems, students frequently utilized the computational skill that had been studied in the first part of the chapter. For example, if the students had been working on subtraction exercises all week, then most of the story problems involved putting the big number on top, the smaller number on bottom, and subtracting to get the *right answer.*

NATIONAL COUNCIL OF TEACHERS OF MATHEMATICS (NCTM)

In response to the *right answer mentality* found in many textbooks and classrooms, NCTM appointed a Commission on Standards for School Mathematics to establish goals for the K–12 mathematics curriculum (1989, p.5). This commission developed the following global goals:

1. All students learn to value mathematics.
2. All students become confident in their ability to do mathematics.
3. All students become mathematical problem solvers.
4. All students learn to communicate mathematically.
5. All students learn to reason mathematically.

In an effort to further enhance students' mathematical expertise, in 2000 the NCTM established *Principles and Standards for School Mathematics* (NCTM, website). The six principles address the following overarching themes:

- **The Equity Principle:**   Excellence in mathematics education requires equity—high expectations and strong support for all students.
- **The Curriculum Principle:**   A curriculum is more than a collection of activities: it must be coherent, focused on important mathematics, and well articulated across the grades.
- **The Teaching Principle:**   Effective mathematics teaching requires understanding what students know and need to learn, then challenging and supporting them to learn it well.

- **The Learning Principle:**   Students must learn mathematics with understanding, actively building new knowledge from experience and prior knowledge.
- **The Assessment Principle:**   Assessment should support the learning of important mathematics and furnish useful information to both teachers and students.
- **The Technology Principle:**   Technology is essential in teaching and learning mathematics; it influences the mathematics that is taught and enhances student learning.

The content and process standards established by NCTM include the following:

Content Standards

Numbers and Operations
Algebra
Geometry
Measurement
Data Analysis and Probability

Process Standards

Problem Solving
Reasoning and Proof
Communication
Connections
Representation

This handbook addresses content standards in a variety of ways. For example: Many facets of numbers and operations are found under the topic Calculations and Computations, while geometry experiences occur under the topic Picture Perfect. An assortment of measurement experiences are found in Measure Mania. An example of a data analysis experience is the Family Broadcasting Network and Polls, Surveys, and Graphs.

This handbook addresses process standards in a variety of ways. For example, in this chapter communication skills are enhanced using math logs, money memoirs, and a personal Guinness book of records. Connections with the everyday world occur in the Gifts and Greetings Gallery, Cookbooks and a Secret Ingredient Cake Shape Cookbook, the Dine 'n' Dash Diner, as well as in the Stock Market Game in Chapter 8.

For each of the NCTM content and process standards, there is a continuum of grade level bands:

Prekindergarten through Grade 2
Grades 3 through 5
Grades 6 through 8
Grades 9 through 12

In this handbook strategy discussions include suggestions for adapting the strategies to meet the developmental needs of students. For example, in Culinary Creations, recipes may be written in rebus form for younger students, while older students may double or divide recipes. The difficulty of questions in Pocket Books for every student participation (ESP) and the story problems for the Holiday Pop-Up Pleaser are based on students' mathematical experiences and appropriate grade level curriculum.

DIFFERENTIATED INSTRUCTION

The equity principal promotes differentiated instruction to support academic needs while continuing to maintain high expectations for success and strong support for all students. Noting that communication is one of the NCTM process standards, Silbey (2003) promotes talking, listening to others, and writing about math problems to promote math understanding and achievement. He finds this approach essential and effective with students who are non-native speakers of English. This handbook includes a variety of communication experiences. A representative experience is the discussion that occurs during the Family Broadcasting Network with polls, surveys, and graphs.

As teachers attempt to design math programs to meet the equity principle, making math meaningful for minority students presents unique challenges. In analyzing this dilemma Franklin (2003) suggests,

> Beset by cultural prejudices, poor resources and frequent misconceptions, many minority students—Hispanic, African American, and Native American alike—"tune out" of math classes at an early age because higher education is not considered a necessity or even an option. Getting them to "tune back in," experts say, often requires changing the way **parents view education**, the way **teachers view their students**, and—above all—the way **students view themselves**. (p. 4; emphasis added)

Franklin suggests a family math night to familiarize parents with math games and strategies to help their children learn. In addition, because linguistic differences may cloud a teacher's perception of a student's mathematical ability, he suggests teachers focus on tying math to a student's cultural traditions. Two culturally meaningful math suggestions he makes for Native Americans are using mathematical information to design a canoe and using the right combination of ingredients and measurements to make clay for pottery.

For differentiated instruction in math, Bintz and Moore (2003) recommend using a literature-based approach that integrates NCTM standards with the Standards for English/Language Arts. A wide selection of math-related literature is used in this chapter. In addition, literature-based mystery math experiences are found in Chapter 8. As was true in the preceding chapters, teachers are encouraged to modify and adapt strategies based on student interest, grade level, curriculum, and literature choices.

MATH QUANDARIES

Martinez and Martinez (2003) identify a major math quandary—in early grades most students enjoy math; however, as they progress through the grades, their enthusiasm wavers, often resulting in *math anxiety* and *math avoidance*. As attitudes about math decline, math anxiety increases. In their analysis of math instruction, they found a predominant use of the *explain–practice–memorize* traditional math approach. As an alternative, they suggest an instructional approach in which students find math problems in their everyday world, invent solutions, and reflect on their own work. For example, students might find math problems in the field of sports. Focusing on a favorite sport or sports figure is motivational. Using this approach, rather than driving students from math, they are drawn into the world of everyday math curiosity and challenge.

Barton, Heidema, and Jordan (2002) discuss the challenges encountered when reading math text and suggest using a variety of graphic organizers (ocular organizers) to enhance math comprehension. This handbook provides an array of visual organizers, including Town House Math, Pie Quivalent and Money Quivalent Wall Charts, Cost Comparison Charts, an assortment of Graphs, and a Class Chart of Records.

How Should You Teach Mathematics?

Willoughby (1990) suggests four steps to better mathematics education that students should follow in developing and solving problems:

1. Derive the mathematics from their own reality.
2. Discover and use the power of abstract thought.
3. Practice.
4. Apply the mathematics to something of interest to them.

Willis and Checkley (1996) emphasize the importance of teaching for understanding. They, along with Stewart (2003), promote the use of manipulatives as a means to bridge the gap between concrete and symbolic realms. They suggest weaving math into students' everyday lives. For students who are "math challenged," cooperative groups in which there is an emphasis on cooperation rather than competition is effective. Of interest is their finding that students do not have to master basic skills, *drill and kill*, before engagement in problem solving. Rather, they master basic skills within the meaningful context of solving everyday problems.

Troutman and Lichtenberg (1995) present concepts at three levels of abstraction in mathematics instruction: (1) concrete level, (2) pictorial level, and (3) symbolic level. These mathematicians, as well as Hyde and Bizar (1989), Smith, Smith, and Romberg (1993); and Tankersley (1993), stress the importance of building a mathematics curriculum focused on relevant problems within meaningful context using hands-on materials and activities.

Based on the research findings of these mathematics educators, the criteria for a mathematics curriculum should include mathematical experiences that are

1. **M**—motivational
2. **A**—authentic
3. **T**—thought provoking
4. **H**—hands on

A *motivational* approach to mathematics begins with personal involvement in a current, relevant, real-life problem set in a real-world context. Within this *authentic* context students are challenged to *think* about the problem and examine personal background knowledge concerning the issue. New information about the problem is assimilated into their current background knowledge thus broadening their knowledge base to create an expanded understanding of the problem. Within this framework, students examine the issue and implement a variety of *hands-on* strategies including concrete manipulatives, pictures, and mental imagery to solve the problem.

A developmental approach to mathematical competence and excellence is the *people and props, proxy, pictures, practice (PPPP) approach*. The PPPP approach includes four sequential steps in dealing with math problems:

1. **People and props:** Personal participation by students in mathematical problems is important. For example, when adding sets, students walk to the front of the classroom and model: *Three people plus two people equals five people.*
   Props or real objects are used in solving problems. For example, *You have a set of ten pretzels. You eat three pretzels. How many are left?*
2. **Proxy:** Objects that represent real people or things are used. For example, a circle may represent a pizza or a rectangle may represent a candy bar. Plastic lids from one-gallon milk containers may represent animals. A small butter tub will hold ten milk lids. Paper clips are tangible objects that may be used to represent people. For example, when dividing 120 paper clips among 6 students, 120 paper clips are placed on the table and then arranged in 6 equal sets: *120 paper clips divided by 6 equals 20 paper clips for each student.*
3. **Pictures:** Pictures or drawings of real objects are used.
4. **Practice:** Students manipulate symbols, calculate, and relate the practice to real-life situations.

The sequential PPPP approach enables students at all grade levels to understand a problem, represent a problem with manipulatives and pictures, and complete symbol manipulation.

In our world there is an ever-increasing need to make decisions based on mathematics. Real-life situations should provide the impetus to seek answers for these problems. Students need to develop *math cognition*, the ability to think about personal, mathematical problem-solving strategies and, through self-monitoring, to assess whether their approach to the problem is reasonable and makes sense. Math cognition is important in *estimation* as students must determine if their estimated answer to a problem is logical.

This chapter is *not* designed to teach students the mechanics of or how to do math. Rather, the emphasis is on strategies to actively involve students in meaningful, motivational real-world mathematical experiences that include participating in math scenarios, creating manipulatives, designing pictorial representations, and providing interesting challenges in problem solving. The five mathematics themes selected for this chapter are based on their universal importance and application across grade level curriculum. These themes are

1. Calculations and Computations (numbers and operations)
2. Fraction Fun (numbers and operations)

3. Dollars and Cents (economics)
4. Picture Perfect (geometry, graphing, and data analysis)
5. Measure Mania (measurement, time, and data analysis)

Artistic Adventures provide a variety of strategies for students to demonstrate and display their work. Ocular Organizers allow students to visualize mathematical relationships and information in graphic forms. Dramatic Debut involves students in real-life scenarios in which mathematics skill is essential. Creative Composition challenges students to think on paper, develop their own problems, and learn through writing about mathematical experiences.

Each Gamut of Games section includes opportunities for *every student participation (ESP)* in which all of the students in the class actively participate simultaneously in learning experiences. ESP activities provide opportunities for *shared math*, a mathematical experience in which a teacher and students work cooperatively to solve math problems. Advantages of ESP include the following:

1. Continuous, active involvement in learning
2. Reduced wait time as all students are participating
3. Immediate feedback as answers are available
4. Increased interest in lesson

Informal *assessment* is ongoing as teachers observe students participating in mathematical experiences and creating mathematical products.

CALCULATIONS AND COMPUTATIONS

Calculations are mathematical methods for determining through computation, reasoning, common sense, and practical experience answers to everyday mathematical dilemmas. These problems may be solved using *computation*: counting, estimating, and figuring to determine a mathematical answer to a problem. As students engage in calculations and computations, they need to know addition, subtraction, multiplication, and division facts. A *firm fact foundation (FFF)* should include addition and subtraction facts to 20 and multiplication facts through the 10 tables. An understanding of our *numeration system*, sets of symbols and rules for symbol combining, is essential in mathematical growth (Troutman & Lichtenberg, 1995).

Traditionally, a FFF was built on practice using the *dittos and drills approach* to learning. Students completed a seemingly endless flow of worksheets. If they were one of the fortunate few who completed a worksheet quickly, their reward was often another worksheet to complete. Procedures were practiced and memorized until they became routine. No wonder many students found math meaningless and tedious.

An alternative strategy for calculation and computation is using the people and props, proxy, pictures, practice (PPPP) approach. When teaching multiplication in second grade, I used the following activities:

Day 1—People and Props: Hula hoops were used to represent the number of sets, and students were used to represent the number of objects in each set. Thus: $3 \times 4 = \square$ was represented by three hula hoops on the floor, four students standing inside each hoop, and counting the number of students in all three hula hoops. *(Note: Hula hoops may be borrowed from the physical education teacher or made using an old garden hose.)*

Day 2—People and Proxy: After repeated experiences with hula hoops and people, students moved to the proxy step, using objects to represent real people or things. For $3 \times 4 = \square$, the students drew three hula hoops on their papers and then glued four gummed stars inside each hoop to represent the four people in each set.

Days 3 and 4—Proxy and Pictures: After repeated experiences with stars representing people, students moved to the picture step. For $3 \times 4 = \square$, the students drew three hula hoops on their papers and then drew four small pictures inside each hoop to represent four objects in each set.

Day 5—Practice: For $3 \times 4 = \square$, the students practiced symbol manipulation doing only five problems at a time. After completing five problems, they colored their answers with a yellow highlighter or a yellow crayon. Then they took their practice sheets to a designated answer station in the room and self-checked their answers. If the answers were correct, they could play a related math game. If the answers were incorrect, they attempted to locate the difficulty or sought the help of the teacher or a peer helper. Students also worked again with manipulatives and pictures before returning to symbol practice. *(Note: Once bad habits are established, they are very difficult to correct.)*

Artistic Adventures

Paper People Practice/Step Book

As students move through the people and props, proxy, pictures, practice (PPPP) stages, a variety of motivational artistic activities provide opportunities for students to develop a firm facts foundation (FFF) through creating proxy objects to manipulate and designing pictorial representations for real-world problems. *Paper people* (see Multiple Men in Activity Appendix A) are useful as proxy manipulatives in math. They may be used to represent the number of people in a set. For example, five rows of paper people with three people in each row represent $5 \times 3 = \square$.

Step books (see Activity Appendix A) with steps of alternating colors provide an exciting opportunity for students to draw pictures to visually represent mathematical numbers and problems. The step book may be organized in different ways. Two possibilities are

1. The answer to the problem appears on the step. The problem is written over the step and under the preceding flap.
2. The problem appears on the step. The solution to the problem and the means for solving the problem are written and illustrated over the step and under the preceding flap.

Literature-Based Examples

After sharing Over in the Meadow *(J Langstaff, 1957), students make step books for the story. Each step is numbered sequentially 1 through 10. The correct number of objects for each number is illustrated under the preceding step of the step book. For example, on page 1 students draw one mother turtle and one baby turtle. Students may compose a song innovation and publish the song in their step books. For example, the following is an innovation for the first verse in* "Over in the Meadow":

> Over in the school where students had fun
> Lived a nice, happy teacher, and her smart student one.
> "Learn," said the teacher.
> "I learn," said the one;
> So he learned and was glad, where students had fun.

Paper people may be used to represent characters in the story and song This Old Man *(P. Adams, 1992). The cutouts in the book provide interest and allow a motivational way to view equations. Number families are represented. On the "five" page there are the following equations: 4 + 1 = 5; 3 + 2 = 5; and 1 + 2 + 2 = 5. The book contains illustrations and equations up to 6. Students may continue the illustrations and equations. Older students may develop a "This Old Man" song and story innovations as well as paper people and pictures for larger numbers and more difficult equations. For example,*

> This old man, he had twenty.
> I know this is really plenty.
> With a nick, knack Paddy whack,
> Give a dog a bone.
> This old man came rolling home.

Paper people are applicable with *One Hundred Is a Family* by Pam M. Ryan (1994). Students use a paper person to represent one person in a family. Two paper people represent two family members and so on. The progression in the story with one additional person on each page continues until there are ten people in a family involved in a variety of activities. The progression then moves in groups of ten, thus the next page in the story deals with twenty people in a family. Students create paper people to represent immediate and extended families as well as examining an ever-expanding definition of the meaning of *family*.

Gamut of Games
Paper Clip Creations/Sticky Note Participation

Paper clips are used as manipulatives in the *proxy* (paper clips represent other objects) step of a math program. Sets of paper clips are used by each student in the class for every student participation (ESP). The advantages in using paper clips include that they are:

1. Readily available.
2. Inexpensive.
3. Easy to join and unjoin for addition and subtraction.
4. A hands-on activity for making chains used in grouping and regrouping (one chain contains ten paper clips).
5. Available in boxes that may be used to represent hundreds; a group of ten boxes represents 1,000.
6. Good visuals for equivalent sets for multiplication and division.
7. Visible on the overhead screen for shared math experiences with ESP.
8. Useful in meeting the needs of kinesthetic learners.
9. Easily stored as individual sets in self-sealing plastic bags.
10. Available in different colors and sizes.
11. Useful in proxy experiences to represent French bread pizza, candy, people, etc.
12. Available at home, so students may use the same manipulatives at home. When not available in the home, take-home kits could be available; or, as incentives, students could earn paper clips to take home.

In a shared math experience, both the students and teacher have paper clips. The teacher places her paper clips on the overhead. For the addition problem $2 + 3 = \square$, the teacher and each student count out a set of two paper clips and a set of three paper clips. Simultaneously, they join the paper clips and count aloud. For the addition problem $21 + 64 = \square$, the teacher and each student count out a set of 21 paper clips and a set of 64 paper clips. Together, they join the paper clips and count aloud.

After determining that counting 85 individual paper clips takes a lot of time, students discover that making chains of ten paper clips provides greater ease in counting. A *chain* is a set of ten paper clips joined together to represent one 10. When several chains (or sets of ten) are shown on the overhead, they may be counted and then placed in a clear cup to conserve space. The purpose of using a clear cup is to allow students to see each chain of paper clips.

Paper clips are especially useful in working with regrouping in addition and subtraction. Hyde and Bizar (1989) suggest that students use a variety of creative approaches in thinking about and solving computational problems as opposed to a single, traditional procedure. For example, when contemplating the subtraction problem $42 - 27 = \square$, examine and solve the equation by answering one of the following questions:

- **How many do I have left?** I have 42 paper clips. I use 27 clips. How many do I have left?
  Step 1: Place four chains and two clips on a desk.
  Step 2: Check and discover that in order to use 27 clips, one chain must be unclipped.
  Step 3: Unclip one chain (there are now three chains and twelve clips).
  Step 4: Remove two chains and seven clips.
  Step 5: Count how many are left to determine that there are one chain and five paper clips or fifteen paper clips left. (see Figure 6.1) *(Note: Emphasize unclipping as this enables students to understand regrouping.)*
- **How many more do I have?** Emelora has 42 paper clips. Ginger has 27 paper clips. How many more paper clips does Emelora have than Ginger?
  Step 1: Place four chains and two clips on a desk.
  Step 2: Place two chains and seven clips on a desk.

FIGURE 6.1   How many do I have left?

$$42$$
$$-27$$

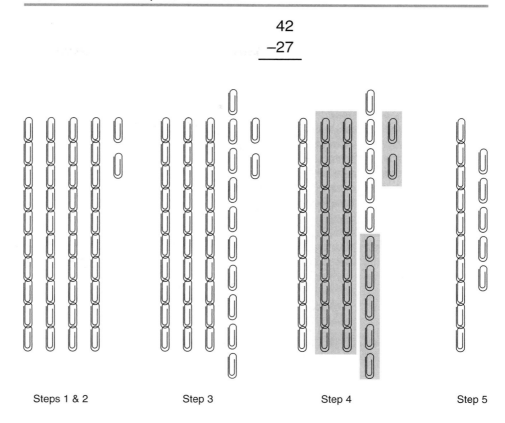

Steps 1 & 2   Step 3   Step 4   Step 5

Step 3: Check and discover that in order to match 42 to 27, one chain in the 42 must be unclipped.

Step 4: Unclip one chain of the 42 (there are now three chains and twelve clips for the 42).

Step 5: Match and remove seven single clips from each set.

Step 6: Match and remove two chains from each set.

Step 7: Count to determine that Emelora has one chain and five clips or fifteen paper clips more than Ginger (see Figure 6.2).

● **How many more do I need?** Cloud has 27 paper clips. She needs 42 paper clips. How many more does she need?

Step 1: Place four chains and two clips on a desk.

Step 2: Place two chains and seven clips on a desk.

Step 3: Check and discover that in order to match forty two to twenty seven, one chain in the forty two must be unclipped.

Step 4: Unclip one chain of the forty two (there are now three chains and twelve clips for the forty two).

Step 5: Pair the single clips from each set.

Step 6: Pair the chains from each set.

Step 7: Count to determine that Cloud needs one more chain and five clips, or fifteen more paper clips to complete the pairs (see Figure 6.3).

Literature-Based Examples

After reading One Hundred Hungry Ants *(Pinczes, 1993), students use paper clips to represent ants in the story. They line up their 100 paper clips. Then as the story is read, they chain their 100 paper clips to represent two lines each with fifty ants. Eventually, they*

FIGURE 6.2   How many more do I have?

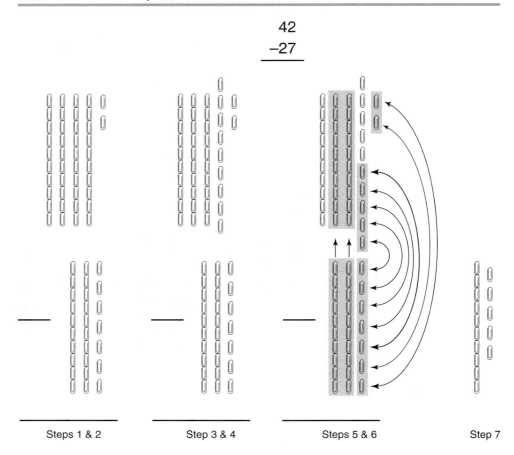

Steps 1 & 2   Step 3 & 4   Steps 5 & 6   Step 7

regroup their ants into four lines of twenty-five. After some more regrouping, the ants end up in rows of ten. Students will enjoy the story as well as the opportunity to experience division kinesthetically.

Senefer: A Young Genius in Old Egypt (Lumpkin, 1991), introduces students to the history of mathematics and mathematical symbols. As they read about Senefer, they use small paper clips to represent strokes and a large paper clip to represent ten strokes or one ten. An even larger clip is used to represent 100. Students will enjoy the mathematical challenges presented in the book.

Sticky Note Participation

Students each get ten sheets of sticky note paper and make a set of participation sticky notes, by writing numbers from 0 to 9, one number on each of the sticky notes. These sticky notes, are placed in a row across the top of the desk. A second set of participation sticky notes, may be created to allow answers such as 33 or 144. As students sing math ditties, they decide the correct answer to a math question in the song and move the appropriate sticky note/s down. Examples of math ditty experiences include:

Title: Matter-of-Fact Math*
Tune: "Frere Jacques" or "Are You Sleeping?"

3 times 4; 4 times 3; Equals 12; Equals 12
3 times 4; 4 times 3; Equals 12; Equals 12

(Note: Student has sticky notes "1" and "2" moved down and side by side to make 12. Participation innovations continue with verses for addition, subtraction, and division.)

FIGURE 6.3   How many more do I need?

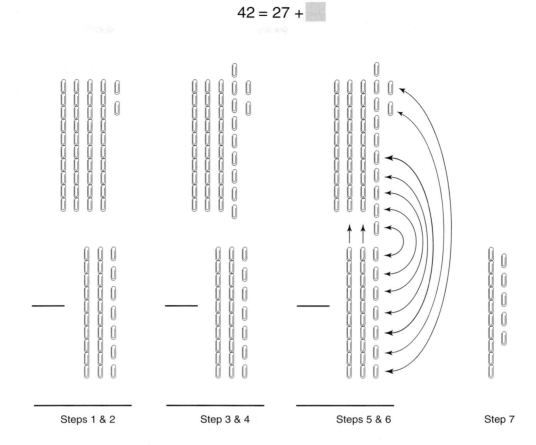

$$42 = 27 + \blacksquare$$

Steps 1 & 2   Step 3 & 4   Steps 5 & 6   Step 7

Title: Marvelous Math*
Tune: "Saints Go Marching In"
Oh 10 minus 7; oh 10 minus 7
Oh 10 minus 7 equals 3
I know my subtraction facts
Now that is plain to see.

(Note: stickynote "3" has been moved.)

Literature-Based Example

Ready to tackle a more challenging problem? Coordinate a literature selection, math manipulatives, and a familiar tune to create a math ditty. For example, after reading, The Doorbell Rang *by Pat Hutchins (1986), for math manipulatives use small circles as cookies and move at appropriate times while singing:*

Title: Divide and Conquer
Tune: "This Old Man"

Mom made cookies. We must share.
She had one dozen there.
We will each get 6 to eat.
They are really a neat treat.

The doorbell rang. Two friends came.
We must share and have the same.

We will each get 3 to eat.
They are really a neat treat.
(continue innovation)

How about a Math Mania Celebration on the 100ᵗʰ day of school? Create or collect 100 manipulatives. For a number of exciting math ideas, check out The 100ᵗʰ Day of School *(Medearis & Holub, 1996).*

Title: We Won One Hundred
Tune: "When Johnny Comes Marching Home"
The days go marching one by one, Hurrah! Hurrah!
The days go marching one by one, Hurrah! Hurrah!
We'll count pennies as the days go by
We'll substitute dimes and heave a big sigh
And we'll never cry when the days go marching by.

(Note: Change lines 3 and 4 to include other classroom "100" activities.)

Ocular Organizer

Town House Math

Reading and representing large numbers correctly is a challenge students face as they move up through the grades. Creating and working with town houses (see town house with notches in Activity Appendix A) enables students to meet this challenge with confidence. After making a set of four town houses, label the townhouses with family names from right to left: *Units, Thousands, Millions,* and *Billions.* Each town house has three driveways. Label the driveways for each town house from right to left *Ones, Tens,* and *Hundreds.* Beginning on the right side of the number, line up the digits in groups of three with a space or comma between each grouping. Read the number from left to right. For example, 12365487293 is organized as 12 365 487 293. Each of the numbers is lined up on a driveway of the town houses. The number reads, twelve billion, three hundred sixty-five million, four hundred eighty-seven thousand, two hundred ninety-three.

For convenience in reading large numbers use individual number squares or cut $1\frac{1}{2}'' \times 2''$ sticky note paper in half ($1'' \times 1\frac{1}{2}''$). Make one or more number sets (see sticky note possibilities earlier in the chapter) writing single digits from 0 to 9 on each sticky note strip. Place number squares or sticky note strips on each of the driveways. Thus, 12 365 487 293 is represented by the town house and numbers in Figure 6.4.

FIGURE 6.4   Town House Math

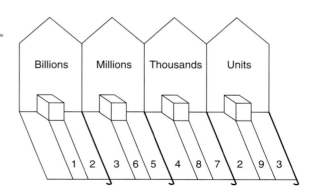

Literature-Based Examples

After sharing Anno's Mysterous Multiplying Jar *(Anno & Anno, 1983), using their town houses, students write and read numbers represented by factorials in the book. For example, there are 7! or 7 factorial rooms in the houses. 7! is $1 \times 2 \times 3 \times 4 \times 5 \times 6 \times 7 = 5{,}040$ rooms or five thousand forty rooms. There are 10! jars or 3,628,800 jars or three million, six hundred twenty-eight thousand, eight hundred jars.*

After reading How Much Is a Million? *(Schwartz, 1985), students write and read the numbers (or line up the numbers) on each driveway for information given in the author's notes. For example, one million gallons of water is equal to 133,333 cubic feet of water, which reads one hundred thirty-three thousand, three hundred thirty-three feet.*

Dramatic Debut

Card Capers/Card Caper Corner

Card Capers are card games that allow players to practice symbol manipulation in a variety of card games some of which require computations and calculations. Using cards in the practice step of the people and props, proxy, pictures, practice (PPPP) approach to math has many advantages. Cards are

1. Readily available.
2. Inexpensive.
3. Motivational.
4. Available at home as well as school.
5. Easily stored in self-sealing bags.

(Note: If commercial decks of playing cards are incongruent with community or family values or are not readily available, use index cards on which suits are circles, squares, rectangles, and triangles).

A *card caper corner* is a corner setting in a classroom that is decorated with large *card suit shapes*, black clubs and spades and red hearts and diamonds. Red and black streamers are draped across the corner to add atmosphere. A card table (check garage sales) is set up for groups of four players. An old TV tray or small table covered with red and black contact paper and decorated with old playing cards covered with clear contact paper provides a playing surface for pairs of players.

Card capers allow integration of language arts and math as students perfect their *card cabulary*, terminology related to card games. Display card cabulary on the suit shapes. Card cabulary words that might appear on these shapes include the following: ace, deal, dealer, deck, discard, draw, pack, face cards, face down, jack, king, pair, queen, round, shuffle, solitaire, suit, tie, wild cards. Many of these words have multiple meanings. For example, "suit" could mean slacks or a skirt with a jacket or a set of cards in either hearts, diamonds, spades, or clubs. Card cabulary phrases that could be displayed include the following: *cut the deck, he's a card, in the cards, play one's cards, play our cards right, put our cards on the table, I have another card to play.*

Choices of card capers for the classroom are based on age appropriateness, grade level curriculum, and students' interest. Face cards (jacks, queens, and kings) may be removed from the deck for some card capers or counted as 10 points each. Aces may be removed from the deck or counted as 1 or 11. Jokers may be removed from the deck or used as wild cards. Card capers with directions include the following:

Sift and Sort

Game Goal: Sort cards based on a given attribute.

Directions: Younger students may sift and sort cards in several ways including:

1. Sort by color (all red and all black).
2. Sort by the number or letter on the cards (group all 2s, 3s, jacks).

3. Sort by suit (all spades, clubs, diamonds, hearts).
4. Sort by suit and arrange in numerical order.

Can You Top This?

Game Goal: Player with the largest number of cards wins and becomes the dealer.

Dealer's Directions:

1. Remove jokers from the deck.
2. Deal all cards in the deck equally to all players.

Players' Directions:

1. Place your cards in a stack face down.
2. Turn over your top card.
3. The player with the highest number wins all the cards. If there is a tie, the players who are tied turn over a second card to determine the winner of all the cards.
4. Continue playing until all cards are played.
5. The player with the most cards wins and becomes the dealer.

Variations

1. **Addition:** Each player turns over two cards and adds the two numbers on the cards together. The player with the highest sum wins all the cards.
2. **Multiplication:** Each player turns over two cards and multiplies the two numbers on the cards together. The player with the highest product wins all the cards.
3. **One Won (Subtraction):** Each player turns over two cards and subtracts the number on the second card from the number on the first card. The number closest to 1 wins the cards. For example,
   Player 1 turns over 6 and 3.
   Player 1's difference is 3.
   Player 2 turns over a 9 and a jack (10).
   Player 2's difference is −1.
   Player 2 is closer to 1 and wins all the cards.
   Note: A number line is helpful for this game.
   Younger students may subtract the smaller number from the larger number. The student with the largest difference wins all the cards.

Cardcentration

Game Goal: Player with the largest number of cards wins and becomes the dealer.

Dealer Directions: Spread the cards out on the table face down.
Player Directions:

1. Player 1 turns over two cards.
2. If the cards have the same number, you have a match and win the pair.
3. If the cards do not match, turn them face down, and try to remember where the cards are located.
4. Player 2 turns over two cards and tries to have a matching pair.
5. Continue taking turns and playing until all cards have been matched in pairs.
6. The player with the most cards wins the game and becomes the dealer.

Variation

1. **Equivalent Equationtration:** Cover the face of each card with a small piece of construction paper and laminate. Write an equation on the face of each card. Follow the directions for cardcentration and make matching pairs. For example:

$$3 + 2 = \square, \text{ and } 4 + 1 = \square$$

$$9 \times 8 = \square, \text{ and } 2 \times 4 \times 9 = \square$$

$$20 \times 4 + (5 \times 4) = \square \text{ and } 80 + 20 = \square$$

Other Possibilities

There are a variety of books available explaining card games including *Crazy Eights and Other Card Games* (Cole & Calmenson, 1994).

Creative Composition

Math Log/Thumbprint Thoughts

"Children who process subject matter by writing learn to think in that discipline" (Noyce & Christie, 1989, p. 253). Thinking on paper provides students an opportunity for organizing their thoughts. A math log provides a place for this writing and thinking. A *math log* is a journal in which students record mathematical information including math terms, math algorithms (steps for problem solving), and math story problems. Students often devise their own story problems to demonstrate authentic, real-world application of computation and calculation skills being discussed in class. They relate these stories to their own personal experiences as well as to theme and literature classroom focus. Students often create their personal stories in a riddle format in an attempt to stump their friends. Story problems are an integral and essential component of a math program and not an *add on*.

One possibility for making a math log is using the journal jacket technique (see Activity Appendix A). Commercially available spiral bound notebooks are also useful as math logs. A simple math log may be constructed using a folded piece of construction paper for a cover with paper stapled between the covers.

Thumbprint thoughts may be expressed using thumbprint illustrations. Thumbprint art is an easy way for even the most reluctant artist to illustrate math problems. *Ed Emberley's Great Thumbprint Drawing Book* (1977) is an invaluable resource for drawing people, animals, bugs, birds, and a myriad of other creatures.

Literature-Based Examples

After sharing The Very Hungry Caterpillar *by Eric Carle (1969), younger students use thumbprints to make the caterpillar as well as to represent the fruit eaten by the hungry caterpillar. Make a story innovation in which the hungry caterpillar eats a different vegetable each day. Make the vegetables with thumbprints. Create story problems and illustrate with thumbprints. For example, the hungry caterpillar ate three pieces of fruit on Wednesday and four pieces of fruit on Thursday. How many pieces of fruit did he eat altogether on these two days? These story innovations and story problems are entered in math logs.*

With older students, read A Grain of Rice *by Helena Pittman (1986), in which a farmer convinces the emperor of China to allow him to marry the princess after he all but bankrupts the kingdom. The farmer uses his mathematical wisdom in asking for only a grain of rice for curing the princess of an unknown disease. However, at the emperor's insistence, he suggests that the amount of rice be doubled every day for a hundred days. Thumbprint people are made to represent the characters in the story. Using thumbprints to represent each grain of rice, students will quickly discover the enormous amount of rice required.*

FRACTION ACTION

Fractions are an important part of everyday life. They are used in counting money, telling time, measuring fabric, indicating the amount of ingredients in recipes, and many other everyday situations. *Fractions* are names for:

1. **Parts of Whole Objects**
   Carmen, Lei Ling, and Roberto equally share a pizza.
   How much pizza will each person receive?
   Answer: One-third

2. **Parts of a Set of Objects**
   There are six people, and three of the people order tortillas for lunch. What fraction of the people ordered tortillas for lunch?
   Answer: Three-sixths

The possibilities for providing meaningful, hands-on experiences with fractions are abundant. Pizzas, pies, tortillas (flat, round pieces of bread), candy bars, paper pies, and fraction bars are easily cut into *equivalent pieces*, pieces of the same size. These items provide real and proxy manipulatives for *parts of whole objects*. People, popcorn, paper clips, pom-poms, M&Ms®, and paper people (see Multiple Men in Activity Appendix A) are grouped into *equivalent sets*, sets of the same size. These items provide real and proxy manipulatives for *parts of a set of objects*.

Students often face situations in which they are not given a *fair share*. The importance of dividing a whole object into equivalent parts may be emphasized by dividing a paper pizza into three unequal parts and distributing the pizza to three students. Ask the student with the largest piece, "Are you satisfied with your share of the pizza?" Ask the student with the smallest piece, "Are you satisfied with your share of the pizza?" Ask the class, "Is this a *fair share*? How could we make each piece of pizza a *fair share*?"

To demonstrate the importance of dividing a set of objects into equivalent sets, repeat the experience with popcorn that is unequally divided into three cups. Give one student a cup that is overflowing with popcorn, another student a cup that is half full of popcorn, and a third student a cup with a couple of pieces of popcorn. Ask each of the students, "Are you satisfied with your share of the popcorn?" Ask the class, "Is this a fair share? How could we distribute the popcorn fairly?"

Artistic Adventures

Parts Pictures

Parts pictures are pictures made from shapes and equivalent parts of shapes arranged and attached to a backdrop. These shapes may be circles, squares, rectangles, triangles, or other shapes. A die-cut machine is a time-saver when cutting shapes. Be creative and experiment with a variety of colors.

To make equivalent parts, the initial shape is folded in half or thirds one or more times and cut. For younger students, precut equivalent parts. To make parts pictures the following are possibilities:

1. Use one shape and equivalent parts of that shape. For example, use one or more circles (see Figure 6.5).
2. Use two or more different shapes and equivalent parts of these shapes. For example, use circles, squares, and equivalent parts of these shapes (see Figure 6.6).
3. Make a picture using a given number of shapes. Any of the shapes may be cut into equivalent parts. For example, make a picture using one-fourth of a large circle, three squares, and three hexagons (see Figure 6.7).

Guide students in listing the number of whole shapes and equivalent parts of the shape that are used. Add the parts together to determine the fraction for the total number of shapes used. For example, create a picture using a circle and equivalent parts of a circle. Make a list of the parts used and determine the resulting fraction.

1 Circle

2 Half-circles

3 One-fourth circles

_____

2¾ Circles used

FIGURE 6.5 Parts Pictures: One Shape and Equivalent Parts of that Shape

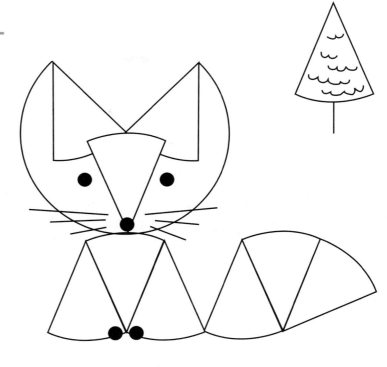

FIGURE 6.6 Parts Pictures: Circles, Squares, and Equivalent Parts of These Shapes

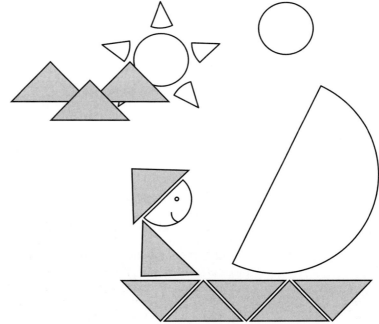

Literature-Based Example

After sharing Ed Emberley's Picture Pie: A Circle Drawing Book *by Ed Emberley (1984), make parts pictures using circles and parts of circles. Relate the pictures to a classroom thematic unit. If the class is studying oceans, experiment with fish pictures. If the class is learning the song "Old MacDonald Had a Farm," make barnyard animals. Expand on Emberley's suggestions and artistic innovations by encouraging students to invent their own parts pictures.*

FIGURE 6.7   Parts Pictures: One-Fourth of a Circle,
Three Squares, and Three Hexagons

Gamut of Games

Parts of Whole Objects/Parts of a Set of Objects

Without grasping math fundamentals, students are unable to progress to the next level of math comprehension. Every student participation (ESP) in the math content area is effective in its ability to provide teachers and students with immediate feedback. Teachers will know whether their students are understanding and progressing in math basics. The following ESP experiences with fractions provide active participation with manipulatives and provide motivational learning experiences.

Teach *parts of whole objects* with pies made from paper, felt, or flannel. Make individual sets of pies using the following color scheme:

1. One whole pie (green for key lime pie)
2. Two pie halves (red for cherry pie)
3. Four pie quarters (yellow for lemon pie)
4. Eight pie eighths (blue for blueberry pie)
5. Three pie thirds (pink for strawberry pie)
6. Six pie sixths (brown for chocolate pie)
7. Twelve pie twelfths (orange for peach pie)

Note: Fraction bars may be made from rectangles of construction paper using the same color scheme.

The number of fractional pies in each individual set is determined by grade level, student ability, and the mathematics curriculum. As students progress in fraction study, pies are added to the individual sets. Label each pie with its fractional name (e.g., each pink pie piece is labeled 1/3). Store individual paper pie sets in self-sealing plastic bags.

During ESP, each student places pie pieces on a sheet of black construction paper or a file folder. The black paper or file folder provides a work area as well as a contrasting background on which the pieces are easily seen. Better yet, cover one side of a file folder with black felt and use as a work area. The other side of the file folder may be covered with chalkboard contact paper, thus making a reversible chalkboard/felt board.

During a shared math experience, the teacher has a set of transparency pie pieces that follow the same color scheme as the paper pies. These pieces are placed on the overhead to demonstrate the use of paper pies and to provide immediate feedback to students.

Literature-Related Example

Teacher: "How many thirds of a pie are equal to one whole pie?"
Student: (Places three pink thirds together to form a whole pie.)
Teacher: "Which is larger, two-thirds or three-fourths of a pie?"

Student:	(Places two pink thirds on top of three yellow fourths to determine that three-fourths is larger.)
Teacher:	"There is three-fourths of a pizza. Two-thirds of the pizza is eaten. How much of the pizza is left?"
Student:	(Places three yellow pie fourths. Places two pink thirds on top of the three yellow fourths. Determines that one orange twelfth will cover the remaining space on the yellow fourths.)
	"One-twelfth of the pizza is left."

Teach *parts of a set of objects* using four popular manipulatives: paper clips, popcorn, pom-poms, and M&Ms®.

The appeal of these items is that they are easily divided into equal sets. Pom-poms work especially well on felt and flannel boards.

Literature-Based Example

Teacher:	"We have just finished reading *The M & M's® Brand Chocolate Candies Counting Book* (McGrath, 1994). Let's practice. You have 12 M&Ms. Share your M&Ms equally among six friends. How many M&Ms will each friend get?"
Student:	Divides M&Ms into six piles.
	Determines that each person has two M&Ms.
	Determines that each person will get 2/12 or 1/6 of the M&Ms.

Note: Repeat experience with 12 M&Ms divided equally among three people, four people, and two people.

 Ocular Organizers

Pie Quivalent Wall Chart/Money Quivalent Wall Chart

Equivalent fractions are two or more fractions that name the same number. For example, 2/8, 4/16, and 8/32 are all fractions that name 1/4. Students will enjoy creating a *pie quivalent wall chart*, a large chart that shows equivalent fractions using paper pies made from construction paper (see Figure 6.8). Cut out pies from construction and label each piece with the fractional name.

A *candy bar quivalent wall chart* is a large chart that shows equivalent fractions using candy bars (fraction bars) made from construction paper and following the same color scheme as the paper pies.

Literature-Based Example

Develop a money quivalent wall chart, a chart that displays equivalents for different fractional amounts of money after reading Fraction Action *by Loreen Leedy (1994). In this book, Tally reduces the price of lemonade by one-fourth of a dollar or 25 cents. This amount could be displayed as one quarter, five nickels, two dimes and one nickel, one dime and three nickels, and various combinations with pennies.*

Large brown and gray circles of appropriate sizes may be labeled as penny, nickel, dime, and quarter. Display money quivalents for other fractional parts of a dollar (e.g., 1/2 dollar, 3/4 dollar, etc.). For individual money quivalent charts use money stamps to represent individual amounts of money.

 Dramatic Debut

Culinary Creations

Many thematic and literature-based units in the curriculum incorporate cooking and math experiences. A multicultural thematic unit might include recipes from many ethnic groups.

FIGURE 6.8   Pie Quivalent Wall Chart

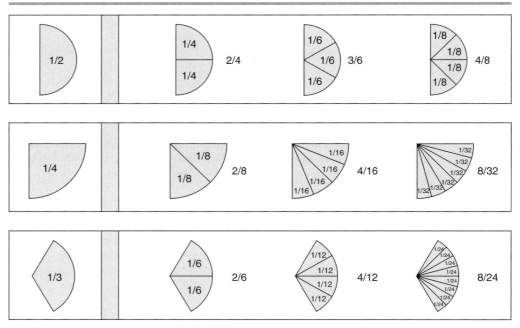

Making tacos is motivational when studying Mexico. A focus on friendship could result in a *friendship salad*, a fruit salad to which each student makes a contribution. The folktale *Stone Soup* by Marcia Brown (1947) lends itself to a crockpot full of vegetable soup. Cut the vegetables so that students add 1 1/2 carrots, 1 1/4 onions, and so forth. Holiday occasions provide abundant opportunities to prepare food. A Thanksgiving feast planned by all the fourth-grade classes in a school invites each class to contribute one dish to the celebration. Even an unbirthday party based on *Alice's Adventures in Wonderland* by Lewis Carroll (1866, 1986) provides opportunities to prepare refreshments.

"*Culinary Creations*" is a television show designed to demonstrate the preparation of culinary creations for the connoisseur of gourmet cuisine. "Culinary Creations" provides students with opportunities to cook as well as eat. What better way to have authentic, real-world experiences with fractions than to train as a chef and create culinary masterpieces? Recipes provide practical, progressive experiences for working with fractions in *doing*, *doubling*, and *dividing*. Younger students follow the recipe exactly, thus they are *doing*. Directions may be written in rebus form. Older students increase or decrease portions thus they are *doubling* and *dividing*.

Participants on "Culinary Creations" wear chef hats made from white construction paper. Provide aprons made from used shirts and blouses. Use pinking sheers to remove the sleeves and collars.

Safety is a special consideration in "Culinary Creations" because a source of heat is likely to be used. Solicit the cooperation of the cafeteria staff. If this is not possible, place crockpots and tabletop ovens in a workroom away from students or with the cords safely tucked and taped behind tables. Another alternative is the microwave oven. There are many no-bake recipes that do not require heat, and they are especially good choices for younger students.

Literature-Based Example

Chef Franquez:

Welcome to "Culinary Creations." I, Chef Franquez, a graduate of the Chefs' Institute of Culinary Arts, am proud to tell you that you are about to view a unique television show designed for the most sophisticated connoisseurs of gourmet cuisine both here and abroad. "Culinary Creations" caters to the gourmet with a refined palate.

Chef Yan

Chefs on "Culinary Creations" tastefully prepare the most delectable dishes. Of course, all the chefs participating on "Culinary Creations" are trained at the Chefs' Institute of Culinary Arts. Our chefs use only the finest ingredients, the most sophisticated baking terminology, and the most accurate measuring utensils. Each measuring cup and measuring spoon is carefully calibrated to measure precisely. To prepare our culinary masterpieces, I have in front of me not one, not two, not three, but four, count them, FOUR, of the finest measuring cups in the world. Here, too, is a set of the world's most accurate measuring spoons. At "Culinary Creations" we use only the BEST!

Chef Perez:

Chef training at the Chef's Institute of Culinary Arts involves many hours of specialized instruction. Apprentice chefs develop skills in careful and accurate measuring of liquids so as not to spill even a drop. They also learn to double and even quadruple recipes. For smaller servings, they practice dividing recipes in half so as not to waste even a bit of the expensive, exotic, imported ingredients. They become culinary artists and can divide hors d'oeuvres so that 144 delectable peanut-butter stuffed celery bites, 60 flaky honey croissants, and 120 delicious gummy worms are evenly divided and artistically arranged on twelve silver serving trays. At graduation, chefs receive special chefs' hats and aprons as symbols of their ability to create culinary masterpieces.

Chef Ottanelli:

As you can see, we have several graduates of our institute ready to prepare a delicious, delectable delicacy for you. Each of these graduates is capable of preparing culinary masterpieces that range from hors d'oeuvres to entrees to desserts. You may request any delicacy, and they will prepare it for you.

Chef O'Sullivan:

We have had a request from our audience. They wish our chefs to tastefully prepare our world famous Delicious Dirt, a recipe created by gourmet chefs, Marlene Beierle and Teri Lynes (1992), for *Book Cooks: Literature-Based Classroom Cooking*. This culinary creation is just one of many delightful dining delights for Worms-a-la-Wow, our personal collection of inspirational worm cuisine creations to accompany *How to Eat Fried Worms* by chef Thomas Rockwell (1993). Chefs, are you ready?

All Chefs:

We are ready!

Note: Recipes for younger students may be written in rebus form with the amount of each ingredient indicated with fraction shapes (i.e., 1 cup with a picture of one cup and 1/2 cup with a picture of a half cup).

Creative Composition
Cookbooks/A Secret Ingredient Cake Shape Cookbook

Students make individual, class, and school cookbooks as they focus on measuring proportionate amounts of ingredients for recipes. Sources of recipes include favorite home recipes, cookbooks, and creative innovations of real or imaginary recipes. Individual recipes may be written on a step book (see Activity Appendix A). A class cookbook is a compilation of favorite recipes from each student in the class. A school cookbook includes favorite recipes from all the teachers and staff at the school including the principal, media specialist, cafeteria workers, coaches, secretaries, and custodians. The journal jacket technique (see Activity Appendix A) or a spiral plastic binding machine may be used to make the cookbooks.

Shape book cookbooks are fun (see Shape Books in Activity Appendix A). For example, cookie recipes may be compiled in a cookie shape cookbook. Multiple copies of class cookbooks and school cookbooks make wonderful holiday gifts.

Literature-Based Example

Share The High Rise Glorious Skittle Skat Roarious Sky Pie Angel Food Cake *(HRGSSRSPAFC) by Nancy Willard (1990). Discuss the importance of the secret ingredient that is hidden in a special place and written in code (mirror image). Make a step book for the angel food cake recipe with six steps that include:*

> **Title Page**
> **Step 1:** Collect and measure ingredients
> **Step 2:** Beat egg whites until...
> **Step 3:** Continue beating until...
> **Step 4:** Fold in...
> **Step 5:** Add the* secret ingredient
>
> **EVOL-EVOL-EVOL**
>
> **Step 6:** Bake

Follow this activity by constructing a secret ingredient cake shape cookbook. Encourage students to bring favorite cake recipes with secret ingredients to school. Compile the recipes into a class secret ingredient cake shape cookbook. Write each secret ingredient in code and hide it somewhere within the book. For example, the secret ingredient in one recipe might be,

SGUH-SGUH-SGUH

Another recipe might refer the reader to a different page number to find the secret ingredient. For example, look on page 14 to find the secret ingredient for this recipe. On page 14, the reader would find,

RETHGUAL-RETHGUAL-RETHGUAL

DOLLARS AND CENTS: ECONOMICS

Dollars and cents sense, an understanding of our money system, is essential in everyday life. Students have daily experiences with money in real-life situations as they shop for groceries, clothes, and toys. Do they understand the value of coins and paper money when paying the bill at a convenience store or a fast food restaurant? Can they count out the correct amount of money for a purchase and be sure they receive the correct change? Are they able to shop wisely and make cost comparisons? Students often hear and ask questions such as (1) How much does this cost? (2) Is this a good price? (3) Do I have enough money?

There are many opportunities to provide authentic money experiences for students. Some schools have implemented a banking system with personal checking and savings accounts. Students earn play money that they deposit into their accounts. The money may be earned for successful completion of academic assignments as well as outstanding behavior. There is a school store where students spend the money they have earned. Other schools have implemented a stock market investment plan in which students receive a given amount of play money to invest in the stock market. Students keep records of their gains and losses in the market.

Students enjoy researching the history of our money system. There are a number of books that present this information in an interesting and informative manner. *The Go-Around Dollar* by Barbara Johnston Adams (1992) contains information on the symbols, seals, and pictures on both the front and back of the dollar bill. There is also information on how money is made and circulated. Each double-page spread in the book contains a fictional story involving the trip a single dollar bill makes as it travels from person to person as well as a separate section with facts about the dollar bill. *The Story of Money* by Betsy Maestro (1993) explains the history of the bartering system in trading for goods and services, some of the problems involved in bartering, the development of our metal and paper money system, and the use of credit cards and checking accounts. In this information book, as well as in *If You Made a Million* (1989) by David Schwartz and *Eyewitness Books: Money* by Joe Cribb (1990), there are many interesting historical and current facts about money along with supportive illustrations.

Note: See Chapter 8 for Sleuth Station and Case Costs. The difficulty of case cost math problems is determined by the grade-level math curriculum and the developmental appropriateness for the student; Sleuth Cyclers—grade/developmental level appropriate math problems are related to recycling.

Artistic Adventures

Pop-Up Pleaser/Holiday and Twelve-Month Pop-Up Pleasers

Design a *pop-up pleaser*, a pop-up book with different items mounted on the notches on each page (see Pop-Up Techniques in Activity Appendix A). Design a *holiday pop-up pleaser*, a multipage pop-up book for a selected holiday in which each successive page has an increasing number of items on the notches. Each item has a monetary value. Sources of pictures for the notches include catalogues, newspaper advertisements, junk mail, and coloring the items on small pieces of paper.

Students may work in cooperative groups to design a holiday pop-up pleaser. Each group designs one or two pages for the book. Younger students plan a page for each day and focus on increasing the number of items in each set by one. Intermediate and middle grade students get so excited about this project that they often prefer to develop their own personal books. They enjoy keeping a running total of the amount of money being spent. They are also able to develop story problems such as the following:

If the item on Day 1 cost $4.95 and the items on Day 2 cost $3.99 each, how much money is spent on these two days? If a 20-dollar bill and a 5-dollar bill are used to make the purchases, how much change will the buyer receive?

Literature-Based Example

After learning the tune for "The Twelve Days of Christmas," students create a song innovation and design a holiday pop-up pleaser. The song with appropriate pictures on the notches for days one and two might include:

Page 1: On the first *holiday*, my true love gave to me *a ruby red racing bike.*
Notch: Picture of bike
Cost of bike is written below or under the notch.

Page 2: On the second *holiday*, my true love gave to me *two Grand Prix cars and a ruby red racing bike.*
Notch: Picture of two Grand Prix cars.
Cost of one bicycle, two Grand Prix cars, and running total of items for day 1 and day 2 is written below or under the notch.
Note: Continue sequence for days 3-12.
The number of days may vary. Holiday names such as Christmas, Hanukkah, and Kwanzaa may be substituted in place of the term, "holiday."

In The Money Tree *by Sarah Stewart (1991), Miss McGillicuddy allows friends and strangers to share in her bountiful wealth from the money tree that grows in her yard. The story focuses on months of the year, sharing, and contentment. As students discuss the value of sharing throughout the year, they compose a song innovation and a* twelve-month pop-up pleaser *such as*

Page 1: On the first day of January, we gave to the homeless *a gigantic, roasted turkey.*
Notch: Picture of turkey.
Cost of the turkey is written below the notch.

Page 2: On the second day of February, we gave to the homeless *two cherry pies and a gigantic, roasted turkey.*
Notch: Pictures of the cherry pies.
Cost of turkey, two pies, and a running total is written below the notch.
Note: *Continue sequence for March through December.*

Gamut of Games
Bingo

An opportunity for every student participation (ESP) with money is a bingo variation. In this game students use commercial bingo cards. Each problem includes students' names in real-world situations, and the difficulty of the problems is based on grade level as well as students' ability. Immediate feedback is available when students give answers to the problems. All students in the class are involved simultaneously in playing the game, and motivation is high and often noisy.

Literature-Based Example

After reading A Chair for My Mother *by Vera Williams (1982), a story about a family saving money to replace a chair that was burned up in a fire, the students and teacher make up questions about the money. The students answer the questions by putting bingo chips on the correct answers on their bingo cards. The following questions are related to the story:*

Question 1: I earned $2.10 helping Josephine at the diner. I was paid in dimes. How many dimes did I put in the jar to save for a new chair? (answer: 21)
Question 2: My mother received a quarter and four dimes as a tip from one of the customers at the diner today. She is saving this money for our new chair. How much did she put in the jar? (65 cents)
Question 3: Grandma saved fifty cents on tomatoes and thirty-five cents on bananas. We put the money she saved into the jar. How much did she put into the jar? (85 cents)

Ocular Organizers
Cost Comparison Charts

Students are highly motivated to determine the best buy for fast food restaurants, pizza places, clothes, books, and games, especially when their allowances are making the purchases. A collection of catalogues, newspaper advertisements, brochures, and menus makes cost comparison motivational. Students make cost comparison charts to determine best buys. As they analyze prices on the chart, they will find that sometimes determining the *best buy* can be very challenging. However, if consumers want the most for their money, they must be willing to expend time and effort.

The following cost comparison chart allows students to determine best buys at three local fast food restaurants:

	Hamburger Haven	Hamburger Heaven	Hamburger Hut
1/4 lb. beef burger	0.99	1.25	1.00
Medium french fries	0.99	1.00	1.00
12-oz. soft drink	0.99	0.75	0.90
Combo: Burger, fries, & drink	2.89	2.95	2.75

Dramatic Debut
Dine 'n' Dash Diner

Are you discouraged, dissatisfied, and disgusted by dark, dirty, dismal diners? Are you depressed and despondent over dull dinner deals? Denounce despicable dining disasters! Demand dining delight! Based on dollars and cents sense, discriminating diners have determined that the Dine 'n' Dash Diner should be your dining destination. You deserve the best! At the Dine 'n' Dash Diner you get a dynamite dining deal! Dinners are designed to dazzle both your wallet and your palate. You have delightful, delectable dinners and desserts that don't cost you an arm and a leg! You will definitely decide that dickering and discounts are not necessary due to our ever-popular dining deals designed for those who desire to defeat high dining costs. Definitive studies declare our meals are priced at bare-bones cost. There is no dilly-dally in delivery of your dinners as our servers are trained to dash. At the Dine 'n' Dash Diner you defy soaring dinner costs, detect detailed determination to deliver your delicious dinner without delay, and devour divine delicacies.

Students will enjoy creating commercials for the Dine 'n' Dash Diner. A dictionary and thesaurus are indispensable resources in composition. Figurative language, such as "cost an arm and a leg" and "bare bones," adds interest and imagery. Use of *alliteration*, words beginning with the same initial sound, is an ear-catching, advertising technique. Words beginning with the "D" sound are used in the Dine 'n' Dash commercial.

Atmosphere for the Dine 'n' Dash restaurant is created by using tablecloths or placemats (watch garage sales or use bulletin board paper), napkins, centerpieces, background music, and menus. Menus are designed using samples from popular eating establishments as models. The trifold brochure and banner book (see Activity Appendix A) are suggested for menu-making. Attire for servers, cashiers, and cooks includes aprons, name tags, and perhaps hats made from construction paper. Order pads and calculators to compute the cost of the meals are authentic props that provide realistic math experiences.

Customers order meals that the servers write on order pads. The cost of the meal is computed and written on the pad. The customer must count out money to the server for the meal. The server counts out the money to the cashier. The cashier counts out change to the server. The server returns and counts out the change to the customer. Both the server and customer determine whether the amount of change is correct.

Design menus to allow cost comparison. Customers will determine whether it is more economical to order *à la carte* (each item priced individually), a complete meal, or the daily dinner special. Discussion will ensue about whether a beverage is worth the added cost or if water is a better choice. If the customer has only $10.00, is this enough to pay for a balanced meal? Older students compute the cost, tax, and tip. Younger students have menus that include the tax and tip in the price of the meal.

Literature-Based Example

In Pigs Will Be Pigs *by Amy Axelrod (1994), the pigs decide they are hungry, and they want to go out to eat. There is a problem: no money. The pigs search the house and find various amounts of money in different places. They then dine at the Enchanted Enchilada, choosing the daily dinner special listed on the menu, which is included in the book. Provide opportunities for students to calculate the following:*

1. How much money did the pigs find?
2. How much did the pigs pay for four daily dinner specials?
3. How much money did the pigs have left?
4. How much money did the pigs save by ordering the daily dinner special?
5. Select other meals for the pigs and calculate the cost.

6. Will the pigs need more money for these meals?
How much?

Using the pigs' escapades, dining experiences, and menus at the Enchanted Enchilada as a model, design dining experiences that require similar dollars and cents calculations.

Creative Composition
Money Memoirs/Money Memoirs Circle Story

Money memoirs are chronicles of memories and dreams about money the author used to have. Writing these memoirs enables the author to reflect on fame and fortune and provides a means by which to deposit memories and dreams into a treasury of past experiences. A bank account into which students deposit money terminology has words and phrases available for easy access and immediate withdrawal as needed for composition. Some of the money phrases on deposit include *a dollar saved is a dollar earned, a fool and his money are soon parted, cough up a dollar, fat cat, feel like two cents, flat broke, filthy rich, fritter away, high on the hog, hit the jackpot, keep the wolf away from the door, money burns a hole in your pocket, money doesn't grow on trees, on Easy Street, money's worth, rolling in money, salt away, strike it rich,* and *time is money.* On deposit are synonyms for money such as *bread, bucks, big bucks, cabbage, cash, chicken feed, currency, dinero, dough, gravy, greenbacks, jack, lettuce, loot, moolah, peanuts,* and *small potatoes.*

These memoirs may follow a given format such as:

1. I *used to be* rich when . . .
   But now I am . . .
   I *used to be* rich when I had a dollar,
   But now I spent my dollar, and I am broke.
2. I *used to be* broke and . . .
   But now I . . .
   I *used to be* broke and didn't have any money,
   But now I get an allowance and save my money.

Note: For added interest substitute "Once upon a time" for "I used to be."

A *money memoirs circle story* contains chronicles of memories and dreams about money the author used to have with a plot containing a series of events that end where they began. This circle story is composed and illustrated on a roll over and over book (see Activity Appendix A). For this activity the circle story is divided into a beginning event, six intervening events, and an ending event that stops at the same point in the plot as the beginning event. Illustrate monetary experiences using coin and dollar ink stamps. To retain a positive relationship with students' parents, be sure that ink-pads have washable ink, rather than permanent ink. Color-coding coins—for example, red for nickels and green for dimes—will stimulate interest and reinforce the value of each coin.

Literature-Based Example

Students create personal money memoirs circle stories for times when they used to be rich or times when they used to be broke. They keep a running total of the money spent and money left as the story progresses. Students examine ways to obtain money such as earning money, losing teeth, recycling, and receiving presents. They also determine ways to spend money.

Students will enjoy creating stories incorporating the names of their friends. The following is a money memoirs circle story that includes the names of professors who have had a significant impact on my life.

Page 1: Fran was flat, busted broke. She wanted to go to the school book fair but. . . . Just as she was bemoaning her fate, the mail arrived with a birthday card from her grandmother. Inside was a check for $20.

Page 2: Fran went to the book fair with her friends. Kathy pointed out two Newbery Award winners for $3.99 each. Fran bought them. ($12.02 left)

Page 3: On the way home from the book fair, she saw a yard sale at Dan's house. Evelyn pointed out three Caldecott Award winners for 25 cents each. What a bargain! Fran bought the three books. ($11.27 left)

Page 4: Her friend Janell suggested that they stop at the corner convenience store to get a soda and candy bar. The soda cost 59 cents and the candy bar was 48 cents. At this rate her birthday money was disappearing quickly. ($10.20 left)

Page 5: With a rapidly diminishing supply of funds, Fran asked her Aunt Yvonne what she could do to earn some money. Fortunately, Aunt Yvonne was willing to pay her $2.00 to rake the yard. ($12.20 with money earned)

Page 6: Fran and Nancy each got ice cream cones on the way home. Fran spent 78 cents for her treat. ($11.42 left)

Page 7: Fran's friend Connie came by and suggested they make a trip to the recycling plant to sell aluminum cans they had collected. Fran received $4.50. She hit the jackpot! ($15.92 with money earned)

Page 8: With this money burning a hole in her pocket, she decided a shirt with the school logo was essential. She asked the school store clerk, Leon, the price of a shirt. Shirts cost $15.92. Did she have enough money? Fran looked in her wallet. She had exactly enough money for a shirt. After this purchase, she was once again flat, busted broke.

After developing personal examples of money memoirs circle stories, read *Alexander, Who Used to Be Rich Last Sunday* by Judith Viorst (1978). Alexander is flat busted broke with only a few bus tokens to his name at the beginning and end of the story. There are several intervening events. Students could create a money memoirs circle story about Alexander.

PICTURE PERFECT: GEOMETRY, GRAPHING, AND DATA ANALYSIS

"Knowledge of geometry and construction of graphs, tables, and charts are closely related basic tools for organizing data" (Charlesworth & Lind, 1990, p. 398). *Geometry* is an area of mathematical study that includes identifying, classifying, and drawing or constructing two- and three-dimensional shapes. *Graphing* is the use of visual organizers with lines and shapes to display a collection of data and provide opportunities for *data analysis*. Both geometry and graphing encompass the use of pictures, drawings, and concrete models in learning experiences for students, thus the title "Picture Perfect" for this section of the math chapter.

Geometry enables students to develop spatial sense. "The purpose of teaching geometry in the elementary and middle school is to help children acquire abilities to be used in describing, comparing, representing, and relating objects in the environment as well as learn to mathematically justify and explain discoveries they make" (Troutman & Lichtenberg, 1995, p. 418). Geometry includes *flat figures*, two-dimensional plane figures, and *fat figures*, three-dimensional space figures. Geometry is used to answer questions and solve problems that involve shapes. Willoughby (1990) stresses the importance of student experiences with both two-dimensional and three-dimensional concrete objects and pictures. Troutman and Lichtenberg (1995) suggest six skill areas for geometry activities:

1. Identifying geometric figures
2. Listing the attributes of geometric figures
3. Comparing geometric figures to see how they are alike and how they are different
4. Identifying the results when geometric figures undergo change
5. Identifying representations for geometric figures
6. Describing relationships among geometric figures (p. 419)

Charlesworth and Lind (1990) emphasize the importance of a basic understanding of shape and space that students apply as they develop graphing skills. Graphs provide a way to organize and visually represent a collection of data. For example, each student in a classroom writes his or her birthday on a sticky note. A class graph is constructed, and these notes are organized chronologically by month and then by day of the month on the graph. Based on this data display, students are able to analyze the information and determine in which month there are the most birthdays, in which month there are the fewest birthdays, who is the oldest in the class, the youngest, etc.

*Note: See Chapter 8 for **Shipology and Ordered Pairs:** In the game "Victory at Sea," students develop pre-algebra skills as they plot coordinates of an ordered pair of numbers to identify a letter point on a graph.*

Artistic Adventures

Three-D-Geometry

Three-D-geometry includes art projects that are constructed using readily available or easily made three-dimensional geometric shapes. These 3-D figures, or fat figures, are found in both the school and home environment. To label these shapes, students count the *faces*, flat surfaces; *edges*, each line where two faces meet; and *vertices*, points or corners (*vertex*: one point or corner).

There are many three-dimensional objects that are readily available for use in three-D-geometry. The following are suggested:

1. **Cylinders:**   toilet tissue, paper towel, and wrapping paper tubes; fruit juice cans; fruit and vegetable cans
2. **Rectangular Prisms:**   packing boxes, shoe boxes, cereal boxes, other food boxes
3. **Cubes:**   cube-shaped boxes, number cubes or dice, blocks
4. **Cones:**   paper cups for water dispensers, ice-cream cones, and party hats
5. **Spheres:**   styrofoam balls, tennis balls, and golf balls

For three-D-geometry art projects, construct three-dimensional shapes by tracing the faces of a figure and adding tabs for gluing as needed. Make cubes, tetrahedrons, and cones using the three-D-geometry patterns in the Activity Appendix A. Create story boxes and fold-a-buildings for three-D-geometry (see Activity Appendix A). Decorate these three-dimensional shapes with scraps of paper, markers, and other craft materials to make people, animals, and buildings.

Literature-Based Example

After reading The Village of Round and Square Houses *by Anne Grifalconi (1986), create a village of round and square houses. Use cylinders and cones for round houses and cubes for square houses.*

Other Possibilities

Construct and decorate three-D-geometry shapes to make ornaments for Christmas trees as well as other holiday decorations.

Gamut of Games

Tangram

A *tangram* is an ancient Chinese puzzle that is made from a square cut into seven standard geometric figures (see Tangram in Activity Appendix A). Each individual piece is called a tan. Tans are flat figures. The seven tans include:

- 1 square
- 1 parallelogram
- 5 triangles (2 large congruent triangles, 1 medium triangle, and 2 small congruent triangles).

Chinese storytellers used a set of tans to form people, animals, and objects as they told stories. As the tale progressed, the tans were rearranged several times to introduce a different person, animal, or object. In this shape-shifting, the storyteller used all seven tans each time. The tans touched but did not overlap.

Assist students in making and using individual sets of tans to tell stories. A set of tans for use on the overhead projector allows the teacher to provide a model for every student participation (ESP) shared tangram experiences. Younger students may use fewer than seven tans or overlap their tans to create pictures.

Literature-Based Example

Grandfather Tang's Story: A Tale Told with Tangrams by Ann Tompert (1990) is a tale told with tans. As Grandfather tells the story of the fox fairies, he arranges and rearranges a set of tans as the fox fairies transform into a variety of animals. His granddaughter, Little Soo, is fascinated with the tans, and at the end of the story both her tans and her grandfather's are combined to form a family picture. As the story is read, students arrange and rearrange their tans to form the fox fairies' transformations. As an extension of this activity, students create more transformations for the fox fairies through shape-shifting.

 Ocular Organizers

Graphs

Graphing is an important life skill. Graphing provides a means of organizing information into a meaningful visual pattern for data analysis and problem solving. According to Charlesworth and Lind (1990), students' most popular graph choices for displaying data are picture graphs (pictographs), bar graphs or histograms, line graphs, and circle or pie graphs.

Graphing experiences should involve students in topics of high interest and personal meaning. For example, each student draws a picture of his or her favorite pet. Afterwards students stand in parallel lines, each line representing one of the favorite pets. To determine which is the favorite pet and the least favorite pet, students count the number of persons in each line. Then students line up their pictures on the floor and step back to examine their pet preferences on their floor pictograph or pet preference pictograph.

Discuss, "How can we permanently display our pet preference pictograph?" Students may suggest designing a wall pictograph on large bulletin board paper and mounting their drawings (see Figure 6.9). After experiences with pictographs, many students make the transition from pictographs to bar graphs (see Figure 6.10).

Literature-Based Example

The Very Hungry Caterpillar by Eric Carle (1969) provides a wonderful opportunity to graph the hungry caterpillar's daily diet. As the story is read, assign different students to draw each piece of fruit or food the caterpillar eats (one student draws an apple for Monday, two students draw pears for Tuesday, etc.). After discussing how to show what the caterpillar eats each day, students line up next to signs for each day of the week and create a floor graph. Placing their pictures on the floor and stepping back provides a view of the caterpillar's daily diet. Students can answer questions such as:

Teacher:	What happened to the caterpillar's diet from Monday to Tuesday?
Student:	He ate one more piece of fruit.
Teacher:	What about from Tuesday to Wednesday?
Student:	He ate one more piece of fruit.
Teacher:	What happened on Saturday?
Students:	On Saturday he was really hungry, and he doubled the number of pieces of food in his diet.
Teacher:	What happened on Sunday?
Student:	He must have been full, because he ate only one leaf.
Teacher:	Which day did he eat the most food?
Student:	Saturday.
Teacher:	Which day or days did he eat the least food?
Student:	On Monday and Sunday, he ate only one piece of food on each of these days.

FIGURE 6.9   Pet Preference Pictograph

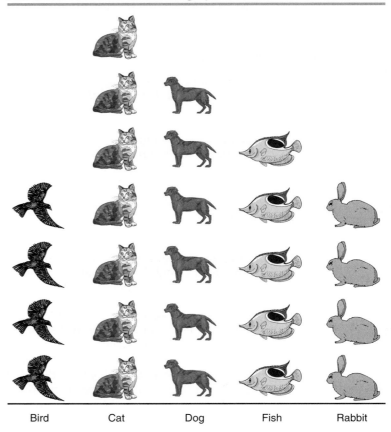

Bird   Cat   Dog   Fish   Rabbit

FIGURE 6.10   Pet Preference Bar Graph

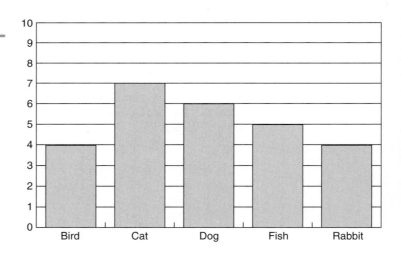

Students make a pictograph of the caterpillar's daily diet. A bar graph may also be created to represent the hungry caterpillar's daily diet.

As part of a nutrition unit, students progress from graphing experiences with the hungry caterpillar to creating personal weekly graphs to represent the number of fruit and vegetable servings eaten daily. Compile this data and create a class pictograph or bar graph to depict weekly fruit and vegetable consumption for the class. The graph allows students to examine whether they are eating the recommended number of servings of fruits and vegetables.

Anno's Counting Book by Mitsumasa Anno (1975) is a delightful, wordless book to introduce students to counting, bar graphs, and months of the year. The first page in the book shows a bare, snowy landscape; the numeral zero; and an empty bar graph created from ten blocks. The next page depicts January with one block on the bar graph and the numeral one. There are several single objects on the page: one snowman, one child building the snowman, one tree, one bird, and so forth. On each subsequent page the number of blocks on the bar graph increases by one, the numeral increases by one, and there are sets of objects to represent that numeral. On the page for December, there are twelve fir trees, twelve bare trees, twelve houses, twelve reindeer, and so forth. The challenge on each page is to identify the different sets of objects. After reading Anno's book, students may design their own books for months of the year with bar graphs, numerals, and sets of objects.

Dramatic Debut

Family Broadcasting Network/Polls, Surveys, and Graphs

Encourage students to participate in polls, interpret the results, and present their findings in a variety of graphic forms. Conducting polls using survey forms, tabulating the information, and presenting the information follows the alphabetical research writing sequence presented in the informational writing section of the writing chapter:

A-ssess class interest (television programs)
B-uild background knowledge (discuss types of shows on television)
C-hoose a topic (time spent watching and type of television shows)
D-ivide the topic into research sections (time spent each day; types of shows: cartoons, drama, game, movies, news, sitcom, and sports)
E-stablish guidelines for collecting information (develop a survey for conducting a poll)
F-ind Facts (take the survey home and encourage the family to complete)
G-roup Information (compute the amount of television viewing time each day and tabulate the types of programs watched)
H-uddle and Write (create charts and graphs)
I-nform Others (present information on a television program)

After a week's survey of family television program preferences in which each class member's family has participated, students appear on a television show. Each class member takes the part of a roving research reporter who has surveyed his own family.

Darrell:	Good evening! Thank you for joining us here on FBN, the Family Broadcasting Network, where our aim is to provide you with the finest in television news and entertainment for the entire family. Tonight, headlines from our news desk in Rochester, New York, with roving research reporter, Lucinda Mirinda. Lucinda?
Lucinda:	Yes, Darrell. What a day this has been. After weeks of intensive research, the widely publicized Famlop Poll results are in! You'll recall, Darrell, that FBN set out to determine family television program preferences from 3:00 P.M. to 9:00 P.M. Well, the conclusions drawn by our researchers are nearly tallied. But first, a revealing, behind the scenes look at how all the necessary information was gathered.
Richie:	Lucinda, Darrell. Good evening, and how are you this evening? Here at Famlop Headquarters is Professor Jeff Hager and his team of researchers who have spent the last few weeks gathering and graphing all essential data necessary for this poll. Professor, explain to our audience what precise method you used to determine family television program preferences during afterschool hours.
Professor Hager:	Well, Richie, we first designed a Famlop Poll Survey Form for family television program preferences (see Figure 6.11). Each team member, along with his family, participated in the poll. The poll was conducted from Monday through Sunday during

FIGURE 6.11   Famlop Poll Survey Form for Family Television Program Preferences

Name: _____

Date: _____

Instructions: As you sit down to watch TV, note when and what type of television show you are about to watch. Place the corresponding letter in the appropriate time slot. At the end of the day, total the number of hours you watched television.

	PROGRAM PREFERENCE						
	Monday	Tuesday	Wednesday	Thursday	Friday	Saturday	Sunday
3:00 PM							
3:30 PM							
4:00 PM							
4:30 PM							
5:00 PM							
5:30 PM							
6:00 PM							
6:30 PM							
7:00 PM							
7:30 PM							
8:00 PM							
8:30 PM							
TOTAL HOURS							

Types of Programs

C = Cartoon	G = Game	N = News	SP = Sports
D = Drama	M = Movie	S = Sitcom	

a given week. Each family kept a survey sheet near the family television set, and while watching television programs, a family member jotted down the type of program.

Darrell: Let's hear from research reporter Jessica and the survey results for her family.

Jessica: Good evening, Darrell, Lucinda. With us tonight here at Famlop headquarters are my parents Mr. and Mrs. Piercefield. Dad, what personal discovery came from our family's participation in the Famlop Poll, family television program preferences?

Mr. Piercefield: Well, Jessica, as we looked at the survey showing the time spent watching television, we were surprised at the number of hours the television set was on each day.

Mrs. Piercefield: We also realized how much we watch TV on school nights when the kids should be doing their homework. We watch the news a lot, and my husband enjoys the weekend ball games.

Jessica: After completing a program preference data chart of the types of shows we watched each day, the chart reveals that our family television program preference is watching the news (see Figure 6.12).

Mr. Piercefield: Jessica even designed a program preference bar graph to depict our family television program preferences (see Figure 6.13).

FIGURE 6.12   Famlop Poll Program Preference Data Chart for the Piercefield Family

	PROGRAM PREFERENCE							
	Monday	Tuesday	Wednesday	Thursday	Friday	Saturday	Sunday	TOTAL
Cartoon	1	1	1	1	1	0	0	5
Drama	1	0	0	0	1	1	0	3
Game	0.5	0.5	0.5	0.5	0	0	0	2
Movie	0	0	0	0	0	2	0	2
News	1	1	1	1	1	0.5	0.5	6
Sitcom	0	0.5	0.5	0.5	0	0	0.5	2
Sports	0	0	0	0	0	1	2	3
TOTAL HOURS	3.5	3	3	3	3	4.5	3	23

FIGURE 6.13   Famlop Poll Program Preference Bar Graph for the Piercefield Family

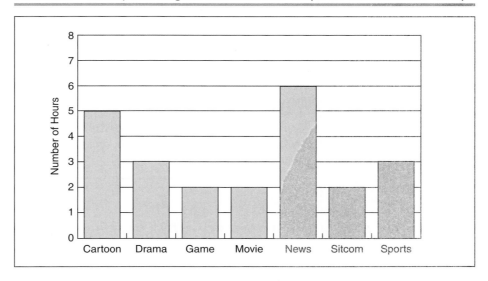

Richie: Thank you Mr. and Mrs. Piercefield and Jessica. Well, Bud, Lucinda, on our next few broadcasts we will share survey results from other families. We will discover the television program preferences of other families surveyed by the Famlop Poll.

Darrell: As you can see, we have just touched the tip of the iceberg in presenting this information to you. Tune in to FBN tomorrow night, when our roving research reporters will continue their interviews with individual families participating in the Famlop poll. Professor Jeff Hager will also have his researchers compile the information from the surveys of the thirty-two families participating in the Famlop Poll. They will share the research results of combined viewing times and program preferences for these families. These researchers are preparing a wide array of graphs with information that has been organized into meaningful, visual patterns for data analysis and problem solving. Professor Hager and researchers, thank you.

Note: Younger students may conduct a survey, discuss results, and prepare graphs for one day's viewing rather than a week.

Creative Composition
Tantalizing Template Tangles/Tantalizing Template Tales

Challenge students of all ages to create and write about their *tantalizing template tangles*, designs made by creatively arranging and mounting shapes drawn from templates. *Templates* are stencils made by tracing shapes on a piece of poster board or the front of a file folder, cutting out the shapes, and leaving the outlines of the shapes. Templates are placed over a piece of paper or a piece of paper slides inside the file folder, the inside of each shape is traced, cut out, and mounted on paper of a contrasting color. Shapes are combined to form a tantalizing template tangle. For example, students trace and cut out three equilateral triangles, one rectangle, and a star using the file folder templates. Arrange the shapes to form a Christmas tree (see Tantalizing Template Tangle in Activity Appendix A). Make decorations, presents, and a background using scraps of paper. Compose a *tantalizing template tale*, a story about the tantalizing template tangle.

Literature-Based Example

Illustrations in The Secret Birthday Message *by Eric Carle (1972) have shapes that are mounted on the page, cut out of the page, or lift up from the page. The story involves the reader in looking for shapes, looking over the shapes, or looking through the cutout shapes while seeking the birthday surprise that is hidden at the end of the reading obstacle course. Use templates to create illustrations and compose a similar story.*

After reading Color Zoo *by Lois Ehlert (1989), older students will rise to the challenge of using Ehlert's format in which three pages, each with a different template shape, are overlaid to form an animal. When the top template is removed a second animal is revealed, and when the top two templates are removed a third animal is seen. A tantalizing template tale could be designed to include each of the animals. Students could design template overlays to form a variety of people, animals, and objects and compose tantalizing template tales about their tantalizing template tangles.*

⟳ *MEASURE MANIA: MEASUREMENT TIME, AND DATA ANALYSIS*

Measurement, the process of describing and comparing using standard units, is an important life skill. In our world, we measure to determine how tall we are, how much we weigh, how much water we drink, how much carpet is needed to cover a floor, how hot or cold a room is, and how long it is until lunch. Thus measurement is concerned with length, weight, volume, area, temperature, and time. Telling time is yet another measurement experience. "Probably the best way for students to deal with numbers and to understand arithmetic operations conceptually is to measure" (Hyde & Bizar, 1989, p. 104).

Students often begin measuring experiences by comparing two objects. For example, students place two pencils side by side to determine which is longer and which is shorter. To determine exactly how long each pencil is, the width of a thumb is sometimes used. However, after using different students' thumbs a problem becomes apparent: Some thumbs are wider than others. Since thumbs are nonstandard sizes, they are not equal units of measure.

Perhaps using objects of the same size is a good idea. Paper clips are a nonstandard unit of equal size that may be used to measure the pencils. However, after experimentation in measuring objects, students will find that paper clips are cumbersome to use, especially when measuring long objects.

Some students may suggest using a ruler to measure the pencils. Rulers are marked in centimeters or inches that are standard and equal units of measure. In the United States many students learn to measure using the traditional English units: inch, foot, yard, mile, and so forth. However, most of the world uses the metric unit of measure, which is developed on the base ten: centimeter, meter, kilometer, etc.

For measurement experiences in addition to those in this chapter, see Chapter 8: Mystery of Flight and Travel Trials and Tribulations, a math card game that focuses on distance and elapsed time and The Stock Market Game and Investment Investigators in which students participate in graphing ups and downs of stock investment.

Artistic Adventures

Clock: What Time Is It?

What time is it? How much longer until lunch? When will your work be finished? All these questions make us conscious of the importance of time in our lives. Students learn when they enter school that each classroom day has a schedule with special times designated for lunch, computer center, media center, and so forth. In fact, many teachers use large cardboard clocks with times set for special events. Students soon learn to calculate how many minutes until music, media center, time to go home, and so on.

Making clocks (see Clock Creation in the Activity Appendix A) and using them in a variety of every student participation (ESP) experiences provides students opportunities to tell time. Divide these clock faces into quarters of different colors to facilitate discussion and understanding of *quarter after*, *half-past*, and *quarter to*. Write each number for the clock on a flap. Under the flap is the corresponding number of minutes after the hour (e.g., under the 1 is a 5, under the 2 is a 10, under the 3 is a 15, and so forth). Label the short hand with a short word, *hour*; this hand moves slowly. Label the long hand with a long word, *minute*, this hand moves more rapidly. Students may indicate with animals or objects which hand moves slowly and which hand moves quickly (e.g., a turtle on the hour hand and a rabbit on the minute hand).

Literature-Based Examples

While sharing Brindle Bear Telling Time *by John Patience (1993), students set their clocks and change times as the story is read. Students determine elapsed time between activities. For example, at a quarter after 11 Brindle waters flowers until a quarter to 12 when Brindle picks apples. How much time did it take to water the flowers? Students answers questions at the end of the book and make up more questions to ask their friends.*

While listening to The Grouchy Lady Bug *by Eric Carle (1977), students set and change times on their clocks as the grouchy lady bug travels throughout the day visiting different animals. Students will enjoy writing a parallel story following the text pattern and making a book using the step book format of* The Grouchy Lady Bug *(see Step Book in Activity Appendix A).*

Anno's Sundial, *by Mitsumasa Anno (1987), contains a great deal of historical information on the development of clocks. Older students will enjoy the challenge of making a sundial using directions in the book. The pop-up illustrations and flaps with facts under them will appeal to students of all ages.*

Gamut of Games

Treasure Measure Hunt/Pocket Books

Treasure measure hunts are treasure hunts using measurement for time, perimeter, area, and other math skills. Students participate simultaneously in measuring time and objects. After measuring at their desks, students go on a treasure measure hunt to find and discover the measurement of objects on a list.

For some of the ESP activities each student will need a set of **ESP number cards**, a set of index cards each numbered with a single digit from 0 to 9 and a pocket book (see Appendix A). Label the pockets on the pocket book from right to left *unit, ten, hundred, thousand*. Using color-coded number cards with a designated color for each number allows the teacher to quickly scan the room and determine whether or not each student has the correct answer. Older students may use two sets of number cards. As the teacher asks a question, the students indicate the answer with their number cards by sliding them into the correct position in the pocket book. After several ESP experiences, the students go on a treasure measure hunt.

Perimeter

Perimeter is the distance around a figure. Students determine the perimeter by using rulers or meter sticks to measure the sides of a figure, a flat figure. Questions the teacher might ask include:

> What is the perimeter of the index card on your desk?
> What is the perimeter of your desk top?
> What is the perimeter of your math book?

Area

Area is the number of square units within a figure. Students begin experiences with area using small square centimeter pieces of paper to determine how many square centimeters it takes to cover a given surface. Students progress to using rulers or meter sticks to determine area.

> What is the area of the index card on your desk?
> What is the area of your desk top?
> What is the area of the cover of your math book?

Time

Use commercial clocks, paper plate clocks, or a clock creation made using directions in the Activity Appendix A. Set times and answer questions such as the following:

> What time does school begin?
> What time is lunch?
> You must be home at 4:00. It takes 30 minutes to walk home. What time must you leave?
> What time is _____ on television tonight?
>   *Note: Show transparency with television program guide on the overhead.*
> Your bedtime is 1 1/2 hours after this show begins. What time is bedtime?

Challenge older students to learn about time zones (see *Anno's Sundial* (1987) and *Geography for Every Kid* by Janice VanCleave (1993).

Ocular Organizer

Class Chart of Records/Class Book of Records

The Guinness Book of Records (Matthews, 1994), first published in 1955, is second only to the Bible as the world's all-time best-selling book. The book was originally designed as a resource to use in resolving arguments concerning facts and figures. Major divisions in the book are earth and space, living world, human beings, science and technology, buildings and structures, transport, business world, arts and entertainment, human world, human achievements, and sports and games. Because of the wide array of topics encompassed in the book, it is an invaluable resource for research within thematic units.

Many of the topics and events in the book employ measurement. Students may look for examples of different types of measurement. For example:

Weight	Heaviest human brain	5 lb. 1.1 oz.
	Lightest human brain	2 lbs. 6.7 oz.
Volume	Blood required in surgery by one patient	1,900 pints
Time	Longest presidential term Franklin D. Roosevelt	12 years 39 days
	Shortest presidential term William Henry Harrison	32 days

Students who have ambitions to establish, achieve, and break class records should examine *The Guinness Book of Records* and choose events of interest, create modifications of events, or design new events. Participation results are entered on a *class chart of records*, a visual organizer that displays team and class records. These charts may be compiled in a *class book of records*.

Students may work in cooperative groups to participate in individual and team events. For example, a team with four members could participate in individual events. Each team member draws a number to determine in which event to participate. Students may determine how long it takes to go a set distance using a stopwatch. A team class chart of records would resemble the following:

Team Class Chart of Records

Team Name: _____
    Event Title: _____ Time: _____

1. Balancing book on head while walking
2. Running backwards
3. Carrying egg on spoon while walking fast
4. Hopping on one foot

After determining team records, a Class Chart of Teams' Records provides comparison information for all of the class teams.

Class Chart of Teams' Records

Event Title	Teams' Time				
	1	2	3	4	5
1. Balancing book on head while walking					
2. Running backwards					
3. Carrying egg on spoon while walking fast					
4. Hopping on one foot					

Dramatic Debut
Gifts and Greetings Gallery

A *gifts and greetings gallery* is a card shop where students use careful and precise measurement to create greeting cards, stationery, note cards, frames for photos and pictures, and gift wrap. Creating gifts and greetings provides opportunities for students to have meaningful, measurement experiences. The gifts and greetings gallery may be set up as four learning centers. An artisan for each center is trained to facilitate experiences at the center thus freeing the teacher to move about the classroom and help where needed. Older students may be trained as artisans to facilitate gifts and greetings experiences for younger students.

The gifts and greeting gallery is especially motivational during the holiday season or before Mothers' Day. Students produce stationery, note cards, pictures, frames, and the like as gifts; create gift wrap; and design greeting cards to accompany each gift.

As a prelude to a gifts and greetings gallery experience, students practice the following skit (or an adaptation of the skit). Their focus should be on enthusiastic "selling" of each gallery experience to their peers.

Nancy: Welcome to the Gifts and Greetings Gallery where you will find exhibited exciting, exclusive, exquisite, exhilarating, exceptional gifts and greetings to please even the most discriminating recipient. Each gift and greeting in our gallery is unique and custom designed by artisans whose ingenious designs are gift and greetings' masterpieces.

Sihoki: Our gallery opens into four mini galleries:
(1) greeting cards, (2) stationery, (3) frames, and (4) gift wrap. In each of these mini galleries, you may design or purchase stunning, one-of-a-kind gifts and greetings. These distinctive treasures will be cherished keepsakes for years to come.

Salvador: At the Gifts and Greetings Gallery only the finest quality materials are used to create our masterpieces. Our master crafters are trained in minuscule measurement so as not to waste one iota of our priceless resources. Our measurement specialists include the following:

1.   **Perimeter Pursuit Professionals** who take pride in precise perimeter pursuit. After much practice, these professionals are proficient in precise perimeter measurement and waste not one particle of our precious, priceless products. Their prudence in perimeter planning for the trim on greeting cards, the edging on stationery, and the borders on frames provides precise measurement of lace, ribbon, and other decorative items for our gifts and greetings.

2.   **Accurate Area Analysts** have admirable aptitude for angling and aligning our exclusive, priceless card stock, parchment, wallpaper, and fabric so that maximum use is made of each of these costly items. These analysts accurately analyze the Gifts and Greetings Gallery's card surfaces, stationery surfaces, frame surfaces, and gift wrap size to determine the area to be covered.

Charley: Please allow our mini gallery artisans to share their exclusive showcase displays with you.

Artisan 1: Welcome to our greeting card gallery, where our greeting cards are designed by talented artisans who have a flare for devising clever creations for every special occasion. We have available a variety of card stock, parchment, and colored paper that can be measured and folded into different size greeting cards. We have birthday cards, congratulations cards, get well cards, holiday cards, thank you cards; in fact, cards for any occasion. Illustrations are innovative and ingenious with precisely measured pop-ups,[†] flaps, windows, doors, and a variety of shapes. Decorations for the perimeters of our cards are planned by our perimeter pursuit professionals. Our greetings and salutations contain memorable messages. Greeting cards in our Gifts and Greetings Gallery are designed based on our motto, *don't rest until you send the best.*

Artisan 2: Welcome to our stationery gallery where note cards and stationery are handcrafted using a distinctive variety of customized techniques. Area analysts accurately angle and align our priceless card stock, parchment, and wallpaper to create our note cards and stationery.

Envelopes are measured and devised using our secret enveloptionery[‡] design. Unique and interesting envelopes are fashioned using newspaper. Our analysts, after great deliberation, have discovered that the size of an envelope into which a note card will slide is determined by measuring the longest side of the note card and doubling that measurement for the length of one side of a square to be used in making the envelope. For example, to create the envelope for a 3-inch X 4 1/2-inch note card, a 9-inch square is needed.

Stationery and note cards are personalized with initials, names, and logos using elegant penmanship. Stationery in our Gifts and Greetings Gallery is *designed with you in mind.*

Artisan 3: Welcome to our frames gallery where each frame[§] is fashioned and fabricated with care and precision. Our photo frames and picture frames allow you to display prominently at home, office, and school those photos and pictures you love and value. Our perimeter pursuit professionals precisely measure picture perimeters to determine the size of framing or matting needed for our priceless frames. Frames from our Gifts and Greetings Gallery will allow you to permanently *make a memory.*

[†]Note: See Pop-Up Techniques in the Activity Appendix A.
[‡]Note: See Enveloptionery in the Activity Appendix A.
[§]Note: See Frames in the Activity Appendix A.

Artisan 4: Welcome to our gift wrap gallery where each elegant gift wrap, gift bag, and gift box# promises to tantalize the recipient. Each festive feature of our gift wrap promises enchanting secrets enclosed within the packaging. Our gift wrap is precisely measured by accurate area analysts. The designs are created by stamping with sponges, fruit, and other objects dipped in only premium paints. Dimensions for our gift bags are determined by disassembling a commercial gift bag, measuring, and increasing or decreasing the measurements proportionately to produce a bag of the proper size. Our finest bulletin board paper is used for constructing these bags. Handle length and placement is determined after careful measurement. The distinctive designs on the gift wrap from our gifts and greetings gallery tell the recipient that the gift comes *wrapped up in love*.

Creative Composition

Personal Guinness Book of Records in a Teeny Tiny Book

Establishing a personal Guinness book of records provides a meaningful, motivational approach to measure mania. Participants determine skills that they would like to improve upon and develop a timetable to record the improvement (e.g., 2 days, 1 week, a month, etc.). These skills may be academic (e.g., math facts, spelling words, science facts), physical (e.g., jumping rope, sit ups, running track), or social (e.g., verbal *warm fuzzies*, cards, social actions). Students may want to decrease the amount of time in which to perform a task (e.g., repeat a multiplication table correctly within a shorter amount of time), increase the frequency within a given time (e.g., increase the number of multiplication tables repeated in 3 minutes) or increase the frequency over time (e.g., increase the number of verbal *warm fuzzies* over the period of a week). Participants are competing against themselves.

A *personal Guinness book of records* is a six-page book that delineates the steps to take in a total workout to achieve a personal Guinness goal (see Teeny Tiny Book in Activity Appendix A). A personal Guinness book of records would be organized as follows:

Page 1: Total *Left Side Write:*
The **total** number of _____ I am performing now is _____
(establishes baseline for skill)
Page 2:
Right Side Write:
Focusing on this task is important to me because_____
Page 3: Work *Left Side Write:*
Some ways I could **work** to improve this skill are _____
Page 4:
Right Side Write:
The intervention I like best is _____
Page 5: Out *Left Side Write*
The **total work out** number of _____
I am performing is _____
Page 6:
Right Side Write:
My *total workout* improvement in _____ is _____ more than I was doing before the intervention.

#Note: See Story Boxes in the Activity Appendix A.

Literature References

Adams, B.J. (1992). *The go-around dollar*. New York: Four Winds Press.

Adams, P. (1992). *This old man*. Singapore: Child's Play.

Anno, M. (1975). *Anno's counting book*. New York: HarperCollins.

Anno, M. (1987). *Anno's sundial*. New York: Philomel Books.

Anno, M., & Anno, M. (1983). *Anno's mysterious multiplying jar*. New York: Philomel Books.

Axelrod, A. (1994). *Pigs will be pigs*. New York: Four Winds Press.

Beierle, M., & Lynes, T. (1992). *Book cooks: Literature-based classroom cooking*. Cypress, CA: Creative Teaching Press.

Brown, M. (1947). *Stone soup*. New York: Scribner's.

Carle, E. (1970). *The very hungry caterpillar*. New York: Scholastic.

Carle, E. (1972). *The secret birthday message*. New York: Harper & Row.

Carle, E. (1977). *The grouchy ladybug*. New York: Harper & Row.

Carroll, L. (1866, 1986). *Alice's adventures in wonderland*. New York: Macmillan 1866; Knopf, 1984.

Cole, J., & Calmenson, S. (1994). *Crazy Eights and other card games*. New York: William Morrow.

Cribb, J. (1990). *Eyewitness books: Money*. New York: Alfred A. Knopf.

Ehlert, L. (1989). *Color zoo*. New York: Lippincott.

Emberley, E. (1977). *Ed Emberley's great thumbprint drawing book*. Boston: Little, Brown.

Emberley, E. (1984). *Ed Emberley's picture pie: A circle drawing book*. Boston: Little, Brown.

Grifalconi, A. (1986). *The village of round and square houses*. Boston: Little, Brown.

Hutchins, P. (1986). *The doorbell rang*. New York: Mulberry/Greenwillow Books.

Langstaff, J. (1957). *Over in the meadow*. New York: Harcourt Brace Jovanovich.

Leedy, L. (1994). *Fraction action*. New York: Holiday House.

Lumpkin, B. (1991) *Senefer: A young genius in old Egypt*. Trenton, NJ: Africa World Press.

Maestro, B. (1993). *The story of money*. New York: Clarion Books.

Matthews, P. (Ed.). (1994). *The Guinness book of records 1994*. New York: Bantam Books.

McGrath, B. (1994). *The M & M's® brand chocolate candies counting book*. Watertown, MA: Charlesbridge.

Medearis, A.S., & Holub, J. (1996). *The 100th day of school*. New York: Scholastic.

Patience, J. (1993). *Brindle Bear telling the time*. New York: Derrydale Books.

Pinczes, E.J. (1993). *One hundred hungry ants*. Boston: Houghton Mifflin.

Pittman, H.C. (1986). *A grain of rice*. New York: Bantam Books.

Rockwell, T. (1993). *How to eat fried worms*. New York: Yearling.

Ryan, P.M. (1994). *One hundred is a family*. New York: Hyperion Books for Children.

Schwartz, D.M. (1985). *How much is a million?* New York: Lothrop, Lee & Shepard Books.

Schwartz, D.M. (1989). *If you made a million*. New York: Lothrop, Lee & Shepard Books.

Stewart, S. (1991). *The money tree*. Canada: Harper Collins.

Tompert, A. (1990). *Grandfather Tang's story: A tale told with tangrams*. New York: Crown.

VanCleave, J. (1993). *Geography for every kid: Easy activities that make learning geography fun*. New York: John Wiley & Sons.

Viorst, J. (1978). *Alexander, who used to be rich last Sunday*. New York: Aladdin Books.

Willard, N. (1990). *The high rise glorious skittle skat roarious sky pie angel food cake*. New York: Harcourt Brace Jovanovich.

Williams, V. (1982). *A chair for my mother*. New York: Greenwillow Books.

Professional References

American Heritage Dictionary of the English Language (4th ed.). (2000). New York: Houghton Mifflin Company.

Barton, M.L., Heidema, C., & Jordan, D. (2002). Teaching reading in mathematics and science. *Educational Leadership, 60*(3), 24–28.

Bintz, W.P., & Moore, S.D. (2002). Using literature to support mathematical thinking in middle school. *Middle School Journal, 34*(2), 25–32.

Charlesworth, R., & Lind, K.K. (1990). *Math and Science for young children*. Albany, NY: Delmar.

Commission on Standards for School Mathematics. (1989). *Curriculum and Evaluation Standards for School Mathematics*. Reston, VA: National Council of Teachers of Mathematics.

Franklin, J. (2003, Fall). Unlocking mathematics for minority students. In *ASCD Curriculum Update*. Alexandria, VA: Association for Supervision and Curriculum Development.

Hyde, A.A., & Bizar, M. (1989). *Thinking in context: Teaching cognitive process across the elementary school curriculum*. New York: Longman.

Martinez, J.G.R. & Martinez, N.C. (2003, March). Raising middle school math standards without raising anxiety. *Middle School Journal, 34*(4), 27–35.

National Council of Teachers of Mathematics. *Principles and Standards for School Mathematics*. Retrieved February 14, 2008. www.nctm.org

Noyce, R.M., & Christie, J.F. (1989). *Integrating reading and writing instruction in grades K-8*. Boston: Allyn and Bacon.

Silbey, R. (2003, April). Math out loud: Heard the word? Talking and writing about math boosts understanding in a big way. *Scholastic Instructor*, 24–26.

Smith, S.Z., Smith, M.E., & Romberg, T.A. (1993). What the NCTM standards look like in one classroom. *Educational Leadership*, 50 (8), 4–7.

Stewart, M. (2003, April). From tangerines to algorithms. *Scholastic Instructor*, 20–23.

Tankersley, K. (1993). Teaching math their way. *Educational Leadership*, 50 (8), 12–13.

Troutman, A.P., & Lichtenberg, B.K. (1995). *Mathematics— A good beginning: Strategies for teaching children* (5th ed.). Pacific Grove, CA: Brooks/Cole.

Willis, S. & Checkley, K. (1996, Summer). Bringing math to life. In ASCD *Curriculum Update*. Alexandria VA: Association for Supervision and Curriculum Development.

Willoughby, S.S. (1990). *Mathematics education for a changing world*. Alexandria, VA: Association for Supervision and Curriculum Development.

Additional Literature/Professional Resource Suggestions

Cave, K. (1991). *Out for the count: A counting adventure*. New York: Simon & Shuster Books for Young Readers.

Demi. (1997). *One grain of rice: A mathematical folktale*. New York: Scholastic.

Kiyosaki, R.T., & Lechter, S.L. (1998). *Rich dad; Poor dad*. New York: Warner Books.

Merrill Lynch (and/or other brokerage houses). Investment Packets for Stock Market Savvy.

Moscovich, I. (2001). *1000 play thinks: Puzzles, paradoxes, illusions and games*. New York: Workman Publishing.

Scieszka, J., & Smith, L. (1995). *Math curse*. New York: Viking.Weltman,

Weltman, B. (1999). *The complete idiot's guide to raising money-smart kids*. New York: Macmillan.

Websites

Ask Dr. Math

Interactive site devoted to answering math questions

http://forum.swarthmore.edu/dr.math/

Funbrain

Games and a quiz lab with teachers receiving email result

www.funbrain.com

McRel

Interdisciplinary site with links to literature, Fibonacci numbers, women in math info

www.mcrel.org/connect/math.html

National Council of Teachers of Mathematics (NCTM)

Information from the National Council of Teachers of Mathematics including principles and standards for school mathematics.

www.nctm.org

CHAPTER 7 TOPICS	Artistic Adventures	Gamut of Games
Tree-mendous Trees	Adopt-a-Tree Four-Flap Flip-Fact	Leaf Lore and Leaf Shape Books Leaf Lab
Kittens and Kings	Cat Habitat in a Plate-arama	Catardy
Weather Watch	Season Scenes in Shallow Shadow Boxes Snowflakes	Weather Station
Gateway Drugs	Fold and Tear Adventures	Drugologists Drug Digs and Drug Diagrams
Hard Drugs	Slit-Slot-Slide Book (SSS) and Pepi Profile SSS Book	What Would I Do If (WWIDI) Challenges, Choices, Consequences

Science

Ocular Organizers	*Dramatic Debut*	*Creative Composition*
Find-a-Tree and Show Me	Chamber Theater The Giving Tree: The Giving Me	Poet-Tree Is-Because Poetry
Cat Clusters	Zooks Zoo Cat Habitat Diorama	Cationary
Three-Flap Flip-Flop Clouds	Prepare, Don't Panic	Haiku/Tanka/Lanterne Poetry
Current Events Collage Killer Kollage	Discuss, Debate, Deliver	Analyze and Advertise Problem, Product, Promises, Propaganda, Position
Brains, Bodies, 'n' Behavior (BBB) BBB Organizer	Dr. Drug-Be-Gone Teams of Surgical Specialists	Dear Diary Drug-etry Patterned Poetry

OVERVIEW

Science is the systematic study of life, earth, and our physical world. "Science as a way of knowing involves systematic ways of asking questions, making careful observations of the world around us, and forging connections between present knowledge and new discoveries as they unfold" (Wellman, 1991, p. 159). Science should be viewed as a *verb,* a process of inquiry, rather than as a *noun,* a product or collection of facts.

The *aim* of the science curriculum is for each student to develop scientific literacy and critical thinking skills. The *goals* for school science are to educate students who are able to:

- Experience the richness and excitement of knowing about and understanding the natural world.
- Use appropriate scientific processes and principles in making personal decisions.
- Engage intelligently in public discourse and debate about matters of scientific and technological concern.
- Increase their economic productivity through the use of the knowledge, understanding, and skills of the scientifically literate person in their careers. *(Website, National Science Education Standards [NSES], 2004 Chapter 1, p. 2)*

Traditionally, science instruction in the classroom was textbook focused. Students read chapters in the textbook, memorized innumerable scientific facts and terms, and took tests. Some students viewed science as a giant vocabulary list (Charlesworth & Lind, 1990). Occasionally, teachers presented or students performed an isolated experiment from a textbook using the cookbook approach and following step-by-step directions. Science was considered a separate subject apart from the rest of the curriculum. Thus, science learning experiences were text and test-driven.

As teachers considered the vast amount of information to be covered in science, they were overwhelmed. Each year this seemingly insurmountable mountain of knowledge increased significantly. Many felt inadequate or incompetent to even begin tackling this subject. Questions such as: What should I teach? Which information is the most important for students to know? What if I don't know the answers to all the students' questions? and other questions concerned teachers. Teachers knew intuitively that students should be involved in hands-on experiments and felt guilty when they were not. However, experiments often required equipment and supplies that were not readily available, so teachers had to locate and then pay for them out of their own pockets. To add to the problem, experiments were often time consuming and messy.

NATIONAL SCIENCE EDUCATION STANDARDS (NSES)

In the midst of curriculum chaos and concern, scientists from across the United States met over a period of time and developed the National Science Education Standards (NSES, 2004). Principles guiding the development of these standards emphasized the importance of science for all students with a focus on equity, inclusion, and excellence. Educators were cautioned,

> *Learning science is something students do,*
> *not something that is done to them. (Chapter 2)*

NSES chapter information with representative comments includes:

- **Standards for Science Teaching** (Chapter 3)
  What students learn is greatly influenced by how they are taught.
- **Standards for Professional Development for Teachers of Science** (Chapter 4)
  Skilled teachers of science have special understandings and abilities that integrate their knowledge of science content, curriculum, learning, teaching, and students.
- **Standards for Assessment of Science Education** (Chapter 5)
  Assessment tasks must be developmentally appropriate, must be set in contexts that are familiar to the students, must not require reading skills or vocabulary that are inappropriate to the students' grade level, and must be as free from bias as possible.

- **Standards for Science Content** (Chapter 6)
  There are eight categories of content standards. Within each category, information is organized by grade levels K-4, 5-8, and 9-12.
  1. Unifying Concepts and Process in Science
  2. Science as Inquiry
  3. Physical Science
  4. Life Science
  5. Earth and Space Science
  6. Science and Technology
  7. Science in Personal and Social Perspectives
  8. History and Nature of Science
- **Standards for Science Education Program** (Chapter 7)
  School and district science programs for all students should be developmentally appropriate, interesting, and relevant to students' lives; emphasize student understanding through inquiry; and be connected with other school subjects.
- **Standards for Science Education Systems** (Chapter 8)
  Coordination of action among the school, district, state, and national educational systems is essential when supplying society with scientifically literate citizens.

SCIENCE AS AN INQUIRY EXPERIENCE

The ideas we tend to retain
Are those we create for ourselves.

Colburn, 2004

"Full inquiry involves:

- Asking a simple question
- Completing an investigation
- Answering the question
- Presenting the results to others"
  (NSES, 2004, Chapter 6, p. 3, reformatted)

Students move from a *product focus*, memorization of a prepackaged collection of information, to an *inquiry focus,* active involvement in hands-on, minds-on experiences. As students focus on creating their own questions and then searching for answers to these questions, problem-solving and critical-thinking skills develop. Curious and inquiring minds lead to scientific literacy growth. No longer can we be satisfied with a textbook-focused approach to science. As Wellman (1991, p. 163) states,

Tired science demonstrations, canned laboratory exercises, and reading aloud from stilted textbooks will not create a community of questioning learners. If we want to engage students in the pursuit of science as a valid intellectual goal, then we must focus our teaching and learning energies on meaning-making activities that bring students' hearts and minds into the science learning cycle.

Zemelman, Daniels, and Hyde (1998) emphasize a *constructivist approach* to science in which the emphasis is on activating students' prior knowledge about a phenomenon, encouraging their questions, helping them gather information, and guiding them as they build their own concepts. Caine, Caine, and McClintic (2002) agree that students should seek to construct personal meaning and make sense of their world. The challenge for teachers is to link (1) what students want to know with (2) what we want students to know.

KWL is a quick and easy-to-implement inquiry strategy (Ogle, 1986). Using this strategy, the teacher is able to identify students' prior knowledge as well as their questions and concerns about a topic. For example, when studying magnets, the class or cooperative group's initial entries on a KWL chart might be:

What do you <u>K</u>now about magnets?	What do you <u>W</u>ant to know about magnets?	What are you <u>L</u>earning about magnets?
Magnets pick things up	Why do magnets pick up some things but not other things?	

For additional information about the KWL strategy see the reading, writing, and social studies chapters.

SCIENCE AS AN INVESTIGATIVE EXPERIENCE

Participation in investigation should involve students in process skills that actively engage their minds and provide concrete, hands-on experiences. Sensory intrigue should capture the investigator and entice thrice through

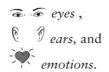 *eyes*,

ears, and

emotions.

Process skills include the following:

1. **Observing:**   Using the five senses to obtain information
2. **Comparing:**   Looking at similarities and differences in objects
3. **Classifying:**   Grouping and sorting objects by categories such as color, shape, and size
4. **Measuring:**   Quantifying observations using numbers, time, temperature, and so forth
5. **Communicating:**   Describing and sharing a phenomenon orally and in writing using pictures, graphic organizers, and extended text
6. **Inferring:**   Recognizing patterns and expecting them to recur
7. **Predicting:**   Making reasonable guesses based on observation or data
8. **Hypothesizing:**   Using an If... Then... statement to explain cause and effect
9. **Defining and Controlling Variables:**   Ascertaining which variables in an experiment should be investigated and which should be controlled (Charlesworth & Lind, 1990)

SCIENCE AS A COMMUNICATION EXPERIENCE

Teachers are often uncomfortable and intimidated when faced with the challenge of teaching science. El Hindi (2003) suggests, "Teachers may feel more comfortable supporting science instruction if they have concrete means for integrating science with everyday literacy instruction" (p. 536). She shares ideas for talking about, reading about, writing about, and connecting knowledge across content areas.

Talking About Science

As students endeavor to solve real-world problems of significance to them, they need to talk: talk to themselves, to peers, and to the teacher. Ongoing discussion results when students working within cooperative groups assume rotating roles during science experiments. These role responsibilities might include discussion leader, recorder, materials organizer, and reporter.

El Hindi (2003) suggests that students pose questions, articulate observations, disseminate findings, and talk through their understanding, confusion, and concerns. Learning experiences designed with collaboration in mind provide opportunities for sharing information and stimulating academic growth.

Reading About Science

When investigating current, controversial science-related issues, a middle school science teacher introduces her students to primary source material: magazines and newspaper articles, pamphlets, brochures, and the Internet (Topping & McManus, 2002). The students discover more detailed information about these issues than is available on television or radio news programs. This teacher's classroom is filled with science-related books often purchased at yard sales, thrift stores, used bookstores, and from book clubs. To entice her students to read a book, she often gives a quick sales pitch or commercial. To assure that her students have time to read these books, students participate in a daily **DIRT** experience: Daily Independent Reading Time.

When introducing scientific topics, one motivational possibility is sharing an appropriate book from Joanna Cole's *Magic School Bus Series*. Students will revel in reader-friendly travel experiences. Bristor (1994) encourages the introduction of a wide variety of books to learn about science. She suggests using magazines and newspapers that contain science information. As students' understanding of their world expands, they will develop positive attitudes toward seeking new information. Recommendations for science nonfiction and fiction trade books are found on the websites listed at the end of the chapter.

Writing About Science

Once a week the entire student body at a middle school participates in Sustained Silent Reading (**SSR**) (Topping & McManus, 2002). Students then write a response to their reading, often a science selection, including something that is amazing, surprising, or humorous. Sharing these written responses with teachers and peers is a highlight of the SSR experience.

To stimulate scientific writing, El Hindi (2003) suggests introducing students to ecological mysteries such as *The Missing 'Gator of Gumbo Limbo* by Jean Craighead George (1992), a focus mystery in Chapter 8. As students delve into the organization of ecological mysteries, they will become sleuth-writers in which their own mysteries revolve around ecological problems, and nature provides clues for finding solutions to the problems.

Look for ideas and suggestions for informational writing in the writing chapter. There you will find five text patterns along with graphic organizers and examples focusing on bugs. Students can write bugographies, make entries in bug logs, and learn a lot about bugs. Ecology is the theme for persuasive writing. Conservation of natural resources is essential, and writing experiences revolve around reduce, reuse, and recycle. Spin off from these examples with curriculum-appropriate experiences.

Connecting Knowledge

To meet students' diverse needs for differentiated instruction, the teacher should (El Hindi, 2003):

- Preview the topic.
- Introduce available materials including trade books at a variety of reading levels.
- Provide, or develop as a class, graphic organizers on which to make entries.
- Give *lecturettes* stopping periodically to let students jot a note or two.
- Tie math and other appropriate content areas to the topic.

Bristor (1994) found that all basic language arts/reading skills may be taught using the science textbook. When focusing on in-depth science instruction in conjunction with reading skills, at-risk students, as well as regular and above-average students, displayed positive attitudes and self-confidence toward both science and reading both in and out of school.

SCIENTIFIC MISCONCEPTIONS

Students' scientific misconceptions often interfere with learning. Crocket (2004) notes the necessity of having students share personal background knowledge about a topic. Once misconceptions are identified, the teacher guides students in re-reasoning their approach to a problem, recognizing a misunderstanding, reformulating their understanding, and reviewing information to be sure that it now makes sense.

Crocket (2004) uses the *carousel strategy* for brainstorming students' initial ideas about a topic. In this cooperative group experience, students meet in small groups around tables. On each table is a large piece of poster board. In the center of each poster board is a different question about the focus topic.

Group members dump (jot) all of their ideas about their question on the poster board. Once each group has made entries about their question, they rotate to the next group's table to answer a new question. After they have rotated through the tables, they return to their original table and summarize all the different groups' ideas in response to their initial question.

How Should You Teach Science?

INSTRUCTIONAL GUIDELINES

Integrating qualities of best practices in teaching science identified by Zemelman and colleagues (1998) with findings from innumerable scientific studies summarized by Willis (1995) results in the following instructional guidelines for teaching science:

- Learning of concepts should be emphasized over memorization of terms and facts.
- Students should have ample opportunities for hands-on inquiry to build investigative skills. Concrete experiences with actual phenomena should precede more abstract lessons.
- Science instruction should be inquiry-based, at least in part. Students should have opportunities to post their own questions, design and pursue their own investigations, analyze data, and present their findings. Students should be *doing science* through questioning and discovering—not just covering material.
- Teachers should explain concepts thoroughly before introducing the terminology associated with them to ensure real understanding rather than parroting.
- Teachers should teach fewer concepts, in greater depth, rather than covering a great many topics superficially. *("Less is more.")* Students should build a knowledge base focused on essential concepts, rather than disconnected topics or bits of information.
- Students should have opportunities to apply science knowledge and to make connections between what they learn and their everyday lives.
- Teachers should build on students' prior understandings and prod them to rethink their misconceptions through active investigation. Meaningful science study will aim at developing thinking, problem solving, and attitudes of curiosity, healthy skepticism, and willingness to adjust, adapt, or change misconceptions.
- All students should become science literate, not just the college-bound. Schools should prepare science-literate citizens, not just future scientists.
- Educators should begin to integrate the various science disciplines (biology, chemistry, physics), as well as integrating science with other subject areas. Learning science means integrating reading, writing, speaking, and math.
- Students need to consider the application of science and technology.
- Good science teaching involves facilitation, collaborative group work, and a limited, judicious use of information giving.
- Meaningful assessment of students' learning in science must promote the objectives of a good science curriculum and not undermine them.

THEMATIC INTEGRATION

Thematic units provide opportunities for learning about science while integrating related language arts components and concepts from other content areas. This chapter focuses on active student investigation of scientific themes through a variety of enjoyable and meaningful educational experiences. Set within a context with which they are familiar, students are able to insert new information into the familiar context of their everyday lives.

Investigative experiences proliferate, involving students in concrete, hands-on, up-close-and-personal interaction with readily available objects, materials, and everyday experiences: trees, cats, weather, gateway drugs, and hard drugs. There is a related science experience for each mystery in Chapter 8: Mysteries Across Content Areas. Certainly, scientific inquiry is essential in the lives of detectives and law enforcement officials.

Expansion possibilities have a ripple effect, an ever-widening array of opportunities. For example:

Representative Themes	Expansion Possibilities
Trees	Ecology/Rain Forests
Cats	Humane Society/euthanasia and protection
Weather	Where would I choose to live based on weather for that geographical area? Why?
Gateway Drugs	How does the use of gateway drugs impact our law enforcement agencies?
Hard Drugs	What is the impact of increased drug use on families and society?

TREE-MENDOUS TREES

What contributions does a tree make to my life?
Why are there so many different kinds of trees?
How can I identify different types of trees?
Why do some trees lose their leaves?
What contributions can I make to the life of a tree?

These questions, as well as others like them, are the beginning of scientific inquiry into the topic of Tree-mendous Trees. Trees are all around us providing opportunities for meaningful, relevant, hands-on experiences. There is ample opportunity to observe, compare, classify, and measure trees and their component parts. Their leaves, bark, twigs, buds, fruit, and cones can be examined and used in a variety of scientific experiments and artistic experiences. Through research students discover that trees are indispensable to life. They must recognize our responsibility to conserve trees, one of our most valuable natural resources.

Artistic Adventures

Adopt-a-Tree/Four-Flap Flip-Fact

Each student chooses a tree to adopt that is growing on the school grounds, at home, or in the surrounding neighborhood. As the adoptive parent of a very special prodigy, each proud parent prepares an adoption announcement to proclaim a claim on a special tree. Included in the announcement are many unusual and unique features of this special tree that are determined by careful observation using the five senses and making note of these findings. Each tree is classified based on leaf shape as well as other identifying characteristics. A certificate of adoption is displayed in front of the tree's picture (see Certificate of Adoption in Activity Appendix A). An example of entry information for a personal tree might read:

Certificate of Adoption
This certifies that <u>Annie Oak Tree</u> is proudly adopted by <u>Kelly Jones</u> on this <u>19th</u> day in the month of <u>January,</u> year <u>2009</u>.

This <u>Wild Turkey Oak</u> tree grows proudly at <u>117 Patten Heights Boulevard</u> in the community of <u>Lake Hollingsworth, Florida.</u>

A picture of an adopted tree is featured on a four-flap flip-fact (see Four-Flap Flip-Flop in Activity Appendix A). The adopter creates a four-part picture of the adopted tree and includes information about each part under the flap on which the part is drawn (see Figure 7.1). The following are picture parts for a tree with some information entries. Appearance will vary depending on the specific tree adopted.

FIGURE 7.1   Four-Flap Flip-Fact

Flap 1:   **Leaves**
Under Flap 1:

    Appearance:

    Importance to Tree: Turn sunlight into food, take in carbon dioxide.

    Contribution to Life: Give off oxygen; provide shade, nesting, and clean air.

Flap 2:   **Branches, Twigs, and Buds**
           Seeds in Cones, Nuts, or Fruit

Under Flap 2:

    Appearance:

    Importance to Tree: Branches and twigs support leaves; transport water to and sugar from leaves and buds; seeds produce more trees.

    Contributions to Life: Source of food for people and animals, primary ingredient for medicine and spices.

Flap 3:   **Trunk**
Under Flap 3:

    Appearance:

    Bark Mark: Place a piece of paper securely over the bark and rub on the paper with the side of a wax crayon. The bark mark is akin to an identifying foot or fingerprint.

    Girth: The distance around the trunk of the tree that is measured about three feet above the ground. For many trees, each inch indicates approximately one year of age for the tree.

Importance to Tree: Protects the inside of the tree. Lenticels, slits in the bark, allow air to pass in and out, thus cooling the tree.

Contribution to Life: Provides lumber, paper, pencils, and other products important to people.

Flap 4:   **Roots**

Under Flap 4:

Appearance:

Importance to Tree: Extract moisture and minerals from the soil and convey them up through the tree's system.

Contribution to Life: Provide homes for small animals and help prevent soil erosion.

Literature-Based Example:

Three trees that lend themselves to the creation of adoption announcements and four-flap flip-facts are found in The Cherry Tree *by Daisaku Ikeda (1991),* The Gift of the Tree *by Alvin Tresselt (1992), and* The People Who Hugged the Trees *by Deborah Rose (1990).*

Gamut of Games

Leaf Lore and Leaf Shape Books/Leaf Lab

Leaf lore is information about leaves. Leaves are collected when students go on nature walks at school and home. Leaf lore is based on information gleaned from observation, comparison, and classification of the leaves as well as from books. A variety of artistic and experimental experiences with the leaves makes students more aware of their unique characteristics. Findings may be compiled in a *leaf shape book* (see Shape Books in Activity Appendix A).

The following *leaf lab* activities provide opportunities to examine leaves closely, to preserve leaves, and to experiment with leaves.

Leaf Sort: Classify leaves by shape, color, size, or texture.

Wax Paper Preservation: Iron leaves between two sheets of wax paper. Protect the iron and ironing board by placing several sheets of newspaper over and under the wax paper.

Newspaper Preservation: Place leaves between two layers of paper towels. Place several sheets of newspaper over and under the paper towels. Make several layers of leaves and newspapers. Place heavy books on top of the stack. Leave for two to three weeks.

Leaf Rubbing: Turn a leaf upside down so that the veins are on top. Place a piece of paper over the veins. Rub the surface of the paper with the side of a wax crayon to create an imprint of the leaf.

Leaf Painting: Turn a leaf upside down so that the veins are on top. Paint the veins and surface of the leaf. Place a piece of paper over the painted surface and rub to create an imprint of the leaf.

Leaf Skeleton: Place leaves in hot water and simmer slowly for approximately 30 minutes. Remove leaves carefully and place on a piece of cardboard. Use an old toothbrush to carefully brush away everything except the veins of each leaf. Mount leaf skeletons.

Ocular Organizers

Find-a-Tree and Show Me

Develop background knowledge on trees by reading *Trees of North America* from The Science Nature Guides (Mitchell, 1994) and construct a find-a-tree and show me bulletin board by following these steps:

1. **Partition** a bulletin board into three sections.
2. **Label** each section with the name of one of three types of trees:
   a. Broad-leaved
   b. Ornamental—fruits and flowers
   c. Evergreen & Conifers
3. **Trunk:** Form a tree shape for each of the three types of trees by cutting apart large grocery bags and removing the bottom from each bag. Twist the bags to form tree trunks and branches and mount on the appropriate section of the bulletin board for a three-dimensional effect.
4. **Leaves:** Collect real leaves for each of the three types of trees. When real leaves are not available, make leaves using various media techniques (see Media Techniques in the Activity Appendix A). Surround each tree with the appropriate leaf specimens.
5. **Buds, Seeds in Cones, Nuts, or Fruit:** Collect real specimens for each of the three types of trees. When real specimens are not available, make buds, seeds, nuts, or fruit using various media techniques (see Media Techniques in the Activity Appendix A). Surround each tree with the appropriate specimens.
6. **Labels:** Create labels for each of the three types of trees using the following information as a guideline:

   Name of Tree: _____

   Type of Tree: _____

   Location of Tree: _____

   Bark Mark: _____

   Girth: _____ Approximate Age: _____

   Twig Sample: _____

Dramatic Debut

Chamber Theater/The Giving Tree: The Giving Me

Chamber theater is a dramatic experience in which participants read scripts expressively, mime movements theatrically, and use props creatively. Chamber theater uses gestures and movement and is a variation of readers' theater in which participants also read scripts expressively, but in readers' theater there is no movement or attempt to show actions. Both types of dramatic experience emphasize oral language development through practice in expressive oral reading.

In chamber theater, characters carry their script in one hand either in a binder, on a clipboard, or on index cards. The other hand is used for gestures. Stools of varying heights, tables, and screens are used for props to represent trees, a house, steps, etc. Participants wear smocks to indicate that they are part of the production. Smocks are made from large shirts or rectangles of material that have head holes cut in them. Participants read their parts expressively while using gestures and actions. At the end of the play, the actors repeat a line slowly to indicate the end of the production. Shepard (1994) has a number of additional suggestions for chamber theater.

Literature-Based Example

Teachers can easily introduce chamber theater using The Giving Tree *by Shel Silverstein. Write a script for a narrator, the boy, and the tree. The boy wears different hats to indicate aging (or several students may take the part of the boy as he ages). The tree is dressed with a green construction hat, leaves, and apples tied to branches (arms), paper towel tubes to indicate smaller branches, bulletin board paper wrapped around the body to indicate the trunk of the tree, and a small stool for the stump. As an alternative, a tree is made from cardboard and construction paper, and each part is removed at the appropriate place in the script.*

As the narrator reads the script, the boy and tree read their parts and participate in appropriate actions to carry out their parts. At the end of the play, the boy, now an old man, sits to rest on the tree stump (a low stool); the tree sighs; and the narrator and boy repeat slowly with the tree, "I have nothing left to give."

Chamber theater provides an opportunity for oral communication. Using a chamber theater experience with The Giving Tree *as a springboard for discussion, students develop questions such as (1) What does a tree do for me? (2) What do I give a tree? and (3) What are a tree's enemies? Students contribute information from their own background experiences and obtain additional information from trade books, textbooks, and other resources. A record of the brainstorming and research might begin:*

1. **What does a tree do for me?**   A tree provides oxygen to breathe, removal of carbon dioxide from the air, fruit to eat, shade to sit in, wood for building, and air purification. More than 5,000 products are made from trees. Some of these products are artificial vanilla flavoring, books, cardboard boxes, charcoal, furniture, medical chemicals, paint, paper, paper towels, pencils, rubber, toothpaste, toothpicks, and vinegar.
2. **What do I give a tree?**   I can help in the conservation of trees through reducing, reusing, and recycling paper. I can write on both the front and back of my notebook paper. I can create newspaper art projects. I can take newspaper and other used paper to recycling centers. I can plant and care for trees by watering, fertilizing, and cultivating them. I should always follow fire safety precautions.
3. **What are a tree's enemies?**   Some of a tree's enemies are fire, acid rain, hurricanes, woodpeckers, fungi, insects, vines that choke out a tree, and humans.

Using information from class discussion and research, students create their own chamber theater scripts working as a whole class or in small, cooperative groups. They may act out the part of products from the tree; animals seeking protection in the tree; a tree's fears of fire, hurricanes, volcanoes, and wind; and people reducing, reusing, and recycling (see Writing chapter, Persuasive Writing). The following books provide ideas for chamber theater scripts: The Cherry Tree *by Daisaku Ikeda (1991),* The First Forest *by John Gile (1989),* The Gift of the Tree *by Alvin Tresselt (1992),* The Lorax *by Dr. Seuss (1991),* The People Who Hugged the Trees *by Deborah Rose (1990), and* A Tree Is Nice *by Janice Udry (1956). As students become involved in composing scripts, they will develop increasing concerns for nature and the preservation of trees.*

Creative Composition

Poet-Tree/Is-Because Poetry

A *poet-tree* may be a permanent fixture in the classroom and may be used throughout the year to display students' poetry. Write poetry on construction paper leaf shapes and hang on the tree. Use a variety of leaf shapes and colors as seasons and thematic focus change. In the fall leaves may be pumpkin-shaped; in February perhaps the leaves are heart-shaped; and during a tree-mendous tree focus, the leaves have a variety of leaf shapes for different types of trees. Shapes for animals and birds that seek shelter in the tree provide additional possibilities for displaying student work. Students enjoy creating a diversity of shapes to hang from the limbs and trunk of the tree.

There are many possibilities for creating a poet-tree. A real tree or the branch from a real tree has potential as does an artificial tree. If this is not feasible, concoct a tree trunk and branches using long pieces of brown bulletin board paper. To transform the paper into a tree, a student holds one end of the paper taut, and another student stands at the opposite end and twists the paper over and over to give the tree trunk and branches a gnarled appearance. Hang the life-sized trunk from the ceiling to the floor in the classroom. Drooping branches allow the students to reach up and hang leaves. Punch holes in the tops of the leaves and use holiday ornament hangers or partially opened paper clips to hang leaves from the tree.

Students sit under the tree to rest, relax, and read. A carpet of grass under the tree is a sheet of green bulletin board paper or some sample carpet squares. Throw pillows, a bench, and table add to the park atmosphere. Write poems on the leaves in a variety of poetic formats (see Poetry Appendix C).

Literature-Based Example

Is-because poetry is a formula sentence poem that is composed of cause and effect statements. State the effect first, and state the cause last. For example:

Effect: a mother is nice
Cause: she loves you
A mother is nice because she loves you.

A Tree Is Nice by Janice Udry provides the stimulus for writing about trees. She examines the value of trees often starting a series of thoughts with,

"A tree is nice because..."

After sharing the book, students compose is-because poetry. Students write the poem on the front of a leaf to display on the poet-tree. They may tell of a personal experience with a tree on the back of the leaf. For example,

Front of Leaf:
- A tree is nice because you can build a tree house in the branches.
- A tree is nice because you can invite friends to play in your tree house.
- A tree is nice because you can sit in your tree house and read your favorite book.

Back of Leaf:
Once upon a time I had a tree house. My friends would come to visit me. They would climb up the tree and sit in the tree house with me. We would have a picnic lunch and read books. We were sad when it was time to climb down and go home.

KITTENS AND KINGS

What are some different breeds of cats?
Who are some of a cat's relatives?
Which cats could I see at a zoo?
Why do so many people have cats as pets?
Do cats really have nine lives?

Scientific inquiry into the realm of animals is meaningful and motivational. From innumerable animal possibilities, cats were chosen as the example of an animal to study, because students see cats at home, at a relative's house, or in the neighborhood. Thus, they are familiar with cats and bring a wealth of background information to a thematic unit focusing on cats. Opportunities abound to observe, compare, and classify cats. Observing the escapades of a litter of kittens prompts discussion about types of cats and care of cats. Expand cat studies from kittens to the king of the beasts, the lion.

From Disney's *The Lion King* to *The Lion, the Witch, and the Wardrobe* by C.S. Lewis (1951), students are captivated by the ferocious king of the beasts as well as its many relatives. Intrigue with cats is evidenced by the many literary works that include cats. Familiar nursery rhymes, folktales, and fables about cats include "The Three Little Kittens," "Puss in Boots," and "The Lion and the Mouse." Award-winning books about cats range from *Millions of Cats*, a 1928 Newbery Honor Book by Wanda Gag, and *Sam, Bangs, and Moonshine*, a 1967 Caldecott Award Book by Evaline Ness, to *One Eyed Cat*, a 1984 Newbery Honor Book by Paula Fox.

Through observation and interaction with cats we are able to compare and contrast different cats' appearance and traits. Cats make notable contributions to our lives as household pets. Larger cats fascinate us as we observe their strength and intelligence at the zoo, circus, and in documentaries such as those produced by National Geographic.

Artistic Adventures

Cat Habitat in a Plate-arama

Create a *cat habitat*, a cat's natural environment or the story setting for a cat's adventure, in a plate-arama. Make a **plate-arama,** a three-dimensional story or environmental scene, from two paper plates (see Activity Appendix A). Decorate the eating side of one paper plate to form the backdrop for the habitat. Remove the center circle from the second paper plate. Decorate the remaining rim and join to the first paper plate eating sides together to form a frame around the scenery. Cut a cat from the remaining circle and cover with small pieces of torn paper to give a furry appearance (see Media Techniques in Activity Appendix A). Mount the paper cat on a jack-in-the-box spring (see Activity Appendix A) and place in the plate-arama.

Write about the cat and its environment in the circle on the back of the plate-arama. As a research report, the composition about the cat includes information such as type, appearance, habits, care, protection, and importance. If the cat is a story character, the composition contains interesting adventure tidbits or a synopsis of the story. An additional challenge for older students is to write in a circular pattern starting at the outer edge of the circle, writing around and around, and ending the entry in the center of the circle.

Literature-Based Example

After sharing The Kids' Cat Book *by Tomie de Paola (1979), a student might choose to create a plate-arama for a Siamese cat. The Siamese has dark fur on the face, ears, paws, and tail. The rest of the fur is a light tan or gray. The eyes are blue. The backdrop for the Siamese might be a porch with a food bowl, water bowl, and litter box. The research report includes information about the history of the Siamese.*

Suggestions for other books to use as a stimulus for the platearama are:

1. *Sam, Bangs, and Moonshine* by Evaline Ness (1966) sometimes takes place in Sam's bedroom. Bangs scratches at Sam's window when he wants in. Another possibility is the cave, lighthouse, and water at Blue Rock. Write what Sam learns about the danger of lying on the back of the plate-arama.
2. *Big Cats* by Seymour Simon (1991) provides the necessary background information to make a plate-arama for a big cat such as the jaguar. The backdrop is a dense forest. Write information about the jaguar on the back of the plate-arama.
3. *Six-Dinner Sid* by Inga Moore (1991) divides the setting into six scenes. Make a series of plate-aramas, one for each scene. The drawings in each scene depict each of the different homes where Sid eats dinner nightly. The composition on the back captures Sid's ingenuity. Create a vertical chain of the six scenes.

Gamut of Games

Catardy

Catardy is a variation of the popular game show *Jeopardy*. Catardy has six categories with five questions in each category. The difficulty and dollar amount for the questions ranges from ten dollars to fifty dollars. Questions for each category are color-coded using different colored 3-inch × 5-inch index cards (e.g., "paw verb" questions are written on blue index cards; "cat tale" questions are on yellow index cards, etc.). Write a question on the back of each card. A book of lists such as *The Reading Teacher's Book of Lists* (Fry, Kress, & Fountoukidis, 2000) provides information for teachers and students to use in creating questions using homophones, multiple meaning words, proverbs, and other formats. Question cards slip into pockets on a Catardy question board.

An easily stored catardy question board is constructed in a variety of ways such as:

1. Use library pockets and mount on a 24″ × 28″ piece of poster board.
2. Use 3.5-inch × 6-inch envelopes. Seal the envelopes. Cut in half forming two 3.5-inch × 3.25-inch pockets. Mount on a trifold science project board.
3. Use commercially available sentence strip charts.

The catardy board with dollar amount pockets appears as follows:

Cataphones	Kitty Ditties	Cat-a-Breeds	Catabulary	Paw Verbs	Cat Tale Characters
$10	$10	$10	$10	$10	$10
$20	$20	$20	$20	$20	$20
$30	$30	$30	$30	$30	$30
$40	$40	$40	$40	$40	$40
$50	$50	$50	$50	$50	$50

In Catardy two or more class teams answer questions to score points for their team. Rules for Catardy include:

1. Each team member takes turns choosing and answering a question. The team collaborates on the answer.
2. A class scorekeeper keeps a running total of each team's points.
3. Teams take turns answering questions.
4. If a team cannot answer a question correctly, the next team has the opportunity to answer the question and score points before choosing its own question.
5. If that team cannot answer the question, a third team may attempt to answer. However, after that question is completed, with or without points, the team whose turn it is gets to choose the next question.

Note: Older students may play Double Catardy for double dollar amounts. Include daily double questions as well.

Literature-Related Example

The following catardy categories and questions relate to cats:

Category 1 — Cataphones *Cataphones* are *homophones,* words that are related to cats that sound the same but are spelled differently and have different meanings.
Practice: When the judge sentenced the attacking feline, from the law he cited the... (claws clause)
$10 A story of a cat's appendage is a... (tail tale)
$20 To pay a cat for each sound he makes, you must pay... (per purr)
$30 When cats make a brief stop, you have a... (paws pause)
$40 The veterinarian assured the distraught owner about his injured tomcat saying, "Don't worry... (he'll heal)
$50 As the religious leopard faced his adversary, he suggested... (pray prey)

Category 2 — Kitty Ditties *Kitty ditties* are *hink pinks* (riddles with two one-syllable rhyming words for the answer) and *hinky pinkies* (riddles with two two-syllable rhyming words for the answer). When concocting hink pinks, determine the pair of rhyming words first, then make up a question stem to go with the pair. The question stem will generally have synonyms for the rhyming words answer.
Practice: What is a plump feline? (fat cat)
$10 Paw warmers... (kittens' mittens)
$20 The country mouse did not want to see the... (city kitty)
$30 Kittens' babysitter... (litter sitter)
$40 Heavenly cat... (divine feline)
$50 When a cat falls, it will always land on its feet, because it has... (agility ability)

Category 3 — Cat-a-Breeds *Cat-a-Breeds* are hink pinks; hinky pinkies; *hinkity pinkities,* riddles with three three-syllable rhyming words, and so forth, for the answer. One of the rhyming words is the name of a type of cat. Often the number of syllables for each rhyming word is given (e.g., Cat journey... Persian excursion; 2,3).

Practice: Cat meeting…(alley rally; 2,2)

$10 Grumpy cat…(crabby tabby; 2,2)

$20 Cat hug…(Siamese squeeze; 3,1)

$30 From this grateful cat you will receive…(manx thanks; 1,1)

$40 Cat purchaser? (cheshire buyer; 2, 2)

$50 Metropolitan opera songstress? (calico soprano; 3,3)

Category 4 — Catabulary Catabulary questions are answered with words or phrases that have cat in them.

Practice: Organize systematically…(categorize)

$10 An imitator…(copy cat)

$20 A narrow walkway…(cat walk)

$30 Devastation…(catastrophe)

$40 A tomb…(catacomb)

$50 A church…(cathedral)

Category 5 — Paw Verbs *Paw verbs* are short, well known sayings about cats. The literal and figurative meanings for paw verbs are different.

Practice: Torrential gully washer…(It's raining cats and dogs)

$10 Inquisitiveness annihilates…(Curiosity killed the cat)

$20 Divulge a secret…(Let the cat out of the bag)

$30 When the supervisor's away, chaos reigns…(When the cat's away, the mice will play)

$40 Stunned speechless…(Cat got your tongue)

$50 Dazzling appearance…(The cat's meow)

Category 6 — Cat Tale Characters Cat tale characters are found in cat stories.

$10 Rescued by a tiny mouse he had befriended…(the lion in *The Lion and the Mouse*)

$20 He along with Thing One and Thing Two turn a house into shambles…(the cat in *The Cat in the Hat*)

$30 Through ingenuity this cat makes great gain for his master…(Puss in *Puss in Boots*)

$40 He protects the farm mice…(Martin in *Martin's Mice* King-Smith, 1988)

$50 He defeats the powers of evil in Narnia…(Aslan, the lion, in *The Lion, the Witch, and the Wardrobe* Lewis, 1951)

Ocular Organizers
Cat Clusters

Cat clusters are graphic organizers with cat silhouettes on which to categorize cat facts. The nucleus and each major cluster category are cat silhouettes. Laminate these silhouettes so that changes can easily be made, and the silhouettes can be reused. Be sure to use a water-based marker.

A cat cluster may contain general information about a wild cat; for example, a lion (see Figure 7.2). The categories to expand include appearance, habitat, characteristics, food, and protection. The same categories may be used for domestic cats. Students might then expand one of these categories. For example, How does a cat move? (*walk, leap, slink, stalk, spring, scamper, sprawl*). What are characteristics of a cat's mealtime manners? (*devour, lap, lick, sniff, snuff*). Searching for information to expand a category simultaneously expands a student's proprietary vocabulary.

Dramatic Debut
Zooks Zoo/Cat Habitat Diorama

People take trips to zoos to visit animals. Traditionally, zoos had a collection of animals in cages and concrete enclosures. Today zoos have park-like settings and attempt to recreate, as closely as possible, the natural habitats of the animals. A zoo is not only a place to visit

FIGURE 7.2   Cat Clusters: Wild Cat, Big Cat, Lion

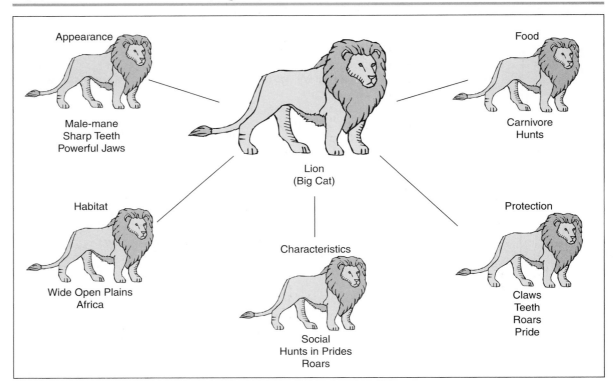

Appearance
Male-mane
Sharp Teeth
Powerful Jaws

Food
Carnivore
Hunts

Lion
(Big Cat)

Habitat
Wide Open Plains
Africa

Characteristics

Protection
Claws
Teeth
Roars
Pride

Social
Hunts in Prides
Roars

animals, but zoos are a center for animal study, animal entertainment, and animal education. Through animal study, zoos have made valuable contributions to saving endangered species. Often the animals' participation in shows benefits the animals by providing a means of exercise. Through education, people become more aware of animals' contributions to our environment.

After sharing *Let's Take a Trip Around the Zoo* by Strong (1992) with younger students or *Zoos* by Daniel and Susan Cohen (1992) with older students, discuss zoo facts and features. As part of a zoology thematic unit, research big cats and their natural environments. Using this information, create cat habitat dioramas.

A *diorama* is a miniature, three-dimensional scene with objects placed in front of a painted background. A diorama is made from shoeboxes, cereal boxes, or gift boxes. Use a variety of media materials, including paint, paper, paper tubes, sand, twigs, rocks, and ribbon, to make scenery and objects (see Diorama and Media Techniques in Activity Appendix A).

A *cat habitat diorama* is a miniature, three-dimensional scene that portrays the natural environment of a wild or domestic cat. Devise tree trunks from paper towel tubes or rolled construction paper. Make tree foliage and grass for the habitat. Suspend vines from the ceiling. Glue sand to the floor to represent sandy terrain. To make cats, use clay or construction paper shapes covered with torn paper to give a furry appearance and mount on stands (see Media Techniques in the Activity Appendix A). Use camouflage colors appropriately. Design a zoo information plaque for each cat that includes unique features, physical appearance, and a range map (see Figure 7.3).

Issue an invitation to other classes to visit your zoo where zoologists, who are animal experts, will conduct tours to each habitat.

> You're invited to Zooks Zoo.
> Where there's fun for me and you.
> Please come at ten; don't be late
> You'll love our cats; they're GR...eat!

FIGURE 7.3   Zoo Information Plaque for the Lion

Unique Characteristics	Physical Characteristics	Range Map
• The lion is the only social cat. • The lion lives and hunts in prides or groups. • The lion roars fiercely. • The mane of the male lion is the only obvious sign of sexual difference in the cat family. • Family: Felidae (mammal). • Order: Carnivore.	• Weight: More than 400 pounds. • Length 9 to 10 feet from nose to tail. • Eyes: Large and round with a wide range of vision. • Teeth: Large, sharp canine teeth. • Tongue: Rough for scraping flesh from bones. • Fur: Two layered, provides warmth, camouflage, carries scent, serves as an organ of touch. • Legs: Long for leaping on prey.	• Central and South Africa on the wide open plains.

Literature-Based Example

After sharing Big Cats *by Seymour Simon (1991),* Eyewitness Books: Cat *by Juliet Clutton-Brock (1991), and other information books, create cat habitat dioramas for a variety of cats. Expand the following script for your class zoo:*

Zoo Guide: Thank you for visiting the Zooks Zoo. Here you will find out about each of the cats in our zoo from world-renown zoologists. Each zoologist is an expert on his or her cat. You will visit lions, tigers, leopards, jaguars, pumas, and cheetahs. As you stop in front of the lion's habitat, our world famous cat expert, Dr. Frederick, is ready to share his expertise with you.

Dr. Frederick: As you can see, the lion is truly the king of the beasts. You will note the zoo information plaque contains information about the lion (see Figure 7.3).

Zoo Guide: Be sure to visit the zoo nursery before leaving. You may also want to become a zoometry expert by examining the measurements of proportionate lengths and sizes of parts of our animals.

Creative Composition
Cationary

A *cationary* is a cat's reference book, or dictionary, in which the definitions are written from a cat's point of view. Choice of entries and definitions are based on:

1. **Cat Search:**   Revealing revelations from research
2. **Cat Antics:**   Funny feline fabrications
3. **Cat Tales:**   Latitude with literary legends

Cationaries are made in a variety of ways. Encourage students to experiment with journal jackets, accordion books, shape books, and teeny tiny books (see Activity Appendix A).

Ed Emberley's Great Thumbprint Drawing Book (1977) has wonderful ideas for thumbprint illustrations that could adorn entries.

Literature-Based Examples

Cat Search: Revealing Revelations from Research

Entries chosen from Big Cats *by Seymour Simon (1991).*

Carnivore	flesh eater
Endangered	scarce; in peril of vanishing
Mammal	gives birth to young; young born alive
Prey (noun)	animal used for food
Pride	group of lions
Roar	utter a deep, loud cry
Stalking	stealthily pursuing prey

Cat Antics: Funny Feline Fabrications

Entries chosen from Catwings *by Ursula K. Le Guin (1988).*

A Hands; A Shoes	a human being
Drool	drip water from mouth in anticipation of food or attention
Knead	massage with paws when happy
Mew	speaking when hungry, wanting to be picked up, or wanting in or out of the house
Mice	delicious entrée
Owl	nocturnal enemy; avoid at all times
Pur-r-r-r	contented sound

Cat Tales: Latitude with Literary Legends

Entries are paw verbs and other expressions selected from Martin's Mice *by Dick King-Smith (1988). Definitions are the related familiar expressions. (Similes, metaphors, interesting terminology, and word pictures are other entry possibilities.)*

A mouse a day keeps the vet away.	An apple a day keeps the doctor away.
Beat you with one paw tied behind my back.	Beat you with one hand tied behind my back.
Mouse to mouse resuscitation	Mouth to mouth resuscitation
Worn my claws to the bone.	Worn my fingers to the bone.

WEATHER WATCH

How can we predict the weather?
How does weather affect our lives?
Why are clouds different shapes?
How can we be safe during storms?
Is there really a pot of gold at the end of the rainbow?

When asked, "What is the weather like today?" replies generally include statements such as, "Hot. Cold. Rainy. Windy. Muggy." *Weather* is the state of the atmosphere, or ocean of air, around us that is affected by temperature, moisture, clouds, wind, pressure, and the sun.

Weather constantly changes. When asked, "What is the climate like where you live?" replies include statements such as, "Hot days and cool nights. Dry summers. Frigid winters. Delightful year round." *Climate* is a weather pattern for a region that is determined over a period of time and is affected by the region's proximity to the equator, bodies of water, and mountains.

Weather affects the way we live: the clothes we wear, the food we eat, the type of house in which we live, and the types of recreation in which we participate. If we live where the weather is hot, we wear lightweight clothes with short sleeves. We like cold drinks and ice cream. We want air conditioning or windows in our house that provide ventilation. We enjoy water activities such as swimming and water skiing. If we live where it is cold, we wear jackets and sweaters. We like soup and hot drinks. We want our home to have a heating system that will keep us warm. Cold weather recreation includes sledding and snow skiing.

A thematic focus on weather provides meaningful and motivational opportunities for students to use their senses in observing weather and determining its unique effects on our lives. Weather is charted; temperature and rainfall are measured. Comparisons can be made with weather in other parts of our country and other parts of the world. Certainly, predicting weather is fun especially when comparing predictions with those of *meteorologists,* scientists who study and predict the weather, on radio, television, and in the newspaper. Verifying, modifying, or rejecting predictions increases interest in weather watching.

Artistic Activities

Season Scenes in Shallow Shadow Boxes/Snowflakes

Designing season scenes in shallow shadow boxes is a creative activity for students of any age. Students work in cooperative groups of four with each group member selecting and creating a scene for one of the four seasons: winter, spring, summer, and fall. Carefully plan scenes to reflect appropriate clothing, food, recreation, foliage, and other characteristics for the season. One side of a gift box or a shallow box that holds soda cans is used for each of the four season scenes. Create three-dimensional pictures using a variety of media techniques (see Diorama and Media Techniques in Activity Appendix A). Arrange and display each group's season scenes.

The following are some season scene suggestions:

1. **Winter:** Snowsuit, hot chocolate, sled, bare tree, snowman. *Note: Try chalk art.*
2. **Spring:** Shorts and shirt, lemonade, swing, flowers, grass. *Note: Try jab art for flowers.*
3. **Summer:** Bathing suits, ice cream, beach, sand castle, sun. *Note: Try sand art for beach and sand castle.*
4. **Fall:** Jacket, soup, rake, tree with colored leaves, squirrel. *Note: Try dab art for leaves.*

Literature-Based Example

After reading All About Snow and Ice *by Stephen Krensky (1994), make snowflakes (see Activity Appendix A). Afterwards, hang the snowflakes from the ceiling, use them for a bulletin board border, or combine three or more snowflakes to make a snowman. Include snowflakes in season scenes. Read and find out more facts about snowflakes, such as most snowflakes have six sides, and no two snowflakes are alike just as each of us is unique.*

Gamut of Games

Weather Station

A *weather station* is a center where classroom meteorologists investigate and share information about weather. They gather, record, and interpret weather information daily. This data should be collected at designated times during the day and includes:

1. Temperature
2. Wind direction

3. Rainfall
4. Cloud formations

This information is compared with findings of professional meteorologists by calling the local weather bureau, checking the newspaper on the following day, or checking online. Be sure class meteorologists chart the paths of storms and hurricanes. Weather reports may be included in closed circuit school broadcasts.

Rain Gauge: How Much Rain Fell?

To determine the amount of rain that falls, the classroom meteorologists build a rain gauge using the following directions:

1. Wash out a clear plastic straight-sided drink container that has a flat bottom.
2. Horizontally cut the container in half.
3. Invert the top of the container and place it in the bottom of the container to form a funnel.
4. Secure the two pieces of the container together with duct tape.
5. From the base of the container, mark the side of the container in one-half inch intervals.
6. Place outside in an open area or mount on a fence post.
7. On rainy days, record the amount of rain and time of day the gauge is read. Then empty the container.
8. Compare records to newspaper, television, and radio reports. *(Note: Commercial rain gauges are available.)*

Windsock: Which Direction Does the Wind Come From?

A *windsock,* a tapered tubular cloth open at both ends, is used to determine wind direction. Windsocks are used at airports and other places where knowing the direction of the wind and the approximate intensity of the wind is important. Wind is identified by the direction from which it blows; thus, a north wind blows from north to south and a west wind from west to east. To make a windsock use the following directions:

1. Cut off one leg from a pair of panty hose.
2. Cut the foot end off the leg, leaving a tapered tubular cloth open at both the thigh and ankle ends.
3. Use lightweight florist wire to reinforce each circular end at the openings of the windsock.
4. On the thigh end of the windsock, attach four 6-inch strings to the wire at equal intervals around the circumference. Gather the strings together approximately 2 inches from the wire and knot.
5. Put a nail in the top of a 5-foot dowel or stick and plant vertically in the ground.
6. Tie a string around the nail.
7. Tie the knotted end of the windsock string to the string on the nail. Be sure the windsock can pivot freely around the nail.
8. Observe the windsock as the wind blows into the thigh hole and out through the ankle hole. The wind is named after the direction the thigh end is pointing to or the direction the wind is blowing from.
9. When the windsock stands out straight, the wind is strong. When the windsock sags, the wind is light. When the windsock drops, there is no wind. *Note: Commercial wind vanes are available to determine wind direction.*

For additional meteorological research, experimentation, exploration, and directions for constructing weather instruments, consult *Exploring the Sky by Day* by Terrence Dickinson (1988), *Eyewitness Books: Weather* by Brian Cosgrove (1991), *Janice Van Cleave's Geography for Every Kid* (1993), *175 More Science Experiments to Amuse and Amaze Your Friends* by Terry Cash, Steve Parker, and Barbara Taylor (1989), *The Usborne Book of Weather Facts* by Anita Ganeri (1987), and *Weatherwatch* by Valerie Wyatt (1990).

Ocular Organizers
Three-Flap Flip-Flop Clouds

Clouds are collections of tiny drops of water or ice suspended in the air. There are three main types of clouds:

1. **Cumulus Clouds:**   Cumulus means "heap" or "pile" in Latin. These clouds are puffy and often change size and shape. They are shaped like a cauliflower and are flat on bottom. They are low in the sky and often seen on sunny days.
2. **Stratus Clouds:**   Stratus means "stretched out" in Latin. These clouds look like layers of blankets. They are low in the sky, gray in color, and may block the sun. Often light rain accompanies these clouds.
3. **Cirrus Clouds:**   Cirrus means "curl" in Latin. These clouds resemble wispy curls of hair and are sometimes called mares' tales because they resemble the tails of horses when the wind blows. They are white and float high in the sky.

Make a three-flap flip-flop book (see Four-Flap Flip-Flop Book in Activity Appendix A). Make each type of cloud with cotton balls that have been pulled apart to give a fluffy appearance. Label each flap with a type of cloud and attach the appropriate cloud over each label. Include appropriate information about each type of cloud under the flap.

Literature-Based Example

After reading The Cloud Book *by Tomie de Paola and* Exploring the Sky by Day *by Terrence Dickenson, make ten-flap flip-flop books (or attach two five-flap flip-flop books) to display appropriate information and illustrations for the ten different types of clouds that include:*

Highest level	Cirrus, Cirrostratus, Cirrocumulus
Mid-level	Altostratus, Altocumulus
Low-level	Stratus, Nimbostratus, Stratocumulus
Tall clouds	Cumulus, Cumulonimbus

Dramatic Debut
Prepare, Don't Panic

Prepare, don't panic is a dramatic activity based on safety information gleaned through class discussion in which students improvise a response for a given weather situation. Participation increases awareness of precautions to take if there is a tornado, hurricane, lightning storm, or other weather phenomenon. In Prepare, Don't Panic, the leader holds up a card with a weather situation such as, "You're at home watching TV when an emergency broadcast signal announces tornadoes have been spotted in your area." Participants improvise their response to the situation.

Literature-Based Examples

The following information may be used for class discussion before Prepare, Don't Panic activities. Many of the suggested safety precautions are found in Storms *by Seymour Simon (1989).*

Tornadoes

A tornado is a very powerful, funnel-shaped cloud with fierce winds that inflicts terrible damage on anything in its path. Tornadoes can uproot trees, lift houses, move cars, and overturn trains. The Wizard of Oz *by Frank Baum (1982) will introduce students to the terrible devastation of a tornado.*

If you know a tornado is coming, then . . .
Stay inside the house or in the basement, in the center of the house, away from windows, under a chair or stairs. Cover up with a blanket or bedspread.

Hurricanes

A hurricane is a big storm that gains intensity as it travels over tropical ocean water. Hurricanes are named alphabetically with alternating male and female names (excluding Q, U, X, Y, and Z). Different names are used each year. Hurricanes crash over barriers, flooding homes, knocking out electric lines, destroying trees, rerouting rivers, ripping up roads, and crumbling bridges. Be cautious of the eye of the hurricane, which is a deceptive time of calm before the rest of the hurricane hits. Hurricanes by David Wiesner (1990) includes some of the precautions to take before and during a hurricane.
If you know a hurricane is coming, then . . .
Have a battery-operated radio. Store drinking water. Have alternate sources of light: flashlight, candles, and lanterns. Have canned food and a hand-operated can opener. Move pets and lawn furniture inside. Tape or cover large glass surfaces.

Lightning

Lightning is an electrical discharge that occurs during a storm. Electricity in the clouds builds up and is released in a "leader" stroke that zigzags to the ground. The return stroke races up the path that was just formed.
If you know there is lightning, then . . .
Go inside a house, building, or car. Don't use the telephone.
If you are caught outside in a lightning storm, then . . .
Stay in a low open space on knees, bend over, and put hands on knees to minimize contact with the ground. Don't get under a tree or on a hill. Don't get near metal. Don't get in or near water.

Creative Composition
Haiku/Tanka/Lanterne Poetry

Students enjoy the challenge of capturing a weather moment through pictures and poetry. Haiku, tanka, and lanterne poetry provide a structure for poetic response (formats in Poetry Appendix C). These forms of Japanese verse focus on nature and provide a concise description of an event. Limitations of line and syllable count challenge the poet to make thoughtful and precise word choices to capture the moment in a word picture. *Haiku* has three unrhymed lines containing seventeen syllables. *Tanka* is an expanded form of the Japanese haiku and has five unrhymed lines containing thirty-one syllables. *Lanterne* has five unrhymed lines containing eleven syllables. The poem forms a Japanese lantern shape.

Employ a variety of media techniques such as dab art, chalk, and crayon resist for illustrations (see Media Techniques in Activity Appendix A). Displaying pictures and poetry in frames from file folders (see Activity Appendix A) adds significance to and recognition of students' compositions.

Literature-Based Example

Cloud formations inspire poetic response. Dreams *by Peter Spier (1986) is a wonderful wordless book that invites creation of cloud poems such as:*

Clouds drifting slowly
Across the sky make pictures
For stories in books
Haiku

Cloud
Floating
In the sky
Like a white ghost
Help!
Lanterne

Sharing the story Storms in the Night *(Mary Stolz, 1988) stimulates stretching the imagination and experiencing storms through poetry.*

A storm strikes swiftly
Thunder crashes; lightning bolts
Streak across the sky
No power, then lights go off.
Are you safe under the bed?
Tanka

GATEWAY DRUGS

In a major drug recovery community, I asked women attending a meeting for those in recovery from drug addiction, "How many of you started on drugs when you were in elementary school?" A lot of hands shot up. "How many of you had a drug prevention program in your school?" Again, many affirmative responses. "What could your teachers have done differently in the classroom to keep you from experimenting with drugs?" The lively discussion that ensued went on for well over an hour. Their responses could be categorized as:

Tell me I forget (good? maybe)

Show me, I remember (better)

Involve me, I understand (best)

Ancient Chinese Proverb

Note: See this same proverb in Chapter 1.
Capturing the essence of their suggestions*:

Involve Me

Involve me in close-up-and-personal encounters of the worst kind via field trips, speakers, and a busy life.

1. Field Trips to where?
   * To a treatment center, guidance clinic, or hospital to see a child ravaged by drugs, a child who will never have a normal life due to the debilitating effects of drug addiction.
   * To a psychiatric ward to see the padded room where an addict tears padding off the wall in a manic fit because there are bugs crawling all over him—he thinks.
   * To a juvenile detention facility, a spot in-the-middle-of-nowhere surrounded by a 12-foot fence, topped off by electric wire with wire-caged walkways between buildings.
   * To a morgue where I can talk to a forensic pathologist.
   * To a cemetery.
   * To a prison (*Note: Prisoners often dig graves and bury bodies for those who die while they are incarcerated.*).
   * To death row.
   (*Note: One of the women who had been incarcerated for thirteen years shared that during a prison visit, her daughter was taken to death row. This daughter, despite an all-but-disastrous childhood, is NOT a drug user.*)
2. Speakers who have been there**
   * Speakers whose appearance has been dramatically, drastically destroyed by drug use.

- Speakers with sores, scars, wrinkles, missing teeth, rotten teeth, sallow complexions, emaciation, a missing leg, on oxygen.
- Speakers who support/ed their habits by dealing, stealing, or prostitution.
- Speakers who are young.
- Speakers who have had their lives destroyed, who have lost their children, who can no longer attain their lifetime goals due to felony convictions or brain damage that prevents them from mentally functioning at a level that is necessary to hold a well-paying job.
- Don't bring in a cop in a nice, clean, shiny uniform.
- Bring in an addict who has lived on the street or in a junked car, or in a roach-infested motel, and let her tell her story.

3. Busy Life
- Involve me in drama that depicts what can happen when I'm not involved in worthwhile activities, what happens when I hang out with the wrong crowd.
- Involve me in worthwhile activities such as sports, band, orchestra, drama, class projects, creating multimedia presentations.
- Involve me in community projects for those in need, especially when those needs are the result of drug addiction; for example, a soup kitchen.

Show Me 👁 👁

- Show me brains with holes in them—brains that will never function at a level that will allow me to hold a job, read a book, function in society.
- Show me brains that are not damaged, that can function, that will allow me to get the job I want, to function in society, to achieve my lifetime goals.
- Show me videotapes/DVDs with first-person stories and information about drug abuse/addiction.
- Share with me books that hit-the-nail-on-the-head, that discuss the impact of drugs in a down-and-dirty way.
- Show me wrecked cars, the result of DUI/Driving under the influence of alcohol and/or drugs.
- Show me pictures of the remains of the inhabitants of these cars.
- Show me kids who hang out with and follow the wrong crowd, "sheeple."
- Show me "frienamies," users who can't stand it when those around them aren't using too.

Tell Me 👂 👂

- Tell me you love me. Tell me you care.
- Tell me to tell-a-teacher, tell-a-parent, tell-a-counselor, tell-a-friend that I'm scared.
- Tell me I may lose everything—my kids, my family, my friends, my job, my house, my car, and maybe my life.
- Tell me to bring my parents to school to participate with me in our down-and-dirty, get-your-attention drug prevention program.
- Combat the "it-can't-happen-to-me" mentality, the "I'm invincible, not-me" attitude. Don't mince words. You're dealing with my life.
- Tell me about what drugs are, what they do, how they can impact my life using the plethora of ideas and suggestions in the drug sections that follow.***
- Delve deep. Surface information won't cut it. Drug use is at an all-time high!
- Don't pussyfoot around. It's too late, almost.

*Note: Although some of these suggestions may not be feasible at the time this is being written, due to the drug pandemic in our nation, they may well be realistic by the time the book is published.

**Note: When looking for speakers, ask for recommendations from Alcoholics Anonymous, Narcotics Anonymous, and faith-based recovery programs.

***Note: Most of these strategies have been shared with women and men in recovery from drug and alcohol addiction.

Drug Overview

Drugs are chemical substances that affect the body both physically and psychologically. Drugs may be *used* or *abused*. In the National Science Education Standards (NSES 2004: Chapter 6), Standard F: Science in Personal and Social Perspectives, there is a section on personal health that includes a focus on substance abuse with drugs such as tobacco, alcohol, illegal drugs, and at times over-the-counter medications that can damage the body and lead to addiction. According to the United States Department of Education (USDOE website), students make crucial decisions about the use of drugs and alcohol while they are in elementary school. The earlier these youngsters begin drug experimentation, they more likely they are to become drug abusers/addicts.

The Centers for Disease Control (CDC, 2005) have researched and identified at-risk behaviors that are detrimental to a healthy lifestyle. Included in this list are tobacco use, alcohol and other drug use, and behaviors that contribute to unintentional injuries and violence. Because healthy lifestyle patterns are usually established early in life and remain throughout adulthood, the CDC recommends an educational focus on these as well as other areas of risk.

> My sixth graders internalized information quickly when confronted with scare tactics. For example, videotapes showing lung surgery with lots of blood and guts, as well as interviews with emphysema patients wearing oxygen back packs, were especially effective in encouraging a "Just Say No" attitude toward smoking. Often the class would squeal and gag during the more graphic parts of the videotape but afterward would beg to watch just once more.

Based on research that finds a healthy lifestyle goes hand-in-hand with increased academic achievement (Allen, 2004; Pateman 2003/2004; Smith, 2003), it is incumbent upon the education profession to establish curriculum to guide students in developing a lifelong healthy lifestyle. Pateman (2003/2004) summarizes innumerable research studies and suggests the following guidelines for promoting healthy behavior and academic achievement:

- Focus on helping young people develop and practice personal and social skills, such as communication and decision making, to deal effectively with health-risk/drug-risk situations
- Provide healthy/drug-free alternatives to specific high-risk behaviors
- Use interactive approaches that engage students and:
  - Are research-based and theory-driven
  - Address social and media influences on student behaviors
  - Strengthen individual and group norms that support healthy/drug-free behavior
  - Are of sufficient duration to enable students to gain the knowledge and skills that they need
  - Include teacher preparation and support

Note: The terms drug-risk and drug-free added.

Early Use Leads to Early Abuse

Gateway drugs are habit-forming substances whose frequent use often stimulates the use of more addictive or more dangerous drugs. Early encounters with gateway drugs are casual, social interactions—a *just-have-fun* experience. Over time the impact of these drugs becomes less satisfying, the conscience barrier breaks down, and the user often moves to more addictive and more dangerous drugs. According to the National Center on Addiction and Substance Abuse (NCASA, 2005), preteens are smoking, drinking, and using marijuana at earlier ages. Adolescents who abuse gateway drugs are at a higher risk of abusing harder drugs. There is a statistical correlation between tobacco and drug use; 12- to 17-year-olds who smoke are eight times more likely to use illicit drugs than non-smoking youth. According to Joseph Califano (2007), "Drug education and prevention should be embedded in elementary, middle, and upper school courses and should address the reasons that kids use drugs" (p. 44).

To introduce students to gateway drugs, have them envision a cemetery whose entrance gate provides easy access to a path that spirals downward into permanent brain damage and possibly oblivion. On the headstone of each grave is an epitaph for the one who chose to enter this drug-invested environment. At the entrance to the cemetery is a gatehouse with a gatekeeper, an armed guard, who keeps watch and warns those of the danger of entering this world of darkness, deception, and disaster. In the gatehouse is a plethora of research along with innumerable stories of those who chose to ignore the warnings of the gatekeeper and enter the gate. On display are posters encouraging the potential visitor to slam the gate shut, about face, and flee.

The gateway drugs focused on in this chapter include Prescription drugs, Alcohol, Inhalants, Nicotine, and Marijuana (the acrostic PAIN and marijuana). Research indicates that *early use leads to early abuse*. Thus, it is imperative to begin drug prevention education in the elementary school because this is when students engage in decisions that will impact them for the rest of their lives. The information on gateway drugs that follows comes from a variety of resources including Mothers Against Methamphetamine Secular/Public School Information Package (website, 2006); "Teens and Prescription Drugs: An Analysis of Recent Trends on the Emerging Drug Threat," Office of the National Drug Control Policy (ONDCP, 2007); Partnership for Drug-Free America (website 2007); "Growing Up Drug Free: A Parent's Guide to Prevention," U.S. Department of Education (USDOE website 2007).

Prescription Drugs
* Most commonly abused drugs among 12- and 13-year-olds.
* Most poisoning deaths due to abuse.
* Readily available in medicine cabinets and from friends and relatives.
* Teen myth: Prescription drugs provide a medically safe high.
* Chronic use leads to physical dependence and addiction.

Alcohol
* Oldest, most used drug of abuse.
* Leading cause of death among 15- to 24-year olds.
* 50 percent of deaths by drowning, fires, suicide, and homicides are alcohol related.
* The majority of fatalities in car accidents are the result of drunk driving.
* Those who start drinking early are more likely to abuse alcohol and other drugs.

Inhalants
* Commonly abused by 10- to 15-year-olds.
* Cheap, readily available, cause severe and often permanent brain damage.
* Described as the teen stalker beneath the sink, the stuff we kept away from toddlers.
* Often lethal—may *die with first try*—Sudden Sniffing Death Syndrome.
* Focus on risks, not specific products, so that you don't give students any ideas about which inhalants to try lest they die.

Nicotine
* 18 percent of high school seniors are daily smokers.
* Chief avoidable cause of death.
* Smokers are ten times more likely to develop lung cancer.
* Smokers are three times more likely to die at early age from heart attack.
* Smokers are at a greater risk for other drug use.

Marijuana
* Most commonly abused, *illegal* drug in the United States.
* Long-term use may lead to significant brain function impairment.
* Users develop an "I don't care" attitude.
* Slows reaction time; decreases coordination and concentration.

Allen (2004) finds that many school districts are successfully integrating health themes into the language arts, social studies, science, and math curriculum. Because topics concerning drugs and drug abuse are up-close-and-personal in students' lives, interest and motivation for learning are high. Open communication with parents and positive adult role models is essential. Guiding students in accepting themselves and others and encouraging positive self-esteem are significant steps in combating a tendency toward drug dependence. Drug abuse/addition prevention is the focus of both the gateway drugs and hard drugs sections in this chapter. Strategies are designed to entice thrice through

👀 eyes

👂 ears

💓 and emotions.

Artistic Adventures

Fold and Tear Adventures

A tragic number of disasters and drug-related deaths occur each year. Experiences in reacting to and rejecting gateway drugs is imperative. Students often find themselves in potentially dangerous situations. Awareness can be increased through a variety of drug-related experiences. For example, in *fold and tear adventures*, the student folds a single piece of paper into three different hats, a boat, and then a vest (see Activity Appendix A). These objects that magically emerge provide interactive reminders about how one should react to drugs.

Literature-Based Example

Implement a fold and tear adventure when using the Kids React to Meth *(2006), a 32-page booklet published by Mothers Against Methamphetamine for five-day lesson plan suggestions. Guide students in determining proper responses to drug experiences while focusing on the REACT acrostic:*

Refuse to use
Exit the situation
Act on what you know
Control your own behavior
Turn away from influences that take away your self-control (p. 8)

Accompany fold and tear adventures and determine how to REACT to invitations to drug experimentation by singing the following:

Title: REACT to Drug Invitations
Tune: "This Old Man"

Verse 1 (sing after folding hat 1) **Refuse: Thinking Hat**
Thinking hat! Thinking hat!
Where is my brainpower *at*?
When asked to use; I'll **refuse.**
I win or lose by the way I choose.

Verse 2 (sing after folding hat 2) **Exit: Fire Hat**
Fire hat! Fire hat!
Exit now from where I'm *at*.
Drugs will burn holes in my brain.
They will drive me quite insane!

Verse 3 (sing after folding hat 3) **Act: Dunce Hat**
Dunce hat! Dunce hat!
Act right; I'll not be a brat!
Though some will say that drugs are cool,
I don't want to be a fool!

Verse 4 (sing after folding boat) **Control: Boat**
In a boat! In a boat!
I choose to sink or choose to float.
I'll be my boss and take **control,**
And not look for a big loophole.

Verse 5 (sing after folding vest) **Turn Away: Vest**
Put on my vest! Put on my vest!
This will be the ultimate test.
Turn away; no slugs* nor lugs.**
I believe in hugs not drugs.

Verse 6 (sing as summary)
Win or lose! Win or lose!
I win or lose by the way I choose.
Think! **REACT!** And I'll be free,
To live my life in sobriety.

Note: Slug: Amount of liquor swallowed in one gulp;
Lug: Slang meaning clumsy fool or blockhead.

Gamut of Games

Drugologists/Drug Digs and Drug Diagrams

Drugologist is a coined term for scientists who participate in *drug digs*. Just as archaeologists dig for artifacts, these scientists

1. Dig up drug data from a variety of resources.
2. Display data on drug diagrams.
3. Distribute data to other interested scientists.

Drugologists use the following sequence in their scientific inquiry:

1. Collect
2. Classify
3. Compare
4. Conclude

Literature-Related Example

The initial data from a drugologist's drug dig for gateway drugs include:

Type of Drug	Examples or Names	Short-Term Effects	Long-Term Effects
Prescription Drugs	Oxycotin Vicodin Valium	Nausea Vomiting Abdominal cramps	Anxiety Death by overdose
Alcohol	Beer Wine Liquor	Relaxed Daring Outgoing	Brain damage Balance problems
***Inhalants**	Glue Hairspray Lighter fluid Paint thinner Spray paint	Dizziness Disorientation Slurred speech Distorted perception	Brain damage Oxygen deprivation Death

Type of Drug	Examples or Names	Short-Term Effects	Long-Term Effects
Nicotine	Cigarettes Cigars Snuff	Feeling grown-up, "cool," and admired; increased blood pressure	Heart disease Lung cancer Yellow teeth
Marijuana	Dope Pot Grass Weed	Increased heart rate; anxiety Distorted perception	Impaired brain function Dependence

*Caution: You may want to avoid having students look for examples of inhalants.

Additional investigative charting possibilities include appearance of the drug, how the drug is used (e.g., swallowed, smoked, chewed, snorted, injected), statistics related to drug use, and consequences not only to the user but also to families and society.

Ocular Organizers

Current Events Collage/Killer Kollage

A *current events collage* is an artistic arrangement of newspaper and magazine clippings related to a current topic of interest that is attached to a background for display. Illustrations and pictures from brochures, magazines, and newspapers add interest to the collage. Markers and paint may be used for outlining and emphasis. A *killer kollage* is an artistic arrangement of newspaper and magazine clippings related to dangerous drugs.

Literature-Related Example

Scour newspapers and magazines for articles related to the use and abuse of drugs. Search for brochures and posters about drugs (see Mothers Against Methamphetamine website). Organize the collection of articles by related topics; for example, automobile accidents where alcohol was involved, death as a result of smoking, and violence involving drugs. Create a killer kollage with a kaption that kaptures the viewer's attention and causes introspection about the wisdom of staying away from drugs. For example,

- *Stay alive! Don't drink and drive!*
- *Don't smoke! Don't puff! Nicotine is terrible stuff!*
- *Sniffing glue messed up his head, and now he's decidedly dead!*
- *Don't mess around with pot; it will hurt your brain a lot.*
- *Taking pills that don't belong to you could cause big problems and usually do.*

Search for "druggate" scandals involving illegal acts and coverups involving drugs. Display appropriate drug diagrams with each killer kollage.

Literature-Based Example

Initially, personally read A Child Called "It" *(Pelzer, 2005), a heart-wrenching autobiography. Have plenty of tissues on hand when you do. Let David Pelzer speak to your heart and later the hearts of mature students who will experience with you the unbelievable physical abuse an alcoholic mother inflicts on one of her sons. Be prepared for lots of tears and lots of questions. Allow the author to remind you in a most poignant way of your responsibility to be alert to the suffering of any one of your students.*

Dramatic Debut
Discuss, Debate, Deliver

As the study of drugs progresses, many controversial topics emerge. Develop a structured oral language plan that will maximize opportunities for each student to have input into the discussion of these topics. Controversy stimulates critical thinking as students introspectively reflect on what they believe and why. *Discuss, debate, deliver (DDD)* is a dramatic experience dealing with controversial topics. DDD employs the following sequence:

Discuss:
- Large group discussion centers around an introductory question that provides the stimulus for controversy as well as a common core of background knowledge.
- One or more class members act as scribes and record the information on the board or an overhead transparency.
- Develop questions for small debate groups.

Debate:
- Small groups meet and debate answers to the questions developed by the large group.

Deliver:
- The large group reconvenes and participants deliver or share their findings and feelings. Expect courtesy and controversy.

Literature-Based Examples

In Go Ask Alice *(Anonymous, 1971), the author goes to a party and unwittingly consumes a soda laced with LSD, a hallucinogen that creates wild, weird perceptions in the mind that have a compelling sense of reality. This initial encounter with drugs is the beginning of the end. (Note: If you choose to use this book in the classroom, be sure you have administrative and parental approval.) Use this literature selection or a similar scenario as a stimulus for a DDD discussion on avoiding an initial encounter with drugs.*

Discuss: How can you avoid getting into a situation where you might be tricked into taking drugs?

Possible Responses: Go to parties that are supervised closely by adults; have friends come to your house; participate in sports and other school activities that the school supervises.

Debate: Why would a friend try to pressure you into taking drugs? What are some dangers of experimenting with drugs? What would you tell your parents if someone tried to get you to experiment with drugs? How would your parents react? Should you associate with people who take drugs? Why or why not? How can you influence your friends not to take drugs?

Deliver: Reconvene in the large group to deliver and share findings and feelings.

Izzy Willy-Nilly *by Newbery Award winning author Cynthia Voigt (1986) begins when Izzy is told, "We're going to have to take it off." Little does Izzy realize the dramatic changes that will take place in her life when they take it off—amputate her leg.*

As Izzy tells the story, her flashbacks reveal that she conned her parents into allowing her to date Marco. She and Marco attended an unchaperoned party. When it was time to leave the party, Izzy realized Marco had been drinking too much. She was offered another ride but was too embarrassed to accept. When the car veered back and forth across the center of the road and smashed into a tree, it was too late! Now they have to take it off.

Use some of the following questions after reading about Izzy or create a scenario similar to the one in the book to stimulate DDD.

Discuss: Why do people drink?

Possible Responses: Everyone else is doing it. Drinking makes me feel grown up. I'm bored. I need to relax.

Debate: What would you say if your friend offered you a drink?
What would you say if your friend, who drove you to the party, had too much to drink and then wanted to drive you home? What are the harmful effects of drinking? Why are

advertisers allowed to promote alcoholic consumption when so many people die in alcohol-related deaths? What are some sources of help for those who are addicted to alcohol?

Deliver: Reconvene in the large group to deliver and share findings and feelings.

Creative Composition

Analyze and Advertise/Problem, Product, Promises, Propaganda, Position

Collect advertisements and, when feasible, actual product packages for alcohol, cigarettes, and prescription and nonprescription drugs. Look in magazines and newspapers for advertisements. Videotape television commercials and audiotape radio commercials or make notes on commercials you see and hear. Sketch billboard advertisements. Organize the collection into categories such as cigarettes, beer, wine, hard liquor, headache remedies, stomach irritation combatants, and so on. Place material for each category in a basket or file folder.

Assign each category to a cooperative group. Each group member's responsibility is to complete a *problem, product, promise, propaganda, position (PPPPP)* form based on the following guidelines:

1. **Problem:**   Select an advertisement or product package and identify a problem that the advertisers have assured their readers and viewers the product will cure.
2. **Product:**   Write the name of the product.
3. **Promises:**   List promises the advertisement makes.
4. **Propaganda:**   Identify propaganda techniques and persuasive vocabulary used to convince consumers to purchase the product. *Note: For additional propaganda information see Commercials in Chapter 2 and Persuasive Writing in Chapter 3.*
5. **Position:**   Take a position on whether to purchase the product. Taking a position involves making choices, an integral part of critical thinking. Suggest alternative solutions to the problem.

Discuss *medicines*, drugs that when used correctly help prevent and cure illness and when used incorrectly may become a gateway to chemical dependence including alcohol and drug abuse. There are two major types of medicines: (1) *over-the-counter drugs*, medicine purchased without a prescription, and (2) *prescription drugs*, medicine that requires a written order from a doctor.

As students learn about medicines and the contributions medicines make to help them *thrive* and *stay alive*, look for information on medicine containers and pamphlets included with the medicine. Research information in reference books such as *Prescription and Over-the-Counter Drugs* (Reader's Digest, 2001). Discuss the types of information available such as dosage, drug interactions, special instructions, possible side effects, and warnings. Special instructions may advise that the medicine be taken while eating or on an empty stomach. Side effects may include dizziness, nausea, sleepiness, and motor problems. Stress the importance of taking medicine only when given by a parent or a person specifically designated by the parent. Do not take anyone else's medicine, because it was prescribed especially for that person based on age, weight, and symptoms. Emphasize, *"Prevention is the best medicine,"* and *"An ounce of prevention is worth a pound of cure."* When drugs are abused, there are negative intellectual, physical, emotional, and social effects.

The following example is based on fictitious *"Go Away Aspirin"* magazine advertisements.

Problem: Headaches

Product: *Go Away Aspirin*

Promises: *Go Away Aspirin* relieves headache pain within 30 minutes without stomach upset.

Propaganda: Leading doctors at Snobby University take *Go Away Aspirin*. (Testimonial technique) More hospitals use *Go Away Aspirin* than any other aspirin. (Bandwagon) When you take *Go Away Aspirin*, even your most severe headaches will Go Away! (Reward)

Position: Even though *Go Away Aspirin* promises miraculous headache relief, taking aspirin may cause an upset stomach. Relying on too many aspirin may stimulate physical dependence. Rather than purchasing *Go Away Aspirin*, try alternatives for making headaches go away: take a walk, lie down and cover your eyes with a wet cloth, or listen to some soothing music. Not only will your head feel better but so will your pocketbook.

Literature-Based Example

After reading and discussing The Usborne Young Scientist: Human Body *by Susan Meredith, Ann Goldman, and Tom Lissauer (1983) and other trade books related to smoking, analyze cigarette advertisements and product packages. Complete a PPPPP for a popular brand of cigarettes. The following is a PPPPP for a fictitious brand of cigarettes:*

Problem: Lack of confidence and self-esteem

Product: *Toughton Cigarettes*

Promises: A mature image

Propaganda: Rodeo superstar Marson Michaels prefers *Toughton.* (Testimonial) All the guys on my crew smoke *Toughton.* (Bandwagon) When you draw on the cool, clean taste of a *Toughton,* you'll draw a crowd. (Reward)

Position: Even though *Toughton* promises me a mature image and lots of friends, I realize that smoking causes lung cancer, stinks up my clothes, and produces bad breath. As an alternative, I can make friends by inviting classmates to a pizza party chaperoned by my parents.

Expand a study of prescription drugs using The Essential Guide to Prescription Drugs 2001 *(Rybacki & Long, 2001) Find a copy in thrift stores to use as a classroom reference. Since OxyContin and Vicodin are the most commonly abused prescription drugs by teens, study the detailed information about each drug including possible benefits, possible risks, possible side effects, possible adverse effects, effects of overdose, and possible effects of long-term use.*

Develop an advertisement or commercial to convince consumers NOT to purchase or consume a particular product and employ some of the same promises and propaganda techniques that the product's advertisers use to sell the product—in other words "coerce in reverse."

HARD DRUGS

Being involved with drugs is a lot like playing Russian Roulette. So little is under your control. Hanging with friends who do drugs. Driving with someone who is high. Depending on people who put drugs ahead of their families and friends.
And then there's you—making a decision to use. The first time it's a choice. After that, it may not be. And sometimes it's hard to know the total consequences of your choice—until it's too late.
You might think
Not me!
Not my body!
Not my friends!
Not my life!
Think twice!!
(JustThinkTwice.com)

Hard drugs are substances that are highly addictive; brain, body, and behavior altering; whose prolonged use leads to deception, destruction, and possibly death. A hard-core, drug-addicted teenager is vehemently opposed to giving up drugs. Because of the continuing decline in the average age of drug users, it is imperative that teachers and parents take a firm stand against the "*say yes*" of drug addiction: (1) **Y**earning, (2) **E**nticement, and (3) **S**eduction. The allure of sophisticated multimedia in the form of music, film, TV, Internet, and other mass market outlets reverberates with a *try-it; you'll-like-it* seduction. A Mickey-Mouse approach to drug prevention just won't cut it. But, a tough love confrontation just might.

As you deal with students who are or might become drug addicts, you must remember that a user's social, emotional, and mental development stops at the chronological age at which addition begins (Holley, 2005). If you are teaching a 14-year-old whose addiction began at 11 years of age, you are in effect teaching an 11-year-old. Thus, in the classroom, you can't instruct a student who is abusing or addicted to drugs at his or her chronological age, but you must deal with that student socially, emotionally, and mentally at the addictive age.

The information on representative hard drugs that follows comes from a variety of resources, including the websites that follow. These sites provide a wealth of reproducible material for classroom use.

- **Just Think Twice** designed for teens; includes a teacher's guide for grades 6 through 12 with modules that focus on the risks of drug use and the effects of drugs on society. Lessons are designed to stimulate students' interest as they engage in interactive research on this website. www.JustThinkTwice.com
- **National Institute on Drug Abuse (NIDA).** contains information on the "Mind Over Matter" series designed to encourage students in grades 5 through 9 to learn about the biological effects of drug abuse on the body and brain. "The Brain's Response to Drugs Teacher's Guide" has lesson plans that include background information, objectives, and activities for a specific drug or drug group. Teens.drugabuse.gov; www.nida.nih.gov.
- **U.S. Department of Education (USDOE)**
  "Growing Up Drug Free: A Parent's Guide to Prevention" includes suggested activities and information by grade levels. Although geared toward parents, the same activities may be modified for classroom use. The appendix contains information on specific categories of drugs as well as resource suggestions. www.usdoj.gov/dea/concern
- **Mothers Against Methamphetamine (MAMA)**
  The secular/public school information package and website includes "Kids React to Meth," "Meth Death," and "Crystal Methamphetamine: The High Is a Lie." www.mamasite.net
  Examples of representative hard drugs with brief bits of information include the following:

Heroin
- Highly addictive; develop tolerance; must use increasing amounts in an attempt to achieve the same intensity or effect user is seeking.
- Most abused and most rapidly acting of the opiates.
- High risk of overdose and death.
- Cheese—mixture of heroin and cold medication is cheap; heart-wrenching stories on the Internet of teen death for those who try this mixture.
- Withdrawal more painful than withdrawal from any other drug.
- Combined with methamphetamine, "speedballing" is more addictive than meth alone.

Cocaine
- One of the oldest drugs.
- Powerfully addictive; high potential for abuse.
- Stimulates violence, erratic thinking, and paranoia.
- 75 to 80 percent addiction rate; only 20 to 25 percent of those who become addicted will be able to overcome this addiction.
- Free-base crack cocaine causes the same severe and rapid brain damage as does meth.

Methamphetamine
- Artificial/manufactured form of cocaine.
- 75 percent initiate meth drug use in teens.
- 25 percent start using under the age of 15.
- Manufactured from drain cleaner, battery acid, antifreeze, and other household products.
- More toxic to the brain than cocaine.
- 95 to 98 percent addiction rate; only 2 to 5 percent of those who become addicted will be able to overcome this addiction.

Why a Meth Strategy Focus?

As a nation, we are facing a meth pandemic, an epidemic of mammoth proportion. Meth is the most addictive substance known to man. *Newsweek Magazine* labels meth "America's Most Dangerous Drug." Headlines scream: "*Meth creates a potent, long-lasting high—*

until the user crashes and too often, literally burns." How did we allow meth to quietly march across the country and up the socioeconomic ladder leaving wreckage in its wake (Jefferson, 2005)? Law enforcement is fighting a losing battle. What can be done?

Every meth addict quits eventually—when he or she ends up in a nursing home, jail, or the morgue. After five years of meth addiction, the user will be brain damaged, in prison, or dead (Holley, 2005). The first time meth use is a choice. After that, there is no choice except to use again and again and again. Meth is habit-forming, mind-altering, and death inviting.

To introduce students to the dangerous, downward spiral of meth addiction:

- Extend the cemetery metaphor from gateway drugs
- Share the poem: "I Am Meth" (see Figure 7.4)
- Show "The High Is a Lie" DVD and complete the accompanying worksheets (Mothers Against Methamphetamine, 2005)

Artistic Adventures
Slit-Slot-Slide Book (SSS) and Pepi Profile SSS Book

King Heroin is my shepherd, I shall always want.
He maketh me lie down in the gutters.
He leadeth me beside the troubled waters.
He destroyeth my soul.
He leadeth me in the paths of wickedness.
Yea, I shall walk through the valley of poverty and will fear no evil
for thou, Heroin, art with me.
Thy needle and thy capsule comfort me.
Thou strippest the table of groceries in the presence of my family.
Thou robbest my head of reason.
Surely heroin addiction shall stalk me all the days of my life
and I will dwell in the house of the damned forever.

Anonymous; 23rd Psalm Innovation
(suggestion: substitute meth or cocaine for heroin).

(Found beside the body of a suicide victim along with a note that said, Jail didn't cure me. Nor did hospitalization help me for long. The doctor told my family it would have been better, and indeed kinder, if the person who got me hooked on dope had taken a gun and blown my brains out. And I wish to God he had. My God, how I wish it.")

Guide students in establishing lifetime personal goals, *destination determination* (*the what*). Decide the purpose or reason for each goal (*the why*), and design the steps necessary to reach each goal (*the how*). Discuss why perseverance is an essential element in the pursuit of these goals.

Make a *slit-slot-slide (SSS) book*, a two-page book in which the slit page slides through the slot page and VOILÀ! as if by magic, the two sheets of paper form a book (see Activity Appendix A). Transform the SSS book into a *Pepi profile SSS book* by cutting out a profile from the center pages. Draw facial features on either side of the profile to create any one of a variety of emotions such as happy, sad, mad, or glad. Portray a different emotion on either side of Pepi, a happy face on one side and a sad face on the other.

When the book is open, have students list lifetime personal goals (destination determination) on the inside of the left cover: **What** do I want to do/be? In the center of the profile list: **Why** do I want to do/be this? On the inside of the back cover list: **How** do I attain these goals. Include the steps necessary for reaching these goals. For added interest decorate this page using a rolling footprint ink stamp.

With younger students, glue the two center profiles together. Then swing the profile back and forth while chanting:

"Say **NO** to **drugs!**"
　　"Say **NO** to **peer pressure!**"
　　　　"Say **NO** to **strangers!**"

Figure 7.4   Poem: I Am Meth

I Am Meth

I destroy homes: I tear families apart,
I take your children, and that's just the start.
I'm more costly than diamonds, more precious than gold,
The sorrow I bring is a sight to behold.
If you need me, remember I'm easily found.
I live all around you—in schools and in town.
I live with the rich; I live with the poor.
I live down the street, and maybe next door.
I'm made in a lab but not like you think.
I can be made under the kitchen sink.
In your child's closet, and even in the woods.
If this scares you to death, well it certainly should.
I have many names, but there's one you know best.
I'm sure you've heard of me; my name's crystal meth.
My power is awesome; try me, you'll see.
But if you do, you may never break free.
Just try me once, and I might let you go,
But try me twice, and I'll own your soul.
When I possess you, you'll steal, and you'll lie.
You do what you have to—just to get high.
The crimes you'll commit for my narcotic charms
Will be worth the pleasure you'll feel in your arms.
You'll lie to your mother; you'll steal from your dad.
When you see their tears, you should feel sad.
But you'll forget your morals and how you were raised.
I'll be your conscience; I'll teach you my ways.
I take kids from parents, and parents from kids.
I turn people from God and separate friends.
I'll take everything from you, your looks and your pride.
I'll be with you always—right by your side.
You'll give up everything—your family, your home.
Your friends, your money, and you'll be alone.
I'll take and take, till you have nothing more to give.
When I'm finished with you, you'll be lucky to live.
If you try me be warned—this is no game.
If given the chance, I'll drive you insane.
I'll ravish your body; I'll control your mind.
I'll own you completely; your soul will be mine.
The nightmares I'll give you while lying in bed.
The voices you'll hear, from inside your head.
The sweats, the shakes, the visions you'll see.
I want you to know, these are all gifts from me.
But then it's too late, and you'll know in your heart,
That you are mine, and we shall not part.
You'll regret that you tried me; they always do,
But you came to me, not I to you.
You knew this would happen; many times you were told.
But you challenged my power, and chose to be bold.
You could have said, "No!" and just walked away.
If you could live that day over, now what would you say?
I'll be your master; you will be my slave.
I'll even go with you, when you go to your grave.
Now that you have met me, what will you do?
Will you try me or not? It's all up to you.
I can bring you more misery than words can tell,
Come take my hand, let me lead you to hell.

Anonymous (Written by a meth addict while in jail)

Literature-Based Examples

Create SSS books for the following literature experiences:

- Read "*Kids REACT to Meth*" (Mothers Against Methamphetamine, 2006). Discuss the character's *what, why,* and *how* goals. What happens to these choices when methamphetamine enters the picture?
- Share "*The Tortoise and the Hare,*" an Aesop fable available in a wide variety of collections including an adaptation by Janet Stevens (1983). The moral of the story in Steven's rendition is *Hard work and perseverance bring reward.* Additional ideas might include *Slow and steady wins the race* or *Keep your eyes on the goal.*
- Discuss *The Billy Goats' Gruff.* Could the troll be a drug pusher who tries to impede each goat's determination to reach its destination and achieve its goals? Focus on the classic, *The Little Engine That Could,* and talk about mountain-climbing-motivation.

Sing about personal potential, "I Am a Promise." Veggie Tales has a lively rendition of this classic. You may want to alter the song slightly by changing the underlined words, "I am learning to hear God's voice, and I am trying to make the right choice," to hear my own voice my parents' voice or my teacher's voice.

Older students could grapple with Dave Pelzer's horrific autobiography, A Child Called "It" *(1995). There appears to be no hope, no lifetime goals for "It." However, there is light at the end of the tunnel as students discover when reading the sequential books in the trilogy,* The Lost Boy: A Foster Child's Search for the Love of a Family *(1997) and* A Man Named Dave *(1999).*

Gamut of Games
What Would I Do If (WWIDI)/Challenges, Choices, Consequences

> *The man who knows right from wrong*
> *and has good judgment and common sense*
> *is happier than the man who is immensely rich!*
> *For such wisdom is far more valuable than precious jewels.*
>
> Classic Proverb

Wise choices, well thought out in advance, allow time for careful consideration of options before facing difficult situations in which choices must be made. *What would I do if (WWIDI)* provides challenges as students vicariously face situations in which they must make choices and live with the consequences of these choices. This *close-encounter-of-the-dangerous-kind* allows students to prepare and practice a cadre of ready responses that lead to conflict resolution. WWIDI is a cooperative group endeavor in which each group is given the same or a different WWIDI challenge.

Make a *challenge, choice, consequence organizer* using masking tape lines on the floor or carpet. Place response cards in the appropriate places.

	Challenge	
	Choice	
Positive Consequence		Negative Consequence
Positive Consequence (chant)		Negative Consequence (chant)
I can! I will!!		I can't! I won't!!
I'll do it!!!		You can't make me!!!

Conduct WWIDI as follows:

Group Leader: Share a WWIDI challenge card with the group.

Each Group Member: Make a choice on how to deal with the situation. Write this individual choice on a card. Write a positive consequence for this choice on a second card and a negative consequence for this choice on a third card.

Challenge, Choice, Consequence Organizer: Place your cards on the organizer in the appropriate places.

Group Discussion: Assess the choice each member has presented along with the consequences. Make additional choice and consequence cards as the discussion progresses. Place your cards on the organizer. Share your findings with the class. Chant the appropriate response for positive and negative consequences.

Literature-Based Examples

Share the following literature selections and expand the WWIDI challenges.

- *Yolanda's Genius* by Carol Fenner (1995, Newbery Honor).
- **What would I do if** a pusher gave me a packet of white powder (cocaine) and told me it would make me feel good?
- **What would I do if** my best friend started screaming that his skin hurts so much that he can't go to the toilet?
- **What would I do if** I was asked where my friend got her drugs?
- **What would I do if** the *power brokers (drug dealers)* grabbed my bike and took off?
- **What would I do if** someone called me a genius?
  (Note: Extension suggestion—What does being a genius have to do with drugs?)
- *The Berenstain Bears and the Drug Free Zone* by Stan and Jan Berenstain (1993)
- **What would I do if** I suspected someone who looked like a crook was a pusher but then I remembered, "You can't judge a book by its cover?"
- **What would I do if** someone called me silly, stupid, uncool, chicken, a baby if I wouldn't try happy pills?
- **What would I do if** a pusher tried to pollute bear cubs' (kids') minds and bodies and turn them into an endangered species?

Ocular Organizers

Brains, Bodies, 'n' Behavior (BBB)/BBB Organizer

Read *Growing Up Drug Free: A Parent's Guide to Prevention* (U.S. Department of Education, 2007) and study the general guidelines that students should know by the end of ninth grade:

- Characteristics and chemical nature of specific drugs and drug interactions.
- Physiology of drug effects on circulatory, respiratory, nervous, and reproductive systems.
- Stages of chemical dependency and their unpredictability from person to person.
- Ways that drug use affects activities requiring motor coordination such as driving a car or participating in sports.
- Family history, particularly if alcoholism or other drug addiction has been a problem (p. 12).

Note that these guidelines incorporate the effects of drugs on brains, bodies, 'n' behavior. Use information from a variety of resources to explore the physiological and psychological effects of drug abuse/addiction on brains, bodies, 'n' behavior. An initial investigation might begin using *Good Answers to Tough Questions about Substance Abuse* by Joy Berry (1990). Display the results of this research in and on the following graphic organizers.

- ***Brains, Bodies, 'n' Behavior (BBB) Organizer*** Create an accordion file folder book (see Activity Appendix A) with four pockets on the front and four pockets on the back (use four file folders). Label the pockets on the front: (1) Beware! (2) Brain,

(3) Body, and (4) Behavior. Use the four pockets on the back to display drug-related creative compositions. Display Drug-etry in the "beware pocket."

- *Slit-Slot-Slide Book: Brain Focus*   Make a slit-slot-slide book with two slit pages (see Activity Appendix A). Write general information about the effects of drug abuse/addiction on the brain on the inside of the front cover. Trace or copy the seven brain figures from the *Mind Over Matter Teacher's Guide* (www.teens.drugabuse.gov). Cut out and paste a figure on each of the next seven pages. Write pertinent information to go with each figure. For example, permanent holes in the brain, battery acid effect. Add more brain information on the last page and the inside of the back cover. Display in the "brain" pocket.
- *Eightfold Person: Body*   Make an eightfold person (see Activity Appendix A). Add a head, hands, legs, and feet to the person. Indicate places on/in the body that are affected by drug abuse/addiction. For example, show the effects on appearance. Put sores on the face and arms. Show a *meth-mouth* with rotten teeth. Indicate chest pain. Display in the "body" pocket.
- *Multiple Men: Behavior*   Create one or more sets of multiple men (see Activity Appendix A). On each individual man, indicate a different effect of drug abuse/addiction on behavior. For example, rage. Add details to the appearance to demonstrate rage. Display in the "behavior" pocket.

Dramatic Debut

Dr. Drug-Be-Gone/Teams of Surgical Specialists

Dr. Drug-Be-Gone and his teams of surgical specialists are ever vigilant when it comes to identifying the symptoms, sadness, and madness of drug addiction/abuse. Their desperate attempts to save lives could be likened to the frontline measures taken by teams on the classic TV show, M*A*S*H. For these teams of world-renown specialists, scavenge props from thrift shops, yard sales, parents, for example. Your collection might include:

Props

- **Scrubs:** hospital scrubs, lab coats, men's shirts
- **Doctor's satchel:** small carrying bag or suitcase
- **Surgical instruments:** cooking tongs, plastic knives
- **Paddles:** chalk/white board erasers
- **Stethoscopes:** locate or create using flexible tubing, a CD headset with earphones, a cardboard circle covered with aluminum foil, and other media materials
- **Blood pressure cuff:** create or locate
- **Shower caps:** collect during hotel visits
- **Shoe covers:** look for at airline security clearance or use paper bags
- **Body:** use large puppet or doll, sheet, operating table
- **Symptoms:** write on 3″ × 5″ index cards. Paper clip on long string at intervals.

Drama Suggestions

During surgical procedures, the body lies on an operating table covered by a sheet. For added interest, have the surgical team of doctors and nurses stand behind the table facing the audience. Surgeons carry on a discussion such as, "We must operate immediately." "Put him under." "Scalpel!" "Incision!" "Look at these symptoms!" "Tongs!" (Use tongs to grab string and pull out slowly revealing one index-card symptom at a time with discussion about each symptom.) "Let me check his blood pressure." "Check his pulse." "Grab the paddles! "Resuscitate!" "We're losing him." "He's Going! Going!! Gone!!!"

Drama Starters

Dr. Meth-Be-Gone

Team Member 1:   Thank goodness for our world renown team of neurosurgeons, brain specialists. Let's go, team! Open up his head!

Team Member 2:	Oh no! It's battery acid effect! This patient has permanent holes in his brain.
Team Member 3:	Look at that brain! He's gone insane!
Team Member 4:	There's nothing we can do! We can't pull him through!
Team Member 5:	Egads! His neurons have gone awry; he's possibly destined to die.
Team Member 6:	He took meth, and that could mean death.

Dr. Crack-Be-Gone

Team Member 1:	Look at the bruises and cuts on this guy. They're horrendous!
Team Member 2:	Apparently he thought he could whip a whole gang and survive. It didn't work!
Team Member 3:	No wonder it didn't work. Look at his brain.
Team Member 4:	I've never seen so much brain damage.
Team Member 5:	You can see why this guy's daughter is terrified! She came home from school, and he tried to kill her. He thought she was going to poison him.
Team Member 6:	Paranoia from cocaine use is unbelievable!

Dr. Heroin-Be-Gone

Team Member 1:	What a blessing to have a team of heroin specialists!
Team Member 2:	Oh no! Quick! He's in withdrawal! This withdrawal is more painful than withdrawal from any other drug.
Team Member 3:	He developed a tolerance for heroin and had to keep taking more and more trying to achieve the level of his first high.
Team Member 4:	When that didn't work, he turned to "speedballing,"* mixing heroin and meth. He may not make it!

Note: combining a depressant with a stimulant; term often used for mixing heroin and cocaine.

Creative Composition

Dear Diary/Drug-etry/Patterned Poetry

Plan *dear diary* experiences in which students write based on their own innerfeelings or grapple with responses to a selected topic, a topic that allows them to explore their innermost feelings, fears, and failures. A dear diary experience allows for:

Daring to express my
Innermost,
Awful,
Rebellious,
Yearnings.

Drug-etry is poetry that provides plenty of possibilities to share facts, feelings, and fears related to drugs. Poetry formats are located in Appendix C. *Patterned poetry* allows the author to use an established poem or song as a model and substitute alternative wording for a selected topic. Display drug-etry in pockets on a BBB organizer (see Accordion File Folder Book in Activity Appendix A). For additional writing opportunities and discussion, see Chapter 3.

Literature-Based Experiences

Lit Starters: Select excerpts from literature as stimuli for dear diary, drug-etry, and patterned poetry experiences.

Dear Diary

*Based on **Go Ask Alice (Anonymous, 1971) diary starters might include*
Dearest Diary,

- Like Alice I yearn to be loved by the people around me. They want me to do drugs with them. I'm tempted but....
- My family loves me. I don't want to hurt them, but the pull of drugs is so powerful that...
- I'm in a lock down facility. I feel awful! There are worms crawling all over me! I've pulled out my hair! I've torn off my fingernails! I'm bleeding! I want to get better but can I?
- Boy is the invitation to that party a temptation. I know what they'll do there. Should I go?
- My life is a roller coaster. One minute I'm up; the next I'm down. Oh when will it end?
- I'm an idiot-stupid. I know what these drugs will do and yet...
- It's the beginning of a new year, the first day of the rest of my life. I'm going to rip out the pages of my life-those in which I used drugs. Dumb! Stupid! Now I...
- I want to go home. So do all the kids on the street who are caught up in the drug scene but...
- I have two choices-commit suicide or help others. Which will it be?
- We need to discuss important things in life-religion, God, parents, our future, and war because...

Stimulated by **The Freedom Writers Diary: How a Teacher and 150 Teens Used Writing to Change Themselves and the World Around Them *(Gruwell, 1999), diary starters might be:*

- I don't want to! But there sits that baggie with the white powder in it. My head hurts! My stomach hurts! My body aches! What should I do?
- My best friend is crystal meth because...
- My worse enemy is crystal meth because...
- I try to get better, but I get worse when...
- I could be called a closet tweeker because...
- What's so bad about becoming an addict is...
- How can I turn back before there is no way out.
- Why are the police at my door?
- I watched that gang beat up that kid. Why didn't I help...
- My teacher called me out in the hall, me, the class dummy, and I knew why... (*Read about a teacher who cares enough to get in a kid's face and yell...*)
- Something is only an obstacle if you allow it to be. I know this because...

*** Note: Be sure to read first. Have both administration and parental approval before using these books in the classroom. The topics are tough; the language is rough; the situations terrifying—though perhaps not enough.*

Drug-etry

Using the book Yolanda's Genius *(Fenner, 1995, Newbery Honor) as a stimulus: students might write a poem about Andrew, Yolanda's younger brother.*

The Mystery of You-niqueness

Who am I?
  I am Andrew.
  I am special.
Sometimes I ask:
  Why does Yolanda warn me to stay away from the *fear makers*?
  Why is that drug stuff bad stuff?
Sometimes other people ask
  Why does that kid distract the hustle?
  Why does the devil dance under Asphalt Hill like a troll in
"The Three Billy Goats Gruff"?
But deep down I know.
  I am able to break the bonds and play the sounds.
  I am a musical genius.
Who am I?
  I am Andrew.
  I am You-nique!

Patterned Poetry

"The House That Crack Built" by Clark Taylor (1992), is patterned after the nursery rhyme "This Is the House That Jack Built." Create a personal patterned poem for a selected drug. For example, students might compose the following poem

This is the house that meth built.
This is the pusher
who lives in the house that meth built.
This is the lab
that's used by the pusher
who lives in the house that meth built.
This is the drug known as meth
that's made in the lab
that's used by the pusher
who lives in the house that meth built.
This is the kid who's damaging his brain
who takes the drug known as meth
that's made in the lab
that's used by the pusher,
who lives in the house that meth built.
This is the grave awaiting
The kid who's damaging his brain
who takes the drug known as meth
that's made in the lab
that's used by the pusher,
who lives in the house that meth built.

Literature References

Anonymous. (1971). *Go ask Alice.* Englewood Cliffs, NJ: Prentice-Hall.

Baum, F. (1982). *The Wizard of Oz.* Illustrated by Michael Hague. New York: Holt, Rinehart & Winston.

Berenstain, S., & Berenstain, Jan. (1993). *Drug-free zone.* New York: Random House.

Berry, J. (1990). *Good answers to tough questions about substance abuse.* Chicago: Children's Press.

Cash, T., Parker, S., & Taylor, B. (1989). *175 more science experiments to amuse and amaze your friends.* New York: Random House.

Clutton-Brock, J. (1991). *Eyewitness books: Cat.* New York: Alfred A. Knopf.

Cohen, D., & Cohen, S. (1992). *Zoos.* New York: Doubleday.

Cosgrove, B. (1991). *Eyewitness books: Weather.* New York: Alfred A. Knopf.

de Paola, T. (1975). *The cloud book.* New York: Holiday House.

de Paola, T. (1979). *The kids' cat book.* New York: Holiday House.

Dickinson, T. (1988). *Exploring the sky by day.* Camden East, Ontario: Camden House.

Emberley, E. (1977). *Ed Emberley's great thumbprint drawing book.* Boston: Little, Brown.

Fenner, C. (1995). *Yolanda's genius.* New York: Simon & Schuster. Newbery Honor.

Fox, P. (1984). *One-eyed cat.* New York: Bradbury. Newbery Honor.

Gag, W. (1928). *Millions of cats.* New York: Coward-McCann.

Ganeri, A. (1987). *The Usborne book of weather facts.* Tulsa, OK: EDC Publishing.

Gile, J. (1989). *The first forest.* Stevens Point, WI: Worzalla.

George, Jean Craighead, (1992). *The missing 'gator of Gumbo Limbo.* New York: Harperm Trophy.

Gruwell, E. (1999). *The freedom writers diary: How a teacher and 150 teens used writing to change themselves and the world around them.* New York: Broadway Books.

Ikeda, D. (1991). *The cherry tree.* New York: Alfred A. Knope.

King-Smith, D. (1988). *Martin's mice.* New York: Dell.

Krensky, S. (1989). *All about snow and ice.* New York: Scholastic.

Le Guin, U. K. (1988). *Catwings.* New York: Scholastic.

Lewis, C. S. (1951). *The lion, the witch, and the wardrobe.* New York: Macmillan.

Meredith, S., Goldman, A., & Lissauer, T. (1983). *The Usborne young scientist: Human body.* Tulsa, OK: EDC Publishing.

Mitchell, Alan. (1994). *Trees of North America.* (Science Nature Series). San Diego, CA: Thunder Bay Press.

Moore, I. (1991). *Six-dinner Sid.* New York: Simon and Schuster.

Ness, E. (1966). *Sam, Bangs & Moonshine.* New York: Henry Holt and Company. Caldecott Award.

Pelzer, D. (1995). *A child called "It:" One child's courage to survive.* Deerfield Beach, FL: Health Communications, Inc.

Pelzer, D. (1997). *The lost boy: A foster child's search for the love of a family*. Deerfield Beach, FL: Health Communications, Inc.

Pelzer, D. (2000). *A man named Dave: A story of triumph and forgiveness*. New York: Penguin Putnam.

Rose, D. L. (1990). *The people who hugged the trees*. Niwot, CO: Roberts Rinehart.

Seuss, Dr. (1991). The Lorax. In *Six by Seuss: A treasury of Dr. Seuss classics*. New York: Random House.

Silverstein, S. (1964). *The giving tree*. New York: Harper & Row.

Simon, S. (1989). *Storms*. New York: Mulberry Books.

Simon, S. (1991). *Big cats*. New York: HarperCollins.

Spier, P. (1986). *Dreams*. New York: Doubleday.

Stevens, J. (1984). *The tortoise and the hare*. New York: Holiday House.

Stoltz, M. (1988). *Storms in the night*. New York: Harper-Collins.

Strong, S. (1992). *Let's take a trip around the zoo*. Los Angeles: Invervisual Books.

Taylor, C. (1992). *The house that crack built*. San Francisco: Chronicle Books.

Tresselt, A. (1992). *The gift of the tree*. New York: Lothrop, Lee & Shepard Books.

Udry, J. M. (1956). *A tree is nice*. New York: Harper & Row. Caldecott Award.

VanCleave, J. (1993). *Janice VanCleave's geography for every kid*. New York: John Wiley & Sons.

Voigt, C. (1986). *Izzy Willy-Nilly*. New York: Fawcett Juniper. Newbery Author.

Wiesner, D. (1990). *Hurricanes*. New York: Clarion Books.

Wyatt, V. (1990). *Weatherwatch*. Addison-Wesley.

Professional References

Allen, R. (2004, Winter). A healthy mind-set: Coordinated efforts focus on the whole child. *ASCD Curriculum Update*, 1-2; 6-8.

Bristor, V.J. (1994, October 15). *Using IDEAS (In-Depth Expanded Activities in Science) to improve the achievement and attitudes of at-risk students*. Paper presented at the annual meeting of the Florida Reading Association, Fort Lauderdale, FL.

Caine, G., Caine, R. N., & McClinic, C. (2002). Guiding the innate constructivist. *Educational Leadership, 60* (1), 70–73.

Califano, J. A., Jr. (2007). *High society: How substance abuse ravages America and what to do about it*. New York: Public Affairs.

Centers for Disease Control (CDC). (2005). Retrieved May 30, 2007. www.cdc.gov/

Charlesworth, R., & Lind, K. K. (1990). *Math and science for young children*. Albany NY: Delmar.

Crocket C. (2004). What do kids know—and misunderstand—about science? *Educational Leadership, 61* (5), 34–37.

El Hindi, A. E. (2003). Integrating literacy and science in the classroom: From ecomysteries to readers' theatre. *The Reading Teacher, 56* (6), 536–538.

Fry, E. B., Fountoukidis, D. L., & Kress, J. K. (2000). *The reading teacher's book of lists* (4th ed.). Englewood Cliffs, NJ: Prentice-Hall.

Holley, M. F. (2005). *Crystal meth: They call it ice*. Mustang, OK: Tate Publishing.

Jefferson, D. J. (2005, August 8). America's most dangerous drug. *Newsweek*, 41–48.

Just Think Twice. (2007). *Just Think Twice Teacher's Guide*. Retrieved May 29, 2007. www.JustThinkTwice.com

Mothers Aganist Methamphetamine (MAMA), 2006. *Mothers Against Methamphetamine Secular/Public School Information Package*. Retrieved May 3, 2007. www.mamasite.net

National Center on Addiction and Substance Abuse (NCASA). (2005). Retrieved May 15, 2005. www.casacolumbia.org.

National Institute on Drug Abuse. (2007). *Mind Over Matter and The Brain's Response to Drugs Teacher's Guide*. Retrieved May 18, 2007. www.casacolumbia.org.

National Science Education Standards. (2004). Retrieved February 20, 2004. www.hap.edu/readingroom/books/nses/overview.html.

Ogle, D.M. (1986). K-W-L: A teaching model that develops active reading of expository text. *The Reading Teacher, 39*, 564–570.

Office of the National Drug Control Policy. (ONDCP). (2007). *Teens and Prescription Drugs: An Analysis of Recent Trends on the Emerging Drug Threat*. Retrieved May 24, 2007. www.whitehousedrugpolicy

Partnership for Drug-Free America, (2007). Retrieved May 24, 2007. www.drugfree.org.

Pateman, B. (December 2003/January 2004). Healthier students, better learners. *Educational Leadership, 61* (4), 70–74.

Reader's Digest. (2001). *Prescription and over-the-counter drugs*. Pleasantville, NY: The Reader's Digest Association.

Rybacki, J. J., & Long, J. W. (2001). *The essential guide to prescription drugs 2001*. New York: HarperCollins.

Shepard, A. (1994). From script to stage: Tips for readers theatre. *Reading Teacher, 49* (2), 184–186.

Smith, J. (2003). *Education and public health: Natural partners in learning for life*. Alexandria, VA: ASCD.

Topping, D. H., & McManus, R. A. (2002). A culture of literacy in science. *Educational Leadership, 60* (3), 30–33.

U.S. Department of Education (USDOE). (2007). *Growing up Drug Free: A Parent's Guide to Prevention*. Retrieved May 24, 2007. http://consumerlawpage.com/brochure/drgfree.shtml.

Wellman, B. (1991). Making science learning more science-like. In A. L. Costa (Ed.), *Developing minds: A resource book for teaching thinking* (pp. 159–163). Alexandria, VA: Association for Supervision and Curriculum Development.

Willis, S. (1995, Summer). Reinventing science education: Reformers promote hands-on, inquiry-based learning. *ASCD Curriculum Update*, 11–8.

Zemelman, S., Daniels, H., & Hyde, A. (1998). *Best practices: New standards for teaching and learning in America's schools* (2nd ed.). Portsmouth, NH: Heinemann.

Websites

American Library Association

700+ amazing, spectacular, mysterious, wonderful websites for kids and the adults who care about them.

www.ala.org/parents

Centers for Disease Control (CDC)

Includes information from several departments concerned with safety and health including health topics and healthy living.

www.cdc.gov/

Children's Literature in the Science Classroom

A collection of web and database resources from The Clearinghouse on English, Reading, and Communication.

http://reading.indiana.edu/ieo/bibs/childsci/html

Drug Enforcement Administration (DEA)

Home Page of the Drug Enforcement Administration (DEA), a component of the US Department of Justice.

www.usdoj.gov/dea/concern/

Just Think Twice

Street smart prevention website produced by the Drug Enforcement Administration (DEA)

www.JustThinkTwice.com

Mothers Against Methamphetamine (MAMA)

Includes information on posters, videos, pamphlets, and books, and some of this material may be reproduced.

www.mamasite.net

National Center on Addiction and Substance Abuse (NCASA)

At Columbia University, think tank that focuses on all forms of substance abuse; includes program designed to help students who are at high risk for substance abuse, delinquency and academic failure.

www.casacolumbia.org

National Energy Foundation

Promotes, and provides resources for education related primarily to energy, water, natural resources, science and math, technology, and conservation.

www.nefl.org

National Institute on Drug Abuse (NIDA)

The mission of the National Institute on Drug Abuse (NIDA) is to lead the nation bringing the power of science to bear on drug abuse and addiction.

www.nida.nih.gov

NIDA for Teens: The Science Behind Drug Abuse

The National Institute on Drug Abuse (NIDA) created the NIDA for Teens Website to educate adolescents ages 11 through 15 (as well as their parents) about drug abuse/addiction.

www.teens.drugabuse.gov

National Science Education Standards (NSES)

Present a vision of a scientifically literate populace. They outline what students need to know, understand.

www.nap.edu/readingroom/books/nses/overview.html

Office of the National Drug Control Policy (ONDCP)

Features White House Drug Policy initiatives, programs, and publications. Includes testimony and press releases. Outlines national drug control strategy.

www.whitehousedrugpolicy.gov

Partnership for Drug-Free America

Obtain pertinent drug abuse and substance abuse information for the partnership for a drug-free America.

www.drugfree.org

Smithsonian

Discover education resources and information, lesson plans, field trips, and fun interactive activities for educators, families, and students.

www.smithsonianeducation.org/

U.S. Department of Education (USDOE)

This is the home page of the drug enforcement administration (DEA), a component of the US Department of Justice.

www.usdoj.gov/dea/concern

CHAPTER 8 LITERATURE SELECTIONS	Reading	Writing
Encyclopedia Brown Boy Detective	ROPE Reading Comprehension	Sleuth Slang Accordion File Folder Book
Windcatcher	Magnify the Mystery	Enigmatist Mystery Puzzles
The Missing 'Gator of Gumbo Limbo	Clue Collection for Inferences and Predictions	Missing Person Poster
The House of Dies Drear	Mysteries of the House Mystery Memos	The Mystery of Prejudice Prejudice Poem
The Westing Game	Tip Terms	Whodunit Suspect Portrait and/or Paragraph

Mysteries Across Content Areas

Social Studies	Math	Science
Hostile Hooligans ABCDo	Sleuth Station Case Costs	Foot and Finger Facts
Shipology Terminology Shipology Terminology Verselets	Shipology and Ordered Pairs Victory at Sea	Treasure Hunt Distance and Directions
The Mystery of You-Niqueness	Sleuth Cyclers Sleuth Cycler Math Problems	Necessary Niche Plate-arama Mobile
You Are There The Mystery of the Underground Railroad	The Mystery of Flight Travel Trials and Tribulations	The Mysteries of Caves and Caverns Cave and Cavern Science Corner
Cooperation Revelation: Two Heads Are Better than One	The Stock Market Game Investment Investigators	Effective Objective Detective Suspect Profile

OVERVIEW

Mysteries are very popular with students. In fact, "Mysteries have won more state children's choice awards than any other type of story, which suggests that mysteries are truly favorites of children" (Lynch-Brown & Tomlinson, 1993, p. 129–130). When asked if they like mysteries, students in many different classrooms respond with a resounding, "Yes!" When asked why they like mysteries, students often mention that reading a mystery is a lot like playing a game. When you plan carefully, you can win by solving the mystery and identifying the culprit.

A *mystery* is a story puzzle that actively involves the reader in putting the puzzle pieces together to find a solution to a problem. Each puzzle piece contains a clue that provides essential evidence for solving the mystery. The reader's responsibility is to identify the clue on each puzzle piece and then place the pieces together in a logical order that gradually reveals the solution to the problem and enables the reader to solve the mystery. Flack (1990, p. 1) says,

> *Good problem solvers and detectives are bloodhounds for facts and clues. They leave no avenue of possible relevance unexplored. They are systematic. Once their data have been assembled, they bring past experience and learning to bear in sorting, saving, and organizing data pertinent to the investigation. A hypothesis or prediction follows which is confirmed or disproved. A denouement or resolution is the final stage. Things are tidied up. The acclaim and awards are enjoyed or disappointing results are acknowledged. The problem solver or detective proceeds to new avenues of research, brand new ventures, or new cases.*

Skillfully crafted mysteries draw the reader into the story. They are designed to create questions in the reader's mind. Searching for clues to answer baffling, intriguing questions such as "Where does the wind come from?" challenges the reader to expend the time and effort necessary to find the answers. Perhaps the most popular type of mystery is a whodunit mystery, a mystery that focuses on solving a crime and identifying the culprit. Case questions for a whodunit mystery include the *5Ws + H*:

1. **What** problem or crime has occurred?
2. **Who** is capable of committing such an act?
3. **Why** would this individual do such a thing (motive)?
4. **When** and **Where** did the problem or crime occur?
5. **How** can the problem be solved?

These questions are included on the ROPE form in the Encyclopedia Brown *Reading* section in this chapter.

Examining the literary elements in mysteries reveals significant information that should be included in a well-crafted mystery. Each mystery is unique. Discuss literary elements as they relate to the mystery on which the class is focusing. General guidelines for literary elements discussion include:

Characters
1. The investigator is a problem solver, detective, police officer, another law enforcement official, or amateur sleuth.
2. The investigator carefully records observations and facts.
3. The investigator has well-developed senses: seeing, hearing, feeling, smelling, and tasting.
4. Many investigators are highly intelligent and well educated with extensive experience in solving mysteries.
5. When suspects are involved, they are carefully developed and have believable motives for committing the crime.

Plot
1. The mystery actively involves the reader in making predictions about solutions to the problem or identifying the culprit responsible for the crime. Making predictions allows the reader to have a vested interest in the outcome of the mystery.
2. Events are fast paced and masterfully orchestrated with intricate twists and turns that provide suspense, tension, and conflict.

3. Foreshadowing in the story provides hints about who or what is responsible for the problem or crime as well as the motive.

Setting
1. The setting is very significant in some mysteries and comparatively insignificant in others.
2. The setting includes the time and place of the problem or crime.
3. Important facts concerning the setting and plot in whodunit mysteries include the following:
   a. Which suspects were on the premises at the time of the crime?
   b. Which suspects have alibis for the time of the crime?
   c. Which suspects have a motive for committing the crime?

Style
1. Vocabulary choices include words that are related to mysteries such as *accomplice, alibi, crime, clue, culprit, deductions, interrogate, investigate, sleuth, suspect*, and so forth.
2. Short sentences are often used for fast-paced action.

Theme
1. One theme prevalent in mysteries is that good triumphs over evil.
2. Another theme found in mysteries is that the brain is more important than brawn.

The mystery is ideal for motivating critical thinking because readers are involved in making judgments and seeking solutions to problems. Readers increase their observation and inferential skills as they examine clues and make predictions. According to Pierce and Short (1995), "Readers discover something about themselves as they work to solve mysteries with the characters of the books" (p. 510). Another value of mysteries is that as readers become engrossed in a mystery, their silent reading speed increases in their eagerness to identify the villain and/or solve the problem.

Use picture books to introduce younger students to mysteries. These initial encounters with mysteries deal with a variety of topics and questions. "The earliest mysteries children solve are the simple questions they ask about their world, questions that often have not-so-simple answers" (Pierce & Short, 1995, p. 508). Information books deal with some of the mysteries and questions about nature. For example, *The Very Busy Spider* by Eric Carle (1985) helps students answer the questions: What is a spider? How does a spider spin a web? Wordless books are mysteries that need young detectives to explain them. For example, *Tuesday*, a Caldecott Award winning book by David Weisner (1991), has flying frogs sailing through a series of adventures in the Tuesday night sky. A police investigator is puzzled by the evidence. Young sleuths are able to help him. The next Wednesday there are pictures of pigs in the sky. What will happen? Super sleuths make predictions. Other picture books deal with mysteries concerning everyday life. In *Miss Nelson Is Missing!* by Harry Allard and James Marshall (1977), students try to unravel the mystery of a missing teacher. Why did the teacher disappear? Will she ever come back? A mystery stimulates curiosity on the part of the reader or listener and provides opportunities to ask questions, make predictions, explain the basis for predictions, and seek answers. The following are examples of picture book mysteries:

Nature: *Hurricane* by David Weisner (1990)
What: What is a hurricane?
Why: Why do we have hurricanes?
Prediction: I predict the following will occur during a hurricane... The evidence for my prediction is...
How: How can I be safe before, during, and after a hurricane?

Note: Answers to some of these questions are not in Hurricane. *Supplementary information books about weather will provide the answers.*

Difficult Phenomenon: *There's a Nightmare in My Closet* by Mercer Mayer (1968)
What: What is a nightmare?
Why: Why is the nightmare hiding in my closet?

Prediction: I predict the nightmare is going to.... The evidence for my prediction is....

How: How can I get rid of that nightmare?

Mysteries provide motivational opportunities for learning in the classroom. A song to introduce "whodunit" mysteries is:

Title: Whodunit?

Tune: "I've Been Working on the Railroad"

I've been looking for the culprit
All the live-long day.
I've been looking for the culprit.
Don't let him get away.
Can't you search to find the clues,
The evidence verify?
Can't you interrogate the witnesses
And answer the question WHY?
What are the clues? What are the facts?
What do my notes say to me?
What are the clues? What are the facts?
Who is guilty?

Mystery series are perennial favorites of young readers. Well-loved classic series that have withstood the test of time include the following:

- *The Boxcar Children Mysteries* by Gertrude Chandler Warner
  The first book in this series was published in 1942. Ms. Warner, a schoolteacher, wrote for the children in her classroom. Inspired by childhood memories of trains and views of the inside of a caboose with a small stove, table, and cracked dishes, she shared dreams about keeping house in a boxcar. There are nineteen titles in the series by Ms. Warner. Because of an overwhelming demand from boxcar mystery enthusiasts, even after Ms. Warner's death, more books are being written for this series (see KidsReads website).
- *The Hardy Boys Series* by Franklin W. Dixon
  First published in 1927, this series includes fifty-nine titles. Many of the original mysteries have been revised (see Hardy Boys website).
- *The Nancy Drew Mysteries* by Carolyn Keene
  Many authors, under the pseudonym Carolyn Keene, have contributed to this popular series. Through the years, modern themes and settings have emerged. There are about 175 titles in the series. The first fifty-six mysteries have been updated and reissued (see Hardy Boys and KidsReads websites).

Mysteries, selected as the thematic focus for a literature-based, across the content area curriculum, stimulate logical and critical thinking and maintain high student interest. A selected mystery, that all students in the class read simultaneously, is the core book around which reading, writing, social studies, math, and science experiences are centered. Pappas, Kiefer, and Levstik (1990, p. 49) state,

Thematic units reflect patterns of thinking, goals, and concepts common to bodies of knowledge. They link together content from many areas of the curriculum and depict the connections that exist across disciplines. Thematic units provide a framework for a community of learners in which all children can continue to learn language and to construct knowledge.

Each of the five mysteries in this chapter provides a core book around which to build a class curriculum. *Reading, Writing, Social Studies, Math,* and *Science* strategies are included for each of these mysteries. Mystery choices include a detective mystery and a treasure hunt mystery for younger readers, an ecological mystery for a little more mature reader, and a historical mystery and a whodunit mystery for older readers. After introducing students to content area strategies, place these activities in a super sleuth station or detective agency learning center. All of the content area investigative experiences have *pick-me-up possibilities* and may be used with a variety of other mysteries.

ENCYCLOPEDIA BROWN BOY DETECTIVE

Encyclopedia Brown is a 10-year-old super sleuth in sneakers who lives in the town of Idaville. The police chief of Idaville is proud of his town's reputation for having no unsolved crimes. What most people don't realize is that the difficult crimes are solved by Encyclopedia, Chief Brown's son. Family dinner table conversations revolve around town troubles. At the mere mention of an unsolved crime, Encyclopedia leans back, closes his eyes, and thinks hard. Soon, often before dessert, he is well on his way to cracking the case.

Encyclopedia Brown Boy Detective by Donald Sobol (1963) is the first in a series of Encyclopedia Brown detective books popular with younger readers. There are ten short mysterious cases to be solved in this book. By the end of each case, reading investigators know that Encyclopedia has solved the crime, but *how* he solved the crime and sometimes who the culprit is still remain a mystery. Reading investigators match wits with the boy detective and answer the question at the end of each story to see if they have made the same observations and arrived at the same conclusions. An example of a question is, "How did Encyclopedia know?" After reflecting on the question and possible answers, reading investigators are referred to a designated page at the back of the book. This page contains the name of the culprit and the observation strategies used by Encyclopedia to solve the crime. Thus, reading investigators are able to evaluate their own observation abilities. Once readers get hooked on Encyclopedia Brown, they will want to match wits with him in further escapades.

Reading

ROPE/Reading Comprehension

ROPE is a reading comprehension strategy for mysteries in which an ocular organizer, which includes the steps **Read, Observe, Predict,** and **Evaluate,** helps the reading investigator solve the problem or crime. Completing a ROPE form increases the readers' awareness of components found in a mystery (see ROPE Form in Activity Appendix A). Just as readers build a *sense of story* from hearing and reading stories, reading investigators build a *sense of mystery* as they hear and read mysteries.

When using *Encyclopedia Brown Boy Detective* as a core book in the classroom, introduce ROPE to the class. Assign one of the cases for all of the students to read. After they complete the reading assignment, complete a ROPE form together. Then assign each cooperative group a different case on which to complete a ROPE form. After working cooperatively, students read other cases and complete ROPE forms independently.

Reading investigators want to solve a problem and ROPE in the culprit. SIFT provides a framework of strategies for sleuths to follow in sifting through the evidence and determining how to solve the crime. SIFT components include:

Senses: Sleuths use their senses of seeing, hearing, touching, smelling, and tasting. Sleuths also develop a sixth sense, *intuition.*

If Then: Sleuths use inferential skills to determine **If** _____ **Then** _____. (**If** *there is smoke,* **Then** *there is fire.*)

Facts: Sleuths collect, organize, and analyze facts in detective notebooks.

Think: Sleuths think analytically and critically about all the evidence using their intellectual ability.

After sifting through the evidence, sleuths predict *who* the culprit is and *why* the culprit committed the crime (modify this Section if there is not a culprit). The sleuths *evaluate* by comparing their observations, predictions, and findings with those of the principle investigator in the case. With Encyclopedia Brown cases, sleuths turn to the designated page at the back of the book and compare their findings with those of Encyclopedia Brown.

FIGURE 8.1   ROPE Form Example—
Case Information

ROPE

The Case of the Happy Nephew
Book or Case Title

Read

What problem or crime occurred?   The crime that occurred was a
robbery.

When and **Where** did it occur?   It occurred one hour before the
Chief was notified. It happened at the Princess Bake Shop on Vine Street.

Observe

How does the sleuth **SIFT** through the evidence and solve the
problem or crime?

Senses   By listening: John said he got home just 5 minutes earlier after
driving for 12 hours. By touching: The car hood was cool to the touch.

If - Then
If   John was telling the truth   Then   the car hood would be hot.
If   Then

Facts   An eyewitness saw John running out of the bakery.
            The baby is able to walk on the cool car hood.

Think   John is lying. He must be guilty.

Predict

Who is the culprit?   John Abbot

Why did the culprit do it?   John needed the money.

Evaluate

Encyclopedia Brown and I agree. We're both observant
super sleuths!

Literature-Based Example

See Figure 8.1 for a completed ROPE form for the sixth story, "The Case of the Happy Nephew," in Encyclopedia Brown Boy Detective.

Writing

Sleuth Slang/Accordion File Folder Book

Sleuth slang is specialized vocabulary used by investigators when solving a mystery and writing reports. This technical lingo allows sleuths to communicate effectively as they seek to ferret out the truth. The super sleuth station has available a readily accessible and visible source of sleuth slang with definitions, examples, and illustrations for investigators to use in writing their reports.

An *accordion file folder book* is an organizer made from file folders joined at the edges to form an accordion book. File folder pockets are placed at the base of each file folder to hold entry cards for sleuth slang. Entry cards, 5″ X 8″ index cards, slide in and out of the pockets for quick and easy reference. The pockets are labeled alphabetically. The accordion file folder book (see Activity Appendix A) stands atop a table or bookshelf and provides ready access to sleuth slang.

Sleuth slang entry choices are secured from:

1. Mysteries used in whole class instruction
2. Mysteries read by small groups or individuals
3. Technical lingo students collect from a variety of other sources such as media, home, and friends.

Literature-Based Example

Students write definitions, examples, and create illustrations for sleuth slang from Encyclopedia Brown Boy Detective. *Some sleuth slang suggestions are:*

arrest	eyewitness	proof
crack the case	foul play	search
crook	lead	snoopers
expenses	leg work	suspect

Entries might include the proper use of may *and* can. Encyclopedia *is constantly reminded by his mother to use these terms correctly. For additional sleuth slang suggestions, see Figure 8.2.*

FIGURE 8.2   One Hundred Sleuth Slang Suggestions

abuse	deduction	indict	scene
accessory	deposition	inexpicable	scrutinize
accomplice	detect	innocent	search warrant
accuse	disguise	inspector	shadow
alias	elucidate	interrogate	shoplifting
alibi	elude	intimidate	slaying
arson	enigma	intruder	sleuth
assailant	ensconce	investigate	solution
assault	evidence	investigator	spy
baffling	extortion	loot	stakeout
battery	felony	modus operandi	statement
blackmail	ferret out	motive	surveillance
burglary	frame	mystifies	suspicious
bust	getaway	offense	tactic
case	grill	off the record	tail
clues	guilty	perpetrator	third degree
code	gum shoe	probe	top secret
compelling	headquarters	profile	track
confession	hearsay	protect	trial
confidence	heist	pursue	undercover
conspiracy	hideout	pursuit	vandalized
conspirator	homicide	raid	villain
crime	hypothesize	ransack	watch
criminal	identity	ransom	weapon
culprit	incriminate	robbery	witness

Another possibility is developing a *detectionary*, a dictionary containing alphabetically arranged entries for sleuth slang with a page for each letter of the alphabet.

Social Studies

Hostile Hooligans/ABCDo

Hostile hooligans are people who cause problems for others. They are bullies, cheaters, tricksters, traitors, or other types of rogues. They may organize themselves in cliques or gangs. As a class, select one type of hostile hooligan from real life and list the characteristics of that particular type of troublemaker. Hypothesize *why* this person would adopt a lifestyle of negative interaction with others. Then discuss *how* to deal with a person who is this type of hooligan using the ABCDo strategy.

ABCDo is a strategy that offers four broad approach possibilities, **A**void, **B**old Front, **C**ommunicate, and **D**o, for dealing with hostile hooligans. ABCDo offers positive action possibilities for students to consider implementing in hostile hooligan encounters. As students incorporate these positive actions into their lives, they develop social skills for living peacefully and productively with others in society. The ABCDo approach involves

1. **Avoid**
   a. Stay away from the hooligan.
   b. Ignore the hooligan.
   c. Flee from the hooligan.
2. **Bold Front**
   a. Face the foe.
   b. Stand tall.
3. **Communicate**
   a. Ask the hooligan why there is a problem.
   b. Issue a command statement such as:
      1. Stop taking my pencil!
      2. Stop looking at my paper!
      3. Stop telling lies about me!
      4. Leave me alone!
4. **Do—Plan Positive Actions**
   a. Maintain a positive attitude such as:
      1. I am important!
      2. I have rights too!
   b. Resolve conflict without physical violence.
   c. Solve problem without retaliating.

Literature-Based Example

One of the hostile hooligans Encyclopedia Brown encounters is Bugs Meany. Bugs, the town bully, leads a gang that tries to intimidate Encyclopedia and others by making them feel like bully bait. Encyclopedia employs a number of effective tactics in dealing with Bugs. Search the cases in Encyclopedia Brown Boy Detective *and list characteristics Bugs exhibits and reasons why Bugs may be a bully. Give examples of how Encyclopedia and others deal with Bugs following the ABCDo strategy.*

Bugs Meany, Town Bully
  What are Bug's characteristics?
  He intimidates others physically (e.g. fists).
  He attacks others verbally (e.g. insults).
  He appears tough (e.g. swaggers).
  Why is Bugs a bully?
  He wants attention.
  He has low self-esteem.
  He is insecure.

ABCDo

1. *Avoid:* Encyclopedia ignores Bugs's insults.
2. *Bold Front:* Encyclopedia faces Bugs bravely.
3. *Communicate:* Encyclopedia often whispers in Bugs's ear to let him know he has been caught and had best make restitution quickly.
4. *Do—Plan Positive Attitudes:* Encyclopedia reminds himself that he has rights upon which Bugs is infringing. He follows the ABCDo approach and does not resort to physical violence or retaliation.
   Reminder: Mysteries have hostile hooligans, and this is the role Bugs plays in Encyclopedia's escapades.

Other Possibilities

1. Compose hostile hooligan scenarios for role-playing.
2. Develop a warm fuzzy mailbox system where students write warm fuzzies to each other. Warm fuzzies enhance positive communication and a caring atmosphere in the classroom.
3. Learn more about crime prevention, precaution, and protection. Investigate local law enforcement agencies' contributions to the community. Invite a guest speaker. Take a field trip. Interview law enforcement officers.

Math

Sleuth Station/Case Costs

A *sleuth station* is a detective agency that charges a fee for solving a problem or crime. A client goes to the sleuth station to retain a detective to solve a problem or a crime. Sometimes the detective incurs expenses that the client must pay for in addition to the agreed upon fee, which is either a daily fee or a flat rate. Of course, there are business expenses in setting up a sleuth station such as signs, business cards, other forms of advertisement, office supplies, and so forth. There are innumerable math problem possibilities for determining *case costs,* costs for solving each problem or crime. The difficulty of case cost math problems is determined by the grade-level math curriculum as well as the developmental appropriateness for each student.

Literature-Based Example

The Encyclopedia Brown Detective Agency charges 25¢ per day plus expenses for case costs. The following are sample case cost questions and answers related to Encyclopedia's cases.

1. In setting up the Detective Agency, Encyclopedia incurred the following expenses: $1.00 for pads of paper, 50¢ for pencils, and 25¢ for markers. How many days will Encyclopedia have to work on cases to recover his business investment expenses in setting up the Brown Detective Agency?
2. If Encyclopedia works 5 hours on one day and solves a case, how much does he earn per hour?
3. Suppose it takes one week for Encyclopedia to solve a case. He incurs 80¢ in expenses. How much does the client owe in case costs? Remember, Encyclopedia does not work on Sunday. If the client gives Encyclopedia a five-dollar bill, how much change is returned to the client?

The teacher and/or students develop other case cost math problems for Encyclopedia Brown's escapades. There are numerous possibilities around which to center problems such as:

1. Encyclopedia is considering putting his money in the bank where it will be safe. How much will he earn in interest at the current rate of interest? Will it make a difference if the interest is compounded daily, monthly, or yearly? If so, what is the difference?
2. Time is significant in many detective cases especially in establishing the credibility of alibis. Create time problems for Encyclopedia's cases.

3. Bugs Meany goes into the detective business in competition with Encyclopedia in the fourth book in the series, *Encyclopedia Brown Gets His Man* (Sobel, 1967). Bugs undercuts Encyclopedia and charges 20¢ per day plus expenses. Create case cost comparison problems.

Science

Foot and Finger Facts

Foot and finger facts are gleaned from scientific investigation and careful observation of footprints and fingerprints found at the scene of the crime. The investigator does careful surveillance of the premises and gathers all relevant evidence pertinent to the crime, being careful not to disturb footprints and fingerprints. *The KnowHow Book of Detection* by Judy Hindley and Donald Rumbelow (1978) and *The Spies and Detectives Cut and Color Book* published by Chatham River Press (1989) provide footprint and fingerprint information.

To become familiar with footprints, collect a variety of shoes and make shoe prints in damp sand. Take notes on the distinctive differences in prints made from each type of shoe. Compare the prints from shoes with heels to those of shoes with smooth soles. Note the size and shape of each heel. Observe ridge patterns from tennis shoes and boots. Measure the length and width of the prints. Make a paper pattern and illustrate any distinctive marks or features. All of this information may be helpful in identifying the culprit.

Fingerprinting is a scientific method for determining who was present at the scene. Each person has unique and distinctive fingerprints that are unlike those of any other person. Make fingerprint records using an ink pad and $5'' \times 8''$ index card. Touch each finger lightly on the ink pad and then place it on the index card. As an alternative to a standard ink pad with permanent ink, use a water-based ink pad or a water-based marker to color the end of each finger. Label the left hand and right hand. Label each fingerprint.

There are four fingerprint types: (1) center arch, which has a hill or arch pattern; (2) center loop, which is a hairpin pattern; (3) center whorl, which has a circular pattern; and (4) mixed, which has a varied pattern. A fingerprint testing kit contains talcum powder for use on dark surfaces; ground pencil lead or cocoa for use on light surfaces; a small, soft paintbrush; clear cellophane tape; and white and dark colored index cards.

To lift a fingerprint from a dark surface, brush carefully with talcum power, place a piece of tape over the print, press down firmly, lift the tape with the print, and place the print on a dark index card. To lift a fingerprint from a light surface, brush carefully with ground pencil lead or cocoa, place a piece of tape over the print, press down firmly, lift the tape with the print, and place the print on a white index card. To compare and identify fingerprints use a magnifying glass and follow these steps:

1. Classify by type
2. Look for identifying marks like scars and cuts
3. Look for other matching small shapes
4. Count the lines or ridges between the shapes to determine if the number is the same.

Literature-Based Example

In "The Case of the Knife in the Watermelon," Encyclopedia is going to buy a fingerprint kit to lift prints from the knife handle and identify the thief. Unfortunately, the knife handle has been wiped clean. Fortunately, the thief does not know this. Encyclopedia will undoubtedly need to use a fingerprint kit in future cases. Challenge students to research the history of fingerprinting and share findings with classmates.

WINDCATCHER

Windcatcher (1991), by Newbery Award winning author Avi, is a sunken treasure mystery. Tony, the protagonist in the story, purchases a Snark, a type of sailboat. He spends his summer vacation with his grandmother in Swallows Bay, where he learns to sail the Snark. He is intrigued by a local legend that there is buried treasure. He soon discovers that the treasure is not buried beneath the earth but beneath the sea. Treasure hunters do not take kindly to his interest in them. What happens? Students will enjoy this easy-to-read treasure adventure with clues from a variety of sources such as characters, the environment, and books in the library. Sailing information is an additional highlight of this mystery. Several exciting content area adventures are suggested to entice students to develop investigative skills while reading *Windcatcher*.

Reading

Magnify the Mystery

Magnify the mystery is an ocular organizer specifically designed to focus on the literary elements in mysteries. Reading investigators increase their sleuth sense as they focus on determining motives, identifying clues, and evaluating evidence. Critical thinking skills are enhanced as these sleuths make inferences about events and predict answers to case questions. In mysteries with a *whodunit* question, reading detectives hypothesize about the guilt or innocence of the culprit or culprits.

Literature-Based Example

A blank magnify the mystery *worksheet on a magnifying glass is in the Activity Appendix A. An example for* Windcatcher *looks like this:*

Windcatcher
(Title)
Where is the treasure?
(Case Question)
Summer vacation at Swallows Bay
(When and Where)
Treasure hunters scuba diving near the island
(Clue 1)
Littlejohn's historic statue points to Money Island
(Clue 2)
Tony sees the sunken ship while diving for tennis shoe
(Clue 3)
Treasure hunters try to bribe Tony
(Clue 4)
Under the water
(Case Answer)

Writing

Enigmatist/Mystery Puzzles

An *enigmatist* is the author of a mystery, a puzzling story, which actively involves the reader in putting the puzzle pieces together to find a solution to a problem. A mystery contains a case question and clues leading to a case answer. To create a mystery, the enigmatist begins with the completed puzzle. Gradually, the enigmatist takes the puzzle apart. Each piece contains a clue for an answer to the case question. The puzzle pieces are arranged in the mystery, so that the reader can place each piece together in a logical order to gradually reveal the solution to the case question and solve the mystery.

To develop a mystery, as an enigmatist, begin at the end of the story and decide what problem or crime occurs, when and where it occurs, and who is the culprit. Next, determine how the crime was committed, the motive of the guilty party, and the incriminating blunder or mistake the culprit makes. Include additional suspects who also have reasonable motives and clues that tend to indict them. Devise a *"red herring,"* diversion or misleading clue, to throw the investigator off track. Create an ingenious super sleuth and instill that investigator with exceptional talents and observation skills. Incorporate super sleuth strategies such as fingerprinting, interrogating suspects, shadowing suspects, and recording alibis. Identify the *blunder finder,* the specific strategy the super sleuth uses to prove the culprit guilty.

Use an enigmatist plan to assist in writing a mystery. An enigmatist plan contains the following information:

> **What** problem or crime occurs?
> **When** and **where** does it occur?
> **Culprit**
> > **Who** does it?
> > **How?**
> > **Why?**
> > **Blunder?**
> **Other Possible Suspects:** *(repeat for each suspect)*
> **Who?**
> > **Evidence?**
> **Red Herring?**
> **Super Sleuth?**
> > **Who?**
> > **Strategies?**
> > **Blunder Finder?**

After developing an enigmatist plan, compose an initial draft for the mystery. Revise and edit the draft. Write the final copy of the mystery on one side of a mystery puzzle (see Puzzle Pleasers in the Activity Appendix A). Draw lines between words in the mystery to form puzzle pieces. On the other side of the puzzle create an illustration for the mystery. Cut the puzzle apart. Label an envelope with the title of the mystery and the enigmatist's name. Place the puzzle in an envelope. Share mystery puzzles with classmates.

Social Studies

Shipology Terminology/Shipology Terminology Verselets

Windcatcher is full of wonderful *shipology terminology*, seafaring nomenclature. Challenge students to detect these terms in the mystery and ferret out their meanings. Commence the search for definitions in the media center where evidence is located in dictionaries, thesauruses, and various information books. Analyze this evidence and compose *terminology verselets*, a pair of rhyming lines that include and define the selected term. When versifying, *Webster's Compact Rhyming Dictionary* (1987) is a valuable tool. Construct ship shape log books (see Shape Books in the Activity Appendix A). Compile a class anthology of shipology terminology and shipology terminology verselets, STVs.

Literature-Based Examples

The following STVs incorporate shipology terminology from *Windcatcher*.

Ship STVs

The back of the ship is called the *stern*
This is shipology terminology that you must learn

On the *bow* of the ship is a figurehead.
She points the way: straight ahead.

Sailing STVs

The zigzag motion is called the *tack*.
Wind makes the boat move forth and back.

Take a starboard *tack* when sailing right.
As under the stars you cruise through the night.

Safety STVs

Don't stand in a small boat; you could drown.
A boat when *capsized* turns upside down.

You must wear a *life jacket* in the boat.
If you fall out, it will help you float.

Math

Shipology and Ordered Pairs/Victory at Sea

In *Windcatcher* Tony visits the Shallows Bay local library to explore and amass evidence on *shipology*, the scientific study of sailing. Throughout the mystery reference is made to the historical significance of different types of ships. Classroom shipologists look *high and low, scan the horizon,* and *go overboard* as they cruise the pages of resource books in search of shipology information. Developing class charts, time lines, and illustrations to display these findings enhances understanding of shipology.

Victory at Sea is an exciting game that combines shipology terminology and ordered pairs in math. This game is similar to the popular commercial game, Battleship. In this game students develop pre-algebra skills as they plot the coordinates of an ordered pair of numbers to identify a letter point on the graph. Pairs of students choose names for five ships and plot these names on individual Victory at Sea game boards. Each letter of the ship's name is plotted and labeled on a point. Each player attempts to sink the other player's ships and win a Victory at Sea.

Game Board Information
1. Make a Victory at Sea game board using graph paper. Put numbers on the X and Y axes (see Figure 8.3).
2. With your partner choose names for five ships.
3. Secretly plot and label the name of each ship on your graph paper. Write the names horizontally, vertically, or diagonally (see Figure 8.3).
4. Use ordered pairs when calling out the coordinates of a letter point to your opponent. Give the number on the horizontal axis (X) first, and the number on the vertical axis (Y) second.

Victory at Sea Directions

Player 1 Calls out an ordered pair of numbers.

Player 2 Responds, "Hit" or "Miss."

Player 1 If Player 2 responds, "Miss," record an M over the point. If Player 2 responds "Hit," record an H over the point.

Player 2 Indicates a Hit from Player 1 with an X over the letter.

Player 2 Calls out an ordered pair of numbers.

Player 1 Responds, "Hit" or "Miss."

Player 2 If Player 1 responds, "Miss," record an M over the point. If Player 1 responds, "Hit," record an H over the point.

Player 1 Indicate a Hit from Player 2 with an X over the letter.

FIGURE 8.3   Victory at Sea Game Board Example

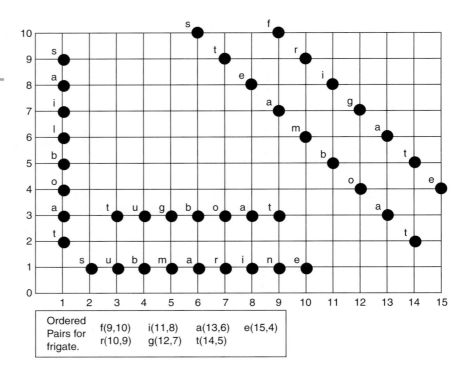

Ordered Pairs for frigate.

| f(9,10) | i(11,8) | a(13,6) | e(15,4) |
| r(10,9) | g(12,7) | t(14,5) | |

Note: *When all the letters in a ship's name are hit by the opposing player, announce the sinking of the ship. Continue playing Victory at Sea until one of the players no longer has any ships. The other player wins a Victory at Sea.*

Science

Treasure Hunt/Distance and Directions

The populace in Swallows Bay mistakenly assumes that the treasure is buried. Treasure hunters in droves search for years in futile attempts to locate the hidden treasure. Tony's investigative sources—books in the library, his grandfather's ship model, and a statue of Littlejohn pointed toward the islands—uncover many clues. As Tony contemplates his observations, the preponderance of evidence points toward the treasure's hiding place. As reading investigators search with Tony for the hidden treasure, they too will want to experience a treasure hunt.

One way to provide this experience is for classroom super sleuths to develop and participate in treasure hunts that incorporate the scientific skills of distance and direction. Plan the experience so that distance is measured using standard or metric units of measure. Use the following information as a guide.

Treasure Hunt Information
1. Challenge cooperative groups to devise treasure hunts that they exchange with other groups.
2. Determine a treasure hunt site: the classroom, media center, cafeteria, or other location.
3. Establish the cardinal directions—north, south, east, and west—at the treasure hunt site.
4. Provide time for each group to independently set up its treasure hunt.

Treasure Hunt Directions
1. Hide a treasure (nickel or another object).
2. Write five clues on separate 3″ × 5″ index cards to locate the treasure.
3. Include a direction and distance challenge in each clue.
4. Hide a clue at each location.
5. Hand clue 1 to treasure hunters as they enter the classroom.

6. Clue 1 leads treasure hunters to clue 2.
7. Clue 2 leads treasure hunters to clue 3, clue 3 leads to clue 4, clue 4 leads to clue 5, and clue 5 leads to the treasure.

Treasure Hunt Example

Clue 1:   Enter the room from the door on the West.

Go *East 2 yards*. Look on page 32 of the blue book at this location for clue 2.

Clue 2:   Go *South 3 yards*. Look down under the furniture for clue 3.

Clue 3:   Go *Northeast 4 yards*. Look behind the furniture for clue 4.

Clue 4:   Go *West 4 1/2 yards*. Look above the picture for clue 5.

Clue 5:   Go *Southeast 5 1/3 yards*. Look 1 foot to the right inside the box to find the treasure.

THE MISSING 'GATOR OF GUMBO LIMBO

The Missing 'Gator of Gumbo Limbo (1992), by the Newbery Award winning author Jean Craighead George, is an *ecological mystery*, a mystery in which nature provides clues for finding the solution to a problem. The reading investigator, as a budding ecologist, revels in a search for Dajun, the protecting dragon and missing 'gator of Gumbo Limbo. Through the eyes, ears, and background knowledge of Lisa K, a homeless woods person, the reader is actively engaged in determining the significance of each ecological clue, locating Dajun, and protecting him from the alligator hunter. Dajun is important to Gumbo Limbo, a Florida Everglades habitat, because he makes significant contributions to the ecosystem balance as well as protection of the homeless woods people who live there.

George skillfully weaves the lives of the woods people with the suspense and tension of saving Dajun from the certain death and doom of the hunter. How can a 12-foot alligator disappear into thin air, leaving no apparent trace of his whereabouts? Clues abound as George integrates information about plants, flowers, trees, animals, fish, birds, and insects indigenous to the Florida Everglades into this suspenseful mystery.

The five homeless woods people who inhabit Gumbo Limbo are seeking refuge from a variety of personal problems. They are hiding from society, social workers, and perhaps even themselves. Each life is a mini-mystery within the larger mystery, Where is Dajun?

Reading

Clue Collection for Inferences and Predictions

Where is Dajun and why did he disappear? Interest is at an all-time high, as reading investigators study the ecological clues in an all-out search for Dajun. The suspense and tension increase each time the alligator hunter returns. Lisa K and the other woods people know that they must locate Dajun soon or he will die. A *clue collection*, an organized list of clues and the significance of each clue, guides investigators in making *inferences and predictions* about Dajun's hiding place.

The following chart contains some of the ecological clues used in determining Dajun's hiding place.

Clue Collection for The Missing 'Gator of Gumbo Limbo

Clue	Significance
No vultures	Dajun is not dead.
Solution pit—plants perky	Dajun is not there. He tramples and flattens plants.

(continued)

Blue-green algae means water is polluted. Dajun would move the algae to shore.	Dajun is not where the blue-green algae is growing.
Canal is full of hydrilla.	Dajun is not in the canal.
Cypress slough is shallow.	Dajun is not in the slough.
Armadillo avoid GL.* (false lead)	There is saltwater intrusion in GL.* (incorrect assumption)
There are no claw or tail marks at the borrow pit.	Dajun is not in the borrow pit.
There are no weeds in GL.* Fish are multiplying. Water is almost clear.	Dajun is in the GL* hole carefully camouflaged.

*Note: Gumbo Limbo-GL

Writing

Missing Person Poster

A *missing person poster* (MPP) is an investigative, advertising procedure that is used when searching for a person who has disappeared. With slight alterations, the MPP is also useful for locating missing places and things. These posters, with information and illustrations, increase others' awareness of the search and enlist their help in finding the missing person, place, or thing. A MPP may be displayed in a frame from a file folder or on a variation of a wanted poster (see Activity Appendix A).

This procedure is useful in classroom cases such as *The Case of the Missing Teacher* (person), *The Case of the Missing Quiet Classroom* (place), and *The Case of the Missing Homework* (thing). The following is a true classroom case.

The Case of the Missing Pencil

Last Known Address: Carlos' desk

Appearance: Orange #2 with an eraser on one end, approximately 6 inches long

Traits: Writes Carlos' stories and math problems

Concerns: Necessary for Carlos to complete classwork

Rewards: Satisfaction in helping Carlos; class reputation for helpfulness and honesty maintained

Note: Include an illustration of the pencil.

Literature-Based Example

This MPP is based on Dajun, the missing 'gator of Gumbo Limbo.

The Case of the Missing 'Gator

Name: Dajun

Aliases: Living dinosaur, protective dragon, reptilian bulldozer, conjurer

Last Known Address: Gumbo Limbo Hole

Appearance: 12 feet long, suit of armor, yellow eyes, teeth: upper jaw 30-40, lower jaw 28-30

Traits: Reptile, cold blooded, comes out during the day and hides at night, can't swallow, holds breath underwater for up to five hours, has to breathe above water

Concerns: Lisa K needs Dajun's friendship.

Priscilla writes poetry about Dajun.

Woods people need Dajun for protection. Environment needs Dajun for ecosystem balance. Alligator hunter wants bounty.

Rewards: Woods people will be safe and secure.

                            Environment will be protected.

Note: Include an illustration of Dajun.

Social Studies

The Mystery of You-niqueness

Each person is a mystery. Each is a unique puzzle with personal pieces that answer questions and precisely fit together to form an amazing whole. The completed puzzle answers the question, "Who am I?" *The mystery of You-niqueness (MOY)* is a personal story each person has to tell that asks and answers the question, "Who am I?" The MOY has fourteen lines with a series of questions and answers that reveal secrets of a unique life with unique problems (see format in Poetry Appendix C). The MOY may reveal the mystery of hurts, habits, and hang-ups. Students develop social sensitivity to others and their problems as they develop an understanding of the fact that each of us is unique.

Display an MOY on the silhouette of a person's head. Make the silhouette by standing in front of the light from an overhead projector or a light bulb and directing the light onto a 12″ × 18″ sheet of construction paper that is taped to the board. Have a friend use chalk to draw around the shadow on the paper. Cut out the silhouette. Write the MOY on a 5″ × 8″ index card and mount it on the silhouette. Display silhouettes on a bulletin board entitled "The Mystery of You-niqueness." Distribute paper question marks randomly around the silhouettes to provide interest. A MOY could also be displayed on an eightfold person (see Activity Appendix A).

Literature-Based Example

The five woods people in The Missing 'Gator of Gumbo Limbo *each have heart-wrenching, personal stories that are intertwined throughout the mystery. Each mini-mystery within the larger story asks and answers questions about why this person and his or her problems are unique. The following list provides insight into a few of the problems the characters face.*

Character	Problems
Lisa K	Fears physical abuse from her father
Charlotte	Struggles to provide a better life for her daughter
James James	Suffers from memories of Vietnam War
Caruso	Envisions himself as a famous opera star
Priscilla	Fears walls and being inside

As students create MOYs about each character in the story, their sensitivity for and understanding about others will increase. The following is a MOY for Priscilla.

Who Am I?
    Line 1: I am Priscilla *(name)*
    Line 2: I am special.
    Line 3: Sometimes I ask:
    Line 4: Why am I afraid of walls? *(question)*
    Line 5: Why can't I put my thoughts into poems? *(question)*
    Line 6: Sometimes other people ask:
    Line 7: Are you crazy? *(question)*
    Line 8: Are you an alcoholic? *(question)*
    Line 9: But deep down I know:
    Line 10: That I care about others.
    Line 11: That one day I will be able to live in a house.
    Line 12: Who am I?

Line 13: I am Priscilla. *(name)*
Line 14: I am You-nique.

Math

Sleuth Cyclers/Sleuth Cycler Math Problems

The cost to the natural world as well as society is overwhelming when natural resources are not conserved. One way to protect the environment is to *recycle*, save used items and take them to businesses who turn them into new products. Lisa K, her mom, and classmates realize the importance of recycling. One of Lisa K's school assignments is to collect glass bottles, plastic bottles, cans, and newspapers and place them in recycling bins at school.

Sleuth cyclers are detectives who collect and separate used items that can be made into useful new products. Sleuth cyclers:

1. Research recycling benefits in ecology literature.
2. Investigate the types of products for which there are community recycling centers.
3. Organize recycling drives.
4. Determine the benefits of recycling the used product into a new product rather than making an entirely new product.
5. Solve sleuth cycler math problems.

Literature-Based Examples

Get sleuth cyclers excited about making contributions to saving the environment. Discover pertinent information in 50 Simple Things Kids Can Do to Recycle *published by The Earth-Works Group (1994). Information from this source is used to create the sleuth cycler math problems that follow. Adjust difficulty of math problems to the class curriculum and students' developmental levels.*

Glass Bottles and Jars
Information:
1. Americans throw out more than 500 million glass jars and bottles each year.
2. Recycling one glass bottle saves enough energy to light a 100 watt light bulb for four hours.

Sleuth cycler math problems:
1. During a recycling project our class collected 159 bottles the first week and 127 bottles the second week. Our goal is 500 bottles. How many more bottles do we need?
2. The 500 bottles we collected save enough energy to burn light bulbs for how long?

Aluminum Cans
Information:
1. In three months, Americans throw away enough aluminum to rebuild all airline planes.
2. Recycling one aluminum can saves enough energy to run a television set for three hours.

Sleuth cycler math problems:
1. Family members watch TV for 12 hours per week. How many cans should they recycle to save enough energy to run their television set for a week?
2. A class TV poll shows the average class member in this class of 30 students watches television 1 hour per day on weekdays and 2 hours per day on weekends. How many cans need to be recycled to provide this energy for a week?
    The teacher and/or students develop other sleuth cycler math problems. There are numerous possibilities around which to center problems such as:
3. Recycling 118 pounds of white paper saves 1 pine tree and 3 barrels of oil. White paper includes notebook paper, copy paper, and computer paper. Separate and weigh class trash. How many days does it take the class to use up a pine tree and 3 barrels of oil? As recycling consciousness increases, weigh trash again. How much has the class improved?
4. Phosphates harm plants and animals. Soap doesn't contain phosphates. Laundry, dishwasher, and dishwashing detergents contain varying percentages of phosphates

that take oxygen out of the water and kill living things. Compare and contrast the percentages of phosphates in different brands of detergents.
Note: See George, p. 91, for additional information.

See the writing chapter for additional information on an ecology theme. Information in this chapter includes three well-known conservation strategies: reduce, reuse, and recycle.

Science

Necessary Niche/Plate-arama Mobile

Each plant and animal occupies a necessary niche and makes a unique and essential contribution to the environment and the balance of the ecosystem. "A *niche . . .* is an ecological term for a place an individual or species occupies in a community of plants and animals" (George, 1992, p. 21). When one or more members of an ecosystem is hurt or destroyed, all other members of the system are affected.

The balance of nature is dependent on *food chains,* which are sequentially linked plants and animals that are interdependent on each other for food to supply energy. For example, the first link in a bird food chain is grass that can manufacture its own food. The grass is consumed by an insect that in turn is eaten by a toad. The toad is consumed by a snake that is then eaten by a bird. When something happens to damage a link in this food chain, the balance of nature is upset. The balance is dependent on the protection of each plant and animal that forms a link in the food chain. Many interrelated food chains form food webs.

George describes Gumbo Limbo as a hammock, a tropical Eden, an island in the woods, a greenhouse. Within this community are numerous microsystems of mutually interdependent plants and animals. As students read about these systems, they construct plate-arama mobiles to depict the necessary niche each member occupies in a food chain within a microsystem. To create this mobile, students make a plate-arama for each member of the food chain they are studying. They write information about each member on the back of the appropriate plate-arama. These plate-aramas form a vertical chain when holes are punched in the top and bottom, and the plate-aramas are tied together with yarn (see Activity Appendix A).

Literature-Based Example:

When constructing a plate-arama mobile for Dajun, each member of a cooperative group contributes one plate-arama to the mobile. The plate-arama mobile is organized as follows:

Top Plate-arama	Dajun
Second Plate-arama	Turtle
Third Plate-arama	Sun Fish
Fourth Plate-arama	Little Fish
Fifth Plate-arama	Algae

Another possibility is constructing plate-arama mobiles to represent a specific species of plant or animal indigenous to the area being studied. Gumbo Limbo possibilities include trees, plants, insects, birds, or animals. Include information about each member on the back of the appropriate plate-arama. Students will also enjoy creating food chain wrap-over books (see Activity Appendix A).

THE HOUSE OF DIES DREAR

The House of Dies Drear, by the prolific African American author Virginia Hamilton (1968), is a historical mystery, a mystery in which a historical setting provides clues for unlocking secrets, supplies answers to questions, and enhances understanding of a particular historical period. This book has received recognition as an ALA Notable Children's Book, "Best of the Best Books" from the *School Library Journal,* and a Mystery Writers of America "Edgar" Award.

This contemporary story with a historical setting is told from the point of view of Thomas Small, the son of an African American history professor who leases the mysterious Dies Drear house. Dies Drear was an eccentric abolitionist whose house provided sanctuary as an Underground Railroad Station to hundreds of runaway slaves during the Civil War era. Sliding walls, moving steps, turning mirrors, tunnels, caves, and caverns intrigue both Thomas and the reader.

Throughout the mystery, Thomas fires a continuous barrage of questions: Does the house look haunted? How do the tunnels fit together? Where do they go? The reader quickly scans the pages searching for the answers. These questions contribute to the fast-paced action of each event. Most chapters end with a *cliff-hanger,* a moment of tension and suspense, which encourages the reader to move hurriedly on to the next chapter.

Within this mystery are complex, intriguing, well-developed characters. Perhaps Mr. Pluto is the most unusual. He is certainly an unbelievable, fascinating giant of a man. Questions surrounding Mr. Pluto include: Who is he? Why does he attempt to scare Thomas and his family into leaving the house? Why does he live in a cave? What is he trying to hide?

As terrifying events occur, Thomas and his family have many questions that plague them: Is the house of Dies Drear haunted? Who jammed the mysterious triangles into each bedroom door? Why is their kitchen vandalized? Can they protect their house and lives from outsiders? Many of these questions are answered, others are not. A sequel to the book, *The Mystery of Drear House* (Hamilton, 1987) provides information for unanswered questions, reveals hidden secrets, and intrigues the reader with unusual twists and turns in tunnels and plot. For additional suggestions on the Underground Railroad, see the Language Arts Chapter. Strategies in this chapter include quilts, lit link centers, lit link legends, felt boards, and a freedom trail.

Reading

Mysteries of the House/Mystery Memos

As historical sleuths read *The House of Dies Drear,* they focus on the historical facts and fiction related to the many mysteries surrounding the house. *Mystery memos,* notes about mysteries, are recorded in a mystery memo mini-book (see Teeny Tiny Book in the Activity Appendix A).

One organizational possibility is an entry page for each of the following topics: appearance, history, legend, and personification. List relevant information and the page number from the story on the appropriate page in the mystery memo mini-book.

Literature-Based Example

- *Appearance of the House*
  The house is sinister, sits on the rise in the wilderness, has an atmosphere of desolation, and is huge, isolated, and unnatural.
- *History of the House*
  The house had been an important Underground Railroad Station, had provided care and concealment of runaway slaves, and from the house secret conductors had returned to bondage to help others escape. (p. 17)
- *Legend About the House*
  The house is haunted by Dies Drear and two slave ghosts and has secrets and treasure.
- *Personification of the House*
  The house reached out for them, pulling them in. The house listened and watched them; the house thinks it's going to get them.

Writing

The Mystery of Prejudice/Prejudice Poem

Mayhew, Mr. Pluto's son, says, "Folks have hated other folks for centuries, and the same business is still with us" (p. 202). Throughout the story there are examples of a wide variety of *prejudices*, unreasonable, preconceived negative feelings, impressions, or opinions. Often these prejudices are based on a misunderstanding of the words, actions, or attitudes of others. Search *The House of Dies Drear* for examples of prejudice and keep a running list on a wall chart in the classroom. Some examples of negative attitudes in the mystery are the prejudices:

1. Between Baptists and Methodists
2. Against new people in the church
3. Against the North
4. Between Presbyterians and Methodists
5. Between Whites and Blacks

Discuss examples of prejudice in the story and prejudice today. Do we have the same types of prejudice as those exhibited by the characters in the mystery? What types of prejudice exist today? Why do we have prejudice? How do we overcome prejudicial feelings and attitudes?

Use the following acrostic as a stimulus for a discussion on the sources of prejudice.

Parents
Religion
Economics
Jealousy
Uniqueness
Diversity
Impressions
Color
Exteriority

Compose a prejudice poem on ways to confront and examine critically negative feelings, impressions, or opinions toward another person or group of people (see format in Appendix C.) A *prejudice poem* is a four-line investigative poem that answers the following questions:

1. What is my prejudice?
2. Why am I prejudiced?
3. How can I change my attitude?
4. What is my attitude now?

An example of a prejudice poem is the following:

I thought all blacks (or whites) were bad,
Because my parents said so.
Then I got to know a black (or white) person really well.
Now I know blacks (or whites) are just like me.

Literature-Based Example

A prejudice poem based on *The House of Dies Drear* reads:

I thought all Methodists were better than Baptists,
Because I grew up a Methodist.
Then I visited a Baptist church.
Now I know we believe many of the same things.

Another possibility is examining the prejudice in *Maniac Magee*, the 1991 Newbery Award winning book by Jerry Spinelli.

Social Studies

You are There/The Mystery of the Underground Railroad

One purpose of historical mysteries is to enhance an understanding of people and events during a particular time period. *You Are There* is a dramatic experience that actively involves participants in events that happened during a particular historical period, so that they can experience vicariously the thoughts and feelings of people living at that time.

Literature-Based Example

Plan a You Are There experience to enhance understanding of the time period and events surrounding The House of Dies Drear. *Set up the classroom as an Underground Railroad route with the mysterious Drear house as the destination.*

Setting
1. Establish the cardinal directions: North, South, East, and West.
2. Construct cabins for slave residences in the south.
3. Create stations, houses, and barns, along the escape route.
4. Custom build the house of Dies Drear in the north using information from the book as a guide.

Suggestions:
1. Use tables, desks, bulletin board paper sketches, and appliance cartons for housing.
2. Create trees, bushes, waterways, and other features using various media materials or bulletin board paper sketches.

Plot and Characters
Write a script incorporating the following suggestions:
1. Include parts for slaves, slave owners, slave hunters, station masters, conductors, and Dies Drear.
2. Link events about slaves who are abused and plan to escape; meetings with a conductor who explains the risks of escaping, the importance of traveling at night and hiding by day; survival tactics such as walking in a stream to hide tracks from slave hunters; and feelings about those who are fleeing as well as those who are helping them.
3. Include events with secret conductors who courageously returned to bondage in order to help their families and friends escape the tyranny of slavery.
4. Integrate truths that all men are entitled to life, liberty, and the pursuit of happiness.
5. Teach cross reading and mark the trail for the Underground Railroad with triangles like those described in *The House of Dies Drear*. (For information on cross reading see pages 234–238.)
6. Use other books about the Underground Railroad to provide information for the script. Some literature suggestions are *Aunt Harriet's Underground Railroad in the Sky* by Faith Ringgold (1992), *Follow the Drinking Gourd* by Jeanette Winter (1988), *Harriet and the Promised Land* by Jacob Lawrence (1993), *Harriet Tubman* by Bree Burns (1992), *If You Traveled on the Underground Railroad* by Ellen Levine (1988), and *Sweet Clara and the Freedom Quilt* by Deborah Hopkinson (1993).

An alternative approach for constructing an Underground Railroad is the utilization of tables, poster board, or a large piece of felt as the base for a miniature Underground Railroad route. Use masking tape for roads. Create people using multicolored pipe cleaners. Make houses and barns using fold-a-building or story box techniques (see Activity Appendix A).

Math

The Mystery of Flight/Travel Trials and Tribulations

When traveling on the Underground Railroad, runaway slaves often traveled at night and hid during the day as they fled for sanctuary in stations such as the Dies Drear house. Despite the dangers, these slaves were willing to risk their lives in a flight for freedom and independence. Many brave people, regardless of color, risked their lives to give assistance.

Computing travel distance and time was a major concern of the slaves as they plotted their journey through an unknown land. Many obstacles stood in their way of escape. Students expand their understanding of this historical event as they construct and participate in *Travel Trials and Tribulations (TTT)*, a math card game that focuses on distance, elapsed time, and hazards of travel.

Divide the class into cooperative groups with four members per group. Each group receives 3″ × 5″ index cards to construct a TTT card game. Each group member is responsible for writing six cards; thus, each cooperative group develops a game with 24 cards. After playing their own TTT, groups swap decks of cards and play a TTT created by another group.

Travel Trials and Tribulations guidelines include the following:

Basic Information

1. Travel time during the day is 7:00 AM–5:00 PM.
2. Travel time at night is 8:00 PM–5:00 AM.
3. Slaves travel 2 miles per hour.
4. Each player creates five question cards and one hazard card.
5. Each card contains a question for one day **or** one night.
6. Each of the five question cards created by a player must be different.
7. Each player keeps a personal flight record on the number of miles traveled that is checked by the player on the left.
8. Calculators are helpful.

Hazard Card Possibilities

Hide from a bounty hunter for the night
Treed by dogs for a day
Sick
Hurt
Overslept

Literature-Related Example

Sample Set of Questions and a Hazard Card

Card 1: A runaway slave traveled from 8:00 PM to 2:00 AM. How long did the slave travel? *(6 hours)* How far did the slave travel? *(12 miles)*

Card 2: A runaway slave traveled from 9:30 PM to 10:00 PM. How long did the slave travel? *(30 minutes)* How far did the slave travel? *(1 mile)*

Card 3: A runaway slave traveled from 7:00 AM to 4:00 PM. Because of a hurt foot, the slave could only travel half as fast. How long did the slave travel? *(9 hours)* How far did the slave travel? *(9 miles)*

Card 4: A runaway slave traveled from 7:00 AM to 4:00 PM. The slave stopped and ate lunch at one of the Underground Railroad Stations from 12:00 PM to 1:00 PM. How long did the slave travel? *(8 hours)* How far did the slave travel? *(16 miles)*

Card 5: A runaway slave traveled from 8:00 PM to 10:00 PM. The bounty hunters closed in, so the slave hid in a tree and took a nap. Travel continued from 1:00 AM to 3:00 AM, but the moon was covered by a cloud, so the pathway was dark. The slave could only travel half as fast. How long did the slave travel? *(4 hours)* How far did the slave travel? *(6 miles)*

Card 6 Hazard: The dogs were out all day, and there was no travel.

Rules

1. Shuffle the cards and place face down in the center of the table.
2. The first player takes the top card and answers the question.
3. If the answer is correct, the player records the number of miles traveled on a personal flight record.
4. If the answer is incorrect, the player does not earn any miles.
5. Play continues in a clockwise direction.
6. If the player draws a hazard card, no miles are earned during that turn.
7. After all of the cards are played, the player with the greatest number of miles wins the game.

Science

The Mysteries of Caves and Caverns/Cave and Cavern Science Corner

Mysteries abound under the ground in *The House of Dies Drear*. Mr. Small explains, "This is limestone country, and always with limestone in this formation you'll find the water table percolating through rock into springs. There are caves, lakes and marshes all around us, all because of the rock formations and the way they fault" (p. 32). As Thomas explores, he discovers a maze of tunnels, secret passageways, moving boulders, slimy walls, streams of cold air, freezing temperatures, brackish water, eerie noises, and chilling screams. He panics! We panic, too, as we travel with him downward toward unknown ghosts and haunted destinations!

As Thomas searches for Mr. Pluto, he enters a 30-foot tunnel that leads to a 25-foot-wide, 30-foot-long, and 15-foot-high cave (p. 178). Descending from the cave is a pathway of enormous, damp stalactites. Their tentacles reach out grasping for him! In the deep, dark recesses of his mind, he vaguely remembers, *"Stalagmite: a calcium carbonate deposit shaped like an icicle and formed by the dripping of percolating calcareous water ... Stalagmite: dripping of percolating calcareous ..."* (p. 184). Further down in the earth, the ramp is warm and dry. Eventually, Thomas enters a gigantic cavern where there is a constant climate that is essential for the treasure of Dies Drear.

Literature-Based Example

Construct a cave and cavern science corner *in the classroom where* spelunkers, *cave explorers, delve into reading and research. Design both the cave and cavern to resemble those described in* The House of Dies Drear. *Include artifacts and furnishings similar to those of Mr. Pluto. The following suggestions are based on information located in Chapter 13.*

Tunnel into the Cave
Long sheets of bulletin board paper hung with very little open space between.

Cave
Cave: Large, cardboard appliance box or bulletin board paper
Carpet: Used carpet or carpet squares
Arm Chair: Old chair or bean bag chair
Table: Old table or upside down cardboard box
Bed: Beanbag chair or pillows
Note: Use various media materials for a forge, photographs, calendar, robe, tree stump, cooking stove, etc.

Ramp from the Cave to the Cavern
Narrow board set up on an incline.

Stalagmites and Stalactites
Twisted strips of bulletin board paper
Note: Stand up from floor or suspend from ceiling.

Cavern
Cavern: Large, cardboard appliance box or bulletin board paper
Desk: Classroom desk with chair
Bookcases: Cardboard boxes or milk crates
Treasure: Plastic bottles for glassware, student paintings, etc.

Books: Cavern Classics: Civil War stories, earth science trade books, and other works of Virginia Hamilton.

After spelunkers search and explore the cave and cavern Science Corner, they select one of the following as a cooperative group project to share with the class.

- ***Cave and Cavern Formation and Experimentation***: Investigate the mysteries of cave and cavern formation. Use *The Magic School Bus Inside the Earth* by Joanna Cole (1987) and *Earth, Sea & Sky* by Tom Stacy (1990) as well as other books to answer cave and cavern questions such as:
  1. How are caves formed? *(from rainwater that has been dripping for a long, long time)*
  2. How are stalagmites and stalactites formed? *(from dripping water that contains tiny bits of invisible limestone)*
  3. What is the difference between a stalagmite and a stalactite? *(stalagmites grow up from the ground and the word has the letter **g**; stalactites grow down from the ceiling and the word has the letter **c**.)*
  4. What happens if stalagmites and stalactites meet? *(they form a column)*

  Experimentation in the cave and cavern corner results in miniature stalactites similar to those found in caves. Share a stalactite experiment with the class using information from Tom Stacy's book, *Earth, Sea & Sky* (1990).
- ***Cave and Cavern Vacations***: Research famous caves and caverns in the United States to visit on vacations. Designate their locations on a large map of the United States. Design a travel brochure for one of these sites (see Trifold Brochure in Activity Appendix A).
- ***Cave Animals***: Investigate types of animals that live in caves. Create a cave diorama (see Diorama in the Activity Appendix A) with a cave information plaque for each animal (see Zoo Information Plaque in the Science Chapter). *Cave Life* (1993) by Christiane Gunzi has information on cave animals.
- ***Cave Safety***: Plan a spelunker adventure through an unexplored cave. Guide fellow spelunkers through an imaginary maze of tunnels, puddles, lakes, and rooms. Make a sound track tape to accompany this tour. Stress cave safety precautions such as:
  1. Determine that the cave is safe to enter.
  2. File a spelunker plan, so that in an emergency, others will know where and when to start looking.
  3. Discuss safety equipment such as hard hat with light, special shoes, jacket, etc.
  4. Stay together.
  5. Listen attentively to sounds and look cautiously at cave creatures.

Additional possibilities include:

- Observe, compare, classify, label, and display collections of rocks in the cave and cavern classroom science corner.
- Study how sound travels and the effects of air currents on sound. Are the sounds that Thomas hears in the cave magnified or distorted? (p. 125).
- Study light and prisms. The glassware Pesty cares for is like a prism (p. 187).

THE WESTING GAME

What happened to Sam Westing? The *Westing Game* is an exciting, suspense-filled, Newbery Award winning, whodunit mystery by Ellen Raskin (1978). The Westing mansion sits on the top of a hill overlooking Sunset Towers. Sixteen residents of Sunset Towers are notified that they are beneficiaries and receive invitations to the reading of Sam Westing's will. The will states that the heirs will be paired to participate in a game, the object of which is to identify the person responsible for taking Sam Westing's life. Each pair of heirs receives $10,000 and a set of clues. The winner of the game inherits the grand prize: $200 million. The heirs recognize the fact that one of them could be the culprit. The game progresses with many twists, tangles, and turns as bombs explode, burglaries occur, and a *mistake* is made. Each pair of heirs plots tirelessly to add to its collection of clues and solve the case.

Because of the unusually large number of suspects, *The Westing Game* provides wonderful investigative opportunities for students to critically examine and evaluate suspects' backgrounds and motives for committing the crime. It is imperative that reading investigators place brown paper sleeves over pages 149–185 of *The Westing Game* to shield both incorrect and correct solutions for "Whodunit?" Remove these sleeves and continue reading only after effective objective detectives have completed the class suspect chart described in the science strategy.

Detective notebooks are an essential component of any sleuth's investigation. These notebooks organize reading investigators' case evidence and might contain suspect profiles, sleuth slang, whodunit culprit portraits and paragraphs, rope forms, a magnify the mystery, a missing person poster, etc. All classroom super sleuths will want to have a detective notebook (see Journal Jacket in Activity Appendix A).

Reading

Tip Terms

Tip Terms is a game in which the goal is to collect vocabulary, or tip terms, from the story that provides important clues for cracking the case. To play Tip Terms, reading investigators collect tip terms and phrases as they search the story. They enter these tip terms on blank word cards and arrange the tip term cards in a variety of patterns in order to make predictions based on this tip term evidence.

Literature-Based Example

The Westing Game *provides the ultimate challenge in playing Tip Terms. In this mystery, the sixteen heirs are divided into eight pairs. Each pair receives an envelope with a set of four word cards each containing one word. Each pair, through stealth, scheming, and cooperation, attempts to add to its collection of clues. While reading the book, play Tip Terms along with* Westing Game *players by following these rules:*

1. Divide the class into eight teams.
2. Give each team thirty-two blank word cards.
3. Enter each tip term on a word card as the term is encountered in the story.
4. Arrange Tip Term word cards in a variety of patterns and interpret the clues these words provide.
5. Compare findings with those of the Westing Game players.

Another investigative challenge is to locate the identities of the bookie, burglar, bomber, and *mistake* in *The Westing Game.*

Writing

Whodunit Suspect Portrait and/or Paragraph

A *whodunit suspect portrait (WSP)* is a ten-question formula poem in which each line answers one of the ten questions (see format in the Poetry Appendix C). A WSP provokes closer examination of a suspect's intellectual, physical, emotional, and social characteristics as well as intense scrutiny of motive, opportunity, and evidence for committing the crime. WSPs have paragraph expansion possibilities. An example of a WSP is

What happened to Sam Westing? (1)
Ask Turtle. (2)
She is a very bright entrepreneur. (3)
She has a braid. (4)
She kicks people in the shins when they pull her braid. (5)
She says, "The braided tortoise strikes again!" (6)
Her mother ignores her and others avoid her. (7)
She has no motive to do away with Sam Westing. (8)

She was on the premises at the time of the crime. (9)
She is not the culprit. (10)

A *Whodunit suspect portrait paragraph* expands information from a WSP into a paragraph. The following WSP paragraph is based on the WSP poem about Turtle.

> *What happened to Sam Westing? If you want to know, ask Turtle. She was on the premises at the time of the crime. Turtle has a braid that friends and family fear to pull as they know the result will be a swift kick to the shins. Most people avoid her. Her mother ignores her, because she rebels against family tradition. Her older sister, Angela, adores her for her bold and daring spirit. Turtle is a very enterprising entrepreneur who invests wisely in the stock market. She has no motive for eliminating Sam Westing. If you want to know what happened to Sam Westing, you will have to play* The Westing Game.

Social Studies

Cooperation Revelation: Two Heads Are Better Than One

Heirs work in pairs in *The Westing Game*. Assigned to a partner, each individual soon learns the value of cooperation in an attempt to crack the case and win the game. Initially, some of the heirs considered working separately. After all, if they solved the case individually, they would not have to split the loot. However, they soon have a *cooperation revelation, two heads are better than one*. In teamwork each partner contributes a unique set of background information and talent to the task.

Interestingly, each pair of heirs playing the Westing Game selects different strategies in the quest to answer the question, "What happened to Sam Westing?" As the mystery progresses, pairs begin to cooperate with each other in sharing word clues that eventually reveal the patriotic song, "America the Beautiful."

Plan a class cooperation revelation experience to decide whether *two heads are better than one*.

Teacher Responsibility
1. Assign each student a partner.
2. Assign each pair a patriotic song.
3. Assign the same patriotic song to two or three groups. (*Suggestions: "America the Beautiful," "America," "The Star Spangled Banner," or "This Is My Country."*)

Cooperative Group Responsibility
1. Plan and creatively present the patriotic song to the class.
2. Decide if the group wants to cooperate with another group in planning the presentation. (*Suggestions: choral reading, singing, illustrations, a play, diorama*)

Class Responsibility
1. Discuss and list the advantages of working cooperatively.
2. Illustrate artistically *two heads are better than one*.

Math

The Stock Market Game/Investment Investigators

Turtle interpreted the wording in the will to mean that the $10,000 they received should be invested in the stock market. Turtle decided the set of word clues she and her partner were given were symbols for three corporations listed on the stock exchange. She discussed this revelation with her partner and then, "returned to her calculations, multiplying numbers of shares times price, adding a broker's commission, trying to total the sums to the ten thousand dollars they had to spend" (p. 43). Later in the game, she adds Westing Paper Products to her list of selected stocks. The fluctuation in stock prices adds excitement to this mysterious game.

As students study Turtle's financial wizardry, they too, become excited about *The Stock Market Game*, a game in which *investment investigators*, who are financial tycoons, select and invest in stocks for financial gain. To play The Stock Market Game, an investment investigator follows these guidelines:

1. Accept $10,000.
2. Select one stock listed on the New York Stock Exchange (NYSE) from the financial pages of the newspaper.
3. Divide ten thousand by the price per share to determine the number of shares to purchase. *Note: Only whole shares may be purchased.*
4. Use quarter-inch squared graph paper.
5. Label the horizontal axis TIME.
6. Let each line represent one day of the week and continue numbering for a predetermined number of days.
7. Label the vertical axis PRICE.
8. Place the initial price of the stock next to the line in about the center of the vertical axis. Above and below this point, label each line in one-eighth increments. For example, if the initial price of the stock is $62\frac{1}{8}$, label the lines going up the axis, $62\frac{1}{8}$, $62\frac{1}{4}$, $62\frac{3}{8}$, $62\frac{1}{2}$, $62\frac{5}{8}$, $62\frac{3}{4}$, $62\frac{7}{8}$, etc. Label the lines going down the axis 62, $61\frac{7}{8}$, $61\frac{3}{4}$, $61\frac{5}{8}$, etc.
9. Chart the stock price each day by making a dot on the graph.
10. Connect the dots to make a line graph.
11. Compute weekly gain or loss.
12. Sell at the end of the predetermined number of days.
13. Compute the total gain or loss.
14. Determine which investment investigator won *The Stock Market Game* by making the most gain on the investment.

Additional possibilities include reading *The Kids' Money Book* (1991) by Neale S. Godfrey to learn more about the stock market. Learn stock market terminology such as bear market and bull market. Invite a financial consultant to speak to the class. Purchase more than one stock for a given amount of money. Allow multiple transactions over a given time period. Deduct 2 percent commission on each transaction (buy or sell). Chart volume as well as price.

Science

Effective Objective Detective/Suspect Profile

An *effective objective detective (EOD)* is a professional sleuth who employs the scientific method of investigative inquiry to determine answers to perplexing questions and thus solve a case. An EOD searches for clues utilizing eight of the scientific process skill strategies (see the Science chapter):

1. Observing
2. Comparing
3. Measuring
4. Communicating
5. Inferring
6. Predicting
7. Hypothesizing

Literature-Based Example

Before the class reads *The Westing Game*, randomly assign the names of each of the sixteen suspects to one or more classroom EODs. Be sure brown paper sleeves are securely in place. Each EOD is responsible for completing a suspect profile on the assigned suspect (see Figure 8.4). The suspect profile is a component of the detective notebook that is constructed

FIGURE 8.4　Suspect Profile

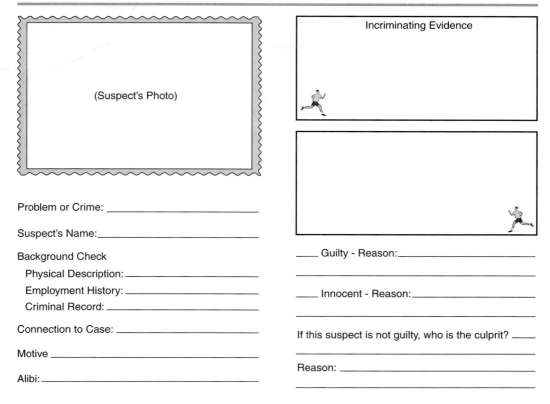

Problem or Crime: _____

Suspect's Name: _____

Background Check

　Physical Description: _____

　Employment History: _____

　Criminal Record: _____

Connection to Case: _____

Motive _____

Alibi: _____

Incriminating Evidence

____ Guilty - Reason: _____

_____

____ Innocent - Reason: _____

_____

If this suspect is not guilty, who is the culprit? ____

_____

Reason: _____

_____

using the journal jacket technique (see Activity Appendix A). Each EOD is responsible for investigative scientific inquiry into the question, "What happened to Sam Westing?" The EOD shadows the assigned suspect throughout the story, making appropriate scientific entries on the suspect profile as relevant information comes to light.

When the EOD encounters the brown paper sleeve that shields the answer to "Whodunit?," the EOD stops reading and completes the suspect profile. The EOD hypothesizes on the guilt or innocence of the assigned suspect. The EOD's hypothesis is based on the preponderance of evidence as detailed on the suspect profile in the detective notebook. If an innocent verdict is rendered, the EOD hypothesizes and names another suspect as the culprit. Reasons for the guilty verdict must be stated.

Guilty votes for each suspect are tallied on a class suspect chart. This chart has the name of each suspect and space for the tally as well as reasons for the guilty verdict. After reaching a class consensus on the guilt or innocence of each suspect, the brown paper sleeves are removed and the EODs complete their reading of *The Westing Game*.

Literature References

Allard, H., & Marshall, J. (1977). *Miss Nelson is missing!* Boston: Houghton Mifflin.

Avi. (1991). *Windcatcher*. New York: Avon.

Burns, B. (1992). *Harriet Tubman*. New York: Chelsea.

Carle, E. (1985). *The very busy spider*. New York: Putnam.

Cole, J. (1987). *The magic school bus inside the earth*. New York: Scholastic.

The EarthWorks Group. (1994). *50 simple things kids can do to recycle*. Berkeley, CA: EarthWorks Press.

George, J.C. (1992). *The missing 'gator of Gumbo Limbo*. New York: HarperTrophy.

Godfrey, N.S. (1991). *The kids' money book*. New York: Checkerboard Press.

Gunzi, C. (1993). *Cave life*. New York: Dorling Kindersley.

Hamilton, V. (1968). *The house of Dies Drear*. New York: Macmillan.

Hamilton, V. (1987). *The mystery of Drear House*. New York: Macmillan.

Hindley, J., & Rumbelow, D. (1978). *The KnowHow book of detection*. Tulsa OK: EDC Publishing.

Hopkinson, D. (1993). *Sweet Clara and the freedom quilt*. New York: Alfred A. Knopf.

Lawrence, J. (1993). *Harriet and the promised land*. New York: Simon & Schuster.

Levine, E. (1988). *If you traveled on the underground railroad*. New York: Scholastic.

Mayer, M. (1968). *There's a nightmare in my closet*. New York: Dial.

Raskin, E. (1978). *The Westing game*. New York: Puffin Books. Newbery Award.

Ringgold, F. (1992). *Aunt Harriet's underground railroad in the sky*. New York: Crown.

Sobol, D.J. (1963). *Encyclopedia Brown boy detective*. New York: Bantam Skylark Book.

Sobol, D.J. (1967). *Encyclopedia Brown gets his man*. New York: Bantam Books.

The spies and detectives cut and color book. (1989). New York: Chatham River Press.

Spinelli, J. (1990). *Maniac Magee*. New York: HarperTrophy.

Stacy, T. (1990). *Earth, sea & sky*. New York: Random House.

Weisner, D. (1991). *Tuesday*. New York: Clarion Books. Caldecott Award.

Weisner, D. (1990). *Hurricane*. New York: Clarion Books.

Winter, J. (1988). *Follow the drinking gourd*. New York: Alfred A. Knopf.

Professional References

Flack, J.D. (1990). *Mystery and detection: Thinking and problem solving with the sleuths*. Englewood, CO: Teacher Ideas Press.

Lynch-Brown, C., & Tomlinson, C.M. (1993). *Essentials of children's literature*. Boston: Allyn and Bacon.

Pappas, C.C., Kiefer, B.Z., & Levstik, L.S. (1990). *An integrated language perspective in the elementary school*. White Plains, NY: Longman.

Pierce, K.M., & Short, K.G. (Eds.). (1995). Mysteries of a child's world. *The Reading Teacher, 48* (6), 508–515.

Webster's Compact Rhyming Dictionary. (1987). Springfield MA: Merriam-Webster.

Websites

ABC Teach

There are thematic units as well as many free printables for basics, research reports, teaching extras, portfolios, flashcards, reading comps, fun puzzles. In addition there are online tools for creating custom documents for shape books, word walls, word searches, word unscrambles, and crossword puzzles.

www.//abcteach.com

Carol Hurst's Children's Literature Site

This website features reviews of books for kids and ideas about how to use the books in the classroom. There are books and activities about particular subjects, curriculum areas, themes, and professional topics.

www.carolhurst.com

The Hardy Boys Unofficial Home Page

This is the most complete and detailed Hardy Boys site on the Internet. Includes **Hardy Boys, Nancy Drew,** Tom Swift, Chip Hilton, Bowery Boys, and much more.

www.hardyboys.bobfinnan.com

Kids' Mysteries

Includes mysteries to solve, scary stories, and magic tricks. MysteryNet's kids try to solve: "The Case of the Ruined Roses." Has kids' mystery authors, brain teasers, brain teaser books, jigsaw puzzles, magic sets, and more.

www.kids.mysterynet.com

KidsReads

Features that will entice readers are the online reading lists. There is information on the **Boxcar Mysteries** and **Nancy Drew Mystery Series.**

www.kidsreads.com

Lesson Plans and Teaching Strategies

Includes a wide variety of lesson plans, teaching strategies, and thematic unit information.

www.csun.edu/~hcedu013/plans.html

Thematic Units in the Classroom

Includes a variety of thematic unit ideas, for the classroom.

www.suite101.com/article.cfm/
english_education_k12/26979

Activity Appendix

(continued)

Note: Hamburger/Hot Dog Folds

To assist in giving directions, use the terms "hot dog bun fold" and "hamburger bun fold." A hot dog bun fold results in an elongated rectangle to accommodate a hot dog. A hamburger bun fold results in a "fatter" rectangle to accommodate a hamburger.

Accordion Book

MATERIALS

12″ × 18″ sheet of construction paper

DIRECTIONS

1. Fold a 12″ × 18″ piece of construction paper lengthwise, making a top fold and forming a 6″ × 18″ rectangle. *(hot dog)*
2. Fold the rectangle widthwise, making a center fold and forming a 6″ × 9″ rectangle. *(hamburger)*
3. Fold each loose end back, on opposite sides, to center fold.
4. Paper should now form a zigzag and make an accordion book.

APPLICATION

Vocabulary: Choose sentences from a story that have interesting vocabulary words. Write a sentence on each page in the accordion book, leaving a blank for the interesting word. List possibilities for the missing word under the sentence. Hide the author's word choice on another page of the accordion book. (Chapter 2, p. 34)

Autobiography: Publish an autobiography in an accordion book. (Chapter 3, pp. 52–53; 58)

Cationary: Create a cationary using the accordion book. (Chapter 7, p. 219)

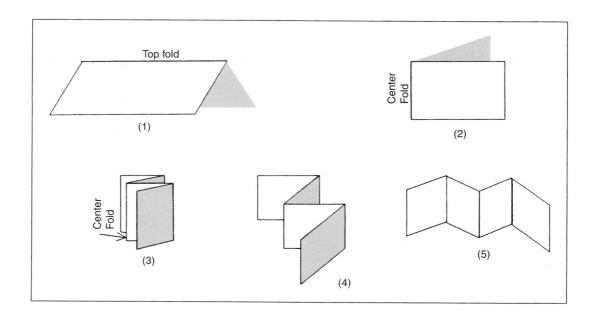

⊚ Accordion File Folder Book

MATERIALS

Twelve letter-sized file folders (multicolored, if possible)
Yarn

DIRECTIONS

1. Fold a file folder in half lengthwise to form pockets. *(hot dog)*
2. Insert an open file folder into the pocket and staple along the outer edges. Repeat for each of the five remaining sets of file folders.
3. Hole punch the ends and lace together with yarn to fashion an accordion file folder book. Tape or metal binder rings serve as adequate substitutes for yarn lacings.
4. To use as an accordion file folder alphabet book, label each pocket of the book with an individual letter. Continue on the back side with the letters M through W. Label the last pocket XYZ.
5. Stand the book atop a table or bookshelf. Use the pockets for specialized vocabulary.

APPLICATION

Brain, Body, and Behavior (BBB) Organizer: Use four file folders to create an organizer with four pockets on the front and four pockets on the back. (Chapter 7, p. 239)

Drug-etry: Display drug-etry in the pockets on the back of the BBB organizer and in the "beware" pocket. (Chapter 7, p. 241)

Accordion File Folder Alphabet Book: Use as an alphabetical organizer for sleuth slang. (Chapter 8, pp. 252–253)

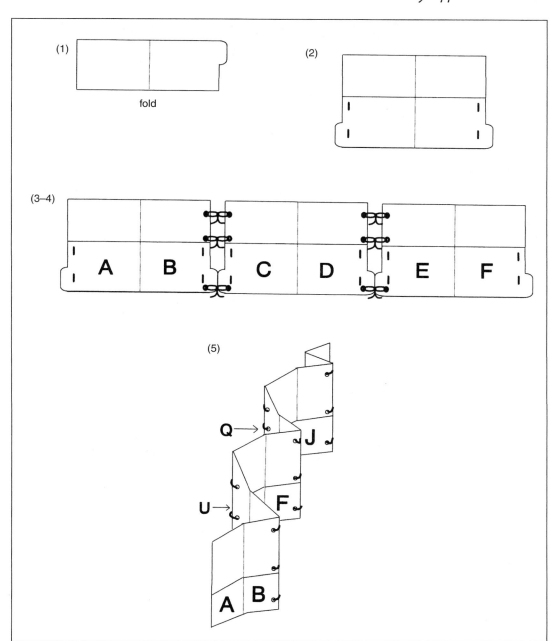

(1)

fold

(2)

(3–4)   A   B   C   D   E   F

(5)   Q→   J   U→   F   A   B

Banner Book and Double Banner Book

Banner Book

MATERIALS

8.5″ × 11″ sheet of paper

DIRECTIONS

1. Fold an 8.5″ × 11″ sheet of paper to form a 5.5″ × 8.5″ rectangle. *(hamburger)*
2. Fold the rectangle to form a 2.75″ × 8.5″ rectangle. *(hot dog)*
3. Open. Along one 8.5″ side of the paper, measure 2.5″.
4. From that mark, draw a diagonal line to the closest corner of the opposite 8.5″ side. Cut along that line.
5. Accordion fold the larger piece of paper along the crease lines in such a manner that the front page opens bookwise (crease on the left).

APPLICATION

Grammacrostics: Publish grammacrostics in a banner book. (Chapter 4, pp. 101–102)
Dine n' Dash Diner menu: Create a menu as one prop for a dramatic debut. (Chapter 6, p. 185)

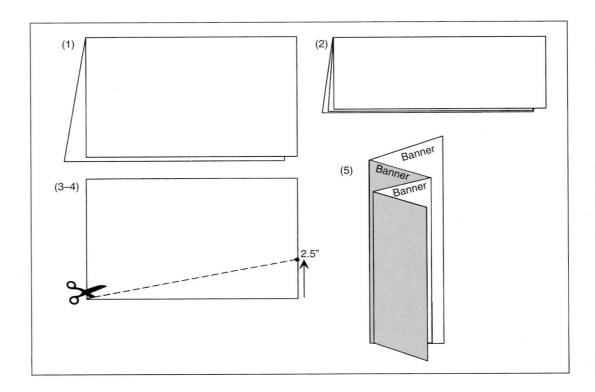

Double Banner Book

MATERIALS

8.5″ × 11″ sheet of paper

DIRECTIONS

1. Fold an 8.5″ × 11″ sheet of paper to form a 5.5″ × 8.5″ rectangle. *(hamburger)*
2. Fold the rectangle to form a 2.75″ × 8.5″ rectangle. *(hot dog)*
3. Open along one 8.5″ side of the paper, measure in 2.5″ from the right and again from the left.
4. From each mark, draw a diagonal line to the closest corner of the opposite 8.5″ side. Cut along that line.
5. Accordion fold the larger piece of paper along the crease lines in such a manner that the front page of the book opens bookwise (crease on the left).

APPLICATION

Double Banner Flip Book: Fold in half parallel with banners *(hamburger)*. Draw a horizontal line on the fold mark to differentiate the top flip and the bottom flip. Label banners on top and bottom with differing points of view (see Figure 5.4, pp. 132; 134).

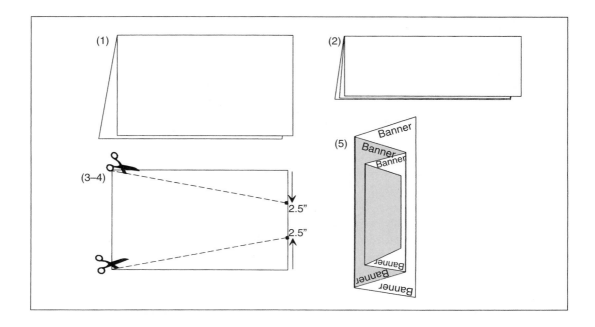

Bingo Board

© Certificate of Adoption

CERTIFICATE OF ADOPTION

This certifies that _____ is proudly adopted

by _____ on this _____ day in the month

of _____, year _____.

This _____ tree grows proudly at

_____ in the community

of _____.

ℰ Clock Creation

MATERIALS

Circular template
Construction paper in seven different colors
One paper fastener

DIRECTIONS

1. Use a dinner plate or circular template to draw four circles in four different colors. Cut out.
2. Fold three of the four circles into quarters.
3. Cut along the crease lines.
4. Use the fourth circle as a base, place three different color quarters on the clock face, each color representing a fifteen-minute segment. Students work in groups and share different color quarters.
5. On a fifth color of paper, measure and cut out twelve $1'' \times 2''$ strips.
6. Fold each strip in half. *(hamburger)*
7. Number the top flaps 1 through 12, and inside flaps to each number's corresponding minute. Example, 1/:05, 2/:10, 3/:15, 4/:20, and so forth.
8. Glue the folded strips in their appropriate places on the clock face.
9. Design and cut out clock hands from the sixth color of paper.
10. Attach the hands to the clock face with a metal paper fastener.
11. Mount the clock on a seventh color of paper to allow both the teacher and students to hold the clock without fingers covering the face.

APPLICATION

Measure Mania: Use for telling time and determining elapsed time. (Chapter 6, pp. 195; 196)

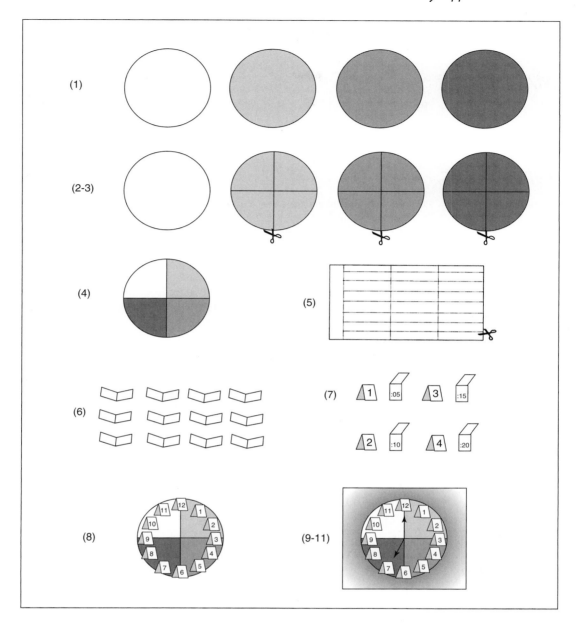

(1)

(2-3)

(4)

(5)

(6)

(7)

(8)

(9-11)

◎ Diorama

MATERIALS

Box: shoe box, gift box, shallow soda can box, cereal box, or others
Decorative materials

DIRECTIONS

1. Orient the box either vertically (using the larger surface as the backdrop) or horizontally (using the larger surface as the floor).
2. Choose a topic for the scene such as an animal habitat, the setting from a story, or a seasonal picture.
3. Create the selected scene inside the box by using various media techniques* in this appendix.
   (a) Use paper or paint to make the backdrop and floor of the diorama.
   (b) Use construction paper rolled in cylinders or paper-towel tubes to make tree trunks or other cylinder-shaped objects.
   (c) Use jab art* to create flowers, leaves, and so forth.
   (d) Use wallpaper to create clothes for people silhouettes.
   (e) Use the torn paper technique* to cover paper animal shapes to give a furry appearance.
   (f) Mount paper figures on stands.*
   (g) Use clay* to make animals and other figures.
   (h) Suspend vines, fish, planets, and other features from the ceiling.
   (i) Use sand* or salt for a sandy terrain.
   (j) Use cotton for clouds.
   (k) Use the fold-a-building technique in this appendix to make houses, stores, and so forth.
   (l) Cover the opening with clear plastic wrap for underwater scenes.
4. Design a plaque to explain the diorama.

See Media Techniques in this appendix.

VARIATIONS

1. **Puppet theater:** Orient vertically. Cut a hole in the top and slide puppets that are mounted on the bottom of tongue depressors through the hole.
2. **Doll house:** Orient vertically. Decorate a box for each room in the house. Stack the boxes, so that they show the rooms in a house.
3. **Sneak-a-peek:** Orient a shoe box horizontally. Remove the lid and cut a small hole in it. Cut a hole in one narrow end of the shoe box. This is the front. Create a scene facing the front of the box. Replace the lid. Sneak a peek through the hole to view the scene.
4. **Sequential scenes:** Create different scenes from a story. Arrange sequentially from left to right.

APPLICATION

Cat habitat diorama: Create a natural environment for a wild or domestic cat. Design a zoo information plaque or animal information plaque for each animal (Chapter 7, p. 218)

Season scenes in shallow shadow boxes: Design season scenes for each of the four seasons. Plan scenes to reflect appropriate clothing, food, and recreation. Chapter 7, p. 221

Cave: Create a cave in which to display cave animals. Create cave information plaques for these animals. (Chapter 8, p. 271)

Dramarama

MATERIALS

One paper plate
Two paper fasteners (optional)
String (optional)

DIRECTIONS

1. Fold a paper plate into quarters.
2. Open the plate and cut to the center along one fold line.
3. Completely overlap the quarters of the plate that are to either side of the cut so as to form a stage floor.
4. Before gluing, stapling, or taping the stage floor into place, decorate the backdrop.

VARIATIONS

1. Join two, three, or four dramaramas back to back with paper fasteners.
2. Make a vertical dramarama mobile by punching a hole at the top of each dramarama and running a string down the backdrop and through the slit in the floor. This should be done before fastening the stage floor into place.

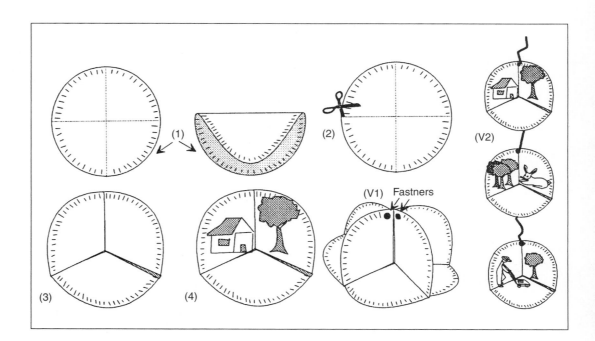

◎ Eightfold Person

MATERIALS

12˝ × 18˝ sheet of paper

DIRECTIONS

1. Make an accordion book.
2. Open the paper up to 12˝ × 18˝.
3. Place the 18˝ edge of paper in front of each participant.
4. Cut the lower left and lower right rectangles off, leaving a T-shirt shape.
5. Fold two arms of T-shirt to the center (forming a rectangle).
6. Make two small triangles for shirt collar.
7. Place two rectangles as arms, open shirt, and staple arms to back of T-shirt.
8. Make a head shape and staple to top of shirt.

VARIATION

To turn the eightfold person into a puppet, make the head using two paper plates. Cut small half circles in each paper plate that are large enough for a hand to slide up into. Match the two half circles, place the eating sides facing each other, and staple the plates around the edges, excluding the half circles.

APPLICATION

Book character: Make a character from a story. Base the character's appearance on information in the story. Write a paragraph or poem about the person to put inside the jacket. (Chapter 2, p. 31)

Autobiography: Design a personal eightfold person. Write an autobiography inside the jacket. (Chapter 3, pp. 53; 58)

Famous people: Make an eightfold person to represent a famous person. Design clothing, hat, and hairstyle that represent the time period and occupation of the person. Place objects related to the person's profession and beliefs in the person's hands. Write a paragraph or poem about the person inside the jacket. (Chapter 5, p. 150). Create a famous person people puppet for a Heroes' Hall of Fame. (Chapter 5, p. 153).

Brains, Body, and Behavior: Indicate places on the body affected by drug abuse/addiction. (Chapter 7, p. 240)

The Mystery of You-niqueness: Display a poem for each class member on individual eightfold people. (Chapter 8, p. 263.)

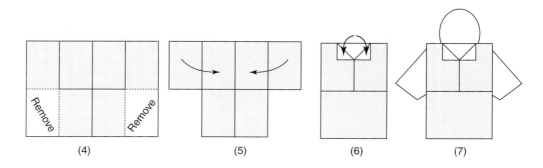

    (4)   (5)   (6)   (7)

℮ Enveloptionery

MATERIALS

8.5″ × 11″ sheet of paper

DIRECTIONS

1. Make an 8.5″ square by folding one corner of a piece of 8.5″ × 11″ sheet of paper to form a triangle. Trim off the 2.5″ × 8.5″ rectangle
2. Leaving the square folded, place the resulting triangle on the table with the fold to the bottom in front of the participant.
3. Open the triangle to reveal a diamond shape. Fold the tip of the corner closest to the participant to the center of the original fold line.
4. Fold over along the original fold line.
5. Fold the left corner over one-third of the way along the original fold. Fold the right corner over one-third of the way along the original fold and overlapping the left-corner.
6. Fold the tip of the right corner up so that it forms approximately a 1″ equilateral triangle
7. Open the pouch formed by the equilateral triangle. Press it flat so as to form a diamond at the base of the enveloptionery.
8. Fold the flap of the enveloptionery, and tuck the tip into the diamond pouch.
9. Decorate.

APPLICATION

Letter Writing: Write a friendly letter on enveloptionery. (Chapter 3, pp. 54–56)
Invitation Poem: Write an invitation poem on enveloptionery. (Chapter 3, p. 82)
Notes in a Nutshell: Write nifty notes to family and friends on enveloptionery. (Chapter 4, p. 118)
Gifts and Greetings Gallary: As a measure mania experience, accurately angle and align priceless card stock, and so forth, to construct enveloptionery for the Gifts and Greetings Gallery. (Chapter 6, p. 198)

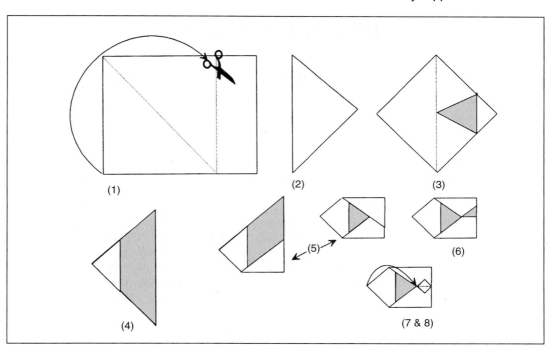

(1)   (2)   (3)

(4)   (5)   (6)

(7 & 8)

@ File Folder Display

MATERIAL

11¾″ × 17¾″ file folder
Two pieces of string, yarn, or fishing line

DIRECTIONS

1. On the folded edge of a file folder, make two parallel cuts of equal length for each notch needed. Depth of cut will determine the size of the notch.
2. Keeping the file folder closed, fold each notch forward and backward, making a sharp crease where the parallel cuts end.
3. Open the file folder slightly and push each notch to the inside of the file folder.
4. Open the file folder so that one side forms a "floor" or base and the other side forms a "wall" to serve as the backdrop. The notches will form "shelves" on which objects are mounted.
5. To mount a file folder display on a bulletin board or wall, the top of the wall and the opposite edge of the floor must be tied together. To do so, cut a 0.5″ slit at the top of the wall 1″ in from the right side of the wall and another 0.5″ inch slit at the top of the wall 1″ in from the left side of the wall.
6. Repeat step 5 on the floor of the folder.
7. Cut two pieces of string, yarn, or fishing line, each about 14″ long. Tie a knot in each end of the two strings. Place one knot in a slit on the wall side with the knot to the back-side of the file folder and run the other end of the string across the open stage, down to the opposite slit on the floor, sliding the knot through the underside of the floor. Do the same for the other side.

APPLICATION

Poems and paragraphs: Design a file folder display with scenery and pop-up figures to represent information in poems and paragraphs. (Chapter 5, pp. 157–158)

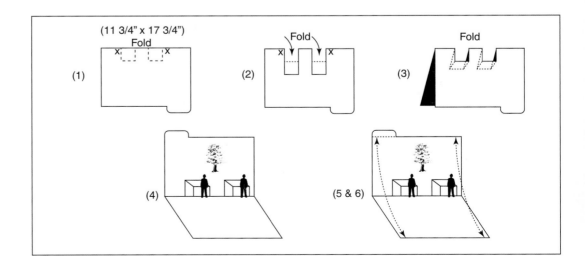

◎ Fold-a-Building

MATERIAL

9″ × 12″ sheet of construction paper

DIRECTIONS

1. Make a 9″ square by cutting 3″ off the long end of a 9″ × 12″ piece of construction paper.
2. Fold the 9″ square in half, making a 9″ × 4.5″ rectangle.
3. Fold in half again, making a 9″ × 2.25″ rectangle. *(hotdog)*
4. Open.
5. Fold in half on adjacent side, making a 9″ × 4.5″ rectangle.
6. Fold in half again, making a 9″ × 2.25″ rectangle. *(hotdog)*
7. Open.
8. Count squares. There should be sixteen squares.
9. On two opposite, outside edges, cut along the fold lines from the edge to the first intersection of the fold lines. There will be six cuts.
10. Overlap end squares B and C to form a diamond (or roof peak). Glue, tape, or staple.
11. Overlap squares A and D approximately halfway on the outside of the diamond to form a square (or end wall). Glue, tape, or staple.
12. Repeat for the other end of the building.
13. Doors and windows can be drawn or cut.
14. Larger and smaller buildings can be made using the same technique.

APPLICATION

Miniature community: Make houses and other important buildings in a community. (Chapter 5, pp. 140–141)

Three-D-geometry: Construct fold-a-buildings to use for three-D-geometry art projects. (Chapter 6, p. 188)

Underground Railroad: Create houses and barns. (Chapter 8, p. 268)

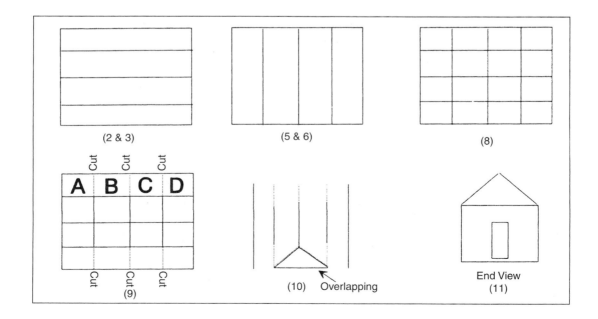

⊚ Fold and Tear Adventures

MATERIALS

12″ × 18″ sheet of construction paper

DIRECTIONS

1. Fold the paper in half to form a 12″ × 9″ rectangle. *(hamburger)*
2. Fold again to form a 6″ × 9″ rectangle. *(hamburger)*
3. Unfold once, returning to the 12″ × 9″ rectangle.
4. Dog-ear each of the two crease side corners to the center crease line.
5. Fold the base flap up. Repeat on the opposite side.
6. Flex open Hat 1. Tuck away the corners of the base flaps.
7. Press together the two tip ends of Hat 1 to form a square.
8. On one side only, fold the tip end of the hat to its uppermost point.
9. Flex open Hat 2.
10. Press together the front and back of Hat 2 to form a square.
11. Fold the remaining tip end of Hat 2 to its uppermost point.
12. Flex open Hat 3.
13. Press together the two tip ends of Hat 3 to form a square.
14. Force open the top points of Hat 3, pulling until the center section raises up and the points create a bow and stern.
15. Tear off the bow.
16. Tear off the stern.
17. Tear off the center point.
18. Unfold to reveal a LIFE VEST.

VARIATIONS

Safety focus: Implement with a unit on safety. Fold a single piece of paper into a pedestrian's hat, a firefighter's hat, a bicycle rider's hat, a boat, and a vest.

Paper size: Implement with an 8½″ × 11″ piece of paper.

APPLICATION

Election Experiences: Create hats for candidates. (Chapter 5, p. 136)

Fold and tear adventures: Fold a single piece of paper into a thinking hat, fire hat, dunce hat, a boat, and vest while singing, "REACT to Drug Invitations." (Chapter 7, p. 229)

(1)

(2)

(3)

(4)

(5)

(6)

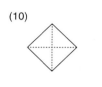

Hat #1 Pedestrian's Hat

(7)

(8)

(9)

Hat #2 Fire Fighter's Hat

(10)

(11)

(12)

Hat #3 Bicycle Driver's Hat

(13)

(14)

(15)

(16)

(17)

(18)

Life Vest

◉ Four-Flap Flip-Flop Book

MATERIALS

8.5″ × 11″ sheet of paper

DIRECTIONS

1. Fold the sheet of paper in half lengthwise. *(hot dog)*
2. Fold in half to form a 5.5″ × 4.25″ rectangle *(hamburger)* and again to form a 4.25″ × 2.75″ rectangle. *(hamburger)*
3. Unfold.
4. On one 11″ side of the sheet of paper, cut along the three crease lines to the center of the paper.
5. Fold the sheet of paper in half lengthwise to form the four-flap flip-flop book. *(hot dog)*

VARIATION

1. Stand the four-flap flip-flop book on end and tape the ends together to create a box. The flaps should open upwards.
2. Create a handle for the box and tape one end each to two opposing panels.

APPLICATIONS

Simile search: Compose original similes using the first half of similes found in the story and writing original endings. Write the first half of a simile found on the top of a flap, and write the original ending and illustrate the original simile under the flap. Write the author's simile on the back of the flap. Compare the original simile to the author's simile. (Chapter 2, p. 39)

Lit link: A four-fold flip-flop with handle provides space for five bits of information about a literature experience. Label the handle with the title, author, and illustrator of the book. Choose one of the following sequences for labeling the flaps:
First, Next, Then, Finally
Characters, Setting, Problem, Solution
Main Character, Event 1, Event 2, Event 3
Draw appropriate illustrations on the back of and under each flap. (Chapter 4, lit link center 2, p. 96)

Four-flap flip-fact: During a study of tree-mendous trees, make a four-flap flip-flop and orient vertically. Label the flaps from the top to the bottom: leaves; branches, twigs, and buds; trunk; and roots. Illustrate each flap appropriately. Write information under the flaps. (Chapter 7, Figure 7.1, p. 109)

Three-flap flip-flop clouds: Use the three sections for cumulus, stratus, and cirrus clouds. Create clouds with cotton to mount on the top of each flap. Another possibility: Make a ten-flap flip-flop book by attaching two five-flap flip-flop books to display appropriate information and illustrations for ten different types of clouds. (Chapter 7, p. 223)

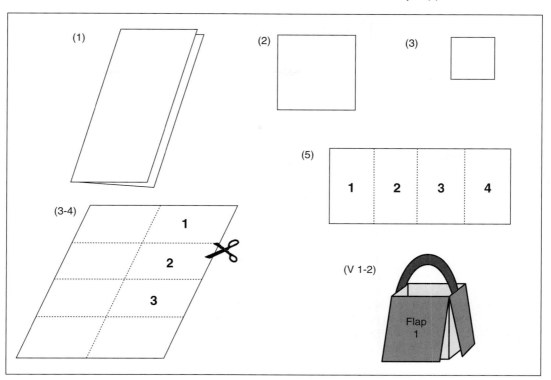

(1)

(2)

(3)

(5)

| 1 | 2 | 3 | 4 |

(3-4)

1

2

3

(V 1-2)

Flap
1

@ Frames from File Folders

MATERIALS

File Folders

DIRECTIONS

1. From the front side of a file folder, cut out a rectangle approximately 6.5″ × 9.5″ leaving a 1″ frame around the opening. *(Note: To facilitate this activity for students, make a pattern for them to trace around.)*
2. When the file folder is closed, tape the edges of each end together then slide pictures, poetry, or compositions in through the top of the file folder.
3. The rectangular opening is a window through which pictures, poetry, and compositions appear.
4. File folder frame displays: To display student work, mount a file folder frame for each student on a bulletin board. Label each file folder frame tab with the student's name.
5. File folder frames provide a permanent bulletin board where student work may be easily rotated weekly or more often by the teacher or students.

APPLICATION

Framed Poetry: Display poetry and paragraphs in frames made from file folders. (Chapter 5, p. 157)

Gifts and Greetings Frames Gallery: Perimeter pursuit professionals precisely measure picture perimeters to determine the size of framing or matting needed for the priceless frames created in the Gifts and Greetings Frames Gallery (Chapter 6, p. 198)

Haiku, tanka, and lantern: Display poetry and related illustrations in frames. (Chapter 7, pp. 224–225)

Missing Person Poster: Display poster in a frame made from a file folder. (Chapter 8, p. 262)

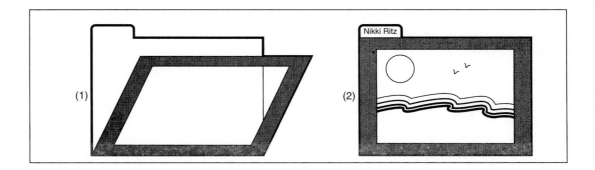

◎ Game Board

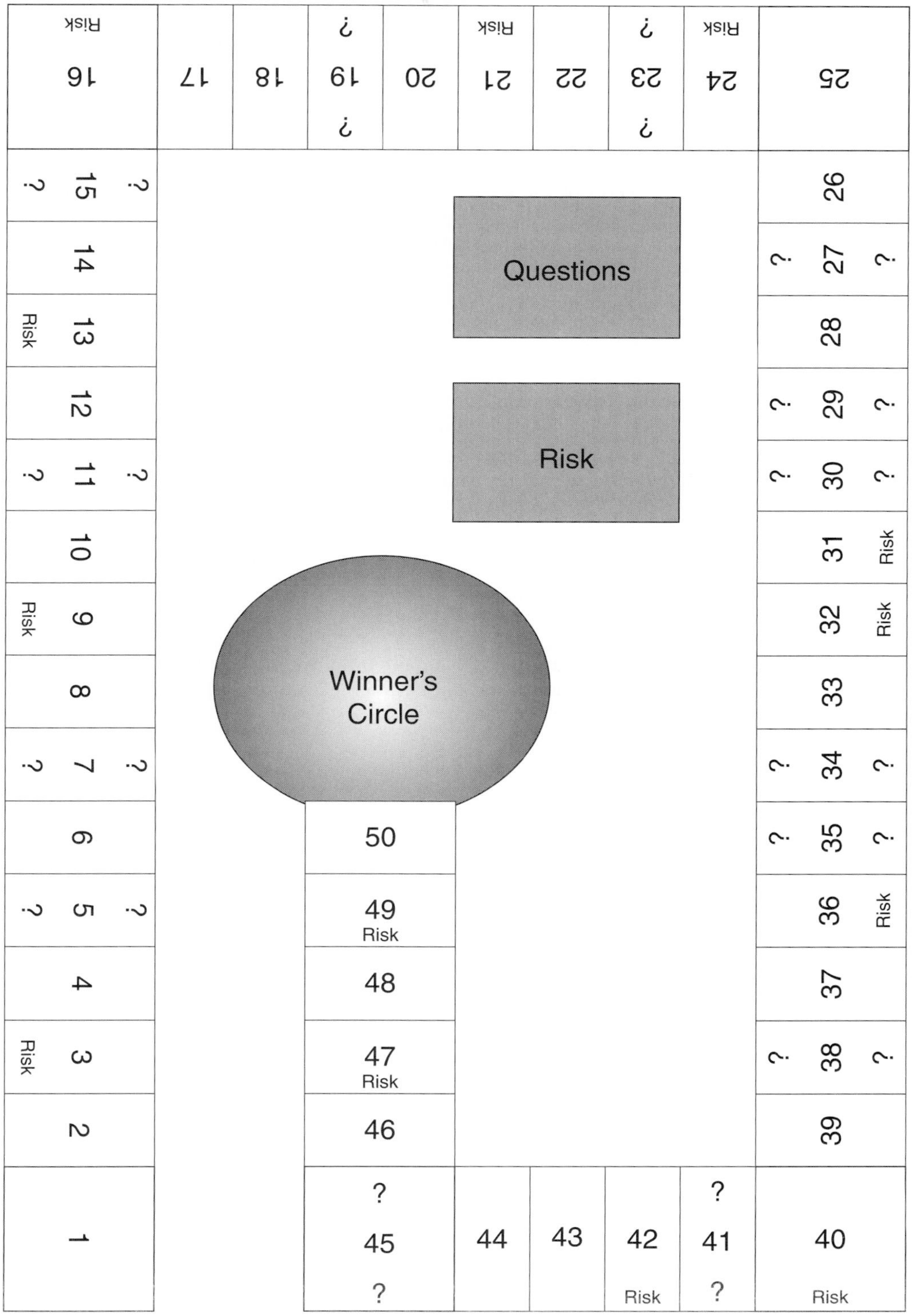

16 Risk	**17**	**18**	**19** ? ?	**20**	**21** Risk	**22**	**23** ? ? Risk	**24**	**25**

Left column		Center	Right column	
? **15** ?			**26**	
14		Questions	? **27** ?	
Risk **13**			**28**	
12			? **29** ?	
? **11** ?		Risk	? **30** ?	
10			**31** Risk	
Risk **9**			**32** Risk	
8		Winner's Circle	**33**	
? **7** ?			? **34** ?	
6		**50**	? **35** ?	
? **5** ?		**49** Risk	**36** Risk	
4		**48**	**37**	
Risk **3**		**47** Risk	? **38** ?	
2		**46**	**39**	
1		? **45** ?	**40** Risk	

44	**43**	**42** Risk	? **41** ?

◎ Jack-in-the-Box Springs

MATERIALS

Two sheets of 9″ × 12″ construction paper, each a different color

DIRECTIONS

1. Cut each sheet of paper into 1″ strips, lengthwise.
2. Place two opposing color strips at right angles to each other.
3. Fold one color over the other and continue folding alternate colors until you reach the end of the strip. Glue, tape, or staple ends.
4. To make longer springs, use longer strips of paper. Repeat steps 1 through 4 as often as necessary until desired length is reached. For longer springs, attach springs end to end.

VARIATIONS

Flowers, sun, and fun: Vary width of strips. Circle to create flowers, a sun, and other three-dimensional objects.
Puppet appendages: Use springs for arms and legs.
Story box pop-outs: Use on the back of pop-out items, so that when the box is opened, the item pops out.

APPLICATION

Plate-arama: Mount people, animals, and objects on springs to give them a three-dimensional appearance. (Chapter 7, p. 215; Chapter 8, p. 265)

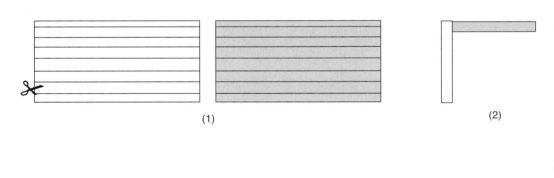

(1)   (2)

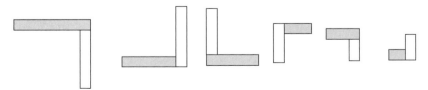

(3)

@ Journal Jacket

MATERIALS

File folder
18″ × 14″ sheet of contact paper
12″ × 18″ sheet of construction paper
11″ × 17″ ditto paper
Paper fasteners (optional)
Stick-on letters or permanent markers

DIRECTIONS

1. Square off a file folder by trimming off the tab.
2. Using the trimmed tab as though it were a puzzle piece, place it into the indented portion of the folder. Tape it into place so as to square off the edge of the file folder.
3. Set the folder aside.
4. Cut an 18″ × 14″ piece of contact paper. (Wallpaper and gift wrap may work equally well, but will require an adhesive.)
5. Peel the backing off the contact paper.
6. Cover the outside of the file folder with contact paper. *(Warning: The 18″ width of the contact paper allows for no overlap. However, as a standard roll of contact paper is 18″ wide, this makes the most economical use of the paper.)*
7. Fold the contact paper to the inside of the folder where necessary and press flat.
8. Use a piece of 12″ × 18″ construction paper to line the inside of the journal jacket. For best results, pre-crease the construction paper and match the crease of the construction paper to the crease of the folder. Glue into place.
9. Stick-on letters or a permanent marker may be used to place the title and name of the author on the cover of the journal jacket. Notebook paper or ditto paper may be used for journal pages. 11″ × 17″ ditto paper works especially well.
10. Pages may be secured to the journal jacket in any of the following fashions:
    (a) Three-hole punch journal jacket and use paper fasteners for notebook paper.
    (b) Staple 8.5″ × 11″ pages to either side of the folder.
    (c) Staple 11″ × 17″ pages along the folder crease.
    (d) Sew 11″ × 17″ pages along the folder crease, using a long machine stitch.

APPLICATION

Autobiography: Create a personalized journal jacket and journal in which to publish an autobiography (Chapter 3, pp. 53; 58)

Personal, dialogue, and simulated journals: Make journal jackets for personal, dialogue, and simulated journals. (Chapter 3, pp. 58–59)

Learning log: Using the journal jacket technique, create a learning log to record facts, findings, and feelings about a particular subject, observation, or issue. (Chapter 3, p. 71)

Chalkboards/Felt Boards: Make individual chalkboards using the journal jacket technique and chalkboard contact paper. Make felt boards using felt. Better yet, make reversible chalkboard/felt boards. Use for Every Student Participation (ESP) experiences. (Chapter 4, pp. 97; 117; Chapter 6, p. 178)

Journey Journal: Develop a journey journal that includes before, during, and after entries for a trip. (Chapter 5, pp. 145–146)

Math log: Create math logs in which students record mathematical information, including math terms, math algorithms, and math story problems. (Chapter 6, pp. 175; 181)

Cookbooks: Design cookbooks using the journal jacket technique. (Chapter 6, p. 181)

Cationary: Compile a cationary using the journal jacket technique. (Chapter 7, p. 219)

Detective notebook: Compile relevant case information in a detective notebook using the journal jacket technique. (Chapter 8, pp. 272; 275)

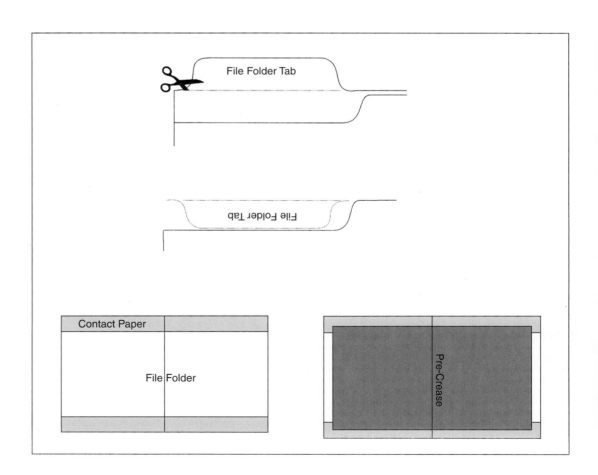

◎ **Magnify the Mystery**

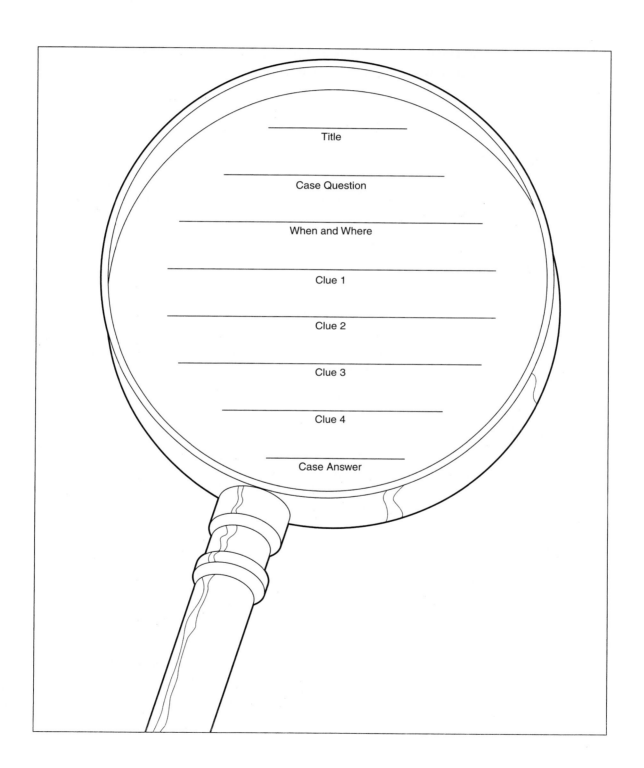

Title

Case Question

When and Where

Clue 1

Clue 2

Clue 3

Clue 4

Case Answer

◎ Media Techniques

CHALK

Chalk on sandpaper	Draw on sandpaper with chalk.
Dry on wet	Spray paper with water or dip paper in and out of container of water quickly. Draw on wet paper with chalk.
Wet on dry	Soak chalk in water for a few minutes. Use chalk to draw on dry paper.
Wet on wet	Draw on wet paper with wet chalk.

Note: Spray finished chalk pictures with hair spray to keep chalk from smearing.

CLAY

Mix two parts flour, one part salt, and a small amount of water to form a mixture of clay consistency. Add food coloring or tempera paint to color. Store in refrigerator in an airtight container.

CRAYON

Crayon etching

Cover an entire sheet of paper with a picture drawn using only a heavy crayon line or splotches. Bright colors work well for this first layer of crayon. Apply a second layer of crayon over the first layer. Choose black for a night scene or blue for an underwater setting. Using the pointed end of a paper clip, scissors, a ballpoint pen without ink, and so forth, etch a design in the crayon.

Crayon resist

Color a picture with crayon. Be sure to make crayon lines very heavy. Paint over the picture with water-diluted paint. The paint will not adhere to the part of the picture that has been colored with crayon. A thin, blue wash makes an interesting underwater scene. A thick black wash makes a night scene.

Crayon rubbing

Place paper over a textured surface. Rub over the paper with the side of a crayon; or sketch a picture and use different textured surfaces to create interesting designs for each component in the picture.

Pointillism

Sketch a picture and fill it in with tiny dots that are made using the end of a crayon. If dots are made with two primary colors, the dots will appear as a secondary color when viewed from a distance. Thus, blue and red will appear as purple, blue and yellow will appear as green, and red and yellow will appear as orange. Use this technique with small pictures or it will become tedious. *(Note: This is a noisy activity. Using fine-line markers is somewhat quieter.)*

PAINT

Blotto art

Fold paper in half. Open. To one side of the crease, drop or spatter dots of paint. More than one color of paint may be used. Carefully refold the paper. Gently blot the dots of paint and press excess toward the outer edges of the paper. Open the paper to reveal an exciting and imaginative creation. Enhance your creation with hand-drawn features. You may want to cut out and mount your blotto on a contrasting color of paper.

Dab art

Dip the tip of a small paintbrush into paint. Put tiny dots of paint on paper. This technique is effective in painting fall scenes and showing leaves in a variety of colors.

Printing

Use sliced onions, green pepper rings, carved potatoes, or sponge shapes. Paint the surface of the vegetable or sponge, or press it on an ink pad. Print on paper. Fingerprints, hand-prints, and footprints also make interesting pictures.

Rolling art

Place paper in the bottom of a shallow soda can box. Dip marbles, matchbox cars, or other rolling objects in a container of paint. Place the rolling object on the paper. Tip the box back and forth to create an interesting design. Use several different colors for special effects.

Straw blowing

Place a small dot of paint on a piece of paper. Using a straw, blow the paint in various directions. The paint will spread out in thin lines.

String painting

Fold a piece of paper in half. Dip a piece of string in paint. Place the string inside, on one side of the folded paper, to create an interesting design. Hold the folded piece of paper tightly with one hand, and pull the string with the other hand. Open the paper to reveal a unique, symmetrical design.

PAPER

Collage

Attach small pieces of paper and objects on a background to form a picture.

Hole punch art

Empty a hole punch tray, and use the pieces to form a picture or cover a pattern. Use this technique for small pictures, or it will become tedious. Punch holes in paper to create unique designs. Hole punch around the edges of a square or rectangle to make stamps or create a scalloped edge.

Jab art

Twist small squares of colored tissue paper around the eraser end of a pencil. Put a dot of glue on the background paper and jab the tissue paper onto the glue. Use jab art for flowers, leaves, and so forth. Use jab art to fill in a pattern—for example, red jab art on a valentine shape.

Mosaic

Cut small pieces of paper and place in various patterns to form a picture, or use small pieces to cover a shape.

Split art

Cut a magazine picture, wallpaper picture, or shape into strips. Mount the picture on a contrasting color with tiny spaces between each strip.

Torn paper

Tear small pieces of paper and attach to a background to form a picture, or tear paper into different object shapes and attach to a background.

SAND

Sand art

Draw a picture on a piece of paper. Spread glue over selected parts of the picture and sprinkle with sand or salt.

STAND

Fold a small strip of tagboard into fourths. Open. Overlap and glue the two ends, forming a triangular stand. Glue paper people and objects to this support to make them stand up.

℮ Multiple Men

MATERIALS

12″ × 18″ sheet of construction paper

DIRECTIONS

1. Fold a 12″ × 18″ sheet of paper lengthwise to form a 6″ × 18″ rectangle. *(hot dog)* Cut on the fold line.
2. Use one 6″ × 18″ rectangle. Fold widthwise to form a 6″ × 9″ rectangle. *(hamburger)* Fold widthwise again to form a 6″ × 4.5″ rectangle *(hamburger)*. Fold the paper once more down to 6″ × 2.25″ rectangle. *(hot dog)*
3. Open the construction paper to the original 6″ × 18″ rectangle.
4. Using the crease lines as a reference, accordion fold the paper down to a 6″ × 2.25″ rectangle.
5. Fold the accordion shut. Lay it on the table with the four-folds on the left.
6. Draw the shape of half a person down the four-fold side. Draw arms and legs over to the opposite side that has three folds.
7. Cut out the person. Be sure to leave part of the three folds uncut or your multiple men will not hold hands, but will fall apart.
8. Open to see multiple men.
9. To increase the number of men, attach the ends of two or more sets of men together.

Note: A variety of shapes may be used. Be sure the shape touches the folds on both sides of the accordion and that part of the folds remain to hold the shapes together.

VARIATION

Safety: Make pairs of people. Design bathing suits. Label: "Always swim with a buddy."

Health: Draw a different body system on each silhouette. Write information about the body system on the back of each silhouette.

APPLICATION

People picture poems: Write people picture poems on multiple men. Each man may contain a different poem, or one poem may be written across two or more men. (Chapter 3, Figure 3.8, pp. 78–80)

Paper people practice: Use multiple men as math manipulatives. (Chapter 6, pp. 167 & 176)

Brain, Body, and Behavior: Indicate behaviors such as anger, rage, and happiness. (Chapter 7, p. 240)

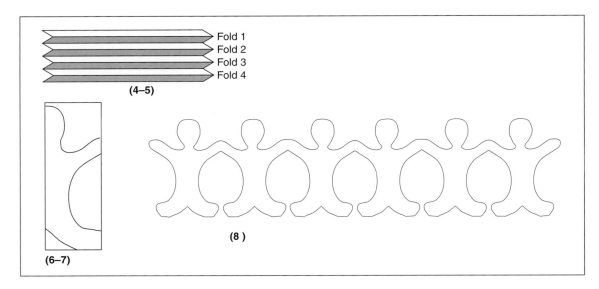

@ Paper Plate Stage

MATERIALS

Paper plates
Construction paper
Popsicle sticks

DIRECTIONS

1. Cut a small half-circle off the outside edge of a paper plate. This plate serves as the stage backdrop. With the half-circle at the base, design scenery on the eating side of the top-half portion of the plate.
2. Cut a second paper plate in half. One half serves as the front of the stage. The other half may be used later as additional scenery.
3. Place the rounded edge of the half paper plate over the small circle at the bottom of the backdrop, eating sides facing each other. Staple the outside edges of the plates together on either side of the hole.
4. Make puppets from construction paper and mount on tongue depressors, craft sticks, or pencils. Different puppets may be mounted on either side of the tongue depressor to make a double-sided puppet.
5. Slide puppets up through the half-circle at the bottom of the stage.
6. To make a change of scenery, color a backdrop on the inside of the remaining half paper plate. Slide in front of the first scenery. Clip at the top.

APPLICATION

Legends: Create puppets and a paper plate stage. Use the puppets to tell a legend. (Chapter 5, p. 149)

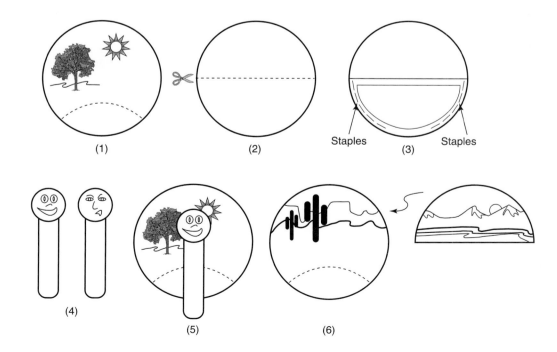

◎ Plate-arama

MATERIALS

Two paper plates

DIRECTIONS

1. On the eating side of one plate, design and illustrate an appropriate backdrop for a particular topic.
2. Cut the center circle out of the second paper plate. Set the center circle aside.
3. Decorate the backside of the rim of the second plate.
4. Attach the rim to the backdrop, eating sides together.
5. Cut a relevant shape from the remaining center circle and decorate appropriately.
6. Using a jack-in-the-box spring from this appendix, mount the shape on the backdrop of the plate.

VARIATION

Metamorphosis: Construct a plate-arama mobile to depict metamorphosis.
Indigenous plants or animals: Construct a plate-arama mobile to represent specific species of plants or animals indigenous to the area being studied.

APPLICATION

Cat habitat: Create a cat's natural environment or the story setting for a cat's adventure in a plate-arama. Write about the cat in the circle on the back of the plate-arama. As a research report, include information such as type, appearance, habits, care, protection, and importance. If the cat is a story character, include interesting adventure tidbits or a synopsis of the story. An additional challenge is to write information in a circular pattern (Chapter 7, pp. 214–215)
Plate-arama mobile: Create a food chain mobile with a separate plate-arama for each member of the food chain. Write appropriate information about each member on the back of the appropriate plate-arama. These plate-aramas form a vertical chain when holes are punched in the top and the bottom, and the plate-aramas are tied together with yarn.
(Chapter 8, p. 265)

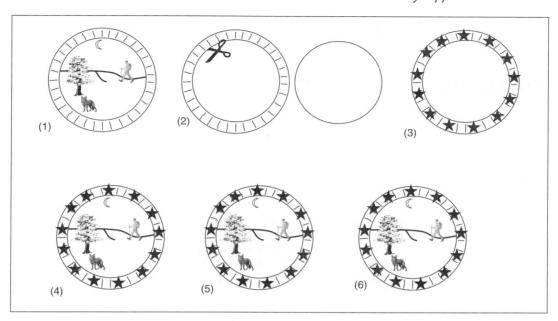

◎ Pocket Book

MATERIALS

12″ × 18″ sheet of construction paper.
3″ × 5″ index cards

DIRECTIONS

1. Fold a 12″ × 18″ sheet of construction paper to form a 6″ × 18″ rectangle. *(hot dog)*
2. Fold again to form a 3″ × 18″ rectangle. *(hot dog)*
3. Accordion fold the rectangle lengthwise into four equal 3″ × 4.5″ panels.
4. Unfold the sheet of construction paper to its 6″ × 18″ size. Place the paper on the table in front of you with the two edges facing you.
5. On one of the edges, cut in approximately 4.5″ along the center crease.
6. Dog-ear the four corners so that they meet and form two triangles.
7. Fold down the tip on each of the two triangles to meet the fold line.
8. Fold each of the tips back up to the center fold line.
9. Vertically staple each tip to the rear panel to form a total of four pockets.
10. Label one of each 3″ × 5″ card with a single digit number, 0 through 9.

VARIATION

Pockets Full of Poetry: Write poems on index cards and fill the four pockets full of poetry.

APPLICATION

Pocket books for Every Student Participation (ESP): Use these card holders for index cards that have individual numbers, letters, coins, or vocabulary words written or stamped on one end. Students slide these cards into the pockets to indicate the answers to questions. Thus all students are participating simultaneously in a shared ESP experience. (Chapter 6, p. 195)

(1)

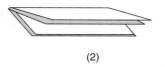

(2)

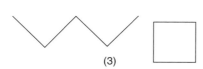

(3)

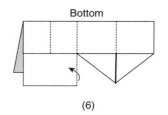

(4)

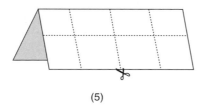

(5)

Bottom

(6)

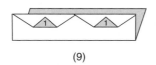

(7)

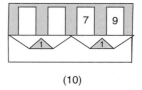

(8)

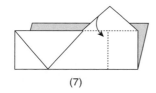

(9)

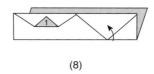

(10)

℘ Pocket Plate Mobile

MATERIALS

Two paper plates
String or yarn

DIRECTIONS

1. Cut one paper plate in half.
2. Place the whole paper plate and the half paper plate together, eating sides facing each other and edges matching.
3. Staple the edges together or punch holes in both plates and weave yarn through the holes.
4. Punch a hole in the top of the whole paper plate. Thread a piece of string through the hole and suspend the pocket plate mobile from the ceiling.
5. The half paper plate forms a pocket in which students place poems, paragraphs, and other written work. Student work may also be mounted on the back of the whole paper plate.

VARIATION

Two pocket plate mobiles may be mounted back-to-back to create a double pocket plate mobile.

APPLICATION

Poetry pocket plate mobile: Write poems and display in and on poetry pocket plate mobiles. (Chapter 3, p. 81–82)

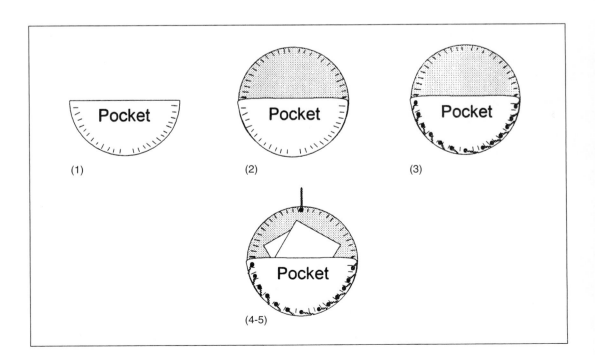

◎ Pop-Up Techniques

MATERIAL

8.5″ × 11″ sheet of paper

DIRECTIONS

1. Fold an 8.5″ × 11″ sheet of paper in half to form an 8.5″ × 5.5″ rectangle. *(hamburger)*
2. Place the fold on your left.
3. Choose a shape from the illustrations that follow and make the appropriate cuts as indicated by the dotted lines.
4. Continue by folding and creasing the shape as indicated by the bold lines in the chosen example.
5. Open the rectangle slightly and push the shape to the inside of the rectangle.
6. To frame the pop-up, choose a slightly larger sheet of paper of contrasting color. Fold the sheet in half, bookwise.
7. Center the pop-up on the larger sheet of paper. Glue the corners of the pop-up sheet to the larger sheet of paper.
8. A pop-up book can be made by joining individual pop-up pages together.

APPLICATION

Autobiography pop-up: Write an autobiography. Plan a pop-up page for each event in the autobiography. (Chapter 3, p. 58)

Pop-up Book: Design a pop-up plan to retell a story. Determine the number of pages needed. Decide which part of the picture will be moving on each page. (Chapter 5, pp. 146–147)

Pop-up pleaser: Mount different items of various prices on the notches in a pop-up pleaser. Compute the cost of two or more items. Younger students can plan a pop-up pleaser in which the number of items on each page increases by one item as the book progresses. (Chapter 6, p. 183)

Gifts and Greetings Card Gallery: Perimeter pursuit professionals plan perimeters of cards and precisely measure pop-ups as well as flaps, windows, doors, and a variety of shapes. (Chapter 6, p. 198)

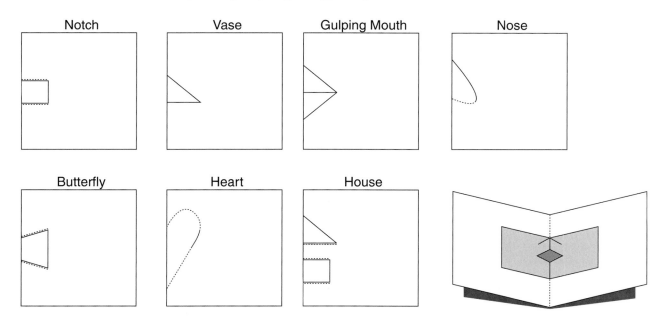

Notch   Vase   Gulping Mouth   Nose

Butterfly   Heart   House

⊚ Puppets

Panty Hose Puppet

MATERIALS

Pliers
Metal coat hanger
Panty hose
Decorative materials
Masking tape

DIRECTIONS

1. Using pliers, pinch the hook of the hanger shut to form a safe handle for the puppet.
2. Bend the triangular portion of the hanger into the desired puppet shape.
3. Stretch one leg of the panty hose over the shape and secure the hook with masking tape.
4. Add features and decorate with paper, fabric, yarn, beads, and baubles.

APPLICATION

Persuasive puppet: Design a panty hose puppet to participate in a persuasive production to sell the audience on a given point of view. (Chapter 3, p. 76)
Puppet productions: Extend reading experiences through puppets and plays. (Chapter 4, p. 96)

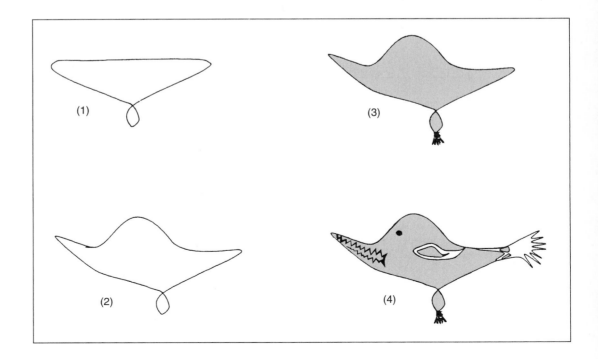

Sleeve Puppet

MATERIALS

9″ × 12″ sheet of construction paper.

DIRECTIONS

1. Fold a 9″ × 12″ sheet of construction paper horizontally, overlapping paper edges approximately 1 inch. *(hamburger)*
2. This will form a 5″ × 9″ rectangular sleeve.
3. Round off the corners on one end of the sleeve to form a head. Glue rounded corners and seam.
4. Decorate puppet.

APPLICATION

Character growth: Make before and after faces on a sleeve puppet to portray a character's attitude before and after growth in a particular situation. The face on the front of the puppet portrays the attitude before growth. The face on the back of the puppet portrays a different attitude after growth. A sentence explaining these attitudes may be written under each face. (Chapter 2, p. 24)

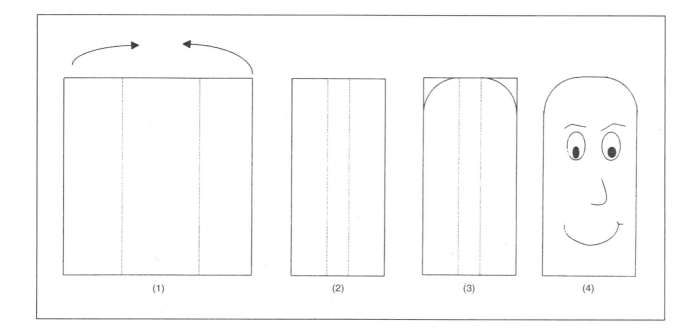

(1)   (2)   (3)   (4)

Sock Puppet

MATERIALS

Old sock
Decorative materials

DIRECTIONS

1. Pull the sock down over your fist and invert the toe of the sock to form a mouth between your thumb and index finger.
2. Add features and decorate with paper, fabric, yarn, beads, and baubles.

APPLICATION

Persuasive puppet: Design a sock puppet to participate in a persuasive production to sell the audience on a given point of view. (Chapter 3, pp. 75–76)

(1-2)

Trifold Puppet

MATERIALS

8.5″ × 11″ sheet of paper
Decorative materials

DIRECTIONS

1. Fold the sheet of paper lengthwise into thirds. *(hot dog)*
2. Fold in half to form a rectangle approximately 3″ × 5.5″. *(hamburger)* To ensure clean lines fold the loose edge to the outside.
3. Fold the open ends back to the crease to form a square. *(hamburger)*
4. Place your fingers in the pocket created by the folds. Add features and decorate with paper, fabric, yarn, beads, and baubles.

VARIATION

Vary the size of your trifold puppet by using different sizes of paper.

APPLICATION

Trifold finger puppets: Create finger puppets, small trifold puppets, to use in puppet plays and songs. A cardboard box may serve as a theater stage. (Chapter 4, p. 96)

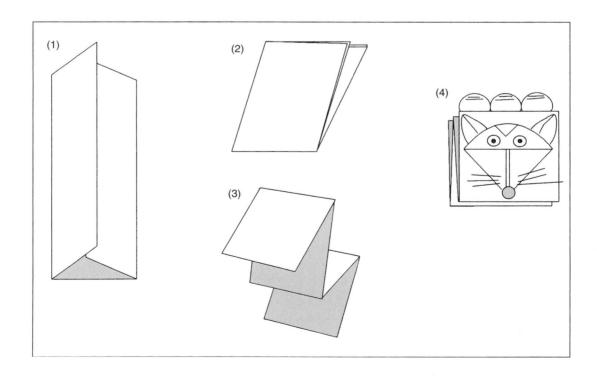

◎ Puzzle Pleasers

MATERIALS

8.5″ × 11″ sheet of poster board
File folder

DIRECTIONS

1. Draw a picture from the story on the front of an 8.5″ × 11″ piece of poster board.
2. On the back of the poster board, write questions about the story. Write answers to the questions adjacent or beneath the questions. Draw lines between the questions and answers; cut on lines, forming puzzle pieces.
3. Draw an 8.5″ × 11″ frame for the puzzle on an open file folder.
4. Put the question/answer puzzle together on the frame; then close the file folder.
5. Hold tightly. Flip the file folder over. Open. See the picture.
6. Store puzzle pieces in a plastic zipper bag that is clipped or stapled to the folder.

APPLICATION

Vocabulary puzzle: On one side of the puzzle draw a picture about the story. On the other side of the puzzle write vocabulary terms and write/illustrate definitions (see Chapter 2, p. 24)

Story puzzle: On one side of the puzzle draw a picture about the story. On the other side of the puzzle write questions and answers about the story. (Chapter 2, p. 24)

Mystery puzzles: Write a mystery on one side of a piece of poster board. Draw lines between words in the mystery to form puzzle pieces. On the other side of the poster board create an illustration for the mystery. Cut the puzzle apart. Label an envelope with the title of the mystery and the enigmatist's name. Place the puzzle in the envelope. (Chapter 8, p. 258)

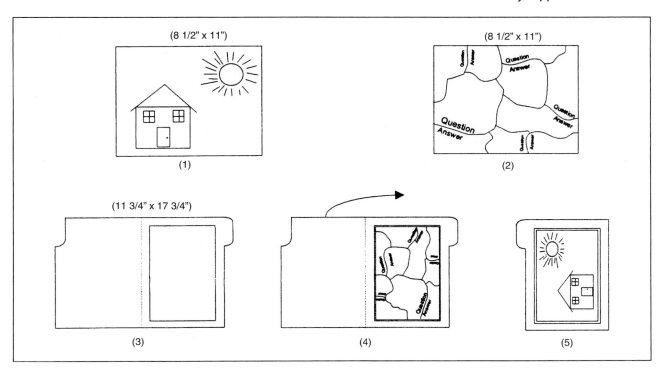

⊚ Roll Over and Over Book

MATERIALS

Two 9˝ × 9˝ squares of construction paper.

DIRECTIONS

1. Fold two 9˝ × 9˝ squares of construction paper into quarters to form eight squares 4.5˝ × 4.5˝ each.
2. Open and place one sheet on top of the other. Cut on the left fold line to the center of each 9˝ × 9˝ square.
3. Place the squares so that the cut edges are to your left.
4. Number each square 1 to 8, beginning with the top left square of the first sheet. Work clockwise so that square 5 is the top left square of the second sheet.
5. Place squares 5 through 8 on top of squares 1 through 4 with the cuts aligned.
6. With cuts aligned, tape the bottom edge of square 5 to the top edge of square 4.
7. Fold square 8 over to face square 7.
   Fold squares 7 and 8 over to face square 6.
   Fold squares 6, 7, and 8 over to face square 5.
   Fold squares 5 through 8 over to face square 4.
   Fold squares 4 through 8 over to face square 3.
   Fold squares 3 through 8 over to face square 2.
   Fold squares 2 through 8 over to face square 1.
8. The back of square 1 becomes the cover of your book.

VARIATIONS

Create with circles, triangles, and rectangles.

APPLICATION

Circle of cinquains roll over and over book: Compose cinquains about one or more legends. Mount a cinquain on each section of the book. The book may be made from two large grocery sacks. (Chapter 5, p. 150)

Birthday biography roll over and over book: Identify eight significant events in a person's life. Arrange these events on the eight sections of the birthday biography roll over and over book. (Chapter 5, p. 153)

Money memoirs circle story: Include chronicles of memories and dreams about the money the author used to have. In the first segment have the initial amount of wealth. In each succeeding segment have catastrophes or purchases that decrease the amount of wealth with calculations to show this loss. (Chapter 6, p. 186)

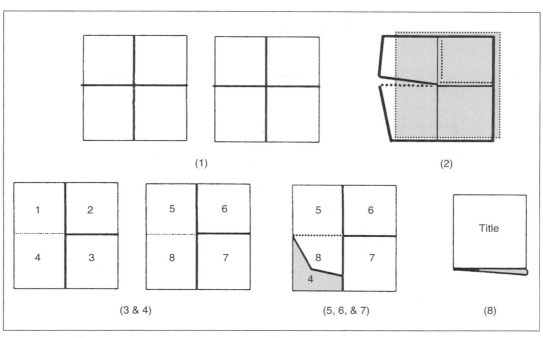

(1)

(2)

(3 & 4)

(5, 6, & 7)

(8)

◎ ROPE Form

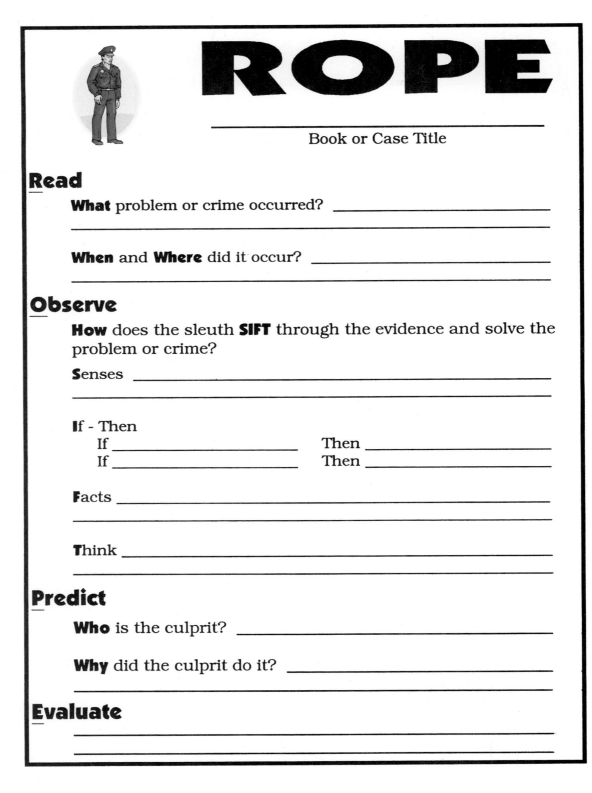

ROPE

_____
Book or Case Title

Read

What problem or crime occurred? _____

_____

When and **Where** did it occur? _____

_____

Observe

How does the sleuth **SIFT** through the evidence and solve the problem or crime?

Senses _____

_____

If - Then
   If _____   Then _____
   If _____   Then _____

Facts _____

_____

Think _____

_____

Predict

Who is the culprit? _____

Why did the culprit do it? _____

_____

Evaluate

_____

_____

☺ Shape Books

MATERIALS

Poster board
Construction paper
Ditto paper
Metal rings
Hole punch

DIRECTIONS

1. Cut two pieces of poster board into the selected shape for the front and back covers of the book.
2. If shaped pages are desired, make a tag board pattern slightly smaller than the covers for the book. Trace and cut construction paper or ditto paper into the selected shape.
3. Include the following pages:
   (a) Title page
   (b) Dedication page
   (c) Text pages
   (d) Author's page (each author contributes a paragraph)
   (e) Read-by page (signature from each person who reads the book)
4. Punch holes in either the side or the top of the book.
5. Slide metal rings through the holes to bind the book.
6. Make individual shape books or class shape books to which each student or group of students makes a contribution.

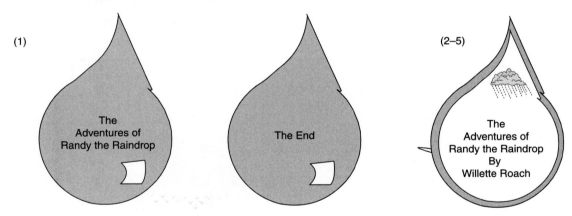

VARIATIONS

Attach-a-shape: Attach an appropriate shape to the front cover of the following:
1. Accordion book

2. Step book

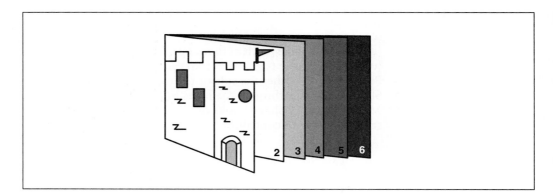

3. Teeny tiny book

Fold-a-Shape: Select a symmetrical shape. Trace on the front of an accordion book. Cut out the shape being sure to leave parts of the folds uncut (see Multiple Men).

APPLICATION

Hopi house shape book: Sketch-to-summarize and illustrate information for each section of the book on individual shape pages (see Chapter 2, p. 28)

Class cloud book: Behind every cloud is a silver lining. (Chapter 3, p. 77)

Castle shape book: Create a castle shape book for medieval times. (Chapter 5, p. 157)

Cookie shape cookbook: When studying fractions, compile a collection of cookie recipes in a cookie shape cookbook. (Chapter 6, p. 182)

Secret ingredient cake shape book: When studying fractions, compile a collection of favorite cake recipes with secret ingredients. Write each secret ingredient in code and hide it somewhere within the book. (Chapter 6, p. 182)

Leaf shape book: Include leaf lore, information about leaves, and leaf samples in leaf shape books. (Chapter 7, p. 211)

Cat shape book: Create a cationary using a cat shape book. (Chapter 7, p. 219)

Ship shape log books: Compile a class anthology of shipology terminology verselets. (Chapter 8, p. 258)

@ Slit-Slot-Slide Book

MATERIALS

Two sheets of 8.5″ × 11″ ditto paper

DIRECTIONS

1. Fold both sheets of paper in half horizontally. *(hamburger)* Unfold.
2. On one sheet of paper, cut along the crease 1″ from each end to form the slits.
3. On the second sheet of paper, cut along the crease line to within 1″ from each end to form a slot (bending paper vertically, *hot dog*, makes cutting on crease easier).
4. Roll the first sheet of paper *(hot dog)* and slide it through the slot of the second sheet of paper.
5. Unroll and secure the slits.
6. Additional slit sheets may be included to make a longer book.

APPLICATION

Pepi profile slit-slot-slide book: Glue the two center pages together. Draw and cut a human profile from the glued page. Draw in facial features on both sides. Include *what, why,* and *how* goals that determine my destiny. Use for the following (Chapter 7, p. 236):
"Say NO to drugs!"
"Say NO to peer pressure!"
"Say NO to strangers!"

Brain focus: Use two slit pages. Create brain drawings on which to indicate drug abuse/addiction impact on the brain. (Chapter 7, p. 240)

VARIATION

"Look left-right-left before crossing the street."

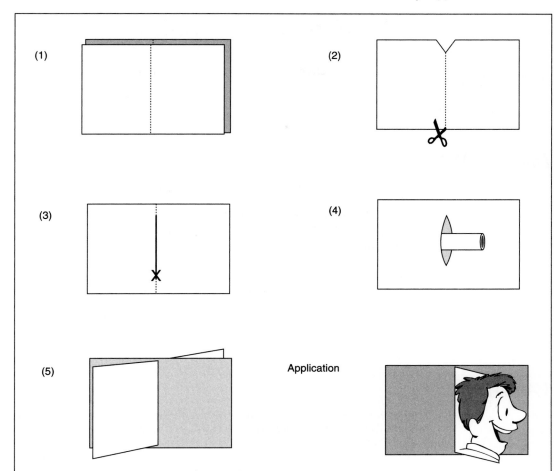

(1)

(2)

(3)

(4)

(5)

Application

⌖ Snowflakes

MATERIALS

8.5″ × 11″ sheet of paper

DIRECTIONS

1. Make an 8.5″ square by folding one corner of the paper to form a triangle. Trim off the 8.5″ × 2.5″ rectangle.
2. Fold the resulting triangle in half.
3. Fold the triangle in half again.
4. Round off the side with the loose edges in a scalloped pattern.
5. Cut out designs on the single fold edge. Be sure to leave part of the single fold uncut or the snowflake will fall apart.
6. Cut out designs on the three-fold edge. Be sure to leave part of the folds uncut, or the snowflake will fall apart.
7. From the scalloped edge, cut a design down toward the center of the snowflake
8. Open to reveal a unique snowflake.

VARIATION

Begin with a circle rather than a square, folding the circle in half, then into fourths, and finally into eighths. Follow steps 5 through 8 to complete the circular snowflake.

APPLICATION

(CHAPTER 7, P. 221)

Season scenes in shallow shadow boxes: Suspend snowflakes from the ceiling in diorama.
Classroom: Suspend from ceiling. Use for bulletin board border.
Snowmen: Stack three snowflakes vertically to create a snowman.
Unique Me: Compare snowflakes and discover that each is unique—just like me.

(1)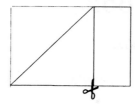

(2)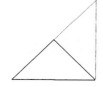

(3)

(4)

(5)

(6)

(7)

(8)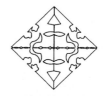

℮ Step Book

MATERIALS

Three 9″ × 12″ sheets of construction paper in three different colors

DIRECTIONS

1. Place a sheet of 9″ × 12″ construction paper vertically.
2. Place a second sheet of a different color on top of the first sheet and approximately 1″ from the top.
3. Place a third sheet of a different color on top of the second sheet and 1″ below the second sheet.
4. Holding the outside edges of the construction paper tightly, fold over until the edge of the third piece of paper is 1″ from its own edge. A step book with a title page and five steps will be formed. Staple on the fold.
5. Example: Step Book Story Organizer using 4 sheet, of paper.

VARIATIONS

Vary number of pages.
Vary paper sizes.
Vary book orientation: (Staples on right; staples on left,) staples on top (most common orientation).
Emergency phone numbers: Make an emergency phone number step book.

APPLICATION

Vocabulary: Write a vocabulary word on each step. Illustrate the meaning of the word over the word and under the preceding step. (Chapter 2, p. 40)

Vocabulary riddles: Devise a riddle with the vocabulary word as the answer. Write the riddle on the step. Write the answer over the riddle and hidden under the preceding step. (Chapter 2, p. 40)

Step book story organizer: Develop a step book story organizer to analyze an author's use of story elements: character setting, problem/goal, events, and resolution. Use a step book story organizer to plan a personal story. (Chapter 3, p. 60)

Research report: Compile information for a research report in a step book. Each step contains a different type of information. (Chapter 5, p. 145)

Picture practice: Use in calculations and computations to illustrate mathematical situations. (Chapter 6, p. 167)

Recipe: When studying fractions, write directions for a recipe in a step book. (Chapter 6, p. 181)

***The Grouchy Lady* Bug story innovation:** Compose a story innovation for *The Grouchy Lady Bug* and publish the story in a step book that has a step for each day of the week. (Chapter 6, p. 195)

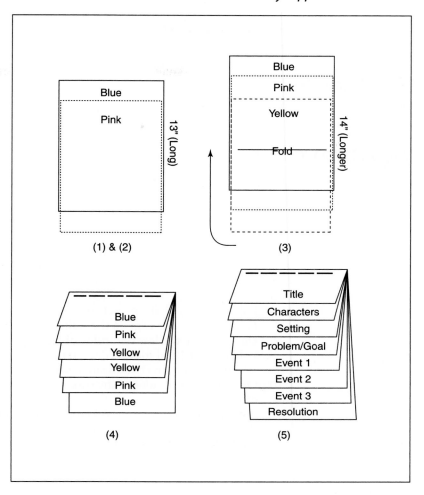

꧁ Story Box

MATERIALS

Two sheets of 8.5″ × 11″ paper.

DIRECTIONS

Box Lid

1. Make an 8.5″ square by folding one corner of the paper to form a triangle. Trim off the 2.5″ × 8.5″ rectangle.
2. Fold the resulting triangle in half.
3. Open the paper to reveal a square evenly divided into four triangles.
4. Fold each corner to the center of the square.
5. Fold back each corner so that the tip meets the center of the edge. *(dog ear)*
6. Fold one edge to the center fold line.
7. Fold the opposite edge to the center fold line.
8. Undo ONLY the last two folds of steps 6 and 7.
9. Fold the third and fourth edges to the center fold line. Undo these last two folds. (Note: When folded correctly, 16 small squares appear on the back.)
10. On the opposite sides of the square, make two cuts on each side as illustrated (a total of four cuts).
11. Pull out the folds on the two edges of the square that were cut into.
12. Raise, fold, and hold in place the third and fourth edges of the square.
13. Fold over and tuck into place the pulled folds of the first two edges so as to form a box lid.

Box Base

1. Make an 8.5″ square by folding one corner of the paper to form a triangle. Trim off the 2.5″ × 8.5″ rectangle.
2. Fold the resulting triangle in half.
3. Trim the open edges of the triangle by about 1/8 inch.
4. Open the paper to reveal a square evenly divided into four triangles, but slightly smaller than the original square used to make the box lid.
5. Follow the directions for making a box lid beginning with step 4.

APPLICATION

Story box with story starters: Place small objects or pictures representing stories for oral storytelling in the box. (Chapter 3, p. 61)

Spuzzle box: Place each set of spuzzle pieces for a spelling word in an individual spuzzle box. The spuzzle pieces and spuzzle box may be color coordinated. (Chapter 4, spelling success center 1, p. 111)

Three-D-geometry: Construct story boxes to use for three-D-geometry art projects. (Chapter 6, p. 188)

Gifts and Greetings Gift Wrap Gallery: Accurate area analysts precisely measure and create gift boxes that promise treasures within. (Chapter 6, p. 199)

Underground Railroad: Construct houses and barns for a miniature Underground Railroad route. (Chapter 8, p. 268)

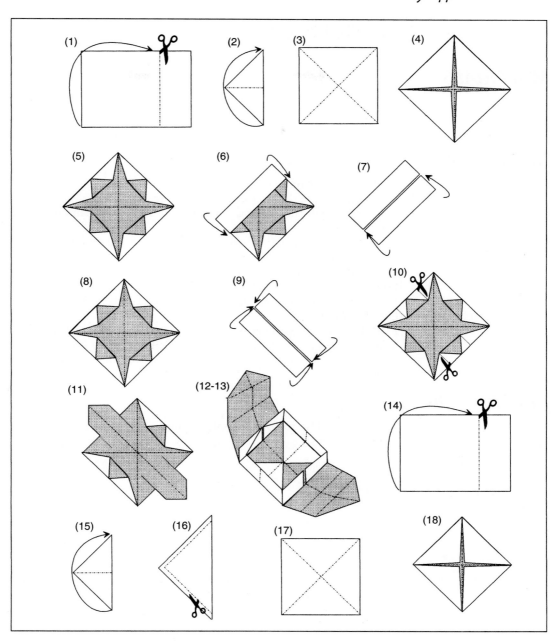

◎ Tangram

MATERIALS

8.5″ × 11″ sheet of paper

DIRECTIONS

1. Fold one corner to form an 8.5″ square. Cut.
2. Cut square along the crease to form two triangles.
3. Fold one triangle in half and cut along the crease to form the two large congruent triangles. Set aside.
4. Place the remaining triangle on the table before you with the longest edge toward you. Fold the tip down to the center of the longest edge. Cut along the crease line to form a quadrilateral and a triangle. Set the triangle aside.
5. Fold the quadrilateral in half. Cut along the crease line.
6. Fold one half of the quadrilateral to form a triangle and a square. Cut along the crease line. Set aside.
7. Fold the other quadrilateral to form a triangle and a parallelogram.
8. The seven shapes, or tans, are used in combination to illustrate story figures.

APPLICATION

Storytelling: Use to form people, animals, and objects while telling a story. (Chapter 6, p. 188)

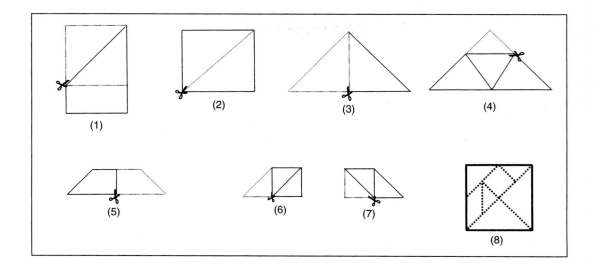

◎ Tantalizing Template Tangle

MATERIALS

File folder
Construction paper of varied colors

DIRECTIONS

1. Open the file folder.
2. Trace and cut out selected shapes from the front of the file folder.
3. Close the file folder.
4. Slide the appropriate piece of colored paper between the front and back of the file folder.
5. Trace the shapes.
6. Repeat as necessary for each color.
7. Arrange the shapes on a contrasting color of paper to form a tantalizing template tangle.
8. Decorate the tantalizing template tangle appropriately.

APPLICATION

Tales for a Template Tangle: Create a picture perfect tantalizing tale for a template tangle. (Chapter 6, p. 194)

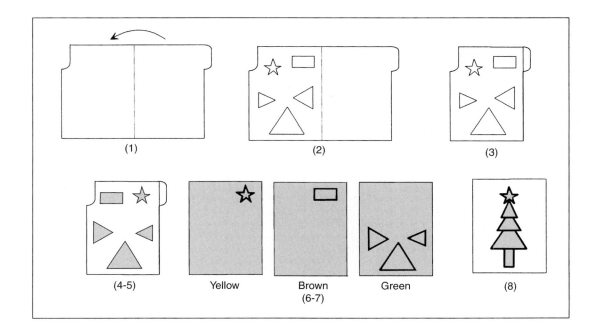

Teeny Tiny Book

MATERIALS

8.5″ × 11″ paper

DIRECTIONS

1. Fold an 8.5″ × 11″ piece of paper into quarters to form four rectangles 4.25″ × 5.5″. *(hamburger; hamburger)*
2. Fold again for form eight rectangles 2.75″ × 4.25″. *(hamburger)*
3. Open to the 8.5″ × 5.5″ rectangle. *(hamburger)* Cut on the crease line from the folded edge to the intersection.
4. Open. Refold on the fold/cut line to form a 4.25″ × 11″ rectangle. *(hot dog)*
5. Push ends toward the center so that the cut edges form a plus sign.
6. Imagine the plus sign over the face of a clock. Fold the 12 o'clock to meet 3 o'clock. Fold 3 o'clock to meet 6 o'clock. Fold 6 o'clock to meet 9 o'clock. Flip over. The 9 o'clock page forms the cover of the book (single fold on the left).
7. These books may be made a BIT BIGGER by using a larger paper rectangle.

APPLICATION

Journey journal: Record daily experiences and observations before, during, and after a trip in a journey journal. (Chapter 5, p. 145)

Personal Guiness book of records: Keep a record of skill to develop and/or improve. Record personal progress. (Chapter 6, p. 199)

Cationary: Create definitions from a cat's point of view. (Chapter 7, p. 219)

Mystery memo mini-book: Keep effective, objective detective notes in a mystery memo mini-book. (Chapter 8, p. 266)

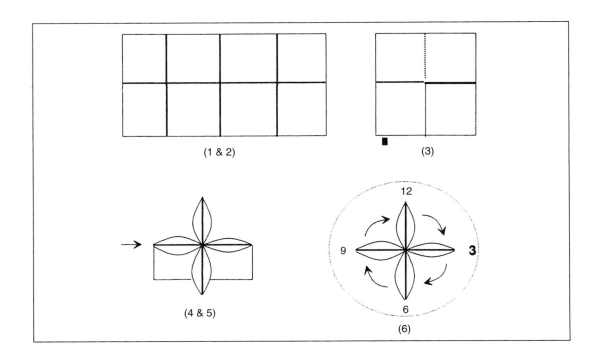

◎ Theater Book

MATERIALS

Two file folders
Six paper fasteners
8.5 ˝ × 11 ˝ sheets of paper for scenery pages and for story book

DIRECTIONS

1. On the tabbed half of a file folder cut out a rectangle approximately 6.5 ˝ × 9.5 ˝, leaving a 1 ˝ frame around the opening. *(Note: To facilitate this activity for students, make a pattern for them to trace around before cutting out the rectangle.)*
2. The rectangular opening becomes a window through which scenery pages for the theater book appear. The window forms the wall of the theater book and the other half of the file folder forms the floor.
3. To the center of the theater book, staple a small story book with 5.5 ˝ × 8.5 ˝ pages.
4. Slip the first file folder inside the second file folder. Three-hole punch the 12 ˝ ends of the file folders and secure with paper fasteners.
5. Illustrate each page of the story book on 8.5 ˝ × 11 ˝ paper. Place the completed illustrations, or scenery pages, behind the window in the order they will appear. As the story is read, the proper scenery page appears in the window. When the story book page is turned, the scenery page slides out of the window and is placed at the back of the stack of scenery pages. *(Note: Laminating each file folder and scenery page facilitates the scenery page changes.)*

APPLICATION

Story Innovation: Compose a story innovation. Write in a booklet and mount on the floor of the theater book. Make scenery pages for each page of the innovation. Change scenery pages while reading the story. (Chapter 3, pp. 62–64)

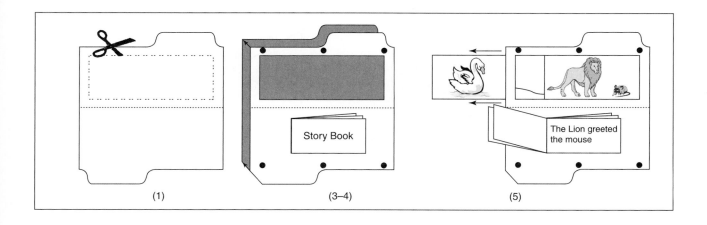

| (1) | (3–4) | (5) |

◎ Three-D-Geometry

Cone, Cube, Square Pyramid, Tetrahedron

MATERIALS

Construction paper

DIRECTIONS

1. Enlarge pattern.
2. Cut out, fold, and glue flaps.

APPLICATION

Three-D-geometry: Construct three-D-geometrical shapes. Decorate with markers, scraps of paper, and other craft materials to make people, animals, and buildings. (Chapter 6, p. 188)

Pyramid poem: Mount one or more pyramid poems on a square pyramid. (Chapter 2, p. 27)

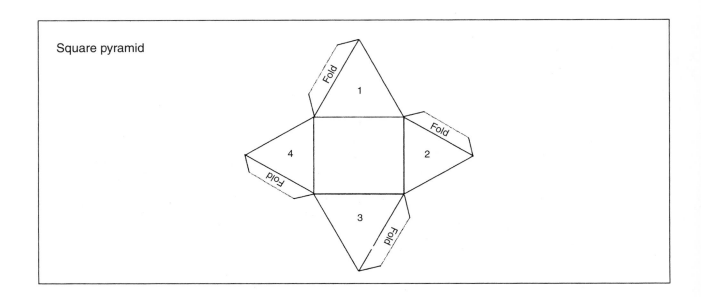

Square pyramid

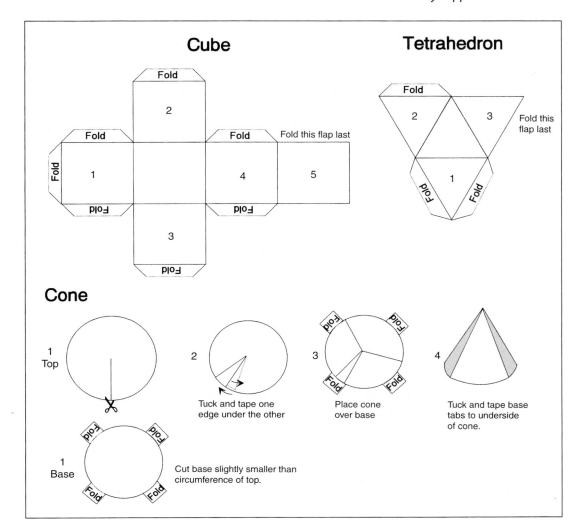

Cube

Fold

2

Fold

Fold

1

Fold

Fold

4

5   Fold this flap last

Fold

3

Fold

Tetrahedron

Fold

2   3   Fold this flap last

Fold   Fold

1

Cone

1
Top

2   Tuck and tape one edge under the other

3   Place cone over base

Fold   Fold

Fold   Fold

4   Tuck and tape base tabs to underside of cone.

1
Base

Fold   Fold

Fold   Fold

Cut base slightly smaller than circumference of top.

☙ Town House with Notches

MATERIALS

12″ × 18″ sheet of construction paper.

DIRECTIONS

1. Fold the sheet of paper in half lengthwise. *(hot dog)*
2. Fold the sheet of paper in half again to form a 6″ × 9″ rectangle *(hamburger)*; then fold again for a third time to form a 6″ × 4.5″ rectangle. *(hamburger)*
3. Unfold. On one 18″ side of the sheet of paper, cut along the three crease lines 2″ deep.
4. Accordion fold the sheet of paper widthwise along the three crease lines. *(hamburger)*
5. Place the folded paper on the table with the slitted side towards you. Mark the halfway point along the 4.5″ end with the slits. From the halfway point, cut to the base of the slits for form four rooftops.
6. Unfold.
7. Fold the sheet of paper lengthwise with the rooftops facing up and the lengthwise fold towards you. *(hot dog)*
8. Starting with the first panel, draw two parallel lines 1.5″ apart and 1″ deep along the base and in the center of the panel. Repeat for the second, third, and fourth panels. Cut along each 1″ line.
9. Fold the resulting notches back and forth to make a sharp crease.
10. Open the sheet of paper slightly and push each notch through to the other side.
11. Turn the sheet of paper so that the front now faces you. The notches will appear as miniature steps. From the base of each of these notches, draw two parallel lines so that the "yard" of each town house is divided into three driveways.
12. Use a wide, felt-tip marker to define the "property line" between each town house.
13. Start with the far left town house and label each town house with a family surname: *Billions, Millions, Thousands,* and *Units.* Decorate the buildings appropriately.
14. Label the driveways for each townhouse, from right to left: *Ones, Tens, Hundreds.*

APPLICATION

Town house math: Line up digits for a selected number from right to left in the correct driveways. Read the number from left to right. Use individual number squares or strips to assist in understanding. (see Chapter 6, pp. 172–173)

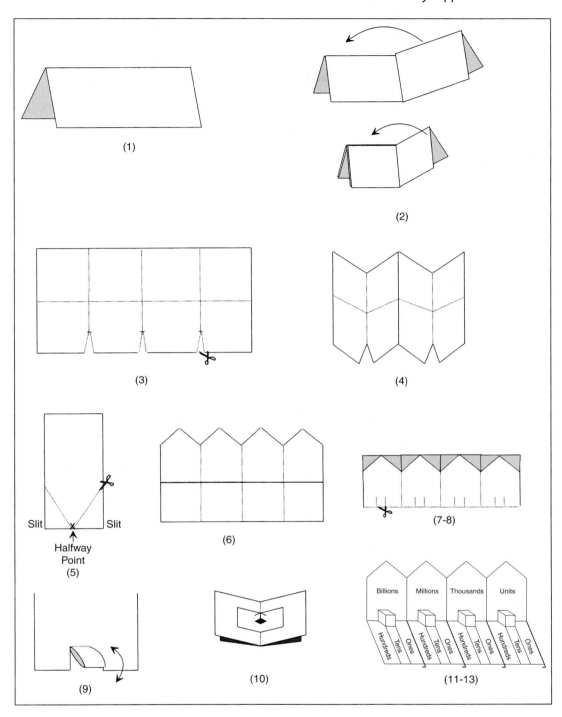

◎ Trifold Brochure

MATERIALS

9″ × 12″ sheet of construction paper

DIRECTIONS

1. Divide a 9″ × 12″ piece of construction paper horizontally into thirds. *(hamburger)*
2. Fold the right third over the center third.
3. Fold the left third over the right third.
4. A 4″ × 9″ rectangular brochure is made.

APPLICATION

Book sale brochure: Design a book sale brochure to sell others on reading the book. Include information about characters, problems, goals, events, and readers' recommendations. (Chapter 2, pp. 35–36)

The power of political persuasion: Sell your candidate to the voters. Grab voters' attention with great graphics and a catchy slogan or two. (Chapter 5, pp. 136; 139–140)

Take-a-tour brochure: Design a tour brochure to sell potential travelers on pursuing a trip to a particular destination. (Chapter 5, p. 144)

Dine n' Dash Restaurant menu: Create a menu as one prop for a dramatic debut. (Chapter 6, p. 185)

Cave and cavern vacations: Entice readers to visit. Provide a map with locations and information. (Chapter 8, p. 271)

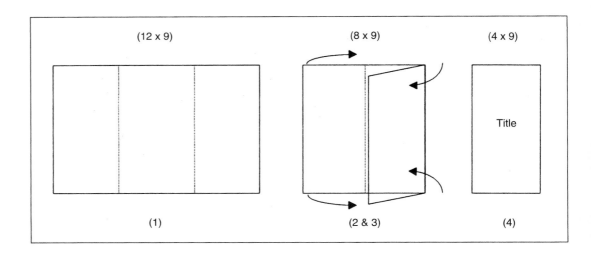

◎ Vest

MATERIALS

Large grocery bag

DIRECTIONS

1. On a large grocery bag, cut lengthwise along the seam to the edge of the bottom of the bag.
2. From the cutting position at the bottom of the bag, cut an oval in the bottom, leaving a 1″ perimeter around the edges. The oval space forms the neckline.
3. On each side of the grocery bag, cut a circle for an armhole.
4. Decorate the vest appropriately.

VARIATION:

Life preserver: Create a life preserver to use in a water safety unit.

APPLICATION

Personal storytelling: Design a storytelling vest with illustrations that contribute to sharing personal stories and/or familiar folk tales. (Chapter 5, p. 148)

Native American vests: Design a vest to wear to a tribal meeting. Decorate the vest with appropriate tribal symbols. The symbols may be arranged to tell a tribal story. Fringe the bottom and front edges of the vest. (Chapter 5, p. 148)

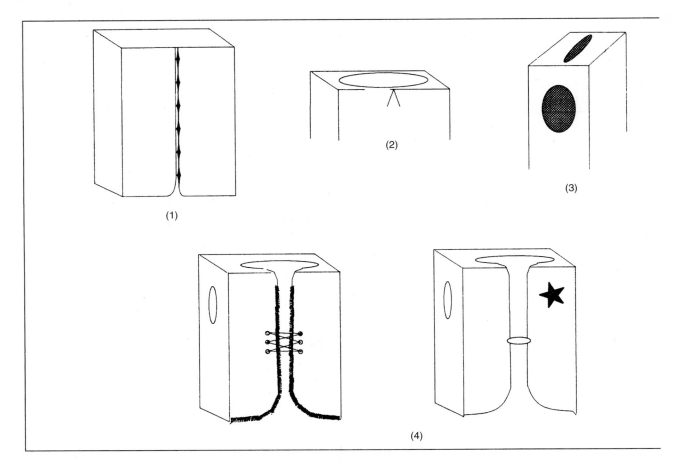

(1)

(2)

(3)

(4)

© Wanted Poster

WANTED
DEAD OR ALIVE

Name: _____

Description: _____

_____

Known For: _____

_____

REWARD: _____

◎ Wrap-Over Book

MATERIALS

9˝ × 12˝ sheet of construction paper

DIRECTIONS

1. Fold a 9˝ × 12˝ sheet of paper to form a 4.5˝ × 12˝ rectangle. *(hot dog)*
2. Open and cut on the fold line.
3. Use one of the rectangles. Fold in half to form a 4.5˝ × 6˝ rectangle. *(hamburger)*
4. Fold in half again to form a 4.5˝ × 3˝ rectangle. *(hamburger)*
5. Unfold. Number the sections 1 to 4 from left to right.
6. Fold section 4 over to face section 3. Fold sections 3 and 4 over to face section 2. Fold sections 2 through 4 over to face section 1.
7. Flip over. Fold on left. The back of section 1 becomes the cover of your book.
8. See the diagram for placement of pictures and story.

APPLICATION

Sentence expansion: Write a kernel sentence. Expand the sentence once using adjectives. Expand the sentence again adding prepositional phrases. As the book unwraps, the kernel sentence expands and the illustrations contain more details. (Chapter 4, p. 108)

Vacation destination wrap-over: Choose three sites to visit on a vacation. Research and write about each site. (Chapter 5, p. 141)

Food chain wrap-over: Create a food-chain wrap-over with sequentially linked plants and animals that are interdependent on each other for food to supply energy. (Chapter 8, p. 265)

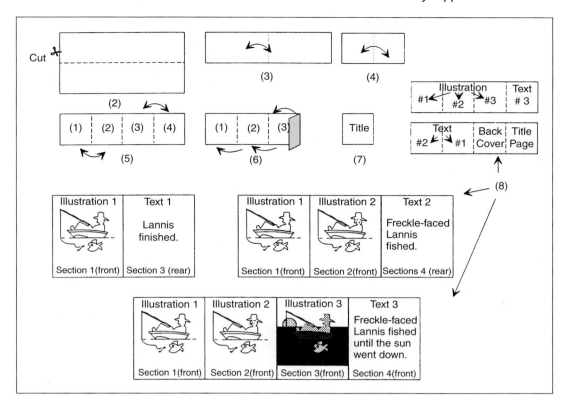

VARIATION FOR A TALL TALE BOOK

MATERIALS

12″ × 18″ sheet of construction paper

DIRECTIONS

1. Follow steps 1 through 7 in Wrap-Over Book activity.
2. A tall tale book should be opened vertically.
3. In the example, the tall tale figure's head is on section 1, the torso and arms are on section 2, the knees are on section 3, and below the knees to feet are on section 4.

APPLICATION

Tall tale: Unwrap the book to reveal a tall tale character for tall tale innovations, personal tall tales, and tall tale tunes. (Chapter 3, pp. 64–65)

Title
Page

(back cover)

Story
Part 1

Story
Part 2

Appendix B

Music Appendix

GUIDELINES FOR CREATING SONG INNOVATIONS

1. Select a topic.
2. Read, research, and collect data about the topic.
3. List significant information about the topic.
4. Select a familiar song (see list on page 354).
5. Determine the rhyming pattern of the song lyrics.
6. Count the number of syllables or beats to determine the pattern in each line.
7. Brainstorm sets of rhyming words that relate to the topic.
8. Compose original lyrics following the rhyme and syllable pattern of the familiar song.
9. Check off each item on the list of significant information as it is incorporated into the lyrics.
10. Share the song innovation with others.

Note: You may experience difficulty fitting the lyrics that other composers create to the selected tune. If this occurs, use lyricist license and modify the words, so that they fit the tune for you. Song innovations are wonderful for introducing, summarizing, or reviewing stories, concepts, and skills.

LIST OF FAMILIAR SONGS*

ABC Song
A Bear Went Over the Mountain
A Hunting We Will Go
A Tisket, A Tasket
Alleluia Chorus
Annabelle
Are You Sleeping?
Battle Hymn of the Republic
Beautiful Dreamer
Bicycle Built for Two
Billy Boy

B.I.N.G.O.
Braham's Lullaby
Buffalo Gal
Bunny Hop
Camp Granada
Camptown Races
Clapping Land
Clementine
Daring Young Man on the Flying Trapeze
Did You Ever See a Lassie?

*This list of familiar songs was compiled by the author. For additional song possibilities, as well as a collection of melodies, lyrics, and chords for more than 600 well-known songs, see *The Fake Book of Everybody's Favorite Songs* (1990). New York: Crescent Books.

Doe, a Deer/Do Re Mi
Down by the Station
Do Your Ears Hang Low?
Eensy, Weensy Spider
Farmer in the Dell
Father Abraham
Five Little Ducks
For He's a Jolly Good Fellow
Found a Peanut
Frere Jacques
Frog Went a Courtin'
Gilligan's Island
God Rest Ye Merry Gentlemen
Halls of Montezuma
Here Comes Peter Cottontail
He's Got the Whole World in His Hands
Hickory Dickory Dock
Hokey Pokey
Home on the Range
How Much Is That Doggie in the Window?
Hush Little Baby
I Know an Old Lady Who Swallowed a Fly
I Saw Three Ships Come Sailing In
I Went to the Animal Fair
If You're Happy and You Know It
I'm a Little Teapot
I'm Dreaming of a White Christmas
In and Out the Window
It Came Upon the Midnight Clear
It's a Small World
I've Been Working on the Railroad
Jesus Loves Me
Jimmy Crack Corn
Jingle Bells
Joy to the World
Lavender Blue
London Bridge
Looby Loo
Mary Had a Little Lamb
Me and My Shadow
Mickey Mouse Song
Miss Mary Mack

Muffin Man
Mulberry Bush
My Bonnie Lies Over the Ocean
Noble Duke of York
Oh, Christmas Tree
Oh, My Darling
Oh What a Beautiful Morning
Old Lady Who Swallowed a Fly
Old MacDonald
On Top of Old Smokey
Oscar Mayer Song
Over in the Meadow
Over the River
Pop! Goes the Weasel
Put on a Happy Face
Row, Row, Row Your Boat
Rudolph the Red-Nosed Reindeer
Sailing, Sailing
Santa Claus Is Coming to Town
Sarasponda
She'll Be Coming Round the Mountain
Shoo, Fly, Don't Bother Me
Sing a Song of Sixpence
Skip to My Lou
Supercalifragilistic…
Take Me Out to the Ballgame
Ten Little Indians
The Ants Go Marching One by One
The More We Get Together
This Land Is Your Land
This Old Man
Three Blind Mice
Turkey in the Straw
Twelve Days of Christmas
Twinkle, Twinkle Little Star
Up on the Housetop
Wheels on the Bus
When Johnny Comes Marching Home
When the Saints Go Marching In
Where Is Thumbkin?
Winter Wonderland
Would You Like to Swing on a Star?
Yankee Doodle Dandy
You Are My Sunshine

LITERARY GENRE DYNAMIC DITTIES

Title: Genre Jive*
Tune: "This Old Man"

Picture Books, Picture Books.   (**Picture Books**)
Illustrations, varied looks.
Text and picture do depend.
On each other to the end.

We have **Multicultural Lit**   (Multicultural Literature)
In each genre it will fit.
Asian, African, Hispanic too.
Native American, which are you?

Traditional Lit, Traditional Lit   (Traditional Literature)
No author will claim it.
That's because it's very old
Through the ages been retold.

    ***Fairy Tales,** Folk line
    Setting, once upon a time.
    Problem, solution, three events.
    Good guys win; Bad guys *didn't*.

    ***Fables,** they are brief.
    Conflict comes to cause some grief.
    Talking animals do teach.
    A moral that does each one reach.

    *Want to know about creation?
    Myths provide an explanation.
    Gods and goddesses abound
    On natural phenomena they expound.

    *King Arthur, Robin Hood
    Each one did what he could.
    To slay evil; conflicts mend.
    Each is called a **Legend**.

    ***Tall Tales,** exaggeration
    Bigger than life through imagination
    Feats enhanced but we believe
    Truth stretched to the utmost we receive.

    ***Traditional Poetry**
    Each of superb quality
    Unnamed authors produce
    Epics, Ballads, Mother Goose

Fantasy, Fantasy   (**Modern Fantasy**)
Each author pens anomaly.
Fantasy, it is not true,
But I believe it; you should too.

    ****Literary Tales,** we know who wrote
    Hans Christian Andersen, we quote.
    An aura of magic does surround.
    Fictional characters abound.

    ****Personified Pinocchio**
    Toys take on an extra glow.
    Animals talk but have true traits.
    Peter Rabbit is first rate.

    ****Little People** we do greet.
    In tiny worlds that are so neat.
    The Borrowers steal our hearts
    Because they are so very smart.

    ****Preposterous Characters,** situations
    Expand and stretch imaginations.
    We meet *Alice in Wonderland*.
    We reach out to take her hand.

Fantasy, High or **Low
To unknown worlds, our quest doeth go.
We suspend disbelief.
Good does win; we have no grief.

We enjoy **Science Fiction.
Where there is a lot of friction.
The plot and setting are high tech
But we enjoy it; what the heck!

****Time Warp**, what is that?
We go forward, and we go back
Historical setting, it is real
Characters solve conflict and have appeal.

Contemporary Lit, Contemporary Lit   **(Contemporary Realistic Fiction)**
Real, it happened, didn't it?
Fiction means that it did not.
This confuses me a lot.

History, History   **(Historical Fiction)**
Means it happened before me.
Most did happen; **Fiction** did not
But I learn an awful lot.

Information, Biography   **(Nonfiction)**
Nonfiction; true as true can be
From each you learn a lot of facts.
As well as some significant acts.

Poetry, Poetry   **(Poetry)**
What does each verse mean to me?
Repetition, Rhythm, Rhyme
Each occurs some of the time.

LYRICS FOR LEARNING LITERARY ELEMENTS

Literary Elements Overview

Title: Literary Elements
Tune: "Do a Deer/Do Ra Mi"

Character: the **who** in a story;
Setting: the **when** and the **where**;
Plot: What happens and **how** it happens; Conflict may occur anywhere.
Style: exciting sounds of language;
Point of view: eyes through which the story is told
Theme: the unifying meaning, and **why** the story is told.

Character

Title: Character Chant
Tune: "Turkey in the Straw" or "Do Your Ears Hang Low"

Do you want to know, a character in a book?
Here are some aspects
At which you should closely look.
Appearance and **Actions**
Attitudes of self—others too.
What is said—**Articulation**,
Reveals this character to you.

Setting

Title: The Setting Song
Tune: "Don't Fence Me In"

Group 1	Group 2
Oh give me books, lots of books Under starry skies above.	That's setting.
Let me ride through the wide open Country that I love.	That's setting.
Let me be by myself In the evening breeze,	Woosh, Woosh,
Listen to the murmur Of the cottonwood trees, Send me off.	Pst...Pst... When?
Forever But, I ask you please,	

JUST LET ME READ!

Plot

Title: Plot Prattle
Tune: "This Old Man"

Part 1	Response
What's a plot? *(two times)* Tell us what a plot has got!	**Foreshadowing**, hints of what's ahead, So the outcome you won't dread.
What's a plot? *(two times)* Tell us what a plot has got!	**Action**, events, excitement, too. What all of the characters do.
What's a plot? *(two times)* Tell us what a plot has got!	**Conflict**, struggles galore, of course, Each against an opposing force.
What's a plot *(two times)* Tell us what a plot has got!	**Tension**, forces in juxtaposition. Finding intense opposition.
What's a plot? *(two times)* Tell us what a plot has got!	**Suspense**, we have uncertainty. We read to solve anxiety.

Style

Title: The Style Song
Tune: "When the Saints Go Marching In"

An author makes
A word choice
Expressing thoughts effectively.
Choosing just the right word from
Proprietary vocabulary.

Point of View

Title: The Point of View Song
Tune: "Clementine"

Point of view, point of view
What does this term mean to you?
The eyes through which we view
And understand the story, too.

Theme

Title: Theme Song*
Tune: "I've Been Working on the Railroad"

Part 1	*Response*
I've been looking for the theme	
	All the live long day.
I've been looking for the theme	
	Just to pass the time away.
Can't you search to find the meaning?	
	The elements unify.
See the characters mature	
	And answer the question, "Why?"
What is the theme?	
	What is the theme?

What is the theme in this story?

What is the theme?	
	What is the theme?

What is the theme to me?

* These songs are from Wynn, Marjorie J. (1994). Experiencing Literary Elements in Stories Through Music and Poetry. *Florida Reading Quarterly, 31*(2), 5–11. Reprinted with permission.

Appendix C

Poetry Appendix

ACROSTIC

An *acrostic* is a series of words or lines of words in which the first, last, or an intermediate vertical line of letters forms a word. (Chapter 4, p. 101–102)

> **S**ensational
> **H**appy
> **A**wesome
> **R**emarkable
> **O**rganized
> **N**ifty

BIOPOEM

A *biopoem* is a personal poem that contains information about a particular person. (Chapter 5, p. 151)

Line 1: First name
Line 2: Three or more describing words
Line 3: Who loved three or more things
Line 4: Who believed in one or more things
Line 5: Who wanted one or more things
Line 6: Who used one or more things
Line 7: Who gave three or more things
Line 8: Quotation
Line 9: Last name

CINQUAIN

A *cinquain* is a formula poem containing five unrhymed lines that describes a subject or tells a story. (Chapter 5, p. 150)

Line 1: Subject
Line 2: Two adjectives describing the subject
Line 3: Three action words related to the subject
Line 4: Four words to express a feeling about the subject (may be a simile or metaphor)
Line 5: Synonym to rename the subject

DIAMANTE

A *diamante* is a diamond-shaped poem that emphasizes contrast and provides an interesting way to develop vocabulary choices and review parts of speech (Chapter 2, p. 30). A diamante poem is sometimes written to contrast a protagonist and an antagonist. (Chapter 3, p. 81)

Line 1: Noun 1
Line 2: Two adjectives related to noun 1
Line 3: Three action words related to noun 1
Line 4: Two nouns related to noun 1
Two nouns related to noun 2 (or a transitional phrase)
Line 5: Three action words related to noun 2
Line 6: Two adjectives related to noun 2
Line 7: Noun 2

5WS + H POEMS

A *5Ws + H poem* is a six-question formula poem in which each lines answers one of the six questions. (Chapter 8, p. 248)

Line 1: Who?
Line 2: What
Line 3: When?
Line 4: Where?
Line 5: Why?
Line 6: How?

FORMULA SENTENCE POEMS

Formula sentence poems have a structure or pattern within which students create their poems. Each line or thought begins with the same words, providing repetition for the poem. (Chapter 3; p. 80; Chapter 7, p. 214)

Is–Are ... (definition poems)

Love is feeling important to someone else.

I Wish

I wish I could go to Walt Disney World.

If I Were

If I were the teacher, I wouldn't give any homework.

I Used to Be...But Now I Am

I used to be unable to read, but now I am able to read lots of books.

Is–Because

A tree is nice because you can build a tree house in the branches.

The Important Thing About Me

The important thing about me is that I help my mom with the housework.

HAIKU

Haiku is a form of Japanese poetry that has three unrhymed lines containing seventeen syllables. The haiku format is as follows: (Chapter 7, p. 224)

Line 1:   Five syllables
Line 2:   Seven syllables
Line 3:   Five syllables

HINK PINKS AND HINKY PINKIES

Hink pinks are riddles with two one-syllable rhyming words for the answer. (Chapter 7; p. 216)
What is a plump feline? (*fat cat*)
Hinky pinkies are riddles with two two-syllable rhyming words for the answer.
What is a grumpy cat? (*crabby tabby*)

INVITATION POEM

An *invitation poem* is a type of 5Ws + H poem. (Chapter 3, p. 82)

Line 1:   Who? (Who is invited?)
Line 2:   What? (What is the occasion?
           For example, a birthday party.)
Line 3:   When? (date and time)
Line 4:   Where? (address)
Line 5:   Why? (Why a party?)
Line 6:   How? (types of games and activities)

LANTERNE

Lanterne is a form of Japanese poetry that has five unrhymed lines containing eleven syllables. The poem forms a Japanese lantern shape. The lanterne format is as follows: (Chapter 7, p. 225)

Line 1: One syllable
Line 2: Two syllables
Line 3: Three syllables
Line 4: Four syllables
Line 5: One syllable

LIMERICK

A *limerick* is a humorous poem with five lines. The words at the ends of lines 1, 2, and 5 rhyme with each other. The words at the ends of lines 3 and 4 rhyme with each other. Often lines 3 and 4 are shorter. Usually line 5 has a surprise ending. (Chapter 3, p. 81)

Line 1: _____ *
Line 2: _____ *
Line 3: _____ **
Line 4: _____ **
Line 5: _____ *

*These lines rhyme with each other.
**These lines rhyme with each other.

MAGNIFY THE MYSTERY

Magnify the Mystery is a patterned poetry format specifically designed to focus on the literary elements in mysteries. Display on the magnifying glass worksheet found in the Activity Appendix. (Chapter 8, p. 257)

Line 1: Title
Line 2: Case question
Line 3: When and where
Line 4: Clue 1
Line 5: Clue 2
Line 6: Clue 3
Line 7: Clue 4
Case 8: Case Answer

THE MYSTERY OF YOU-NIQUENESS

The Mystery of You-niqueness (MOY) has fourteen lines with a series of questions and answers that reveal secrets of a unique life with unique problems. (Chapter 7, p. 242; Chapter 8, p. 263)

Who am I?
Line 1: I am _____
                                    (name)
Line 2: I am special
Line 3: Sometimes I ask:
Line 4: _____
                                    (question)
Line 5: _____
                                    (question)

Line 6:   Sometimes other people ask:
Line 7:   _____
                                    (question)
Line 8:   _____
                                    (question)
Line 9:   But deep down I know:
Line 10:   _____
Line 11:   _____
Line 12:   Who am I?
Line 13:   I am _____
                                    (name)

Line 14:   I am You-nique!

PATTERNED POETRY

Patterned poetry uses an existing poem or song as a model and substitutes alternative words in the model to write a poetry innovation. A patterned poem using "Jack Be Nimble; Jack Be Quick" is as follows: (Chapter 3, p. 82-83)

Tony is thinking;
Tony is smart.
Tony knows his multiplication tables by heart.

PICTURE POEM

A *picture poem* is a poem written in the shape or on the shape of an object. These poems are sometimes called shape poems or concrete poems because the words are written to create a picture characterizing the object. The poem may be *alliterative* (words beginning with the same sound), *alphabetical* (an A word, then a B word, etc), *free verse*, or words on a *shape* that describe the object and create the picture poem. (Chapter 3, p. 78-80)

waves wandering wistfully

whispering whirling waves.

PLOT POEM

A *plot poem* is a poem composed of seven couplets arranged in six ascending stair steps and one descending stair step. The poem is read from step 1 up to step 6 (from the bottom to the top) and then down to step 7 for the last couplet. A *couplet* is a pair of lines in which the words at the end of each line rhyme with each other. (Chapter 3, p. 61–62)

Step 6: Climax
Step 5: Event 3
Step 4: Event 2
Step 3: Event 1
Step 2: Goal
Step 1: Problem

Step 7: Resolution

PREJUDICE POEM

A *prejudice poem* is a four-line investigative poem that answers questions and follows the format: (Chapter 8, p. 267)

Line 1: I thought...(What is my prejudice?)
Line 2: Because... (Why am I prejudiced?)
Line 3: Then I ... (How can I change my attitude?)
Line 4: Now I ... (What is my attitude now?)

PYRAMID POEM

A *pyramid poem* is a pyramid-shaped poem containing five unrhymed lines, each line one word longer than the preceding line. A *pyramid poem for a story summary* has a modified format. (Chapter 2, p. 27–28)

Pyramid Poem
Line 1: One word for the title
Line 2: Two words for contributions
Line 3: Three words for types
Line 4: Four words for different forms or choices
Line 5: Five words for experiences or feelings

Pyramid Poem for a Story Summary
Line 1: Character
Line 2: Two adjectives to describe the character.
Line 3: Three words to describe the setting.
Line 4: Four words to describe a problem.
Line 5: Five words to describe one main event.
Line 6: Six words to describe a second main event.
Line 7: Seven words to describe a third main event.
Line 8: Eight words stating a solution to the problem.

SENSES POEM

A *senses poem* focuses on the sight, sound smell, taste, and touch (feel or feelings) of a person, place, or thing. (Chapter 2, p. 43)

Line 1: _____ *looks* _____
Line 2: _____ *sounds* _____
Line 3: _____ *smells* _____
Line 4: _____ *tastes* _____
Line 5: _____ *feels* _____
Line 6: _____ *is/are* _____

STORY POEM

A *story poem* is a formula poem about a story. (Chapter 5, p. 157)

Line 1: Antagonist
Line 2: One or more problems
Line 3: Protagonist
Line 4: One or more goals
Line 5: Step 1 to attaining goal
Line 6: Step 2 to attaining goal
Line 7: Step 3 to attaining goal
Line 8: Resolution

TANKA

Tanka is an expanded form of the Japanese haiku and has five unrhymed lines containing thirty-one syllables. (Chapter 7, p. 225)

Line 1:   Five syllables
Line 2:   Seven syllables
Line 3:   Five syllables
Line 4:   Seven syllables
Line 5:   Seven syllables

TERMINOLOGY VERSELET

A *terminology verselet* is a pair of rhyming lines that include and define a selected term. When versifying, a rhyming dictionary is a valuable tool. (Chapter 8, p. 258–259)

Don't stand in a small boat; you could drown.
A boat when *capsized* turns upside down.

WHODUNIT SUSPECT PORTRAIT

A *whodunit suspect portrait (WSP)* is a ten-question formula poem in which each line answers one of the ten questions. (Chapter 8, p. 272–273)

Question 1:   What is the dilemma?
Question 2:   Who is the suspect?
Question 3:   What is the suspect's occupation?
Question 4:   What are one or more of the suspect's physical traits?
Question 5:   What are one or more of the suspect's character traits?
Question 6:   What are one or more statements that the suspect made?
Question 7:   How do others feel about the suspect?
Question 8:   What motive does the suspect have for committing the crime?
Question 9:   What evidence is there for or against the suspect?
Question 10:   Is the suspect the culprit?

Appendix D ···

Lesson Planning Appendix

Pickle Picnic Reading/Listening Lesson Plan Format

Objectives: _____

_____

Materials: _____

_____

Purpose: _____

_____

Interest: _____

_____

*Concepts: _____

_____

*Knowledge: _____

_____

Location: _____

_____

Expression Expansion: _____

_____

Prediction Cycles: _____
    Inquire (Questions): _____

_____

    Confirm: _____

_____

    Negate: _____

_____

_____

Inflate: _____

_____

Capsulize: _____

_____

*Concepts are often built by starting with the students' background information and expanding this knowledge base; thus Concepts and Knowledge are often integrated within instruction. Note: acrostic formats serve as reminders to include all components in a lesson plan.

@ Purdom-Wynn Lesson Plan Format

OBJECTIVE (FROM STUDENT'S POINT-OF-VIEW):

In order to _____
I will _____
Resulting in _____

PROPS AND PREPARATION

Introduction: Destination Determination

Purpose—What is the real-world reason for this particular lesson?
Enthusiasm—How are you going to model enthusiasm; get students excited?
Attention—How are you going to grab students' attention?
Review—What previously learned/related concepts are applicable?

Content Presentation: Demonstration and Exploration Participation

Definition—Include name of concept, class term, critical attributes.
Examples—Use real-world, meaningful examples.
Attributes—Differentiate examples from nonexamples.
Nonexamples—Transform nonexamples to examples.
Sequence—Plan logical sequence: do for/do with/do independently.

Stimuli—Use auditory, visual, kinesthetic stimuli.
Transition—Logical step-by-step manner; increasing difficulty.

Follow-Up with Feedback: Self-Evaluation Demonstration

Guided Practice—assistance available.
Independent Practice—may be used for self-evaluation and assessment.
Variety of Practice—entice thrice through eyes, ears, and emotions.
Extension—expand learning relative to lesson's objectives.
Remediation—break down into smaller steps; use different methods/modalities.

Assessment

Self-Evaluation Demonstration—projects, portfolio, discussion.
Self-Evaluation of Teaching—How would I teach the same/differently next time?

Note: acrostic formats serve as reminders to include all components in a lesson plan.

Introduction Format

Introduction (Beginning of Lesson)
Destination Determination
Where am I (the student) going?

_____

_____

_____

_____

<u>P</u>urpose
From the student's point of view:
What is a real-world-reason for this particular lesson?
How is this lesson relevant to my own life?
What's in it for me? Why do I care?

_____

_____

_____

_____

<u>E</u>nthusiasm
How are you, the teacher, going to model enthusiasm?
How are you going to stimulate student motivation?

_____

_____

_____

_____

<u>A</u>ttention
How are you going to grab each student's attention and interest creatively in a
manner that is relevant to the lesson?

_____

_____

_____

_____

<u>R</u>eview
Identify previously learned/related concepts. How will you build bridges from this
current background knowledge to new information?

_____

_____

_____

_____

Content Presentation Format

Content Presentation (Middle of Lesson)
Demonstration and Exploration Participation

<u>D</u>efinition *(What am I learning about? Student's point of view)*
Include name of concept, class term to which concept belongs, and critical attributes of the concept.

_____
_____
_____

<u>E</u>xamples
<u>A</u>ttributes *(included in definition)*

_____
_____
_____

<u>N</u>onexamples *(no nonexamples in math)*

_____
_____
_____

Transformation of Nonexamples to Examples
(no non-examples in math)

_____
_____
_____

<u>S</u>equence *(sequence of lesson)*
Do For *(demonstration/modeling)* _____
Do With *(shared & guided)* _____
Do By Myself *(independently)* _____

<u>S</u>timuli (Teacher Check)

Did I entice thrice through eyes, ears, and emotions?

_____
_____

Did I plan concrete experiences or vicarious experiences?

_____
_____

<u>T</u>ransition *(Teacher Check)*
Did I plan for smooth transitions?

_____
_____

Follow-Up with Feedback Format

Follow-Up with Feedback (End of Lesson)
Self-Evaluation Demonstration

<u>G</u>uided Practice
(assistance available from teacher, peers, or instructional material)

_____
_____
_____
_____
_____

<u>I</u>ndependent Practice
(may be used for self-evaluation and assessment)

_____
_____
_____
_____

<u>V</u>ariety of Practice
(entice thrice through eyes, ears, and emotions)

_____
_____
_____
_____

<u>E</u>xtension
(expand learning relative to the lesson's objective)

_____
_____
_____
_____

<u>R</u>emediation
(break material down into smaller, more manageable steps; reteach using different materials and/or methods)

_____
_____
_____

Self-Evaluation Demonstration
(projects, portfolio, discussion)

_____
_____

Author/Title Index

Subject Index